"To Do Justice to Him & Myself"

Ætatis Suæ
38
Anº 1718

"To Do Justice to Him & Myself"

Evert Wendell's Account Book of the Fur Trade
with Indians in Albany, New York, 1695–1726

Translated and edited by
Kees-Jan Waterman

with linguistic information by
Gunther Michelson

AMERICAN PHILOSOPHICAL SOCIETY ‡ PHILADELPHIA

Lightning Rod PRESS

AMERICAN PHILOSOPHICAL SOCIETY
Held at Philadelphia
for Promoting Useful Knowledge
VOLUME 4

Text and cover design by E. H. Graben.
Set in Minion with Historical Fell Type display by Graphic Composition, Inc., Bogart, Georgia.
Printed and bound in the United States of America.

ISBN-13: 978-1-60618-912-2

LIBRARY OF CONGRESS CATALOGING-IN-PUBLICATION DATA

Wendell, Evert, 1681–1750.
 "To do justice to him & myself" : Evert Wendell's account book of the fur trade with Indians in Albany, New York, 1695–1726 / translated and edited by Kees-Jan Waterman ; with linguistic information by Gunther Michelson.
    p. cm.—(Lightning rod press series ; 4)
 Includes bibliographical references and index.
 ISBN 978-1-60618-912-2 (alk. paper)
   1. Wendell, Evert, 1681–1750. 2. Fur trade—New York (State)—Albany Region—History. 3. Frontier and pioneer life—New York (State)—Albany. 4. Iroquois Indians—New York (State)—Albany Region—History. 5. Iroquois Indians—Commerce—New York (State)—Albany Region—History. 6. Dutch—Commerce—New York (State)—Albany Region—History. 7. Intercultural communication—New York (State)—Albany Region—History. 8. Albany (N.Y.)—Ethnic relations. 9. Albany (N.Y.)—History. 10. New York (State)—History—Colonial period, ca. 1600–1775. I. Waterman, Kees-Jan, 1962– . II. Michelson, Gunther. III. Title. IV. Title: To do justice to him and myself.
  F122.W46 2008
  974.7'420049755—dc22

                                                    2008034423

THIS PUBLICATION was made possible in part by financial support from the following members of the Holland Society of New York:

Hendrik Booraem, IV

Robert G. Goelet

Mr. Robert Ten Eyck Lansing

Hon. Norman F. Lent, Jr.

Robert B. Phelps

Dr. Robert R. Schenck

Anne Tangeman

Mr. Andrew S. Terhune

S. Thompson Viele

Mr. John M. Van Aken

Dr. Robert Labranche Van Dusen

Mr. Arthur W. Van Dyke

Mr. James H. Van Tassel

Mr. John D. Van Wagoner

Mr. John N. Van Wagoner

Mr. Nicholas P. Veeder, III

Dr. John R. Voorhis, III

Mr. Charles W. Wendell

Mr. Edward E. Wendell, Jr.

and by

the New Netherland Institute's Hendricks Manuscript Award

Research for the project was supported by grants from the American Historical Association (Michael Kraus Research Grant) and the American Philosophical Society (Phillips Fund Grant for Native American Research).

About the Original Manuscript and CD-ROM

THE ORIGINAL MANUSCRIPT is in the holdings of the New-York Historical Society, 170 Central Park West, New York, NY 10024. It is cataloged as *Evert Wendell: Account Book, 1695–1726, of Trade with Native Americans,* call number: BV Wendell, Evert, Account Book, 1695–1726. A microfilm edition can also be ordered (Miscellaneous Microfilm Reel #71).

This translation has been published with permission from the New-York Historical Society.

Note that the CD-ROM contains the transcription of the manuscript in Dutch. Files are in Microsoft Word and .pdf format; if you do not have an Adobe Reader, it can be downloaded for free from the Adobe web site: http://www.adobe.com/products/acrobat/readstep2.html.

TRANSCRIPTION CITATION: Waterman, Kees-Jan, trans. and ed. 2008. *"To Do Justice to Him and Myself": Evert Wendell's Account Book of the Fur Trade with Indians in Albany, New York, 1695–1726.* CD-ROM. Philadelphia: American Philosophical Society.

About the Illustrations

COVER AND PLATE VI: *Evert Wendell Account Book of Trade with Native Americans, 1695–1726.* Page 68, digital ID number 79526d. Collection of the New-York Historical Society.

COVER AND FRONTISPIECE: *Portrait of Evert Wendell (1681–1750);* attributed to Nehemiah Partridge (1683–ca. 1737); 1718; oil on canvas, ht. 45″, w. 35¼″, framed, ht. 50″, w. 39⅞″. Inscribed, lower left: "Ætatis suae / 38 / Ano 1718"; Albany Institute of History & Art, gift of Governor and Mrs. W. Averell Harriman, Dorothy Treat Arnold (Mrs. Ledyard, Jr.) Cogswell, Gates B. and Bessie DeBeer Aufsesser, and Richard C. and Marjorie Doyle Rockwell, 1962.48.1.

PLATES (following page 90): Digitally reproduced from *Evert Wendell Account Book of Trade with Native Americans, 1695–1726,* pages 1, 51, 52, 57, 66, 68, 70, 71, 77, 104, 110, and 115. Reproduced with permission from the New-York Historical Society, digital ID number 79526d.

Contents

TRANSCRIPTION, IN DUTCH available from the
American Philosophical Society fulfillment service at *www.dianepublishing.net*

Illustrations

———————

Tables

Acknowledgments

I HAVE BEEN FORTUNATE TO RECEIVE support and assistance from many individuals and organizations during the transcription, translation, annotation, and editing of this manuscript. I am especially grateful for the continued support of Charles Gehring, Jaap Jacobs, and Janny Venema, and for their comments on my drafts. As professionals, and as friends, they never ceased to impress upon me the need to bring the contents of this account book into wider circulation. Among other individuals who were willing to contribute time and knowledge during this project, I want to mention first and foremost Gunther Michelson, who shared his impressive knowledge of the Mohawk and other Iroquoian languages and names. It is sad that he could not witness this book's publication. I remember him with a sense of deep gratitude. George R. Hamell has been very generous in sharing his thorough understanding of Iroquois culture and society, and in identifying Iroquois place names. Blair A. Rudes was of great help in analyzing names of the American Indians who the Wendells referred to as Mahicans. The editorial assistance from Martha Dickinson Shattuck was essential in preparing the manuscript for publication. Others have helped in many ways. Among them I wish to name Robert S. Alexander, Stefan Bielinski, Peter R. Christoph, Ives Goddard, Jos van der Linde, John J. McCusker, Mark Meuwese, Jon W. Parmenter, Harald E. L. Prins, Albert Brett Rushforth, G. J. Rutten, A. J. Scheffers, and David William Voorhees. Romke Rijpkema read the manuscript and provided valuable suggestions for the translation. I am also grateful for the remarks and advice of the reviewers who read the manuscript. Clearly, mistakes and omissions remain mine.

I want to thank the New-York Historical Society for the permission to publish this edition of the account book and for the use of quotations from other manuscript collections. Also, staff at the following institutions assisted me in a professional fashion: New York State Archives, New York State Library, New York Public Library, American Numismatic Society, the Houghton Library, the Pierpont Morgan Library, The Gilder Lehrman Institute of American History, the University Library at Leiden University, and the Municipal Archives of Amsterdam.

I owe special thanks to a number of individual members of the Holland Society of New York. Without their financial contribution the project would have taken considerably longer to come to fruition. The Hendricks Manuscript Award that I received from the New Netherland Institute accelerated the publishing process. Financial support for research, during the initial stages of this project, was provided by grants from the American Historical Association and the American Philosophical Society. Mary McDonald, Editor at the American Philosophical Society, guided this book through its various stages with professionalism and enthusiasm.

Elena supported this project from its very beginning, for which I am thankful. To Federico and Raoul, for their capacity to present refreshing perspectives on the subject that was always around them. Finally, I consider myself most fortunate that Karlijn shares many of my fascinations—both in the field of my studies and in countless other aspects.

———

Abbreviations

AA

Joel Munsell, ed., *Annals of Albany.* 10 vols. (Albany, NY: J. Munsell, 1850–1959).

CCM

Berthold Fernow, comp., *Calendar of Council Minutes, 1668–1783: New York State Library Bulletin 58,* repr. (Albany, NY: University of the State of New York, 1902; repr., Harrison, NY: Harbor Hill Books, 1987).

CMARS

A. J. F. van Laer, trans. and ed., *Minutes of the Court of Albany, Rensselaerswijck and Schenectady 1668–1685.* 3 vols. (Albany, NY: University of the State of New York, 192–1932).

DHNY

Edmund B. O'Callaghan, ed., *Documentary History of the State of New York.* 4 vols. (Albany, NY: Weed, Parsons, and Co., 1849–1851).

DRCHNY

Edmund B. O'Callaghan and Berthold Fernow, eds., *Documents Relative to the Colonial History of the State of New York.* 15 vols. (Albany, NY: Weed Parsons, and Co., 1853–1887).

DSSY

Dutch Settlers Society of Albany Yearbook

ERA

Jonathan Pearson and A. J. F. van Laer, trans. and eds., *Early Records of the City and County of Albany and Colony of Rensselaerswijck.* 4 vols. Vols. 2–4 revised by A. J. F. van Laer. (Albany, NY: University of the State of New York, 1869–1919).

HNAI, vol. 4

Handbook of North American Indians, ed. William C. Sturtevant, vol. 4, *History of Indian–White Relations,* ed. Wilcomb E. Washburn. (Washington, DC: Smithsonian Institute, 1988).

HNAI, vol. 15

Handbook of North American Indians, ed. William C. Sturtevant, vol. 15, *Northeast,* ed. Bruce G. Trigger. (Washington, DC: Smithsonian Institute, 1978).

LIR

Lawrence H. Leder, ed., *The Livingston Indian Records, 1666–1723.* (Gettysburg, PA: Pennsylvania Historical Society, 1956).

NAA

Smithsonian Institution, National Anthropological Archives

NYCM

New York Colonial Manuscripts

NYHS

New-York Historical Society

NYSA   New York State Archives

NYSL   New York State Library

Linguistic Information

BR   Blair A. Rudes supplied a linguistic tool to differentiate
            between Mahican and non-Mahican Algonquian names of
            Indians who the Wendells referred to as Mahicans.

GM   Gunther Michelson translated and helped identify Mohawk
            names of persons and localities. He also provided advice on
            occurrences of other Iroquoian terms and names.

Introduction

THE ACCOUNT BOOK CONTAINS the accounts of hundreds of Indians who traded with Evert, his brother Harmanus, their sister Hester, and possibly a fourth, unidentified relative between the years 1695 and 1726. The bulk of the transactions were dated between 1697 and 1710. By far the largest number of accounts relates to Indian clients of Evert. This translated and edited version of the Dutch manuscript enriches our knowledge of intercultural commercial exchanges on the upper Hudson River with an array of details. Some facets of intercultural trade that have been recognized in the literature were considerably more developed than previously assumed. This pertains particularly to the level of participation by Indian women in the trade. In addition, close examination of the contents of the account book delineates the presence and importance of two elements that have not been described earlier in this manner: the activities of American Indian escorters and guarantors, both men and women, and the use of money that appears both in accounting practices and actual transactions. Also, the entries show evidence of the use of bills that the Wendells issued to some of their Indian clientele.

One of the most rewarding aspects of a study of the manuscript is its potential to provide specific details about issues that have long been among the central questions for ethnohistorians and anthropologists who study intercultural exchanges. Fresh data can now be applied to discussions concerning the use of native agents, the ways in which credit was extended and consumed, the types and quantities of traded goods, origins of native customers, characteristics of the trading season, the use of presents to and special arrangements for Indian customers, the presence of "white" and "black" individuals and enslaved Africans among American Indians in the Northeast, and the level of fluidity of ethnic affiliations in native societies. Still, other aspects are clarified by examining the Wendells' account book. It contains observations on Indian naming practices, the use or lack of tattoos by or among indigenous individuals, indications of the presence of native servants in European households, and numerous descriptions of transactions that were concluded in the country, outside the chartered city of Albany. Finally, through their annotations, the Wendells situated the names of around three hundred individual American Indians in a certain time and place in the history the American Northeast.

The quotation in the title of this book is from page [60] of the account book. On February 1, 1707/8, Evert Wendell made an agreement in Albany, New York, with the male Mohawk trader Aeijewassen to deduct about 20 percent of the Mohawk's debt, provided he would satisfy the account. Wendell's explicit articulation of his desire to continue the mutually profitable relationship is an adequate illustration of the general atmosphere that permeates the account book. It indicates Wendell's recognition of the importance of cultivating agreeable relations with at least a number of his most substantial clients. This assessment is supported by information in other entries as well. Various native traders were allowed to leave sizeable debts unsatisfied for years, and additional credit was routinely extended to them. Native customers could deny the validity of portions of their debt. Approximately two-thirds of the total number of accounts remained entirely or partially unredeemed.

EVERT WENDELL AND HIS FAMILY
IN THE SOCIETY OF ALBANY

Evert Wendell's account book is the earliest known surviving fur trade record dealing with the Indians in colonial Albany, New York. The Indians' purchases were recorded when they visited the Wendells and bought merchandise on credit. On various occasions the authors refer to other ledgers, but if they are still extant they have not yet been located.[1] Evert Wendell was part of the third generation of Wendells to maintain family participation in the fur trade, an activity that started with his grandfather, Evert Jansz Wendell. The first Wendell in the Dutch colony of New Netherland, Evert Jansz (ca. 1615–1709?)[2] emigrated from Emden, Germany. The exact date of his arrival in New Netherland is unknown, but he was a tailor in New Amsterdam in or before February 1643, when he appeared as a defendant in a court case. In 1644, he married Susanna du Trieux in New Amsterdam and they had six children. In October 1648, he received permission to practice his trade of tailoring in the patroonship Rensselaerswijck on the upper Hudson.[3] Sometime thereafter, he moved to Albany. Evert Jansz rose to a position of prominence in the multiethnic community on the upper Hudson River. He served as deacon in the Dutch Reformed Church, magistrate, and orphan master.

Wendell and Susanna du Trieux had a son, Evert, who was three years old at the time of his father's second marriage in 1663. Although this Evert is referred to in documents with some regularity as "Evert Wendell junior," this is not the same individual as the keeper of the account book deposited in the New-York Historical Society. Evert Wendell, Jr. died between November 24, 1690, when he wrote his will, and December 27, 1703, when the instrument was probated. Evert Wendell of the third generation (1681–1750) was the son of Hieronimus, Evert Jansz's seventh child.[4] His identification as main author of the manuscript is further supported by comparing the handwriting in this account book with that of three ledgers, a daybook, and a docket book, also in the possession of the New-York Historical Society. In all these records, which are clearly identified as being kept by this Evert Wendell, a distinctive hand can be discerned. Combined, these ledgers and the daybook cover from 1708 to 1750. Burial records of the Dutch Reformed Church in Albany confirm the attribution to this Evert, as they reveal he was buried on May 4, 1750.[5]

Evert's father, Hieronimus Wendell (1655?–1697)[6,] married Ariaantje Harmense Visscher sometime before 1676. Hieronimus's economic status in the community was respectable.[7] His older brother Johannes (1649–1691/2?) continued the tradition set by their father of broad involvement in local administrative, religious, and political matters. His knowledge of Indian affairs is indicated by his presence at several conferences between Albany authorities and Indian leaders, his presence as translator on various occasions, and appointment as Commissioner for Indian Affairs.[8] After Johannes, the role of family patriarch in the third generation shifted to Harmanus Wendell (1678–1731), the second child and oldest son of Hieronimus and Ariaantje (Visscher) Wendell. A merchant, like his uncle Johannes and most of the other Wendells, he was also an assistant alderman, alderman, tax assessor and collector, and Commissioner for Indian Affairs. Harmanus had three sisters and two brothers, one of whom was Evert, the principal author of the account book.[9] Two entries on the pages of the manuscript confirm Evert and Harmanus were the brothers who kept the fur trade accounts. In 1703, Evert received five beavers from an unnamed Mohawk[10] woman for "brother [Har]manes," and six years later Evert used the same description to refer to a relative for whom he made arrangements to receive merchandise at a carrying place outside Albany.[11] Additional information gleaned from the account book confirms their relationship.[12]

The Wendells were well established in Albany's socioeconomic and political leadership. As a composite of about twenty extended families, almost without exception of Dutch descent, this local elite has been characterized as a "mercantile oligarchy."[13] Throughout the generations, Wendells were present in committees and commissions entrusted to perform a variety of judicious and sensitive tasks. In 1699, for instance, Evert Wendell, Jr., formed part of the committee entrusted with determining which of the town's inhabitants qualified as freemen. Since acquisition of that qualification established one's privilege to trade within the Corporation of Albany, the selection process carried enormous political and economic consequences.[14] Harmanus and Evert continued the Wendells' traditional roles in the local elite.[15]

———

THE WENDELLS' COMMERCIAL ACTIVITIES extended well beyond the fur trade. Accounts of Albany's economic history conclude that, with the possible exception of the 1640s and early 1650s, the fur trade alone could not have sustained the livelihood of the majority of the town's inhabitants.[16] The slow but certain recession had disparate effects on several classes of the town's merchants. Even merchants who had developed extensive networks with Indian customers and agents were eventually forced to diversify their economic activities. The Wendells' various activities were no exception to this long-term evolution of Albany's economic profile. The family's first settler spread his financial risks by dividing his economic activities between his trade as tailor and a sustained effort to slowly penetrate the fur market.

This lesson was not lost on the later generations; nearly all children and grandchildren of Evert Jansz attempted to construct a multifaceted commercial base. The particular branch of the family that included Evert and Harmanus continued to fit this pattern. Both their father and one of Harmanus's sons at least partially provided for their families' livelihood by exercising their trade as a shoemaker. There is limited evidence for a similar approach by Harmanus,[17] but Evert clearly directed his skills to a wider variety of professions and trades. In April 1717 he received a license to practice law from Lieutenant Governor Robert Hunter. Surviving docket books, account books, and the documented cases in which he applied his legal skills testify to his accomplishments as a lawyer.[18] His ledgers contain abundant evidence of trading ventures involving products from Europe and the West Indies for numerous customers in and around Albany and Schenectady.[19] Starting in the 1720s, he built and operated mills, and his 1749 will indicates he operated a brewery. In 1727, he also ventured into a more unusual trade by beginning to sell the first products from a chocolate mill.[20]

CONTACTS AND INTERACTIONS BETWEEN INDIANS AND THE WENDELLS

Evert's grandfather, Evert Jansz Wendell, started the family's involvement in the fur trade. However, in the late 1650s and early 1660s, a sharp decline in the supply of peltry caused the fur trade in Beverwijck to deteriorate. Sharpened competition for the declining trade caused dissension among many of the townspeople, some of whom resorted to illegal and sometimes violent behavior.[21] Increasingly, traders deployed colonists and Indians as brokers to intercept Indians bringing their peltry to the town. Brokers were a common phenomenon in Beverwijck/Albany since at least 1648 when their activities were first described, and into the early 1660s.[22] Later, in 1681, Evert Jansz, his sons Johannes and Evert, and twenty-four other inhabitants signed a petition to the magistrates of Albany, complaining about the state of the "Indian trade[,] caused by various practices to take away one another's trade."[23]

Besides participating in the fur trade, the Wendells were called by both Indians and Europeans to act as interpreters. A letter from Oneida and Onondaga sachems specifically requested Johannes be among four representatives of Albany during a critical council at Onondaga in December 1689.[24] A public display of support for Wendell occurred in June 1691 during a conference with Governor Henry Sloughter when the speaker for the western Iroquois nations desired that Johannes Wendell, Johannes Bleecker, and Robert Sanders Glen attend the proceedings. The unnamed sachem justified the request by stating that these three men "are Maquasse [Mohawks]."[25] In 1699, during the controversy over fraudulent land grants to clergyman Godfredius Dellius and four other prominent inhabitants of Albany, Indian proprietors called upon Johannes's brother, Evert, Jr., Captain Johannes Bleecker, and Abraham Schuyler to serve as interpreters in their contacts with the minister.[26] Evert, Jr., also functioned as one of the commissioners for Indian affairs and helped solidify the neutral stance of the Canadian Iroquois after the peace that concluded King William's War, in 1697.[27] Evert and Harmanus also served on the Board of Commissioners for Indian Affairs after the death of their uncle Evert, Jr. Evert served from 1724 to 1726 and from 1728 to 1734, and Harmanus from 1727 until his death in late 1731.[28] In July 1709 Harmanus was one of seven Albany merchants, all involved in the fur trade, who were requested by four Oneida headmen to accompany them to Canada as interpreters on a military expedition against the French.[29] Two decades later, he was instrumental in acquiring Mohawk land at Tiononderoge.[30]

The Wendells also nurtured alliances with individual Indians. Several entries in the account book reveal that in a number of cases Evert and Harmanus took care of outstanding debts of some of their native trading partners with European traders. In 1709, for instance, Evert redeemed a debt of the Mahican trader Wannanpackes with Andries Jansen for the right to let the Mahican's pig roam on Jansen's island.[31] But their assistance went well beyond such practical, relatively small-scale help. The baptism records of the Dutch Reformed Church in Albany contain numerous cases where a Wendell served as a sponsor at a baptism of an Indian infant. Only thirty-three Dutch individuals are recorded as godparents to Indian children, but the large number of Wendells within this group is significant. Lois Feister lists six, possibly seven, Wendells as sponsors, appearing ten times in that capacity. This represents around a third of all Dutch godparents at Indian baptisms.[32] Neither Evert nor Harmanus was ever recorded as a sponsor, but all the Wendells who acted as godparents to American Indians were close relatives to them. Also, Ariaantje Wendell, mother of the present authors, performed this ceremonial function at least once in Schenectady and an aunt of the brothers, twice.[33]

———

BESIDES THE ACCOUNT BOOK, the brothers' engagement in the fur trade becomes evident from a number of additional sources. Evert petitioned Albany's Common Council on April 29, 1703, for permission to construct the "third Indian house" at the newly created city gate, south of the fort. He proposed financing this with Stephanus Groesbeeck and Gerrit Lucasse Wyngaard, all "being Traders with the Indians," but the request was denied.[34] Correspondence with a contact in Amsterdam provides evidence that Evert himself exported furs to Amsterdam, by way of England.[35] On at least one occasion, he shipped directly to London on his own account.[36] In 1721, his cousin Abraham wrote from New York City requesting beaver furs and raccoons, explaining he was "in need of them for [delivery to] hat-makers."[37] That same year, Evert and Harmanus traveled to a Mohawk village to attend to their business, that of their cousin Abraham, and Nicolaes Schuyler's.[38] Abraham exported large quantities of peltry to London and Amsterdam, but if, and to what degree, he acquired these from Evert or other Wendells cannot always be determined.[39] Evert himself sent furs to Boston and beyond, a practice facilitated by the move of his first cousin Jacob

Wendell, son of Johannes, during the last years of Queen Anne's War.[40] In 1711, for instance, Jacob asked his brother Abraham in New York City to ship 300 pounds of beaver out of the supplies of their cousin Evert, and consign them to Richard Lechmere, a merchant in London.[41]

The presence of kinsmen also facilitated trade with Canada. Ephraim Wendell, a cousin of Evert, is documented as residing in Montreal in 1713. During his stay there, he unsuccessfully attempted to convince the local authorities to relinquish a shipment of merchandise valued at one thousand pounds. Evert had sent the goods to obtain peltry for a common account with Johannes Schuyler, Johannes Bleecker, and Johannes Visser, but the French governor had confiscated the trade items.[42] In 1714, another distinct connection between Evert Wendell and Montreal can be established, again organized through a family contact.[43] In 1722, legislation passed the provincial assembly that required every trader in Albany who was suspected of being engaged in the illegal trade in Indian goods with Canadian merchants to clear their name. One year later, Evert, Harmanus, and the latter's son Jacob purged themselves under oath.[44] In 1724, Jacob had been intercepted en route to Canada with a sizeable quantity of strouds, a coarse woolen highly valued by American Indians. Summoned before the commissioners, Harmanus confessed "he knew Something of Nicholas Schuyler and his own Son [to] whom he had Sold a parcel Strouds and thought perhaps they were going towards Canada, or Tuschachrondie [Detroit]."[45] On at least one occasion, this Jacob received official permission to travel to Canada to collect debts due to him. In June 1729, New York Governor John Montgomerie issued a four-month pass for such purposes to him.[46]

Following the extension of the fur trade to the west, Evert and Harmanus were commissioned to serve in the management of commerce at the new trading house at Oswego after 1726. Evert provided practical services to the colonial government for the establishment and operation of the trade house there. In 1727, Harmanus furnished goods to the officers and soldiers stationed at Oswego and in June 1729 received commissions as official victualer of the garrison for three years.[47] Evert negotiated with Iroquois representatives about the conditions under which the post could be operated and he was able to advise the New York authorities on the necessities to support Oswego.[48] Through an act passed on September 20, 1728, the assembly appointed Evert as commissioner of new duties that were levied on the trade after the fall of Albany's fur trade monopoly.[49]

Interactions between the Indians and the brothers also extended to acquisition of land. In April 1708 Evert bought a tract of undisclosed size from Indians at Cowaseck, a village of the Western Abenakis on the upper reaches of the Connecticut River.[50] Six years later, he made a payment to Schaghnerowane, a Mohawk, for land "given" to Evert, Harmanus, and Abraham Cuyler.[51] And in October 1721 Evert and his associate, Richard Ashfield, petitioned for permission from the provincial council to purchase 2,000 acres of "uncultivated" land from the native proprietors. Neither the location of the tract, nor the prospective sellers were specified.[52]

THE SETTING: LATE SEVENTEENTH-, EARLY EIGHTEENTH-CENTURY ALBANY

From its inception in 1624, Albany, consisting of a settlement (*bijeenwoninge,* later named Beverwijck) and Fort Orange, had been supremely located at an unparalleled position in European and American Indian networks that connected the colonial Northeast. One historian has coined it, persuasively, "the Albany channel" of commerce and communication.[53] Its strategic positioning meant, until the American Revolution, most of the significant diplomatic councils and meetings in the Northeast occurred in Albany.

The strategic, economic, and political fate of Albany and the Iroquois were intimately bound together. In the late 1620s, the Mohawks had waged war against the Mahicans and had driven them away from their homelands, possibly in an attempt to enhance control of trade in Albany.[54] Perhaps since Dutch times, but certainly after around 1675, the Iroquois–Albany relationship was routinely expressed by references to "the Covenant Chain." This alliance constituted a shifting coalition between ever-changing segments and factions from within the nations of the Iroquois Confederacy, the interests and policies of Albany and the New York province, and the larger British imperial drive. Heavily guarded against intrusions by the French to the north, and their schemes with American Indian alliances, the Covenant was revisited at each meeting in Albany, with Indian and European orators and diplomats recalling and refining in ceremonial fashion its genesis and continued importance.[55] In 1686, Albany had been granted a monopoly in trade with Indians on the northern frontier of New York in recognition of its unchallenged position as a place of commerce, alliance, and mediation,. However, leaders of the Iroquois Confederacy had been, and would remain, deeply divided about the wisdom of continued allegiance to British interests and its political and economic profitability.[56] At the Grand Settlement of 1701, the Iroquois took a more neutral stance between the English and the French, signing peace treaties in both Montreal and Albany. In spite of the outbreak of Queen Anne's War the following year, Iroquoia and New York's northern frontier were spared the raids and military campaigns that ravished other areas in colonial North America.

One of the most remarkable features of the history of Beverwijck/Albany is its uninterrupted and peaceful relationship with the local Indians. Occasionally friction would arise—for example, following the killing of pigs or cattle by Indians who found the animals foraging in their unfenced fields, and indigenous orators never tired from emphasizing the need for more military support from the Dutch and English authorities. And although prices of goods were generally much more tolerable in Albany than elsewhere, American Indian leaders routinely complained about exchange rates and, at times, about the trading practices of some of the inhabitants of the town and patroonship. These problematic elements in the relations were never of sufficient importance to pose a threat to the intercultural ties that had been developed. Because of this, the situation differed significantly from the management of Indian affairs to the south, where

Dutch wars against various Algonquian polities resulted in the latter's subjugation and eventual dispersal.[57]

The relatively tranquil and accommodating circumstances created an environment where intercultural communications and exchanges could be developed and sustained. American Indians visited Albany with regularity on diplomatic and other missions and the exchange of goods was regulated by ordinances that the magistrates of the city and county issued annually. Trade was primarily centered in the town itself, as well as its immediate surroundings. Apart from a few expeditions to the west in the late seventeenth century, traders from Albany seem to have rarely ventured deep into Indian country. Early in the eighteenth century, some of the town's inhabitants moved into settlements to the north and northeast of Albany, but if any kind of commercial exchanges with native groups and individuals occurred there (in contravention of the ordinances), these practices would have been carefully hidden from public scrutiny. The same observation can be made about the private patroonship, Rensselaerswijck, which covered wide areas around Albany. In the first decades of the town's existence, native visitors were routinely allowed to lodge with European households, but this practice was increasingly curtailed. Iroquois and other Indian traders had to live in shelters just outside the town, although varying groups (sachems, River Indians, Mahicans, and even Canadian Indians) were exempted from this requirement in the ordinances. Summer was a period of intense activity because during winter, the primary hunting season, native men could dedicate less time to trade and diplomacy.[58]

At first glance, the venue of these intercultural meetings and exchanges was not overly impressive. While the population of the city had risen from fewer than 500 in 1686 to around 710 in 1697, with some 150 (free) householders around 1700, and about 1,100 inhabitants by 1714 (with only 3,300 in the whole county),[59] many visitors commented that the town's stockades appeared wholly deficient. This was particularly apparent at the outbreak of Queen Anne's War in 1702.[60] In many ways, the settlement would not have appeared as an English outpost in the Northeast. In its immediate appearance (its architecture, for instance) and much of its social, less tangible construction, Albany retained many Dutch characteristics.[61] The continuation of Dutch practices was apparent in the composition of the city's population and government, with Dutch names appearing on many of the rosters of various bodies in the city and county. This also applied to the commissioners for Indian affairs, the authority responsible for mediating Indian relations, where most, if not all, commissioners were representatives of Dutch patrician families.

By 1700, although Dutch culture and the influence of its most prominent proponents in Indian affairs was persistent, much had changed since the period of Dutch rule. Economic activities had been diversified to a considerable degree. The fur trade was still, and would remain for quite some time, among the main economic sectors. The slow but unmistakable transition from a frontier town to an integrated artery of interregional, intercolonial, and transatlantic trade resulted in a stronger emphasis on marketable products from the agrarian sector, predominantly various types of grain. The first protoindustrial enterprises were also initiated and, as earlier parts of this introduction have shown, the Wendells (Evert being no exception) were active participants in that process. In town a class of artisans and craftsmen had developed. During the colonial era they never achieved the same social standing of the Dutch merchant families, but their activities would contribute to providing employability and economic sustainability to an increasing number of inhabitants.[62]

As early as the period covered by this account book, the center of the fur trade was beginning to shift westward, away from the privileged market place that Albany had been for several decades. This process intensified during the period immediately after 1726, the year the last entry was recorded in the account book. In fact, that year witnessed the final breakdown of Albany's monopoly in the fur trade, with forts erected in the outlying regions to the west. However, although more transactions with Indians were taking place far away from its city gates, Albany remained a primary stage for diplomatic interactions with indigenous groups and their representatives. The town was increasingly engaged in intercolonial and transatlantic trade and commerce. Merchants in Albany participated in trade with various regions of the British colonial and commercial empire and trade with the Caribbean took on an increasing value. Certainly for merchants in New York City, by the end of the period in this account book, diversified economic exchanges with other colonies and England had become the dominant type of commercial activity.[63] Yet, as the pages of the account book clearly demonstrate, members of some of even the most prominent merchant families in Albany, while partaking in the diversification and broadening of their commercial portfolios, continued to see potential profits in creating credit accounts for their American Indian clientele, well into the eighteenth century. Moreover, Evert's additional ledgers, and other primary sources, show he continued to export considerable quantities of beaver and other peltry.[64]

DESCRIPTION OF THE MANUSCRIPT

The general condition of the account book is excellent. It consists of 120 pages and is bound in a cardboard cover. The inside of the front cover has a list of merchandise and some faded words, while the inside of the back cover was used to make computations and record a list of names. In most cases, the handwriting is clearly discernible and there is only occasional damage at the outer margins of the pages. A note in the case, in which the manuscript is stored, indicates that it was rebound on May 21, 1947.[65] The binding has resulted in a slight loss in the inner margins of the last pages, but did not otherwise affect the physical quality of the book.

The one problem with the account book is that it appears not entirely complete. Five sections appear to be missing from the original. It is possible that this deficiency was a preexisting condition of the account book, before it was rebound. This belief is principally informed by a case where Evert Wendell continued a sentence from the right extremity of a page onto the facing page, forming part of a different section, thereby bridging a gap in the accounts.[66] The missing pages may have been incorporated in another ledger, recording a section of the trade the Wendells desired to administer separately.[67] There are a number of references within the accounts to other trade books, kept, as previously noted, by Evert and some of his immediate relatives. The inclusion of a set of pages of different size, now bound into the volume, also suggests that the manuscript is a composite item.[68] The case in which the account book is kept also contains several handwritten notes by the American historian Dingman Versteeg (1867–1947).[69] Most likely written during the early 1900s, the notes contain transcriptions of Indians' names and origins, lists of peltry and European merchandise, and the outlines of an article.[70] Although Versteeg's writings proceed over some forty pages, they are unorganized.

To facilitate references to pages within the original volume, page numbers that were written on the pages of the account book have been copied. These numbers were not originally written in the account book as they are in Dingman Versteeg's handwriting. The numbers run from 1 to 120, and the translation lists them as pages [1] to [120]. One page has been added, page [121], for the text written on the inside of the back cover. The transcription numbers will be in parentheses and the translation numbers in brackets.

Two sections of the account book, pages [1–20] and [115–119], contain many entries written by Harmanus Wendell. An account on page [119], probably reflecting a purchase on credit from his brother Evert, establishes Harmanus as the author with this particular handwriting. The greatest number of entries in the manuscript, however, were clearly written by Evert Wendell. Another member of the Wendell family occasionally contributed to the account book. Usually undated, these entries appear on the last pages of the book and pertain to transactions taking place during the last years of the period covered by the account book. The identity of this individual cannot be established with any certainty, but it is possible that it is Ariaantje, Everts' and Harmanus' mother. An entry in the unidentified handwriting on page [107] suggests this possibility, as it records a payment by a Mohawk trader to Nicolaes Schuyler, Ariaantje's son-in-law, specifically for her account. And although Hester (1686–1742),[71] a younger sister of Evert and Harmanus, did not personally record debts of her Indian clients, the book also contains accounts of Mohawks who traded with her.

Almost all the pages follow a similar layout. At the top of a page a page number was entered, followed by the date, or year of the first entry on that page. Occasionally, the Wendells created a heading to denote the origins of the first customer on the page. Unfortunately, neither Evert nor Harmanus adhered to this organization in the other accounts on the page. Subsequent entries on the first account, as well as additional accounts with other Indians, were recorded on the remainder of the page. In the left margin of the page the Wendells entered the date of each transaction with a given customer. Typically, the account states the name of the native client, his or her origins, and a list of credit transactions with that particular individual—or those who traded with the Wendells on the account of the main debtor. Included are the kinds of goods that were given on credit, their value, and the expected amount and type of payment. At times, Evert or Harmanus included specific conditions for the settlement of debts arising from the transaction. In addition, the Wendells frequently remarked on elements of a customer's physical appearance. It is possible Evert and Harmanus included such descriptions in order to be able to recognize the debtor more easily when the client returned to pay the account, a part thereof, or to request another credit transaction.

For about 20 percent of the accounts, the Wendells created a column in the right margin of the page in which they kept track of a client's debt. In most of the other cases, the accounts contain a pictographic segment. The Wendells depicted the Indian's total debt in series of small, somewhat crude drawings of the number of animals whose furs or skins the client was required to deliver to satisfy the account. This method was specifically applied to debts of beaver and bear, while smaller animals, such as raccoon and fisher, are often represented by vertical marks. Presumably, this approach permitted the Wendell brothers to present the Indians with a recognizable record of previous transactions. The characteristic elements of the manuscript pages are reproduced in plates I–III. The accounts of several native traders are spread out over a number of pages, reflecting the longevity of their commercial relationship with the Wendells. On occasion, but not consistently, Evert and Harmanus entered references to such other pages. All accounts that were spread out across different pages are indicated in the annotations to the account book.

The setup of the trade book differs from a standard arrangement. Usually, a merchant would organize the accounts by the customers' name: placing the client's acquisitions on the left page of the opened book and the disbursement on the debt on the right page.[72] This is certainly not the case with the Wendells' manuscript. In fact, it is a confusing, somewhat messy account book—to the degree that it makes one wonder how Evert and Harmanus were able to locate specific accounts. It is possible that this manuscript was only the daybook, in which transactions were quickly entered on a day-to-day basis, and that the data would then be copied into an alphabetically arranged account book. But the Wendells never made a reference to such a book, whereas they did do so for other account books or daybooks, such as "small book," "Hester's book," "Indian corn book," "Hester's small book," and a "waste-book."[73] If such an alphabetically arranged account book of the Wendells' trade with their American Indian clientele is still in existence today, it has not been located.

The Wendells made brief entries in the account book, quite likely describing transactions while trading. Such circumstances led them to quickly write down brief sentences and statements. In translating the document, I have opted to maintain the language style of the account book as much as possible. By retaining the straightforward nature of the original text it is possible to convey the immediacy of the situation in which it was written.

THE MANUSCRIPT'S CONTENTS: SIGNIFICANCE AND ANALYSIS

The account book provides detailed insights in the processes and individuals that shaped the fur trade in colonial Albany. It describes in a systematic fashion the transactions between the Wendells and their Indian customers in the late seventeenth and early eighteenth centuries. The partly pictographic entries— numbering almost 1,800—contain revealing information about almost every aspect of the trade in peltries: the involvement of women, both Indian and European, in the commercial exchanges; the patterns and rhythms of trading contacts in Albany with the Iroquois, Mahicans, Ottawas, and other native customers; the role of brokers and agents; the existence of African slaves among Mahicans; adoption in Iroquois communities; and a virtual catalogue of the wide array of European trade goods that American Indians valued.

Traders

Indians who traded with the Wendells came from a wide geographic area: to the northwest by what is now Detroit to the north by native settlements around Montreal, to the northeast by one of the fluid lines distinguishing Abenaki subdivisions along the New England–Canadian border from one another,[74] and to the south by the Catskill River. The entries were recorded during a period of great upheaval. The turmoil of King William's War (1689–1697) does not seem to have impeded the visits by natives to Albany, since the number of newly created accounts increased significantly in 1697. Queen Anne's War (1702–1713) also did not prevent native traders from undertaking the journey to the town. On the contrary, the number and volume of the Wendells' accounts grew most impressively during the latter of the two conflicts between France and England and their respective colonies.

The Wendells extended credit to individuals from Indian communities in the vicinity of Albany, as well as customers who traveled great distances to trade there. In total, the account book contains accounts with, or references to, between 325 and 330 American Indians who can be recognized as individuals. A small number of these were mentioned merely to help the Wendells identify a client for possible return visits. Approximately three hundred identifiable natives developed a debit account with the Wendells. The names of just over forty of these remain unspecified. It should be emphasized that the manuscript reflects transactions with more than the 325 to 330 identifiable traders. However, since the number of additional traders remains obscure, as they cannot be recognized individually, it has not been taken into consideration in the following quantitative analyses.

The great majority of natives listed in the account book were affiliated with Iroquois nations. Mohawk and Seneca traders visited the Wendells' trading house with the greatest frequency. The number of Mahican customers is nearly equal to that of Seneca clients, but the account keepers evidently did not distinguish between all Algonquian groups in New York and New England. Additional documentary sources show that, on at least four occasions, individuals who the Wendells denoted as Mahican were residents of the mixed Indian village Schaghticoke, to the northeast of Albany.[75] Two other cases refer to Catskill Indians, who inhabited a region south of Albany. It is unclear to what degree this practice of the Wendells may also extend to other Mahican individuals.

Application of a basic linguistic criterion reveals that, of the more than fifty Mahican customers, the names of fifteen cannot have been Mahican. These cases have been identified in the annotation to the translation.[76] Since the exact Algonquian groups from which these non-Mahican names were derived cannot be identified, the Mahican category has been maintained in this introduction and in the translation.

Table 1 (p. 45, following this introduction) presents an overview of the origins of the native traders. The determining factor in ascribing a native's place of residence or affiliation is the stated, or obviously deduced, origin of an individual in the manuscript. Thus, an individual listed as Cayuga, and living among the Senecas, has been counted as Cayuga. A number of Iroquois clients were described as Mohawk, Onondaga, and so on, living in Canada; they are listed in table 1 according to their stated (or deduced) origins. The thirteen individuals listed as Canadian, or described as living there, have been incorporated as such. Involvement of American Indians from Canada is clear evidence that intercolonial trade between Montreal and Albany, with native intermediaries from Iroquoia and Caughnawaga (near Montreal), was well in place at the beginning of the eighteenth century.[77] Other elements from the account book indicate that Indians, who may not have been residing in Canada, were also engaged in commercial traffic along the Hudson–Lake Champlain corridor that connected New York and New France.

To what extent the Wendell's renderings of Indian names, and their descriptions of their customers' affiliations were reliable is an important question to ask. It is more than likely that the Wendells, being part of the third generation of families who had a common tradition of deep involvement in trade, diplomacy, and other contacts with the native groups on the northern frontier, had considerable linguistic abilities. These skills were required in order to operate effectively in the fur trade in Albany. This assessment is supported by an observation by Evert Wendell on page [68] of this account book. In an account, opened in June 1706, Evert described a client of Onondaga origins who had been prisoner among the Miami Indians for a period of time, and observed that he "can barely speak Onondaga" anymore. Only an observer with sufficient knowledge and understanding of the languages involved could arrive at such a conclusion. The Wendells were almost always capable of recording the individual names of their clients. Only approximately twelve percent of their customers appear without a name (or names). For Mahican, Mohawk, and Seneca customers, these percentages stand at just 3.7, 6.6, and 10.7, respectively (see table 1).

In quite a few instances, the Wendells provided an individual's name that has been identified as Mohawk while stating that the client was of different origins. In some cases, confirmation has been found in other sources that an individual with a Mohawk name, but who was described as, for instance, Seneca, did indeed appear as a Seneca orator. Moreover, the Wendells' linguistic abilities have been described as "probably better than average," and one assessment of their knowledge in this field was that they "seem to have had a good working knowledge of the Mohawk language."[78] It therefore seems likely "that natives would usually give a Mohawk version of their Onondaga, Cayuga or Seneca name to

Wendell in order to facilitate mutual understanding."[79] Having lodged natives in their own houses, the Wendells must have been in a position to absorb and record their customers' names with a relatively high degree of accuracy. I submit that in most cases it is not the Mohawk name that the Wendells were given by their native customers but the identification by Evert and Harmanus that ought to be the determining factor in identifying them.[80]

Still, ascribing a single affiliation to individual Indians remains a complicated undertaking. Such affiliations may also have fluctuated significantly at the time this account book was in use. One of the most instructive examples of the pliant qualities of Indian ethnic bonds is the listing of individuals who have been incorporated in table 1 as Ottawas. The manuscript contains a small number of accounts of customers who the Wendells described as being Ottawas, or who they reported as living among the Ottawas. Their interactions with the Wendells cover a relatively brief period in this account book: only dates from 1706 (they all show entries from June of that year) or 1707 and only one account covers both years. Interestingly, within this brief period of time, it transpires that of these customers one was a Mahican woman living among the Ottawas; another was an Indian man described in the same fashion, with the addition that he had two Mohawk names; and the third one, a young man, was described as "speaking Mohawk." Only one was described unequivocally as an Ottawa. It could be argued that a fifth customer ought to be included in this overview: the young Onondaga man who was already mentioned in the previous section. He arrived with a group of Ottawa traders in June 1706; unlike them, he did return to trade in 1708 and 1710.[81] To reflect these ambiguities, the number of Ottawa customers in table 1 has been put between two and four.

Individuals other than American Indians, sometimes identified tentatively as such, also appear in the manuscript as trading with the Wendells, and they have not been incorporated into table 1. A note below the table already states that it does not include the account of Jan, a "Frenchman living in Mohawk country."[82] Also, the appearance of two unidentified men, both involved in transactions with Indian men, must be noted. In the case of Gerret (no surname listed), in September 1703, it is entirely possible that this was a Dutch given name for a native man, just like the Mohawk and Mahican men Jan, Cees, and Korneles who appear in this manuscript. The latter cases, however, show a combination of a Dutch given name and the additional descriptor *de wilt(t)* (the savage[83]). Gerret apparently functioned as a sort of guarantor in a transaction with the Mahican man Nietewakam.[84] However, it cannot be determined if the provider of these services was an Indian or European individual—for this reason, he has not been included in table 7 (pp. 52–53)—Occurrences of native guarantors. The case of Jacob d'Schriver, who was sent to Harmanus Wendell with merchandise for a native customer in August 1709 is set in a context that suggests he was a European. Once again, this has not been established with any certainty.[85]

Finally, table 1 shows the total absence of traders from a number of native groups who lived at a relatively short distance from Albany. No individuals were listed from various Algonquian groups south of the Catskill, such as the Esopus Indians or remnants of Algonquian groups that had migrated from the Atlantic

FIGURE 1. Origins of identifiable American Indian customers

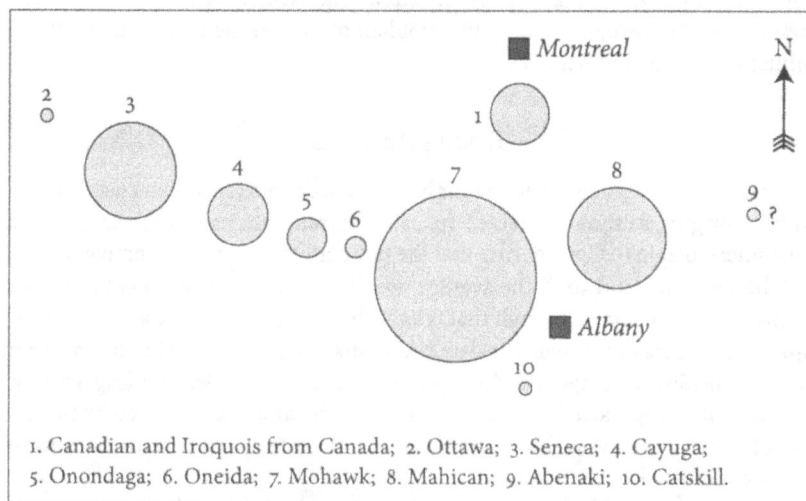

1. Canadian and Iroquois from Canada; 2. Ottawa; 3. Seneca; 4. Cayuga;
5. Onondaga; 6. Oneida; 7. Mohawk; 8. Mahican; 9. Abenaki; 10. Catskill.

Note: Data from Table 1. Canadian customers have been grouped together with
Iroquois clients who were described as "living or staying" in Canada or, for instance,
"Canadian Mohawk."

coast and the Long Island Sound to the interior. However, the Wendells, especially Harmanus, tended to group their Algonquian-speaking customers together, designating them as Mahican. And although some individual Tuscaroras
had, at this time, perhaps migrated to Iroquoia, none can be recognized in the
account book.[86]

Figure 1 shows that the greatest number of the Wendells' native customers were Mohawks. The account book shows eighty-nine identifiable Mohawk
customers, 27.2 percent of the total, which excludes Canadian Mohawks. The
number of clients from the other Iroquois groups tended to rise progressively,
moving to the west from the Mohawk nation. Senecas constituted the largest
contingency of the Wendells' Indian customers west of the Mohawks, and they
rank as the second largest group overall. Fifty-three clients, 16.2 percent of the
total, are described or have been identified as Seneca, excluding those residing
in Canada. Recent estimates put the total number of Mohawks living in Iroquoia, in the period covered by the account book, at around 600. The participation rate among the Mohawks who traded with the Wendells was considerably
higher than that of the Senecas. Estimates of their (the Senecas) population size
in this period range between 2,400 and 4,000.[87]

The localities from which one Shawnee and one English Indian customer
originated cannot be established. As a result, they have not been incorporated
into figure 1. The same applies to the three individuals who appear in the account book as French Indians. The term "French" could relate to a number of Algonquian groups to the north and northwest of Iroquoia. Also, the fact that one

of the three, an unnamed woman, had died at the time the entry was recorded in the account book and that the French Indian Aghsienjaaeijeei was described as living with the Cayugas, adds to the problem of further identifying their ethnic affiliations, or area of habitation.[88]

Trading Accounts

Over time, the Wendells opened four hundred accounts for Indian customers of various origins, as shown in table 2 (p. 46, First transactions on each account, by customers' origins). Considering that the population (n) of active native traders was between 302 and 307,[89] the average number of accounts per client averaged between 1.31 and 1.32. Although that is a moderate figure, a single account could span many years of trading. The data shows that a fair number of accounts were opened in 1697, 1701–1702, and 1704–1709. Years that saw less trading activity, in terms of newly started accounts, apart from the first years covered by the account book, were 1698–1700, 1703, 1710, and the later years toward the end of the account book.

A comparison with the data in graph 1 shows that, although the years 1701–1702 appear to have been among the most active in terms of the participation of American Indians' in trade with the Wendells, the same period reveals a decline in the number of recorded transactions per annum, set against the higher

GRAPH 1. Distributions of transactions ($n = 785$)

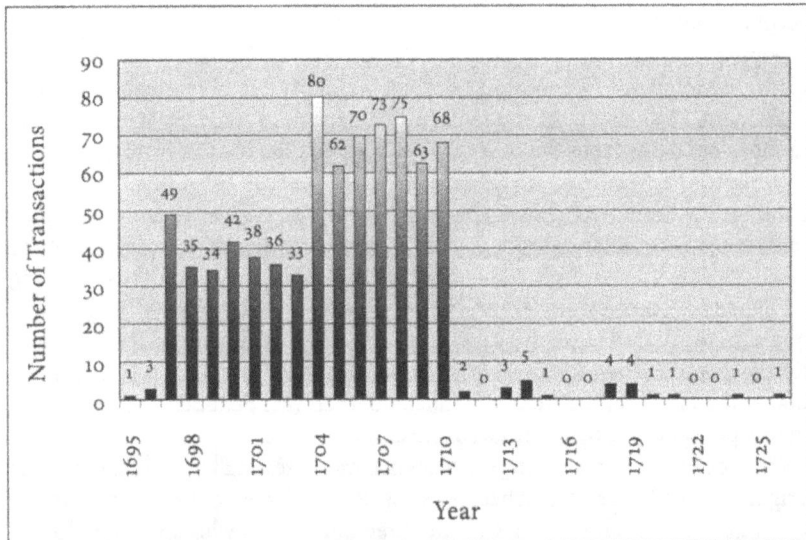

Note: All transactions within one account that were entered in one year have been grouped together as one transaction.

volumes of 1698 and 1700. The most notable years of growth, measured again in terms of the number of transactions in a single year, were 1698 and 1704.

The account book provides a detailed depiction of the overall involvement of Indian women, in commercial exchanges with the Wendells. Table 3 (p. 47, First transactions on accounts in which women were actively involved, by customers' origins) shows that the pattern of their active involvement, in accounts with Evert and Harmanus, closely follows that of all accounts in table 2.

From the total number of accounts in tables 2 and 3, which were maintained by Indians belonging to the groups included in table 2, nearly half contained the participation of one or more women. It is evident from table 4 (p. 48) that the involvement of women in the fur trade was developed most fully among the Mohawks, Senecas, and Mahicans. Iroquois women from other nations were significantly less active. Women, described by the Wendells as being either Canadian or living in Canada (excluding the sizeable group of Iroquois Canadians), also participated substantially with accounts in their own name. However, only seven Canadian women are recorded in this fashion.[90]

The participation of women in commercial exchanges was not a new development. According to Harmen van den Bogaert's journal of his journey into Mohawk country, in the period 1634–35, he encountered three Iroquois women (probably Oneidas) en route to Mohawk villages to trade the salmon and tobacco they carried.[91] On August 13, 1660, the court of Fort Orange/Beverwijck heard evidence concerning an Indian woman who had wanted to trade beaver furs in town and was enticed by an Indian broker to trade them at the house of his employer.[92] Another instance, predating this account book, also relating to direct exchanges with European settlers, occurred in the Catskill area. A deposition dated January 1684/5, reveals that two native women sold Indian corn, of which they were reportedly owners, to a Dutch woman and "an old squaw" functioned as a surety in the exchange.[93]

The sustained involvement of Iroquois and Algonquian women in the trade with the Wendells is evident. Such women, like the (unnamed) wife of the Mohawk Johonnaghquaa who traded on her own account and brought a pack of beavers from Canada to Evert Wendell in October 1708, occur frequently in the account book.[94] Women also appear in other roles, like a Mohawk woman (unnamed) described as "a pockmarked savage [. . .] from Canada," who came to trade with Evert Wendell in December 1705, conveying "greetings from the priest."[95]

Historians of intercultural economic exchanges, in the seventeenth- and eighteenth-century Northeast, have not recognized the high degree of participation by native women in the fur trade, many of whom developed accounts in their own name. Anthropological and ethnohistorical literature on the Iroquois describes complementary, but decidedly separate, economic spheres for men and women. Describing the reciprocal relationships between the domains of Iroquois men and women, but also setting them apart from each other in gendered compartments, such studies tend to portray a static economic arrangement in which men controlled the forest (hunting, warfare, diplomacy, trade) and women were dominant in village economies.[96] The women's sphere of economic activity is often depicted as being restricted to the production, harvesting, and redistribution of food products.[97] The Wendells' account book documents many native women engaging in exchanges that required them to pay their debts by delivering non-agricultural products. Still, analysis of the data from tables 4 (p. 48) and 5 (p. 49) indicates that, among Mahican and Mohawk customers who were active on accounts that were calculated in measures of Indian corn, women were strongly represented. Each account in which these women were active featured (on average) 0.76 Mahican and 0.59 Mohawk transactions involving Indian corn. However, none of the female customers, from the other groups who traded with the Wendells, engaged in transactions that involved Indian corn.

An analysis of the various tables points out that a high number of women figured in, and were active on, accounts with the Wendells. Data on native women as escorters of and guarantors for other customers, as contained in the escorting occurrences in table 6 (pp. 48–51) and the occurrences of native guarantors in table 7 (pp. 52–53), show that of all the individuals who accompanied Indians to the Wendells, fifty percent were women. That figure stands at 37.5 percent for Indians acting as a guarantor for other customers. In addition, half of the natives who the Wendells described as traveling to other Indian communities, sometimes as Evert's agent, and the majority (53 percent) of the individuals who engaged in transactions with the Wendells in the country were women.[98] Also, in the single instance in this manuscript where a debt from one individual was transferred to another, both individuals were women. In 1706 or 1707, the sister-in-law of the Mohawk Oneghriedhaa assumed responsibility for the debt of his wife, her sister, who had died. The payment would be made through another Mohawk woman.[99] In addition, some men traded on their wives' accounts, like the husband of a Mohawk woman entered as "the Limping female savage" in 1701.[100] A higher number of women made transactions on their husbands' accounts.

However, table 3 (p. 47) also indicates that around 1705 a decline occurred in women's participation in the fur trade with the Wendells. Up to that year, accounts with active involvement by women hovered at fifty percent of the total number of accounts (grouped by year). In 1703, the level rose to more than seventy percent. Starting in 1705 these percentages take a steep dive, to levels of between twenty-seven and forty percent. And although 1709 was an exception, with just over fifty percent, a downward trend is shown between 1705–1710. After that, the data becomes too sparse to be analyzed in any systematic fashion.

In general, the Wendells tended to record men's names far more often than those of their female customers. This can be illustrated, most convincingly, by a closer examination of the individuals listed in table 1 as "without name." Allowing for the uncertainty of the identity of one of these persons, the total number reported comes to forty-one or forty-two. All but three customers who appear without a name, and for whom no additional information about their identity has been located in the account book, were women: a remarkable 92.5 to 93 percent.

GRAPH 2. Correlation between the number of first transactions on each account and the number of transactions,* by year

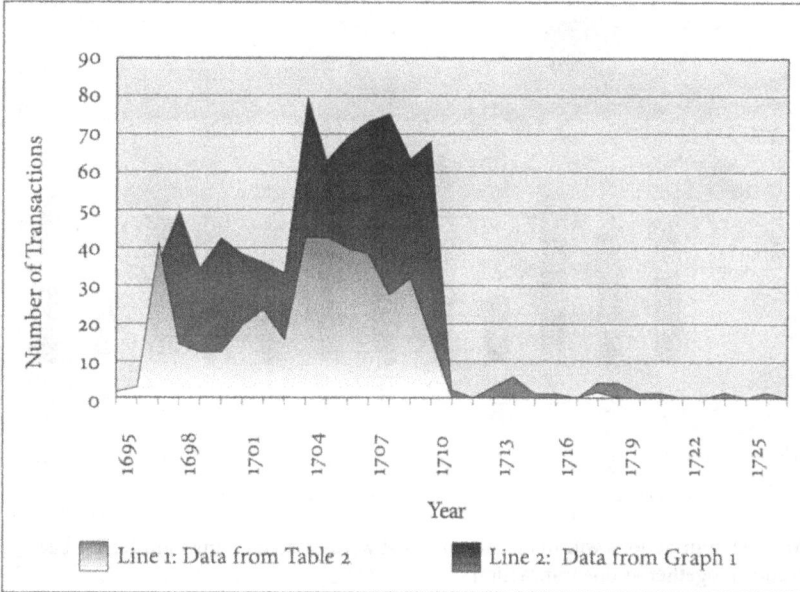

Note: All transactions within one account that were entered in one year have been grouped together as one transaction.

TRADERS IN ALBANY had a distinct advantage over their competitors in Montreal. In Albany, native customers could obtain goods at a cheaper rate and goods, especially textiles, were of a higher quality. By plotting the data from table 2 and graph 1 into graph 2, some observations can be made. Table 2 reflects the number of first transactions on all accounts with native traders by year and they appear as line 1. Line 2 reflects the data from graph 1, showing the total number of transactions in a given year. Variance in graph 2, shown in the area between the two lines, constitutes the subsequent activity on newly opened accounts.

The range between lines 1 and 2 can be used as an indication of the level of the Indian traders' satisfaction with the quality and quantities of goods they could receive on credit from the Wendells or, perhaps, with the conditions on which Evert and Harmanus supplied goods on credit. Apparently, the Wendells achieved a measure of success in retaining their customers after their first transaction. The years the Wendells achieved the highest retention rate among their native clientele were 1705–1708. The number of transactions per year continued to grow, whereas the number of newly opened accounts tended to decrease through the same years. On average, the opening of new accounts, and the prices and conditions under which they were operated, seems to have been sufficiently rewarding to native customers and the Wendells alike. Otherwise, the variance between lines 1 and 2 would have diminished over time.

GRAPH 3. Distribution of transactions ($n = 798$)

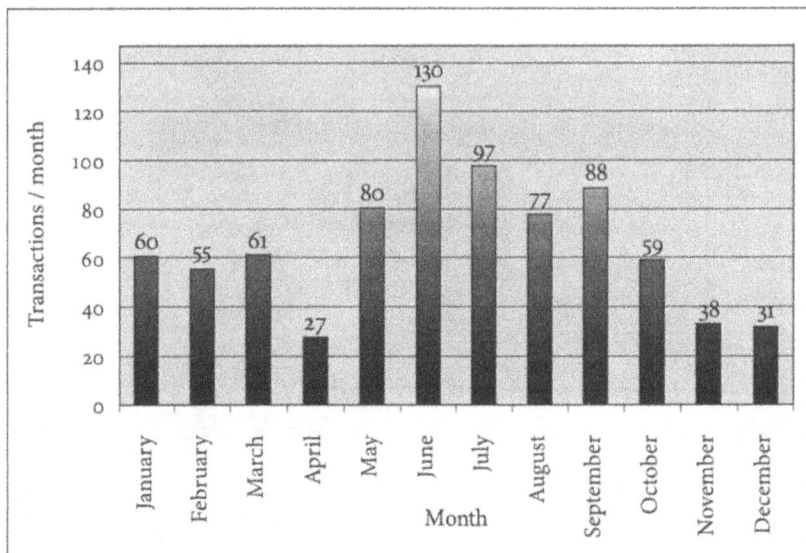

Note: All transactions within one account that were entered in one month have been grouped together as one transaction.

Graph 2 confirms that the outbreak of Queen Anne's War, in 1702, had anything but an adverse effect on the Wendells' trade. Whereas 1702 showed only a slight increase in the number of newly initiated accounts (23 versus 19 in 1701), followed by a less successful year (15 initiated accounts), 1704 and 1705 showed a considerable rise in the number of newly opened accounts (42 for both years). This acceleration was sustained during the next two years and to a lesser extent in 1709. More important, from the Wendells' perspective, was that the opened accounts would result in additional, subsequent transactions. The year 1704 witnessed the highest number of transactions per year, and although it was followed by a relatively unsuccessful year, the number of such transactions then continued to rise again between 1706 and 1708. A similar increase in the volume occurred in 1710.

Assembling data on the specific months in which transactions were made allows us to establish in what periods of the year American Indians were more likely to visit Albany and engage in the trade with Evert and Harmanus Wendell. Information from the Wendells' account book, summarized in graph 3, shows that the trading season extended into September, and even October. The data documents the consistent, year-round presence of American Indians in Albany. There also appears to have been both a summer and winter peak and from January through March there was considerable activity. The Wendells also clearly experienced slow periods in this type of trade, despite long periods of commercial

GRAPH 4. Categories of trade goods

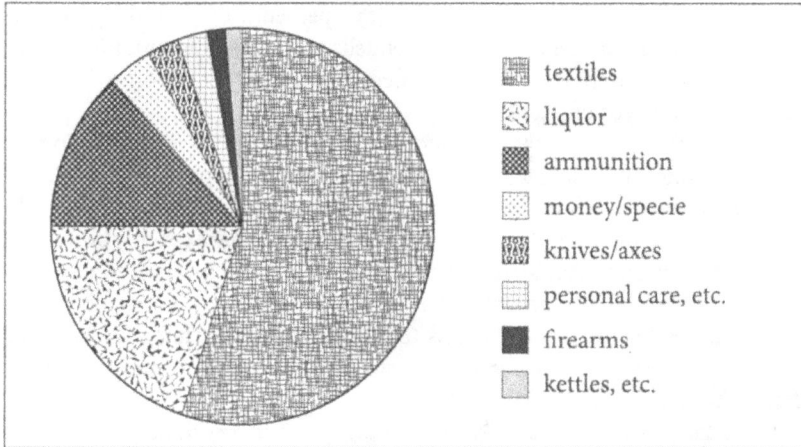

Legend:
- textiles
- liquor
- ammunition
- money/specie
- knives/axes
- personal care, etc.
- firearms
- kettles, etc.

Note: Displayed in percentages. Categories of less than 1% have been excluded.

activity. On average April, November, and December were periods in which few transactions were made.

Traded Goods

Despite the account book's missing pages, and its make-up from several types of folios, the data still provides a catalog of the types of goods that exchanged hands between Evert and Harmanus Wendell and their native customers. One conclusion becomes evident from the data in table 8 (pp. 54–55) and graph 4: more than half (53.8 percent) of the transactions deal with textiles (either fabric, or clothing). Within the category of textiles, three goods enjoyed the highest demand: within the subgroup clothing, shirts (13.4 percent) and stockings (12.9 percent), and within the subgroup woolens, blankets (13.3 percent). The information from the account book contains evidence of a strong preference, among Indians, for dark textiles. In the eighty-five cases where the Wendells described the color of the fabric that they sold on credit, black and red occurred in sixty-seven instances (78.8 percent). Yet, white duffels and other textiles with that color account for 16.5 percent of these cases, and even yellow cloth is recorded twice (2.4 percent).[101]

This profile of goods acquired by native customers is consistent with general conclusions by James Axtell, who identified textiles as the prime type of commodity that exchanged hands:

> the best-selling item in native (as in English and colonial) markets from the seventeenth century on was cloth of all kinds.[102]

Indeed, if one combines the sales of blankets, pieces of cloth, and unspecified woolens, then the conclusion must be that the Wendells' most popular products were various types of untailored textiles (23.3 percent). Data on the participation of women in the trade with the Wendells and the paramount importance of textiles in the overall volumes of traded goods documents women as active selectors of this type of goods.

The second-largest group of products natives purchased was liquor.[103] In fact, the largest single item sold was rum (19.1 percent). Hardly any beer was sold, no brandy, and cider was purchased on credit on only four occasions. The Wendells sold rum on credit, in spite of the fur trade ordinances that explicitly prohibited the sale of rum and other alcoholic beverages to Indians. In August 1709 Evert admitted as much when he noted that such a transaction with a daughter of a Seneca sachem had an element of risk to it, "because selling rum was prohibited then."[104] Not only rum, but also English strouds were the preferences of the Indians who traded with the Wendells.

The total number of sales of firearms, however, was very limited (1.4 percent of all transactions). Even when repairs of guns are added to this number, it still constitutes a small share of the Wendells' trade (2 percent). Ammunition, on the other hand, was in relatively high demand: lead, powder, and shot represent 12.9 percent of the transactions. As such, it constituted the last of the three prime groups of products that native customers acquired on credit; the fourth-largest group, money or specie, is significantly smaller and represents less than 4 percent of all transactions.

The table reveals another interesting fact. The share of a number of items and goods, which have routinely been described as having played a significant role in the trade with American Indians, is rather limited. Items that were traditionally important in native societies (wampum, glass beads, and pipes, together, represent 1.2 percent) only correspond to a very small portion of the goods traded on credit by the Wendells. In addition, a number of items, thought to have substituted traditional native artifacts, do not appear as a significant category for the Wendells either. Metal tools and kettles, for instance, occur in only 0.7 percent of all transactions.[105] The Wendells may have excluded such items as kettles and knives from their offerings to their native customers. When Albany received its city charter, in 1686, it stated explicitly that traders selling "Duffells, Strouds, Blanketts, and other Indian goods of value," a condition that obviously applied to the Wendells, were not allowed to sell "small wares" which were the province of the less well-to-do traders.[106] It is also possible the Wendells recorded transactions of such items in different account books that simply have not survived up to this day. For instance, in this account book the Wendells make several references to other account books. Besides a "small book" and "Hester's book," one of these is named the "Indian corn book," describing a specific account book for the trade in one particular commodity.[107]

Native traders rarely acquired foodstuffs on credit from the Wendells (for Indian corn as natives' debt in the trade, see table 5, p. 49). The description of the single case in this account book where an Indian man may have bought meat, for instance, is not free from ambiguity.[108]

For the Wendells, payments by American Indians on outstanding debts must have been among the most immediate objectives of exchanges in Albany, or in Indian country. The Wendells' account book documents the importance of various types of peltry, which were used to establish the value of Indians' debts and their payments on accounts. Table 9 (p. 55) summarizes the total occurrences of the different types of peltry listed in the manuscript. Furs of small mammals, especially marten (which, in the account book, may also refer to weasel) and, to a much lesser degree, otter, fisher, and raccoon, are named in numerous transactions and tallies.[109] This attests not only to the wide range of furs taken in the trade, but also to the skills of native hunters. Nevertheless, beaver remained the most sought after and valuable pelt of all. Whereas bearskins occur with some regularity in the account book, deer and elk appear only in limited numbers.

Apart from peltries, only two other products were regularly used to compute native customers' debts to the Wendells: primarily, Indian corn appears, while hops was recorded seven times. Indian corn was invariably measured and accounted using a Dutch unit, the skipple (*schepel*). Table 5 shows that it occurs 96 times in the accounts, predominantly as part of debts that were incurred by natives. Especially on accounts of Mahican women, the Wendells regularly listed debts in terms of skipple of corn.

The information in table 5 demonstrates that Indian corn was used as a debit item solely for Mahican and Mohawk traders. Compared to men, Indian women are heavily represented in this specific trade; in both groups, they constitute around ninety percent of the population that traded in corn. The relative importance of the corn trade is nearly equal for both Mohawk and Mahican clients. Table 2 shows that 83 Mahican accounts were opened, and table 5 lists thirty-three transactions on these accounts involving corn, an average of 0.40 per account. For Mohawk accounts, the average is 0.38. However, the data for female traders indicate a more substantial reliance on corn. Information from table 3 shows that, on average, each account in which these women were active featured 0.76 Mahican and 0.59 Mohawk transactions involving Indian corn.

Hops appears in seven cases, and all but one of these occur in the accounts of one Mohawk woman, the unnamed wife of the Mohawk man Aeijewa(e)se(s). The other customer who developed a debt that was to be redeemed in hops was also a woman: the daughter (probably named Wierom Cast) of another Mohawk man, Arijen hotse.[110] All appearances of the native term *notas* in this manuscript are related to quantities of hops. *Notas* was a native word for a pouch, or bag.[111] Finally, one native was charged with two pigs, or hogs in May 1709. The Mahican man WaenEnpackes redeemed this debt in the fall of that year, when the hogs were calculated at eighty Dutch guilders.[112]

Natives' Purchasing Power

The following is a comparison of exchange rates of the same type of fur and merchandise in four years: 1698, 1700, 1704, and 1708. The different circumstances of the four sample years are reflected in the number of accounts that were opened in the account book during these years: in 1697, forty-one new accounts; in 1700, twelve new accounts; in 1704 forty-two new accounts; and in 1708 twenty-seven new accounts.[113] In addition, graph 1 shows that the following transactions were recorded during these years: in 1697, forty-nine transactions; in 1700, forty-two transactions; in 1704, eighty transactions; and in 1708, seventy-five transactions. Both the number of new accounts and the number of transactions per year show higher values in times of war (or in 1697, when peace had been concluded) than in the year 1700, when there was no threat of military campaigns or raids. An overview can be presented of the purchasing power that native customers' products constituted in exchanges with the Wendells. Table 10 (pp. 56–57) reflects the values, or range of values, recorded for transactions for the years 1697, 1700, 1704, and 1708. Typically, an entry lists the exchange rate for all cases within each of those four years, or a range of rates that were current during that year. On many occasions, the Wendells only gave the type of merchandise that Indian customers purchased, without listing specific quantities. Therefore, data is missing from some fields for the years covered in table 10, as they are for inventories of other years.

Diverging circumstances in the years listed above would be expected to cause varying prices in a competitive market, as has been demonstrated for other markets in colonial North America.[114] The data from this account book is substantially different. It shows that, instead of actively fluctuating, prices in commercial exchange based on credit were marked by exactly the contrary: hardly any flexibility can be shown in the value of furs, or those of the main types of merchandise. This stability of prices, at least in terms of their value in natives' arrears, is confirmed by the circumstance that if Indian customers redeemed all or part of their debt years after they had incurred it, the Wendells allowed them to pay the original number of furs that was entered in the account book at the time of the transaction. No evidence has been found to suggest that any of the Wendells ever adjusted the quantity of peltries that was to be handed over in the event of such belated payments.

The last category in table 10 indicates a wide variation of value is attached to peltry when converted to beaver furs. Evidently, this was the result of the differing quality and weight of furs, also between hides of the same type. The mechanics of such comparisons can be established only in rare cases. From one of those, dated 1707, it can be determined that part of the debt of the Mohawk man Caaheghtsiedawee was computed by equating four martens with one beaver weighing two pounds.[115] The same year, a customer made a payment of a beaver weighing one-and-a-quarter pound, which was "credited as 2½ martens."[116] Similar exchanges occurred, but no specification of the peltry's quality or weight was recorded. Accounts from various years equated the value of a beaver that was given in payment with widely varying numbers of martens.[117]

Trading Practices

The majority of the accounts relate to debts of, and disbursements by, individual customers. Many of the Wendells' clients were related to each other, but their transactions do not usually appear on communal or shared accounts. Exceptions can be found, such as in August 1705, when two brothers agreed to pay half of another brother's debt to the Wendells.[118] The total debt of several Indian couples was tallied for the couple, without identifying the individual debt of the man and woman. Clear examples are the entries for the Mohawk Canosedeckhaa, the Mahican Naghnaekamett, and their unnamed wives.[119] In a few other cases, however, a couple's account did show separate totals. That applies, for instance, to the accounts of the Mahican Wannapackes and his unnamed wife.[120]

A comparison of the appearances in the account book provides information on individuals alternating between trading on a shared account and on their personal account. Such is the case with the Mohawk Arija and his relatives.[121] While most accounts where he appears were in his own name, they also contain information on direct involvement of his mother, wife, and son. This small network dealt with the Wendells for the unusually long period between 1697 and 1720. His wife traded on their shared account and maintained her own. His mother was active on a separate account, but also fetched goods for other individuals, while his son is recorded only as being active on his own wife's account. Evidently they also provided services for other individuals and the ensuing debts were entered in the name of the other debtor. A similar pattern can be established for a number of other networks centering on individual men, such as the Mohawks Arijawaasen, Arijenhotsen, and Wagrassero.[122] Only once did the Wendells explicitly refer to a customer's private debt. A daughter of a noted Seneca sachem traded in large quantities during the years 1709–1710, and her first account (of two) shows Evert Wendell maintaining a separate tally of her personal debt. He did not indicate whether the other transactions in her account pertained to another individual or group.[123]

As was customary in trade between European merchants in New York, the Wendells's native clientele could postpone discharges on debts for long periods of time.[124] For example, the debt of one Canadian Mohawk man, started under Evert and Harmanus's father, was not paid until (at least) eleven years after the original transaction or transactions.[125] The account book lists seven additional cases of such arrears, described as being from older, or earlier times.[126] A sizeable number of accounts is marked by the absence of payment for years after a debt had first been developed. In fact, native customers could take out new obligations to the Wendells even if disbursement on all, or a good part, of their debts had not been forthcoming. For example, the earliest recorded trading by Caghneghtjakoo showed an existing debt and additional acquisitions on credit in 1705. Payment was not recorded, yet he took out new credit on two occasions in September 1709, at the value of four fishers, and was able to do so again in July 1710, for "1 beaver or bearskin."[127] None of these additional transactions was accompanied by a recorded disbursement.

Data from the account book points out further characteristics of the ways American Indians dealt with their debts. For Mahican and Iroquois clients, these data are summarized in table 11 (p. 60). Among the Mahicans, overall, only about one quarter of all accounts were fully redeemed and almost half were never paid at all. The Iroquois were initially able to perform considerably better on at least part of their obligations,[128] but over the years their debt management deteriorated considerably. As the Wendells slowly filled the account book with transactions on credit, they faced an increasing number of Iroquois customers who proved to be incapable, or unwilling, to satisfy their accumulating debt. In fact, the later pages of the manuscript show a higher percentage of Iroquois' accounts that were in default than the overall Mahican performance in this regard.[129] The trade book accounts show no apparent cases of the Wendells charging interest on the credit that they extended and only in a few isolated instances was a deadline for the delivery of payment given. Finally, there is no indication in the accounts that the Wendells ever denied their clients the possibility to take out a new line of credit, although they exhibited uneasiness with the debts of a few individuals and requested a surety or pawn from fifteen Indian customers.[130] Indeed, the number of cases where they extended gifts, or special arrangements to individual customers, or showed leniency in collecting debts, exceeded the number of instances discussed previously.[131] Despite ineffective debt collection and deteriorating levels of Indian payments over time, the Wendells continued to trade on credit.[132]

American Indians knew ways to maintain their access to European goods, despite growing indebtedness. One approach was to trade with various European traders. In the period between 1700 and 1709, Evert and Harmanus noted twenty times that a native customer was staying with, or trading at another merchant in Albany at the time they made a transaction at the Wendells' outlet.[133] In a small number of cases, they added the remark that these individuals usually did so, indicating that these were not incidental arrangements. Almost half of those who were mentioned on one or more occasions as staying or trading in the house or shop of another Albany trader were women.

Already in Dutch times, natives were described as moving from one residence or shop to another in search of the most advantageous commercial exchange they could find.[134] It was even expressed as official policy in colonial ordinances.[135] For the Indians this was not easy to attain, as traders applied various techniques to constrain the Indians to their shop (drinks, gifts, enticements). But the practice evidently continued into the eighteenth century. The Wendells also noted in five other cases that a particular customer was staying "here" or "with me"—an unnecessary comment if native clients were expected to trade or barter only at the place of their sojourn.[136] This constitutes one of the cases of Dutch practices in managing commercial exchanges with native customers that survived into the period of English rule.

Escorters and Guarantors

Although, in most cases, the Wendells recorded debts of individual Indian customers, this does not mean natives entered such exchanges on a purely individual basis. Various types of connections between separate customers can be found in the account book. A number of customers escorted and introduced other natives to the Wendells. Evert and Harmanus usually identified such escorters in the accounts. In addition, some natives facilitated trade between the Wendells and Indian customers by offering themselves as a guarantor for the other Indian's debt. On the whole, natives tended to escort individuals of the same ethnicity to the Wendells. The same principle applied to the relationships between Indian guarantors and the individuals they provided that service to (for that data, see tables 6 and 7).

During the years between 1696 and 1710, Evert and Harmanus recorded thirty-seven, possibly thirty-eight, instances of American Indian individuals escorting others to them.[137] Usually such pairs were kinfolk. No cases are recorded for the years 1700–1702. The ethnic affiliation of eleven Mahican escorters, eleven Mohawk (including four from Canada, three of these were men), three Onondaga, three Cayuga, and five Seneca individuals (one living in Cayuga and one probably from Canada, both were women) can be identified. A small group of customers was recorded as having acted more than once in this capacity. The majority of the instances had men escorting men and women escorting women. Compared to women, male customers were only slightly overrepresented in this activity: nineteen men and eighteen women acted in this fashion.

Also, Indian guarantors were active in the trade between the Wendells and their Indian clientele. For the period between 1696 and 1708, the account book contains sixteen cases of American Indian individuals who acted in such a function (see table 7, pp. 52–53).[138] A hiatus exists for a few years, as no cases were recorded for 1699 and 1700. In almost half of these cases (seven of sixteen), the guarantors had also escorted the customer to the Wendells.[139] Wherever the affiliation of the guarantors can be established, it becomes evident that this was a predominantly Mohawk affair in the Wendells' trade: eight Mohawks, including one woman from Canada, five Mahicans, and one Cayuga Indian appear in this fashion. Only one Indian is recorded as having acted more than once in this capacity. Almost without exception, guarantors acted in this manner for other members of their own nation, or group. The account book shows only one unusual instance, when a Mohawk woman acted as guarantor for an Oneida woman. Similar to the practice of escorting, men acted as guarantors for men and women performed this function for female clients. The only documented exception relates to a Cayuga man who acted as a guarantor for a woman, who was almost certainly Mohawk.[140] The role of guarantor was performed more by men than by women (ten men, six women).

Usually, but not always, the person who acted as an escorter of, or guarantor for another customer had the debt (resulting from transactions with the Wendells) added to his, or her own account. In the case of guarantors, this follows naturally from their function. However, even there, on at least three occasions, the newly introduced clients took out a debt on their own account rather than that of their guarantor. These are on pages [28], [43], and [55]; the case on [9] remains ambiguous in this regard.

Native Agents and Peddlers
The account book shows that the Wendells deployed several Indian agents (see table 12, pp. 58–59). Ten other natives may have peddled goods on their own account, as they purchased goods on a single day in sufficiently substantial quantities to suggest such activities. There are fifteen instances where the volume of trade goods purchased in one day suggests this type of trading by indigenous

persons. With the exception of Aekoetts and Aedecaijijkaa, the ten men who traded on these accounts belonged to the Wendells' most frequent customers. They are listed in table 13 (p. 61).

For the period 1697–1707 and the year 1714, table 13 shows that especially (De) Kanasquiesackha and Sakadereiughthaa were active in this fashion, appearing four and three times, respectively. Except for one Mahican man, it is likely that all possible peddlers were Mohawks. One man was listed as a French Mohawk, two had evident ties to Canada (Decakedoorens and Sakadereiughthaa), and a fourth customer (DeCanjaeDeReghtToo) was documented as residing there in 1723/4. Two out of the ten possible peddlers from table 13 also appear as identifiable, documented agents in table 12. Both were Mohawk men: Canosedeckhae and Caaheghtsiedawee.

Bills

The account book contains a number of cases where Indian customers were handed written bills summarizing their debt with the Wendells. This is not to claim that the Wendells were in the habit of writing them a full bill, as they were wont to do in the case of commercial transactions with others merchants in Albany, New York, Boston, or Europe. Perhaps they were mostly a quick overview of the individual's debt tally, showing the same pictographic renderings of the number of a given type of fur that the Wendells had recorded in the account book. In most cases, the Wendells commented specifically that the customer had carried the bill with him or her, but this was a practice the Wendells used predominantly with men. Evert, on one particular occasion, requested of his partners that a native client be asked to show his bill before additional credit was extended and new transactions were to be recorded on that bill. Apparently, some of the customers who had carried a bill were expected to present it on their return. Between 1699 and 1718, the Wendells supplied native clients with bills in eleven cases (listed in 14, p. 60).[141] Only the Mohawk man Caheghtsiedauw/Caaheghtsiedawee received a bill more than once. The practice was applied almost exclusively to Mohawk men; only one Cayuga man (probably from Canada) and two Mahicans received a bill that summarized their debt. The latter two were Wanapakes and his wife. The remaining customers were all Mohawks, and eight from the total group of ten individuals were men.

Pawns

Almost all transactions between the Wendells and their customers lacked any type of assurance that Evert and Harmanus would see a return on their investments. There were some instances where the brothers attempted to develop a secured credit. In such cases, native clients were requested to leave behind a pawn, or security, against their debts. These occurrences are listed in table 15 (pp. 62–63). The Wendells extended this type of secured credit on seventeen occasions, in the years between 1701 and 1710 (one of the instances seems to date from 1699).[142] Only one Indian was requested to provide a security on more than one occasion, but two of the three cases may refer to a single instance. The total number of Indian individuals who were involved in these transactions was seventeen. Twelve of these were men, and Mahican clients were more likely to place a surety with the Wendells. They did so in seven instances, while Mohawk customers provided a security in only five cases. Oneida, Onondaga, Cayuga, and Seneca individuals appear only once in such a way. Requesting pawns from Indian customers was usually prohibited by Albany's regulations for the fur trade,[143] that may help to explain the paucity of occurrences of this practice. However, it is known that the Wendells had few qualms about selling large volumes of rum to their clientele, while that activity was also deemed illegal in the ordinances.

Gifts and Special Arrangements

Between the years 1701–1708, Evert Wendell[144] made gifts, or offered special arrangements to his American Indian clientele in a total of ten cases (see table 16, pp. 64–65). Most likely, he was attempting to ensure that customers would come back for additional transactions. In six of these, Wendell achieved this objective and the customers did indeed return to trade, or to pay all or part of their debts. The result remains unclear in two cases (see the instances on pages [35] and [50]), but two customers did apparently not reappear to trade, or settle their account (on [68] and [81]). Wendell made presents to, or special arrangements with, both Indian men and women (five females were involved and seven males), none of whom he described as Mahican. A relatively large number of cases involved clients from Canada, all of whom were Iroquois: three Mohawks, one Onondaga, and one Seneca man. No individual was the recipient of a gift, or a special arrangement on more than one occasion. In one case, an Indian customer offered the Wendells a present: in July 1700 the Mohawk man Dekanasquiesackha took out a large quantity of merchandise on credit. Evert Wendell noted explicitly that:

> He must not be charged for what follows[,] he has 1 [sic] promised a gift for it. Nor does he carry it with him on his bill.[145]

However, even in the case of specific requests, the Wendells were not always in the habit of accommodating particular wishes, or preferences of their native clientele. Although an arrangement was made in September 1702 for the Seneca man Aeredonquas (see table 16), Wendell showed no additional latitude with him on a later occasion. In August 1709 Aedonquas requested that a certain delivery of goods would be charged to his wife's account. Evert Wendell would not hear of this, and noted:

> I did not want him to proceed like that[,] so that he has it on his own account.[146]

Travels by American Indians

The accounts provide information about cases where Indians set out on trips to the northwest, north, or northeast of Albany. In some instances, the Wendells limited their involvement in these journeys to providing supplies on credit, but other travels were clearly initiated by them. Harmanus, but Evert more so, used Indian customers to bring merchandise to areas near Albany and to more distant regions in the Northeastern woodlands. During the years 1696 and 1700–1710, the Wendells recorded twenty-seven occasions of native clients traveling to or from Albany (see table 12, pp. 58–59).[147] Such trips were undertaken by both men and women, in almost equal numbers (fifteen men and fourteen women; the total number of individuals is higher than twenty-seven, since two couples were recorded in this manner). The great majority involved Mohawks: seventeen men and women. Five Mahicans also appeared in this fashion, as do four Senecas and one Catskill Indian; no other groups were mentioned, and no individual was described as being only Canadian. Only two Indians appear more than once.

Indians acted as intermediaries in the Wendells' trade with native groups, both near and far away from Albany. Only a limited number of Western, "farr Indians" traded directly with the Wendells. The number of these customers is between less than twenty and, more likely, less then ten.[148] Using data from table 1, these figures represent only between 3 and 6 percent of all identifiable individuals in the account book.[149] But the Wendells maintained some indirect trade with Canada, possibly including "farr Indians," through native intermediaries. From the total twenty-seven cases reported in table 12, thirteen can clearly be identified as journeys by eight women and seven men who carried merchandise from the Wendells to sell elsewhere.[150] Three instances contain information on the destination of these native agents, or intermediaries. This also seems to be the case in a fourth instance,[151] and all of them relate to Canada. In five other instances, transactions were recorded with three men and two women without the explicit statement that the native persons were to sell merchandise for the Wendells, but the latter's involvement in the trips is evident. In January 1703, for instance, the Wendells sent rum with an unnamed, "blackish" Mohawk woman to the Oneidas, noting that she went there "to sell the rum."[152] The destination of these trips is known in four cases. They were the areas inhabited by the Abenakis, Oneidas, and Ottawas.[153]

The information from the account book and table 12 refines our understanding of attempts by the Wendells to reach out to native groups to the west. Linking such groups into its commercial–diplomatic arrangements had been a long-standing objective of New York policies. The earliest recorded visit to Albany by delegates from native groups around Detroit dates from 1704, although the sources state that they had been preceded by a delegation in 1702.[154] Full-fledged trade did not occur until 1707[155] but, before that, the Wendells had been involved in trips by three Mahican individuals to Ottawa (in 1701, 1703, and 1704), traded in Albany with a Mahican man and woman (both living in Ottawa),[156] and established an account for an Ottawa man and an individual from Detroit with an extremely complex ethnic history (all in 1706).[157] But although the Wendells also traded with clients from Ottawa in 1707, and continued to do so afterward,[158] the Wendells' account book contains no indication that they ever managed to develop a substantial core of customers to the west of Iroquoia.

Acting as an intermediary in the Wendells' trade with Canada could be a source of considerable income. The manuscript discloses exact payments on three occasions, all involving Mohawk men. Canosedeckhaa's trip in August

1707, earned him fifteen beavers (partially a payment in merchandise, partially a debt reduction). That compensation was comparable to that of Caaheghtsie-dawee, who had fourteen beavers deducted from his debt because of his services in July 1708. The third and latest recorded payment is of quite different dimensions: Daniell received one pair of stockings for his journey in September 1710.[159]

Leeway and Flexibility by the Wendells

The account book shows no evidence of a systematic attempt by the Wendells to collect payments on natives' arrears. On the other hand, examples of a certain degree of flexibility in the Wendells' style of debt management can be inventoried (presented in table 17, pp. 66–67). The Wendells limited their flexibility almost exclusively to their dealings with regular customers. Only once did they offer it in their dealings with Indian women. Table 17 demonstrates that between 1700 and 1710, the Wendells' management of their native customers' debts showed elements of flexibility and leniency in twenty-two cases.[160] Once again, Mohawks appear most often in this regard: ten men and one woman are identifiable as such (directly or indirectly) and three were from Canada. Three customers were Mahican, one a Catskill Indian, and one was either a Mahican, or perhaps an Abenaki. Three Seneca men were treated with leniency, one of whom "used to live in Canada." In addition, one Cayuga man received free repairs of his gun and the debt of another Cayuga man, staying in Canada, was also treated with some leniency. Conversely, on one occasion, an American Indian customer provided leeway to the Wendells in establishing his arrears. They could charge him as they pleased for a small cask of rum when he returned to trade.[161]

Unusual Circumstances with Indians' Debts

Leniency on the part of the Wendells in their debt management was no guarantee that every American Indian customer agreed with the value of a particular transaction. No analysis can be made on the basis of the limited number of occurrences of such disagreements. They pertain to Mohawk clients only, and two women were involved. In one of these cases, Harmanus explicitly urged his partners to record all deliveries to a Mohawk man on his bill, "or he will deny it."[162] Possibly as a means of preventing such disagreements about the exact volume of certain arrears, on three occasions the Wendells intended or decided to approach a client directly and query him or her about their account. One woman was involved in such a case.[163] Saakadesendee, for instance, a Mohawk man who lived among the Senecas, was to be "queried in person" because not all of his transactions had been noted. On occasion, the Wendells also made payments for their Indian clientele on outstanding debts with other Europeans in and around Albany. In one case, Evert Wendell made a down payment, when the Mohawk man Aeijawassen purchased a dog from a soldier (see the case from February 1707, in table 18, pp. 68–69). Between 1705 and 1709, the Wendells provided this type of service in eight instances.[164] The practice was restricted to male clients. More so than others, Mahican customers availed themselves of this service. Two

Mohawk men with strong links to Canada had a debt with another merchant satisfied by the Wendells.

Money in the Trade

Close study of the account book yields a number of findings that detail the way in which money played a role in transactions between the Wendells and their clientele. Without exception, accounts that enumerated the value of transactions or debts in money terms show the use of Dutch currency (guilders and stivers). Not one account of a native customer features the use of English currency.[165] From the total number of accounts 46 of 400 (11.5 percent) show all or part of the transactions or debts computed in Dutch guilders. Some of these accounts are among the most substantial in the account book. Such accounts deal almost solely with Mahican customers. The various groups described by the Wendells as Mahican had, on the whole, less access to furs from the interior. Under these circumstances, their debt was calculated to a smaller degree in terms of peltry than in the case of Iroquois customers. However, being Mahican and amassing a debt calculated in Dutch currency cannot be equated with a destitute economic situation, because some very substantial trading partners and volumes were involved.[166] The use of the Dutch monetary unit in commercial exchanges with American Indians was not restricted to the upper Hudson. In the first quarter of the eighteenth century, guilders and stivers were the exclusive type of currency in accounts of Esopus and other Algonquian-speaking Indians with a trader in Ulster County, located halfway between Albany and New York City.[167] This is not to say that in this account book, or the one from Ulster County, use of the term guilders signified the exchange of hard currency.

The Wendells' account book also contains 111 instances where quarters were used as an accounting unit; in fifty-five of those, natives acquired this item in specie, or as money. "Quarters" were also used in different ways, without the descriptive element of "cash," or money being applied: fifty-one times among Indians' debts for trade goods or services, once as a form of payment by an Indian customer, and on four occasions to describe the balance still due to native customers after they made payments in excess of their debt. In most instances, the accounting unit was used to describe peltry and merchandise: one "quarter" was the equivalent of the fur of one raccoon, two represented the value of one marten, and eight of them amounted to one beaver. It could also be one piece or bar of lead, a knife (sometimes half the value of a knife), and two skipple of Indian corn. A boy's shirt sold for five "quarters," a bottle of rum for two.

This leaves undetermined the exact nature and even the type of currency that was referred to as "quarters." The practice in colonial North America of cutting coins into smaller pieces is well known,[168] and due to the lack of specie in the colonies, foreign currencies were widely used in economic exchanges.[169] The presence of the Spanish piece-of-eight, and quarters thereof, in Dutch and British colonies in the Americas can be demonstrated for both the mid-seventeenth and early eighteenth centuries.[170] But the value of a piece-of-eight (a *peso*, consisting of eight *reales*) does not relate to the value that one-fourth of the coin—a "quarter"—would have represented. A "quarter" in this account book, when clearly used to denominate a monetary value, represented around one-and-a-half Dutch guilders (or thirty stivers); identical to the value listed in other instances on the upper Hudson around 1697–1699, and earlier.[171] Multiplying this by four, the entire coin would have had a value of around six guilders. The Spanish *peso* carried a value of between 12 and 13.50 guilders in New York.[172]

Transactions in the Country

The majority of transactions in the account book took place in Albany. On occasion, however, American Indians purchased goods on credit outside of the trading center, or paid part of their debts there (see table 19, pp. 68–69). Only Mohawks and Mahicans engaged in trade with the Wendells "in the country."[173] Native groups closest to the Wendells' home were more likely to appear in the record in this fashion. By far the greatest number of these transactions occurred with Mohawk customers (fifteen out of twenty-one, including one man who was possibly from Canada), while six were recorded for Mahican clients. Some native women were quite often involved in exchanges in the country: both Catri(e)n, Watcaro(o/s)'s sister, and Marijae, Canosedeckhaa's wife, each appear three times as trading outside of Albany. The account book contains information on one additional transaction with an Indian woman outside of Albany: a Mohawk woman was instructed to pay her debt in Schenectady.[174]

Such trips into the country continued long after the bulk of the recorded cases in this manuscript: in October 1721, Evert and Harmanus agreed on a compensation for Evert's trouble of going into Mohawk country to take care of Harmanus's business there. In this particular case, the journey was related to an attempt to purchase land from the Mohawks.[175] Before that, and also predating these journeys by the Wendells, Iroquois leaders had voiced their concern about commercial transactions outside the city of Albany. In August 1700, they urged Governor Bellomont of New York to restrict the trade to Albany, since "it has always been so." They underlined their uneasiness with such less controlled dealings in their homelands, stating:

> When your people come to our country wee must pay a Bever skin for a few spoons full of rum, and a Beaver for a pair of childrens stockings.[176]

They expressed the desire that Burnet "for the future forbidd peoples coming to trade in our country."[177] It is evident that the Wendells did not always honor that wish of the Iroquois leadership. Trading during these trips was also in direct contravention of trade regulations contained in Albany's 1686 city charter. The Wendells may have initiated such journeys for various reasons. It is very likely that they intended to circumvent the trade regulations in Albany. Certainly for the years around 1720, some sources state that traders from the city went westward and left merchandise in the country—hidden, or stored in Mohawk longhouses or hunting camps—until it could be picked up by native intermediaries from Caughnawaga.[178]

ADDITIONAL SIGNIFICANT ASPECTS OF THE MANUSCRIPT

The previous paragraph described the practices of the Wendells and their Indian clients that shaped the contours, habits, and characteristics in the fur trade in Albany. Besides such observations, the Wendells' account book also presents data that sheds light on various other circumstances and situations that, while not always in direct relationship to the trade, may help to further delineate aspects of native societies in the Northeast during the late seventeenth century and the first decade of the eighteenth century.

Native Ethnic Fluidity

The document contains numerous examples of fluid Indian ethnic affiliations. Various Iroquois individuals were described as living in Canada, or as exhibiting strong liaisons with places like Caughnawaga. The multiethnic nature of native settlements near Montreal has been observed in a number of studies.[179] Table 1 presents an inventory of all cases where Canadian residence of Indian traders can be established in this account book. The multiethnic composition of the communities there also extended to the most intimate bonds. For example, in June 1707, Evert Wendell noted that a young Mohawk man, Decannoessoekee, "lived in Canada [. . .] and had an Oneida woman as his wife."[180] The account book also contains evidence of native individuals migrating back and forth between the Iroquois' homelands and Canada. A young Seneca man with various names (Sacksareeij/Annahriesaa/TaenNaahariesie/Annahriese, the latter of which he used as his new name, in 1707) is once identified, in an account probably dating from 1706, as living in Canada and another entry states that he had returned to live in Seneca country in 1708. He was clearly described as a Seneca, while his father and brother were listed as Mohawks, residing in Canada—or living in Canada and Seneca country.[181] In addition, a number of customers are listed as usually staying or living in a community or among a named group of people, suggesting either that this community differed from their own, or that they alternated residence between the two, or possibly both.

A number of additional cases document the degree of mobility that characterized the lives of some native individuals. Among the more striking examples was the Mahican man, Maghcoes, who was described in (July?) 1706 as living in Ottawa, or among the Ottawas, and who reportedly had both an Algonquian and a Mohawk name.[182] A young man of Onondaga origins, D'waddierhoe (also Dewadierhoe), who had been a prisoner among the Miami Indians, lived (in June 1706) at or around Detroit, and traveled with a group of Ottawas to Albany.

Perhaps not surprisingly, Evert Wendell noted that the latter could hardly remember the Onondaga language.[183] Decakedoorens (also d'Cackkeedooren), a Mohawk man described as living in Canada and Seneca country, shows signs of dual residence. Like Sacksareeij (Annahriesaa) mentioned previously, this individual appears with a new name in the account book: Canaghquajeese.[184]

The permeability of native ethnic demarcations is evidenced also in other ways. The very first account in the manuscript witnesses a Sounos (also listed, later on the same page, as Souwenos)[185] man who was described by Harmanus Wendell in June 1699, as staying among the Onondagas. Summarizing this, and nine additional cases where Indians were described as residing, staying, or living in communities that were extraneous to their own ethnic entity (excluding apparent migrants to Canada), it becomes apparent that: Seneca individuals were described six times in this fashion, the largest number of individuals were reported to have relocated among the Cayugas (six times), and that men were mentioned significantly more often (eight instances) than women as having migrated outside their ethnic group.[186] The Wendells were sometimes undecided about the affiliation of a certain customer. In one instance, Harmanus ascribed two, quite different, identities to Waelekeiet, a female customer: she is first described as a Mahican and later, only two lines below that, as an Ottawa.[187]

Black and White American Indians

In four cases, the Wendells described Indian customers as black (*swart*), or blackish (*swartigh; swartaghge*). Three out of the four are women.[188] The manuscript contains more references to white Indians (*blanck; blank*) than to black ones (eight, against four). Seven of the eight references are to women (three of those to the same woman, and the other four are four different women), only one (the eighth) to a man.[189] As described in the notes to the translation, there is documentary evidence of Evert dealing with another "black [male] savage" on at least one additional occasion.[190]

There is little doubt that these cases refer to individuals exhibiting mixed racial backgrounds, or who had been removed to American Indian communities.[191] In all instances, the Wendells ascribed to them the racial epithet of savage, adding, in most cases, their affiliation or their place of residence. This clearly implies that they were living in Indian communities and suggests that they dressed and behaved as American Indians. By the early eighteenth century, there had been decades of frontier warfare, in which numerous black and white individuals had been captured and carried back to Indian villages. Most of such documented cases, however, relate to the second half of the eighteenth century.[192] This account book is significant in situating at least ten individuals in Albany during the first decade of that century, who were seen as being different in their complexion from other native visitors.[193]

To the white and black savages straddling the demarcations between fixed racial categories, the English Indian Peckwanck, with close connections to

Seeckaet (various spellings), can be added. He is listed (on page [10], and an account partially repeated on page [11]) as a native customer "with red hair."[194] He is the only native customer described in this fashion. Red hair not being among the expected external features of American Indians, it may be assumed that he was the child of a European and an American Indian.

African Slavery

By 1709, the Mahican Wannenpackes (various spellings), and his unnamed wife, had developed a substantial debt with the Wendells, especially with Evert. They traded on a shared account, but occasionally specific transactions were recorded with only one of them. In one such instance, the native woman informed Evert Wendell that she intended to redeem part of her debt by selling a "Negro boy."[195] Some evidence exists of escaped or abducted Africans in the area. In 1705, New York proclaimed an act "to prevent the flight of Negro slaves from Albany." It was stated at the time that some slaves had already run away.[196] At times, authorities and major merchants in Albany were called upon to aid in the release of abducted slaves who were now in Southern colonies along the Atlantic coast by paying a ransom to the slaves' new native "masters," or by other, more diplomatic, methods.[197] Still, the fate of most escaped or abducted Africans, who may have sought refuge in American Indian villages—or were kept there against their will—cannot be established.[198] Some decades before the previously mentioned case, runaway slaves with basic linguistic skills, which enabled them to survive among native communities, have been documented.[199] But the unambiguous occurrence in the this manuscript of a person of African descent in bondage to an American Indian individual is the earliest, for the Northeast, that I have encountered. In addition, it is noteworthy that it is the woman of this Mahican couple who makes this particular statement. It is an established fact that matrons in Iroquois society decided on the fate of new additions to their communities, when such individuals were abducted during raids on European or native settlements and brought into villages, but no documented case is known where proprietary rights regarding a "Negro" individual fell to a woman—certainly not among the Mahicans.

"Our savage"

In a few cases, Evert Wendell and, to a lesser degree, Harmanus registered a type of relationship between European individuals and their native clientele, the exact nature of which remains unclear. On six occasions (three in the hand of Harmanus), the Wendells recorded transactions with a woman, or others directly related to her, who they referred to as "our young female savage."[200] The unnamed Mahican woman appeared in accounts between 1698 and February 1710.[201] Also, between 1704 and October 1709 Evert detailed commercial exchanges with a Mohawk woman, who he described as white, and (initially) young, adding that she was "our Susanna's female savage" (referring to his older sister). However, both a slightly earlier account, and one that covers the period between October 1709 and May 1715 lack the possessive qualification and recorded merely that she "stayed with our Susan." In addition, these entries identified her as living in Canajoharie, or the "upper [Mohawk] castle," and stated that she had peltry in the country that she would use to redeem part of her debt. The latter two accounts are also in Evert's hand.[202] Two other instances document Evert Wendell applying a description alluding to a proprietary position of Europeans in their relationship with native individuals. Both cases relate to men. He opened an account for an Oneida and an Onondaga man (the latter living in Canada), who he identified respectively as being "of" Stephanus Groesbeeck and as "a brother" of an Indian client "of" Johannes Lansing.[203] Taken together, these eleven statements may indicate that these natives were in a state of unspecified servitude to the Wendells and other prominent merchants in Albany.

The existence of Indian slaves in colonial New York is undisputed. Although in 1679 Governor Edmund Andros held that enslavement of American Indians constituted an illegal practice, and the Assembly officially outlawed it that year, several historians have observed that it continued to exist in the colony.[204] There are indications that Indian slaves were included in at least two wills from the decades before and after 1700.[205] Among the slaves who were convicted for their participation in a revolt in New York City in 1712, several were described as being "Indian slaves."[206] Also, two ordinances for Albany County explicitly proscribed certain actions by "negro or Indian slaves" in the mid-1720s.[207]

One source of bonded American Indian labor was native groups who had been defeated in colonial wars with the English to the south. A recent estimate is that, in the period 1670–1715, 24,000 to 50,000 Indians from the Carolinas were sold into slavery to the West Indies and various northern colonies, including New York.[208] But whereas various of the Wendells' wills specifically redistributed African slaves among relatives, none of these instruments contains a reference to "Indian" slaves.[209] In discussing the presence of American Indian men and women in colonial households on the northern frontier, Jacobs noted that up to, at least, the 1680s such cases were few and scattered, and that they pertained to children only. Noting that it is impossible to determine if these minors were indeed slaves, he suggests that they may have been raised in a colonist's family in an effort to convert them.[210] In general, it has been observed that bonded native labor occurred far less frequently in New York than in New England.[211]

Considering the above, the exact status of such native individuals who the Wendells described as "our," or as "our [sister] Susanna's," or as being "of" another merchant, must remain undetermined. They may have been attached as servants to colonial households. The duration of such servitude would have extended over a certain prearranged period of time, or up to the decease of one of the parties in the arrangement. That could explain the relationship between Susanna Wendell and "her" unnamed Mohawk customer. For a period of time between the instances where she was described as merely "staying with" Susanna, the young Indian woman may have been engaged as a servant in Susanna's household. Before and after that, she may have lived in Canajoharie, a

Mohawk village. The existence of Indians as indentured servants in European households has been documented for the Northeast, although their numbers seem to have been minor in New York.[212]

Tattoos, Sketches, Portraits, and Marks

In ten cases, the Wendells remarked on a customer's tattoo or, more often, the lack thereof.[213] Adding instances where they drew a quick sketch, or a more detailed portrait of the face (and, at times, the upper chest) of a customer, but did not comment on markings presented therein, the total comes to fifteen.[214] Two observations can be made from the combined instances. First, all references are to men. Second, they are all related to customers from areas at a distance farther removed from Albany, as none refer to Mahican, Mohawk, or Oneida clients. Male tattooing was a widespread practice in the Northeast, the Great Lakes area, and elsewhere in North America.[215] Individuals from the Oneida, Mohawk, and Mahican groups would also have had facial and body tattoos.[216] Their absence from the list of individuals whose ornamental or ceremonial markings were described by the Wendells seems unclear. Evert and Harmanus included this aspect of a customer's physical appearance as an added element in describing customers who they had fewer opportunities to meet on a regular basis. It may have served as a feature that assisted the Wendells in recognizing such individuals at their anticipated return to Albany, whereas such an added element was apparently not required in meeting and trading with natives who were from the vicinity, who were already known, or who the Wendells met (or expected to meet) with some regularity in other circumstances.

One instance is more complicated. In April 1702 Evert Wendell noted that the young "blackish" Cayuga Aijadatha had "not yet" been "tattooed on his face": the only occurrence of this description in the account book.[217] Whereas the remark that a customer had no tattoos appears more frequently (six times), the description of the young Cayuga men suggests that the presence of such a physical mark was part of a young person's transition from one phase in life to another. This ties in with the observation that, in nine out of the fifteen cases, the Wendells specifically stated that a customer either did or did not have a tattoo and was young; it probably served as a marking point in the evolution of Indian men through various stages of their lives, both in a physical and social sense.[218] This is supported by one of Evert Wendell's remarks when, perhaps somewhat surprised, he described a Seneca as being without a tattoo, and observed "but he has 2 moustaches at his mouth."[219]

Other graphic elements in the manuscript are marks by Indian customers; they appear on pages [1], [57], and [66].[220] The first is by a *sounos* or *souwenos* (Shawnee) customer, Tankarores, and depicts an animal, most likely a turtle. He may have also placed a second mark in the same account. The nature of the subject in the second mark, by Josquassoe or Tennessocthaa ("a young Seneca"), is not intelligible. Like the first mark, the third depicts an animal, but it is difficult to ascertain the exact type. The mark, described by Evert Wendell as the customer's hand, was placed by DeCanjaeDeReghtToo, a Mohawk man with strong

Canadian connections. Perhaps, although the Wendells never stated it, the customers placed these markings to signal that they had understood and agreed to the value of a certain transaction, or their total arrears at a given point in time. The Wendells made numerous sketches and markings in the manuscript. They include pictographic renderings of the animals, which native customers were expected to deliver in furs as payment. Some of these are included in plates I, II, and III. Some additional examples are not reproduced there, because at times the Wendells drew oval shapes to represent furs of raccoons, deer, and elk. They also made crude sketches of a gun and a pistol that were delivered to Indian customers.[221]

Native Naming Practices

The text of the account book contains a number of instances regarding individuals' names. Three cases were discussed earlier.[222] Evert Wendell made a similar observation regarding a Seneca man. In July 1702 Evert opened an account for this customer with the words: "his name [is] Dekanesthejendaghqua[.] His new name [is] Aewaenaccoo[or -anoo?]."[223] Adding the other two cases of Indians listed with a new name, it becomes apparent that all customers described in this manner were men, but belonged to different native groups; two out of three (the ones discussed earlier) had links to various Iroquois nations, sometimes contemporaneously. A considerably larger number of clients were recorded with two names, without the remark that one of these was new, and this occurred almost invariably within the same account. Cases where two names for a single individual (a customer, or a relative) are documented and appear eleven times. An example is the Seneca client Tannassecha, whose account states this name, but also lists Kawessat.[224] In addition, there are five cases where it remains uncertain if the Wendells actually recorded two different names for a single person. These instances may constitute natives' references to their place of residence, or the slight variations of the recorded names leave room for the interpretation that they were simply two renderings of the same name.[225] The few cases of individuals who were described as having three names must be added. They are two Seneca men: Aeredonquas/Onissonda/Thanawese, who "lives in Canada among the Mohawks," and Josquasso/Aennesochtaa/Anadeias.[226]

This overview excludes the case where Harmanus evidently wrote out two variations of a single name (a Mahican named "kahaeckan or kaeghakan," on page [2]), and instances where an alternate name is clearly a European given name, or likely a nickname (Sam and Aberham are the sole examples of the first type).[227] It is not certain if Hoedsewerke was actually a Dutch name, as Evert recorded on page [112]. Conversely, although Evert did not state so on page [72], a second name listed for an Oneida man, Hottentot, may certainly have been Dutch. Examples of apparent nicknames, used alongside native names, are: the Greyhead, the Bold Boy (or the Naughty Boy), Flatfoot, and the small Thickhead.

Finally, there is the case of an Indian woman, about whom Harmanus noted dryly that she had no name. However, he did provide her origins (Cayuga), added her sister's name, and may have anticipated additional exchanges with her, because he left quite some space empty within the lines separating her account from the following one on that page. My note in the translation suggests some possible explanations for this instance.[228] As in other cases, the Wendell account book perhaps does not present completely new observations, but is unique in that it documents such practices for recognizable historical native actors in and around Albany.[229]

Native Adoptions: the Wendells' Descriptions of Indian Kinship

On a few occasions, the Wendells' descriptions of their clientele provide information on adopted individuals, and all instances refer to men. In two cases, this aspect of a customer's position in his native society was stated explicitly. In January 1706 Evert Wendell started the account of Thaijadoores, an Indian man who he described as "a prisoner given to Arijenhotsen" (a Mohawk man). He also entered, in October 1709, an account of an Oneida man, Orghiakeuwaghkaa, and added that the latter was "the adopted brother of Canaghcoonia" (an Oneida war leader, later sachem).[230] In two additional instances, the information is somewhat more ambiguous. In 1703 (month unknown), "a young boy[,] Caeiewamp" made modest transactions with Harmanus Wendell, at which point the latter remarked that "Ouwee suckwans has always h[a]d" him. The ethnic affiliation of these two men has not been determined. Finally, when the account of a native man, "ThiocaghneeRadeie, living in Canada," was entered in the book in August 1707 Evert added the observation that "he belongs to Carghiaedsiecoo" (a Mohawk from Canada).[231] Thaijadoores was the only adoptee to return and trade with the Wendells. His account was quite voluminous, and shows entries up to November 1710. Such individuals traded on their own account, indicating that some adoptees were allowed to initiate and maintain commercial bonds with European traders from their position within the fabric of new family, clan, and kinship relations.

Regularly, the Wendells situated their customers in family or clan relationships. When documenting a customer's family situation, or mentioning an individual's kin in any other sense in the account book, they showed a strong propensity to record the male lines of descent, connecting natives through their male family members. When women appear in the account book, the Wendells often described them simply by referring to their husbands' name, and did so exactly one hundred times. Conversely, unidentified men were described by means of their wife's name in just seventeen instances. A customer's brother, when described in relation to his direct kin, appears sixteen times as a man's brother, and only once as a woman's brother. A different situation exists in the descriptions of younger men: while only eight boys or young men were identified by naming their father, the Wendells used their mother twice as often to place young native men in a parent–child relationship.

At times, the Wendells encountered complications in determining their customers' position within a kin structure. Finding themselves compelled to make use of stepping-stones in constructing a network of kinship around an individual, they consistently followed the direct female line. This can be discerned most clearly in cases where the Wendells defined a person by his or her relationship to the spouse or partner of one of their customers. This occurs thirty times, and none of these instances witness the use of a male relative as an instrument to link individuals through various degrees of kinship. Thus, eleven young men and boys are described as an Indian man's wife's son, but none as a woman's husband's son. Also, on seven occasions a woman was recorded as an Indian's wife's mother, and none as a mother of a woman's husband.[232]

Once again, some indications exist of the degree to which the Wendells were informed about the personal circumstances of their customers.[233] Evert and Harmanus were aware of, or informed about, the death of three individuals' partners: the Mohawk Oneghriedhaa's wife, the husband of an unnamed Onondaga woman, and the Seneca Oekedee's wife.[234] Also, they described a payment by a Mohawk woman (Catrin, Watcaroos's sister) as pertaining to her "last husband's" debt.[235] The Wendells recorded the purchase on credit of white stockings by an Indian man, and described him as the stepfather of the Mohawk Daniell.[236] They identified Dekanijadereghkoe as the brother-in-law of the Canadian man Dewannighrijeie, and the Mohawk SoeHaahies (from Canada) as the son-in-law of the Mohawk Senjaad'riesen.[237] Desochenjoda appears as the nephew or cousin of Kanasquiesackha (both men were Mohawk). And the Wendells were able to discern that the Mohawk Caaheghtsiedawee's present wife was the daughter of Tanenjores's wife (Tanenjores was probably also Mohawk).[238] To these cases, giving evidence of the degree of the Wendells' familiarity with their customer's backgrounds and family ties, the case of the Cayuga man Aennaedsoenes may possibly be added; Evert Wendell perhaps used the Seneca term for the customer's grandmother.[239]

The Wendells were also knowledgeable of the familial connections of the native woman they referred to as "our" (see the previous section, "Our savage"). Combining the entries on various pages in the account book allows for the observation that the Wendells' Mahican woman was married to the Mahican man Naghnacamet[240] and that they had a son named Osawaanans/OsSaawaanaens. Although she remains unnamed, her sister is also identifiable. She was married to Jan the Savage. Also their son, probably called Waskaemp, traded with the Wendells.[241] No information of this kind was listed for the Mohawk woman who Evert described as "our Susanna's female savage."

Prominent Indian Individuals

In the years between 1704 and 1710, the Wendells noted on thirteen occasions that a client either lived or stayed in the house of a person identified as a native, or that individuals acted as witnesses to certain arrangements, and in one case reported that a customer belonged to another Indian. These instances could signify that such individuals held a position of some prominence in an Indian nation or clan. These thirteen cases, listed in table 20 (pp. 70–71), involve a total of fourteen or fifteen individuals, none of whom are mentioned more than once in this fashion.[242] Of these, only four names have been reported in other sources as pertaining to individuals with representative or leading roles in native societies—usually in political or military capacities or both. They are Arija (a Mohawk war leader and sachem), Nietewakam (likely a Mahican, or River Indian sachem), Caienquaragtoo (a Seneca sachem, possibly a war leader), and Coghcaaradawen (a Seneca sachem).[243] The latter is also listed in the account book as Ceghcaareedawee and is described as the "highest sachem of the Seneca country."[244] He is the only person who is described explicitly as a sachem by the Wendells.

Having made an inventory of the appearances of (possibly) prominent individuals, several inferences can be made. Where the name and, in most cases, sex of an individual has been determined, it may be concluded that only one of these individuals (a Mohawk) was from Canada. Of the remainder, three were Mahican, three were Mohawk (not from Canada), and two can be identified as Seneca. None of these individuals were women. One individual, TiocaghneeRadeie, a young Indian man who lived in Canada, is described as being related to a possibly prominent person in more than one way. These descriptions occur simultaneously in one account. He is the only individual to appear more than once in the table.

Whenever the ethnic background of these (possibly) prominent individuals and their protégés can be described with a sufficient degree of certainty, it becomes evident that ethnic connections dominated such liaisons. For example, the three possibly prominent Mohawk individuals are described in relation to Mohawk protégés, and the Mohawk individual from Canada is recorded as the person to whom a young individual who lives in Canada belongs. In addition, all Mahican individuals are described as exhibiting a possible relationship of dominance over Mahican customers.

More ambiguous are the four cases where the Wendells described their clients as "big." They were all Seneca customers (although this identification is tentative in one case), referring to two men and two women, and appear in entries dating between 1705 and 1708. The manuscript contains no indications that these individuals occupied positions with an elevated level of status, so that the appellation may have simply described these persons' physical stature.[245] The latter seems likely, because Evert and Harmanus described an equally small number of customers as being of small bodily constitution, like the woman in 1705 who Evert depicted as being "an old[,] small female savage."[246]

Besides the possible and ambiguous identifications discussed above, the notes to the translated manuscript contain cases of certain or likely identifications of sachems, orators, and war leaders. For easy reference, they are listed in table 21 (p. 72). In numerous instances, the identification of Mohawk leaders was greatly facilitated by Gunther Michelson's linguistic expertise. Note that no attempt has been made in the inventory to reflect the inherently tentative process of describing persons in this fashion; for further details, consult the notes to the translation.

Clearly, Mohawk leaders (all male) were listed most often in the account book as they appear fourteen times, representing almost half of the twenty-nine cases reported in the table. That number does not include the Canadian Mohawk sachem Senjaad'riesen, or Orghjaedikhae, who was either a Mohawk or Canadian sachem. Sachems and leaders of groups other than the Mohawks occur in far smaller numbers: three or four Onondaga chiefs, two or three Seneca leaders, two or three Scaghticoke/Mahican sachems, two prominent Oneida men, and one from the Cayuga, Catskill, and River Indian groups.

Concluding Remarks

The Wendells' account book is a rich source for the study of the intercultural fur trade in Albany, New York, during the late seventeenth and early eighteenth century. A detailed analysis of its contents has yielded numerous observations and extrapolations concerning the activities of the Wendells and their Indian clients. By far the greatest group among the Wendells' customers was the Iroquois (70 percent of all identifiable individuals), among whom the Mohawks and Senecas were the most significant (30.2 percent and 16.2 percent, excluding Canadian Mohawks and Senecas). Mahican customers, from the Mahicans proper and other Algonquian groups, constituted another significant entity (16.5 percent). More than 10 percent of all clients were described as Canadian, as living there, or have been identified as residing in Canada (35–37 individuals, 10.6–11.2 percent of all identifiable American Indians). Sporadically, customers from more distant areas appear, including Ottawa, Abenaki, and French Indians. From an inventory of all transactions on credit, totaling almost 1,800, it becomes apparent that Indian clients purchased large quantities of textiles (30.5 percent of all transactions), followed by liquor (19.9 percent) and ammunition (12.9 percent).

The turmoil of King William's War (1689–1697) and Queen Anne's War (1702–1713) had disparate effects on the volume and intensity of the Wendells' trade. While a correlation has been found between the end of the first conflict and the number of newly created accounts in the account book, renewed English–French warfare in the first decade of the eighteenth century did not prevent Indian traders from undertaking the journey to trade with the Wendells. In fact, the number and volume of the Wendells' accounts grew impressively during Queen Anne's War.

Only a few of the revealing aspects that derive from a close examination of this manuscript have been incorporated into anthropological, historical, or ethnohistorical studies. Although Evert's account book is mentioned twelve times in secondary literature, only three studies offer substantial discussion of its contents, and these contain misconceptions.[247] Thomas E. Norton, for instance, maintains that only 20 percent of the Wendells' customers were women, a contention repeated by Robert Grumet and David A. Ezzo.[248] My analysis strongly indicates a considerably higher level of participation by female traders. In general, participation by women in the fur trade in the Northeast has not been described in the literature.[249]

The Wendells developed close commercial relations with a select group of

Iroquois traders, and a few Mahican intermediaries. Such agents provided a disproportionate share of the Wendells' revenues. It is evident that a considerable group of Iroquois and Mahican individuals successfully established themselves as mediators in the trade between the Wendells and native customers with the same ethnic affiliation. They escorted a significant portion of the native clients who are recorded in the account book. My characterization of these individuals as mediators is confirmed by an additional service they rendered to both the Wendells and their native clients. At times the escorters also agreed to act as guarantors for the person they introduced to the Wendells, thus facilitating further extensions of the trade network in which they were already incorporated. Such extensions could include the guarantor's direct kin, but were not restricted to relatives. The passages above suggest that by moving from a macro- to a micro-level, and by studying and interpreting the almost daily exchanges described in this account book, the observation can be confirmed that the effects of native participation in the fur trade "cannot be applied as a formulaic constant."[250] Individual Indians, like those in any other society, discerned possibilities and opportunities in participating in commercial exchanges.

Nothing in the preceding sections is intended to question the long-term detrimental effects of the increasingly widespread influence of European, capitalistic relationships on native societies and economies. The historical outcome of that process has invariably been a decline of native autonomy, and growing dependency. Generally, economic exchange tended to be in the disadvantage of the American Indians bringing products and services to the market. Moreover, natives had few possibilities to directly affect exchange rates.[251] Information exists about an Indian leader from Schagticoke who lamented, in 1698–1699, about the dire position of his people. Badgered by Albany traders for their debt, they had no means to comply with their obligations.[252] For the Iroquois the situation is more complex, as no comparable statements by their leadership were recorded. One historian claims that, as early as the mid-seventeenth century, the degree of their economic dependency on European trade goods constituted a threat to their very survival.[253]

Tables

TABLE 1. Origins of American Indians, recognizable as individuals

	A = total		Of A, without name		Of A, from Canada	
	n	%	n	%ᵃ	n	%ᵃ
Mohawk	106	32.1	7	6.6	17	16.8
Oneida	15	4.5	4	26.7	1	6.7
Onondaga	21	6.4	1	4.8	1(2?)	4.8 (9.6?)
Cayuga	33	10.0	5	15.2	1?	3.0?
Seneca	56	17.0	6	10.7	3	5.4
Iroquois, total	231	70.0	23	10.0	22–24	9.5–10.4
From Iroquoiaᵇ	207–209	63.0	21	10.1	n.a.	n.a.
Mahican	54–55	16.5	2	3.7	1–?	1.8–?
Canadianᵈ	13	3.9	3	23.1	13	100.0
Catskill	4–5	c. 1.4	1–2	?	——	——
Ottawa	2–4	c. 1.0	——	0	[all?ᶜ]	?
Abenaki	4	1.2	1	25.0	?ᶜ	?
Frenchᵉ	3	.9	1	33.3	[all?ᶜ]	?
English	1	.3	——	0	——	0
Shawnee(?)	1	.3	——	0	——	0
Unknown origins	12–13	c. 3.9ᶠ	10	c. 75.0	——	0
	325–330 [1% = 3.3]	99.4ᵍ	41–42	c. 12.3	35–?ʰ	——

ᵃ Percent of total n in the first column.

ᵇ Total n of Iroquois traders, excluding Canadian Iroquois.

ᶜ Members of these groups lived both in Canada and elsewhere. In these cases, the Wendells did not specify their customers' residence.

ᵈ Individuals counted here were listed, by the Wendells, as living in Canada, without stating an additional affiliation. Those living in Canada with a known ethnicity are listed in the third column.

ᵉ While a fourth Frenchman is mentioned in the manuscript, as "Jan or Aedewackhaa[,] a Frenchman who lives in Mohawk country," it appears unlikely that Evert traded with an Indian in that instance (see page [63], and the note there).

ᶠ For computation, n set at 13.

ᵍ The deviation from 100.0% is caused by the small number of individuals in some of the groups, and their effect on rounding off the percentages.

ʰ Total n of Iroquois from Canada, plus other natives from Canada without ethnic identification. An undetermined number of clients who may have been from Canada is not included in the total. Thirty-seven represents the total confirmed cases from the first two categories mentioned before; 10.9 is the percentage of the total n of Indian traders from the first column.

TABLE 2. First transactions on each account, by customers' origins

Year	Groups[a]														Total
	1	2	3	4	5	6	7	8	9	10	11	12	13	14	
1695	1	—	—	—	—	—	—	—	—	—	—	—	—	—	1
1696	1	1	—	—	—	1	—	—	—	—	—	—	—	—	3
1697	10	30	—	—	—	—	—	—	—	1	—	—	—	—	41
1698	6	7	—	1	—	—	—	—	—	—	—	—	—	—	14
1699	—	9	—	—	—	1	1	—	—	—	1	—	—	—	12
1700	1	6	1	1	2	—	1	—	—	—	—	—	—	—	12
1701	1	15	1	—	—	1	—	—	—	1	—	—	—	—	19
1702	—	8	1	—	6	8	—	—	—	—	—	—	—	—	23
1703	3	9	—	—	2	—	—	—	—	—	—	—	—	1	15
1704	13	12	2	—	4	10	—	—	—	—	—	—	—	1	42
1705	18	10	—	—	3	3	6	—	—	1	—	1	—	—	42
1706	5	8	5	2	2	8	1	3	—	—	—	1	2	2	39
1707	3	18	—	4	—	4	2	1	2	1	—	—	—	3	38
1708	3	11	—	—	5	2	4	—	1	—	—	—	—	1	27
1709	8	5	1	1	7	8	—	—	—	1	—	—	—	—	31
1710	3	5	1	3	—	2	1	—	—	—	—	—	—	1	16
1718[b]	1	—	—	—	—	—	—	—	—	—	—	—	—	—	1
1724[b]	—	1	—	—	—	—	—	—	—	—	—	—	—	—	1
1726[b]	—	1	—	—	—	—	—	—	—	—	—	—	—	—	1
n.d.	6	8	—	1	—	1	1	—	—	—	1	1	—	3	22
	83	164	12	16	31	52	11	4	3	5	2	3	2	12	400
Groups[a]	1	2	3	4	5	6	7	8	9	10	11	12	13	14	Total

[a] 1 = Mahican, 2 = Mohawk, 3 = Oneida, 4 = Onondaga, 5 = Cayuga, 6 = Seneca, 7 = Canadian, 8 = Ottawa, 9 = Abenaki, 10 = Catskill, 11 = Shawnee, 12 = French Indian, 13 = English Indian, 14 = Unknown affiliation.

[b] Break in chronological order.

TABLE 3. First transactions on accounts in which women were actively involved, by origins

Year	Groups[a]									Total
	1	2	3	4	5	6	7	...[b]	14	
1695	1	—	—	—	—	—	—		—	1
1696	1	—	—	—	—	—	—		—	1
1697	2	17	—	—	—	—	—		—	19
1698	2	4	—	—	—	—	—		—	6
1699	—	5	—	—	—	—	—		1	6
1700	1	—	1	—	1	—	—		—	3
1701	1	8	1	—	—	—	—		—	10
1702	—	4	—	—	1	2	—		1	8
1703	1	10	—	—	—	—	—		—	11
1704	7	8	—	—	4	9	—		—	28
1705	12	4	—	—	1	4	—		1	22
1706	1	4	3	—	—	2	1		—	11
1707	—	7	—	1	—	3	1		2	14
1708	1	3	—	—	—	1	3		—	8
1709	3	4	—	1	3	5	—		—	16
1710	1	3	—	—	—	1	1		—	6
1718[c]	1	—	—	—	—	—	—		—	1
1724[c]	—	1	—	—	—	—	—		—	1
1726[c]	—	1	—	—	—	—	—		—	1
n.d.	3	11	—	—	—	—	1		1	16
	38	94	5	2	10	27	7		6	189
Groups[a]	1	2	3	4	5	6	7		14	Total

[a] 1 = Mahican, 2 = Mohawk, 3 = Oneida, 4 = Onondaga, 5 = Cayuga, 6 = Seneca, 7 = Canadian, 14 = Unknown affiliation.

[b] Participation by women from the other groups included in Table 2 is not computed. The limited number of accounts for these groups makes a compilation irrelevant.

[c] Break in chronological order.

TABLE 4. Accounts with participation by native women, by customers' origins ($n = 189$)

Mahican	Mohawk	Oneida	Onondaga	Cayuga	Seneca	Canadian	Unknown	Total
45.8	57.3	41.7	12.5	32.2	51.9	53.9	50	49.6[a]

Note: All numbers are in percentages.

[a] This is the total number of accounts with involvement by women, from Table 3, for the native groups listed in Table 4, divided by all accounts from Table 2, for the same groups.

TABLE 6. Escorting occurrences

Page	Date: M/Y	Escorter	Name or description	Sex
[17]	?[a]/1696	{Mahican}[b]	Wassewaecke, the Greyhead	m
[17]	1696?	{Mahican}	Wassewaecke, the Greyhead	m
[6]	8/1697	Mahican	Walitgaes	m
[22]	?/1697	Mohawk	{Catrin}, Watkaroos['s] sister	f
[31]	1/1698	Mohawk	Sohoonachqae	m
[18]	10/1698	Mahican	Jacob De Willt [the savage]	m
[5]	?/1698	Mahican?	?, "our young female savage"	f
[34]	?/1699	Mohawk	Roetsieijoo or Dekaweeijeendigtachkoo	f
[116]	3/1703	{Mohawk}	Aeijewasee's wife	f
[115]	5/1703	{Mohawk}	Onghnedicha's wife	f
[22]	9/1704	Mohawk	{Catrin}, Watkaroos['s] sister	f
[38]	?/1704	?	Cattquierhoe	m
[38]	?/1704	Seneca, "lives in Cayuga"	Oskeea	f
[119]	1703/1704?	{Mohawk}	Groetie, Area's wife	f
[2]	1704?	Mahican	Wamosie	f
[5]	2/1705	Mahican	Naghnaekmet	m
[7]	2/1705	Mahican	Naghnakamet's sister	f
[18]	6/1705	Mahican?	?	f
[57]	9/1705	Cayuga	Aennaedsoenes	m

TABLE 5. Indian corn in transactions with native traders

	Mahican	Mohawk	Others
1. Occurrences as natives' debt	26 [24][a]	53 [46]	——
2. Payment by natives	4 [4]	10 [9]	——
3. Acquisition by natives	3 [1]	——	——
Total *n*, occurrences	33 [29]	63 [55]	——

[a] Transactions with Indian women are within brackets [ ].

Escorted	Name or description	Sex	Remarks
{Mahican}	Nannalamit	m	Same escorter as the other case on [17]; here, also acts as guarantor
?	?	m	Same escorter as the other case on [17]
?	?	?	——
?	?	f	Same escorter as the other case on [22]; here, also acts as guarantor
Mohawk	Saqaenakarie	m	——
?	?	m	——
Mahican	?, Neemam[et's] wife	f	——
?	?	f	——
?	?	?	Also acts as guarantor
?	?	f	Also acts as guarantor
?	?	f	Same escorter as the other case on [22]
Seneca, lives in Cayuga	Oskeea	f	——
?	?	f	——
?	?, small, old female savage	f	——
Mahican?	?, her sister	f	——
Mahican?	?	f	——
?	?	f	Repeated from [5], but "sister" added
?	?	f	——[c]
Cayuga?	Radewackeree, his *aensoet/achsoet*	?	Also acts as guarantor

(continued)

TABLE 6. (*continued*)

Page	Date: M/Y	Escorter	Name or description	Sex
[62]	12/1705	Mohawk {from Canada}	?	f
[18]	6/1705?	Mahican?	?	f
[18]	6/1705?	Mahican	?	f
[59]	?/1705?	Seneca	Oquenjonquas	m
[62]	5/1706	Mohawk	?	f
[64]	6/1706	Seneca {from Canada?}	Aeraedonquas's sister	f
[71]	7/1706	Seneca	Coetsiessee	f
[55]	8/1706	Seneca	?	f
[36]	9/1706	{Mohawk}	"Our Susanna['s] female savage"	f
[75]	?/1706	Mahican	Sanpatijs	m?
[79]	6/1707	Onondaga	Oranij	m
[79]	6/1707	Onondaga	Oranij	m
[84]	8/1707	Mohawk, from Canada	Carghiaedsiecoo	m
[57]	10/1707	Seneca	Josquassoe, Tennessocthaa	m
[88]	6/1708	{Mohawk, from Canada}	Oghseaknoendoo	m
[94]	11/1708	Cayuga	Aedewanienoo	m
[90]	6?/1708	Mohawk, from Canada	Carghiaedsiekoo	m
[16]	1708?	{Catskill}	Sanhaquisquaas	m
[98]	2/1709	Cayuga	Eghnidaa's mother	f
[112]	6/1710	Onondaga[d&e]	Dewadierhoe	m

[a] The ? indicates that data have not been conclusively ascertained.

[b] Information within brackets { } has been deduced from other entries or different sources.

[c] It cannot be established with certainty, but it appears that in all these three cases the escorter was Waeleghlauwett's wife. Her name has not been determined, but he was a prominent Schaghticoke Indian.

[d] He had been a prisoner of the Miami Indians, now traveled to Albany with the Ottawas, and lived in Detroit.

[e] According to Wendell, "his name in Dutch."

Escorted	Name or description	Sex	Remarks
Mohawk {from Canada}	Warhoose Rode	m	Woman escorting her son
Mahican?	Seghstawaesqua	f	——c
Catskill	Sou waes	f	——c
French	Schoeoendees	m	——
Oneida	Thehoghtaghqueesren's sister	f	——
?	?	f	——
Seneca	Jaadoendoeiee	m	——
?	?	f	Uncertain if transaction occurred
Oneida	?	f	——
Mahican?	Cattenarockes	m	——
?	Awanaaceere	f	Same escorter as the other case on [79]
Onondaga	Secqua-Riesera[s?]	m	Same escorter as the other case on [79]
?, "lives in Canada"	Tiocaghnee-Radeie	m	He "belongs to" the escorter
?	?, "a big savage"	m	——
{Mohawk}	Dekaquarendightha	m	——
?	?	m	——
?, Canadian	?	f	——
?	?	m	——
Cayuga	D'canjadereghtoo's wife	f	——
?	Hoedsewerke^c	m	Also acts as guarantor

TABLE 7. Occurrences of native guarantors

Page	Date: M/Y	Guarantor	Name or Description	Sex
[17]	?[a]/1696	{Mahican}[b]	Wassewaecke, the Greyhead	m
[17]	?/1696	{Mahican}	Wassewaecke, the Greyhead	m
[6]	8/1697	Mahican	Walitgaes	m
[5]	?/1697	Mahican	Jan Seeps	m
[22]	?/1697	Mohawk	{Catrin}, Watkaroos's sister	f
[28]	?/1697	{Mohawk}	Dekarijhondie	m
[33]	?/1697	Mohawk, from Canada	The Limping female savage	f
[29]	?/1698	Mohawk?	Wagrassero's mother	f
[43]	5/1701	Mohawk	Arija's wife	f
[23]	?/1701?	Mohawk	Sagnirroowanne	m
[116]	3/1703	{Mohawk}	Aeijewasee's wife	f
[115]	5/1703	{Mohawk}	Onghnedicha's wife	f
[9]	9/1705	{Mahican}	Atesoghkamen	m
[57]	9/1705	Cayuga	Aennaedsoenes	m
[55]	9/1708	Seneca	Caghquena	m
[112]	6/1710	Onondaga[c]	Dewadierhoe	m

[a] The ? indicates that data have not been conclusively ascertained.

[b] Information within brackets { } has been deduced from other entries or different sources.

[c] He had been a prisoner of the Miami Indians, now traveled to Albany with the Ottawas, and lived in Detroit.

[d] According to Wendell, "his name in Dutch."

Using a guarantor	Name or Description	Sex	Remarks
{Mahican}	Nannalamit	m	Same guarantor as following instance
Mahican?	?	m	Same guarantor as preceding instance
?	?	m	——
Mahican	Kaloolet	m	——
?	?	f	——
{Mohawk}	{Sahorackwaghte}	m	——
?	?	f	——
{Mohawk}	Kadareonichtha	f	——
Oneida	Cresteia's wife	f	——
Mohawk?	Kanaetsakigto	f	——
?	?	?	——
?	?	f	——
{Mahican}	Nietewakam	m	——
Cayuga?	Radewackeree	f?	——
{Seneca}	Oekaedee	m	Customer states that Caghquena acts as guarantor
?	hoedsewerke[d]	m	——

TABLE 8. Categories of trade goods, acquired in transactions on credit by Indians ($n = 1,785$)

Category	Items		Transactions	% of total n
1. Textiles			**953**	**53.8**
1.a *Clothing*			540	30.5
	1.a.1	shirts	237	13.4
	1.a.2	stockings	229	12.9
	1.a.3	coats	60	3.4
	1.a.4	shoes	8	.5
	1.a.5	headgear	6	.3
1.b *Woolens*			413	23.3
	1.b.1	blankets	236	13.3
	1.b.2	pieces, cloth	153	8.6
	1.b.3	unspecified	24	1.4
2. Liquor			**352**	**19.9**
	2.a	rum	339	19.1
	2.b	beer	9	.6
	2.c	cider	4	.2
3. Ammunition			**228**	**12.9**
	3.a	gunpowder	112	6.3
	3.b	lead	99	5.6
	3.c	shot	14	.8
	3.d	flints	3	.2
4. Money or specie			**68**	**3.8**
	4.a	"quarters"[a]	55	3.1
	4.b	in specie	9	.5
	4.c	money	4	.2
5. Knives/axes/harpoons			**51**	**2.9**
	5.a	knives[b]	33	1.9
	5.b	axes	14	.8
	5.c	harpoons	4	.2
6. Personal care/ wampum/beads			**47**	**2.7**
	6.a	personal care[c]	28	1.6
	6.b	wampum	9	.5
	6.c	beads	7	.4
	6.d	shells	3	.2
7. Firearms			**25**	**1.4**
	7.a	guns	22	1.2
	7.b	pistols	3	.2
8. Kettles/pipes/tools/ wire			**22**	**1.2**
	8.a	kettles	11	.6
	8.b	pipes	5	.3
	8.c	copper wire	4	.2
	8.d	tools[d]	2	.1
9. Tobacco			**14**	**.8**
	9.a	tobacco	10	.6
	9.b	tobacco boxes	4	.2

(continued)

TABLE 8. (*continued*)

Category	Items	Transactions	% of total *n*
10. Repairs		11	.6
	10.a guns	9	.5
	10.b other	2	.1
11. Deerskin		6	.3
12. Foodstuffs		6	.3
	12.a corn	3	.2
	12.b grits	1	.05
	12.c meat(?)[e]	1	.05
	12.d peas	1	.05
13. Transport		2	.1
	13.a canoes	2	.1
TOTAL		1,785 (2x)	100.4[f] (2x)

Note: Some items that were sold only once are excluded from Table 8. They include: 1 clock, 1 small cup, 1 small sword, and some buttons.

[a] The total number of transactions in which native customers acquired "quarters" is 55. Additional appearances are not incorporated in Table 8. "Quarters" were recorded 51 times among Indians' debts for trade goods or services, four times as accounting unit to determine the level of overpayment by a native client, and once as a form of payment by a native customer.

[b] Knives includes the occurrence of 3 specific types of knives.

[c] Personal care includes: dye (14 transactions); looking glasses, large and small (10); buckles (3); and one comb.

[d] Tools consist of beaver scrapers, and an awl.

[e] This instance is ambiguous, see the discussion in the Introduction.

[f] The deviation from 100.0% is caused by the small number of some of the types of goods, and their effect on rounding off the percentages.

TABLE 9. Types of peltry listed and depicted in the accounts

Marten	1,081	Fisher	74
Beaver	885	Raccoon	65
Lap	39	Deer	34
Drieling	8	Elk	23
Parchment	1	Fox	4
Beaver, total	934	Mink	3
Otter	89	Cat	1
Bear	80	TOTAL	2,387

Note: Data do not reflect actual volumes or numbers of furs; they constitute the *number of times* the category was used to describe or depict transactions or outstanding debts.

TABLE 10. Purchasing power of Indian corn and main types of peltry

Type of product ▶ Value, as credit ▼	Peltry: Beaver	Marten
MONEY		
Guilders	———	1700: 3 guilders
TRADE GOODS		
TEXTILES:		
Shirt		1697: 3m; 4m = 1 shirt (1 occasion: 2m)
	1700: 1b = 1 shirt 1704: 1b = 1 shirt 1708: 1b; 1b + 1m = 1 shirt	1700: 5m = 1 shirt 1704: 5m = 1 shirt 1708: 3m; 4m; 5m = 1 shirt
Blanket	1697: 1b; 1b + 1 o; 1b +1m; 1b + 2m = 1 blanket *duffel.* 2b = 1 blanket *stroud.* 1700: 1½b = 1 blanket; 2b = 1 blanket *stroud.* 1704: 1b; 1 large b = 1 blanket 1708: 1b + 1 o = 1 blanket; 2b = 1 blanket *stroud.*	——— ——— ——— ———
LIQUOR:		
Rum	1697: 1b = 1 small cask; 1 cask 1700: 1b = 1 small cask 1704: 1b = 1 cask 1708: 1b = 1 cask	1697: 1m = 1 bottle; 5m = 1 cask; 6m = 1 cask 1700: 1m = 1 bottle 1704: 1m = 1 bottle; 5/7/8m = 1 cask 1708: 1m = 1 bottle
AMMUNITION:		
Gunpowder	1697: 1b = 1 small bag 1700: 1b = 1 bag 1704: 1b = 1 bag 1708: 1b = 1 bag	1697: 1m = 1 small bag ——— ——— ———
Lead	——— ——— ———	1697: 1m = 1 bar 1700: 1m = 1 bar 1704: 1m = 1 bar; 1m = 2 bars
EQUAL TO		
Other furs	——— ——— ———	1697: 7m = 1b 1700: 6m = 1b 1704: 5m = 1b; 3m = 1b

Note: b = beaver; m = marten; sk = skipple; o = otter.

Otter	Fisher	Other: Corn
	1708: 3 guilders	
1704: 1 o = 1 shirt	1700: 1f = 1 shirt 1704: 1f = 1 shirt	1700: 5sk = 1 shirt 1704: 5sk = 1 shirt 1708: 5sk = 1 shirt
	1708: 1–1½f = 1 blanket	
		1697: 1sk = 1 bottle
		1708: 1sk = 1 bottle
1697: 1 o = 1 bag		
	1704: 1f = 2m	

TABLE 12. Travel of American Indians, on their own account or as intermediaries

Page	Date—M/Y	Traveler/intermediary	Name or description	Sex
[17]	?[a]/1696	{Mahican}[b]	Nannalamit	m
[33]	?/1700	Mohawk, from Canada	The Limping female savage	f
[8]	6/1701	Catskill	Schewas quawas	m
[34]	8/1701	{Mohawk}	Rotsie's daughter	f
[119]	1/1703	Mohawk	?	f
[9]	6/1703	{Mahican}	Nietewakam	m
[116]	7/1703	Mohawk?	Onogradieha	m
[10]	?/1704	{Mahican}	Niettewapwae	m
[8]	9/1705	Mahican?	Segh nae waes quae	f
[20]	9/1705	Mahican	WaenEnpaeckes	m
[76]	9/1706	Mohawk	Thotquariesen's wife	f
[97]	4/1707	{Mohawk}	Aeijewasen's wife's mother	f
[81]	6/1707[c]	Mohawk	Thowaa-Hodieshenthoo	m
[77]	8/1707	Mohawk	Canosedeckhaa	m
[86]	10/1707	{Mohawk}	Aeijewaesens's wife	f
[65]	2/1708	{Mohawk} {from Canada?}	Aequaenaghthaa, or the small Thickhead, and his wife	m, f
[76]	3/1708	Mohawk	Thotquariesen's wife	f
[76]	4/1708	Mohawk	Thotquariesen, and his wife	m, f
[87]	4/1708	{Mohawk}	Arija	m
[87]	5/1708	{Mohawk}	Arija	m
[83]	7/1708	Mohawk	Caaheghtsiedawee	m
[92]	9/1708	Seneca	Josquassoo or annosktoo	m
[85]	10/1708	Mohawk {from Canada?}	Johonnaghquaa's wife	f
[98]	8/1709	Seneca	Schadseeaaee	f
[103]	9/1709	Seneca	Ossenant	f
[103]	9/1709	Seneca	Dekaeont	f
[107]	9/1710	Mohawk	Daniell	m

[a] The ? indicates that data have not been conclusively ascertained.

[b] Information within brackets { } has been deduced from other entries or different sources.

Destination/origins	Wendells' involvement	Consequence
"Annaekonccoo," went with the Greyhead	Limited delivery of merchandise	Redeemed most of the debt; 5/1707
Canada	A "French kno"	Redeemed small part of debt; 1701
The Otttawas, by way of Schenectady	Substantial delivery of merchandise	Paid about half of his debt
Canada (with her mother?)	Supplies only	Redeemed most of small debt
Oneida	Sent rum with her	Probably succeeded, paid debt
The Ottawas	Supplies only	——
Canada, went with Aquerase	Limited delivery of supplies?	Not redeemed
The Ottawas, goods were carted to Schenactady	Limited delivery of merchandise	Pawned gun in Schenectady, Wendell sold his belt; 6 & 7/1706
?, went with Nietewaekam	?, not described	——
?, went with Metewackam	?, not clear	Paid his debt completely
?	Gave blanket to sell on Evert's account	Debt was redeemed
?	Gave clothing to sell	Debt was almost completely redeemed
Came "by way of the Ottawas"	Obscure, Wendell may have attempted to use him as an agent	——
Canada	Sent him there "for" Evert	He received 15 beavers in payment and against his debt
?	Gave textiles to sell "for" Evert	Probably did not succeed, debt remained unaltered
Canada?	Sent 25 small "tonties" with them, to sell on Evert's account	Goods returned, 7/1708; debt canceled
?	Gave clothing, possibly to sell on Evert's account	Debt was crossed out
?	Gave clothing to sell on Evert's account	Debt was crossed out
"the country" (probably Canada), see also below	Sent large quantity of merchandise with him, to sell on Evert's account	Did not succeed, returned merchandise; 6/1708
"the country," see above	Exchanged some of the goods	See above
	from other case on [87]	
Canada	Sent him there, Evert paid him	He earned 14 beavers against his debt
?	Sent 19 "tonties" with him, to sell "for" Evert	Probably did not succeed, debt remained almost completely unaltered
Canada	Evert received "pack of beavers from Canada" from her	Part of the woman's debt canceled
?	Sent 70 small "tonties" with her, to sell "for" Evert	Debt was satisfied, or rearranged (see the account)
?	Sent 41 "tontieties" with her, to sell on Evert's account	Probably did not succeed, debt remained unaltered
?	Sent 70 "tonieties" with her, to sell on Evert's account	Probably did not succeed, debt remained unaltered
"Proceeded to Canada"	Sent merchandise with him	He earned 1 pair of stockings

^c This instance is also reported in Table 16.

TABLE 11. Long-term developments in discharges on Mahican and Iroquois debit accounts

1. Segment, predominantly Mahican	Unpaid	Partly paid	Paid
pages [1]–[18] appr. 1695–1710; 78 accounts	36 = 46.2%	19 = 24.4%	23 = 29.5%

2. Segments, predominantly Iroquois	Unpaid	Partly paid	Paid
pages [19]–[37] appr. 1696–1705; 67 accounts	19 = 28.4%	32 = 47.8%	16 = 23.9%
pages [38]–[75] appr. 1698–1710; 111 accounts	41 = 36.9%	38 = 34.2%	32 = 28.8%
pages [76]–[114] appr. 1707–1710; 80 accounts	47 = 58.8%	17 = 21.3%	16 = 20.0%
Average, Iroquois:	41.6%	33.9%	24.9%

Note: Considering the diverse origins of native customers with accounts on pages [115] to [120], data from those pages are not included.

TABLE 14. Occurrences of carried bills

Page	Date: M/Y	Carrier	Name	Sex	Remarks
[19]	{?[a]/1699}[b]	Mohawk	Kanossoodickhae	m	Same as man on [48]
[42]	6/1700	Mohawk	Dekanasquiesackha	m	——
[24]	9/1701	{Mohawk}	Sohnerowane	m	——
[49]	6/1702	Mohawk	Watjandondieijo	m	——
[48]	2/1704	Mohawk	Canosedeckhae's wife	f	Man, same as on [19]
[58]	10/1705	Mohawk	Caheghetsiedauw	m	Same as on [83]
[66]	6/1706	Cayuga?, from Canada?	DeCanjaeDeReghtToo	m	——
[67]	6/1706	Mohawk?, from Canada?	Sakadereiughthaa	m	——
			Sakadereiughthaa	m	——
[83]	3/1708	Mohawk	Caaheghtsiedawee	m	Same as on [58], but different bill
[112]	5/1718	Mahican	Wanapakes	f	Same account as below
[112]	5/1718	Mahican	Wanapakes's wife	m	Same account as above

[a] The ? indicates that data have not been conclusively ascertained.

[b] Information within brackets { } has been deduced from other entries or different sources.

TABLE 13. Occurrences of likely native peddlers

Page	Date: M/Y	Agent/peddler	Name	Sex	Remarks
[21]	2/1697	{Mohawk}[b]	Kahonckhae	m	——
[39]	?[a]/1699	{Mohawk}	Dekanasquiesackha	m	——
[42]	7/1700	{Mohawk}	Dekanasquijesackha	m	——
[45]	10/1700	{Mohawk}	Dekanasquiesackha	m	Same as on [39] and [42]
[66]	6/1706	Mohawk? {later, in Canada}[c]	DeCanjaeDeReghtToo	m	——
[67]	6/1706	Mohawk? {from Canada?}	Sakadereiughthaa	m	Two additional appearances, below, also at [67]
[70]	6/1706	Mahican, "from below [Albany]"	Aekoetts	m	——
[72]	10/1706	"French Mohawk"	Aedecaijijkaa, "correctly said aedecanijhaa"	m	——
[83]	6/1707	Mohawk	Caaheghtsiedawee	m	This is a different, earlier instance than the one reported in Table 12.
[78]	7/1707	Mohawk, "lives in Canada and Seneca country"	Decakedoorens	m	——
[77]	11/1707	{Mohawk}	Canosedeckhae	m	This is a different, later instance than the one reported in Table 12.
[67]	10/1708	Mohawk? {from Canada?}	Sakadereiughthaa	m	——
[67]	1/1709	Mohawk? {from Canada?}	Sakadereiughthaa	m	——
[95]	12/1714	{Mohawk}	Waghrosraa	m	——
[42]	?	{Mohawk}	Kanasquiesackhe	m	——

[a] The ? indicates that data have not been conclusively ascertained.

[b] Information within brackets { } has been deduced from other entries or different sources.

[c] For evidence for his later residence in Caughnawaga (January 1723/4), see the note on page [41].

TABLE 15. Occurrences of putting down a security

Page	Date: M/Y	Provider	Name
[1]	?ª/1699?	Mohawk?	Karehadee
[45]	7/1701	Mohawk	Canossedeckha
[45]	6/1702	{Mohawk}ᵇ	oghquese or Canaghquese
[50]	9/1703	{Mohawk}	Thrghijoores
[3]	7/1704	Mahican	Paemoelt
[2]	?/1704	Mahican	Wamossij
[2]	?/1704	Mahican	Cees Dewelt [the savage]
[20]	9/1705	Mahican	WaenEnpaeckes
[62]	1/1706	Mohawk, from Canada	WaerhoesRoodee and his mother
[10]	6/1706	Mahican	Niettewapwae
[10]	7/1706	Mahican	Niettewapwae
[72]	8/1706	Oneida	Sattkattstoghka, or anetsondeian, and his wife
[14]	8/1706	{Mahican}	Nietewapewa
[69]	10/1706	Cayuga	HanNaaRoncoo
[57]	10/1707	Seneca	Josquassoe, Tennessocthaa { ,Aennossockte}
[100]	9/1709	Cayuga	Sasiendes
[79]	1/1710	Onondaga	Cananouwejaae

ª The ? indicates that data have not been conclusively ascertained.

ᵇ Information within brackets { } has been deduced from other entries or different sources.

Sex	Security	Remarks
f	Six pieces, wampum? ["sijven"]	——
m	Two hands of (a) wampum belt(s)	——
m	Gun	Later, Wendell bought it
m	Gun	——
m	Old blanket	Confusing description
f	Not described	Probably redeemed
f	Blanket	Wendell bought it, one week after security had been provided
m	Belt (and gun, harpoon?)	Confusing description
m, f	Axe	Boy "put down" the axe, mother redeemed it
m	Wampum belt	——
m	Gun	Security had been left with Anties Moll (Schenectady)
m, f	35 "pipes" [wampum]	Man "put down" the pipes, wife paid off all debt (redeemed them?)
m	Belt and a gun	Security (from two other cases, on [10]) used to redeem debt
m	Gun	——
m	Hand [of wampum?] belt	——
m	Bracelet	Wendell may sell it in the spring
m	Gun	——

TABLE 16. Instances of gifts to, or special arrangements with, native customers

Page	Date: M/Y	Affiliation/residence	Name	Sex
[35]	1/1701	Mohawk	Tanijijooris, and his wife	m, f
[22]	9/1702	Mohawk	{Catrin}[a], Watcaros's sister	f
[54]	9/1702	Seneca, "lives in Canada"	Onissonda[b], Aeredonquas, or Thanawase	m
[50]	1/1704	{Mohawk}	Arijenhotens's daughter	f
[20]	5/1705	Oneida	?[c]	f
[68]	6/1706	Ottawa	Mackkockwassien	m
[62]	7/1706	{Mohawk, from Canada}	Waerhoes-Roodee, with his mother	m
[65]	1/1707	Mohawk, from Canada	Aequaenaghthaa, or the small Thickhead, and his wife	m, f
[81]	6/1707	Mohawk	ThowaaHodieshenthoo	m
[90]	6/1708	Onondaga, from Canada	Ashareiake	m

[a] Information within brackets { } has been deduced from other entries or different sources.

[b] On [54], he was described as a Seneca, living in Canada, but on [64] he appears to have migrated back to Seneca country in Iroquoia.

[c] The ? indicates that data have not been conclusively ascertained.

Present arrangement	Conditions/remarks	Outcome
1 shirt	They must return to buy merchandise, or pay; if they turn to another merchant, must pay a heavy beaver	? (repeated on [54], not listed here)
1 deerskin borrowed	Had to pay 3 martens, if deerskin not returned	That debt crossed out
1 shirt, 1 pair of stockings	Could retain merchandise, if he returned to trade with Wendells	He did return
1 quarter in money	"For free," if she returned to trade with Wendells	?
1 large shirt at lower? price	Wendells would honor the deal, if she returned to trade	She returned
1 pair of stockings at lower? price	Had to return to trade with Wendells	Does not reappear
For him: 1 piece of strouds, "for free"	No condition given	They paid all debts
Various foodstuffs, rum, and quarters	If they did not return to trade with Wendells, they had to pay for it	She paid
Unclear arrangement, 6 beavers	Had to return to trade with Wendells	Does not reappear
Lead at lower? price	Had to return to trade with Wendells	He did return

TABLE 17. Indications of leniency in the Wendells' management of native customers' debt

Page	Date: M/Y	Affiliation	Name	Sex
[42]	7?[a]/1700	{Mohawk}[b]	Dekanasquiesackha	m
[8]	6/1701	Catskill	Schewas quawas	m
[29]	8/1701	{Mohawk}	Wagrassero	m
[49]	1/1703	{Mohawk}	Canosedeckha	m
[47]	9/1703	Cayuga	Aijadatha	m
[41]	10/1703	Cayuga(?[d]), "stays in Canada"	Dewannighrijeie	m
[25]	10/1705	Mohawk	Aberham, Cenderijokee	m
[58]	?/1705	Mohawk	Caheghetsiedauw	m
[74]	8/1705?	{Mohawk}	Aeijewases's wife	f
[13]	12/1705?	{Mahican}[c]	Naghnaekamett's wife's son	m
[14]	8/1706	{Mahican}	Nietewapewa	m
[60]	2/1707	{Mohawk}	Aeijawassen	m
[17]	5/1707	Mahican	Nannalamit	m
[80]	6/1707	Mohawk, from Canada	Waerhosradee's father	m
[76]	9/1707	?, Mohawk name; see the entry	Thaijadoores	m
[91]	7/1708	Seneca, "used to live in Canada"	Annahariesen	m
[94]	9/1708	Mohawk, from Canada	D'waerhoeseeRaguqu[a?]	m
[93]	8/1709	{Mohawk}	Decaregjaghiaghquaa's son	m
[6]	1/1710	Mahican?/Abenaki?	Retsert	m
[92]	3/1710	Seneca	Josquassoo or annosktoo	m
[38]	7/1710	Seneca	Aeshaerijkoo	m
[110]	7/1710?	{Mohawk}, from Canada	Carghiedsiekooe	m

[a] The ? indicates that data have not been conclusively ascertained.

[b] Information within brackets { } has been deduced from other entries or different sources.

[c] The transaction was made by using a trusted, native intermediary.

[d] The ethnicity of "Dewannighrijeie" remains tentative; throughout, I have incorporated him as Canadian.

Description	Observation/outcome
Part of his debt is not on his bill, promised Wendell a "present" for that	Wendell accepted open-ended proposition from customer
"Ordered" rum, while away	Development of debt by absent[e] client accepted
Customer may decide what to pay for an item	Price-setting by customer
Borrowed gun, returned it after 3 months	No charges for this loan
Repair to gun	No charges
After being indebted 3½ years, customer's brother-in-law paid part the debt	Duration of debt; partial disbursement
Wendell provided gunpowder in the Mohawk country, as he was "very destitute"	Consideration for customer's situation [this debt not disbursed, others were]
Borrowed gun. Wendell: "if it pleased him he should give 3 beavers for that or otherwise [return] it."	Outcome unclear, but decision left at discretion of customer
Payment (in hops) "may be established at that moment" [of payment]	Open-ended agreement
Borrowed (acquired?) gun, to hunt with	No debt, charges recorded
Had given items as a security against his debt; he and Wendell agreed that these would settle the account	Arranged for in the presence of two native witnesses
After customer admitted debt, Wendell intended to "return to him the value of 19 martens[,] to do justice to him and myself"	Wendell seeks to arrive at arrangement with significant customer
After having been indebted 10 years, customer paid part of the debt	Duration of debt; only partial disbursement
A debt with Hieronymus Wendell, 10 years old, was noted again	Duration of debt
Borrowed a gun. Wendell: "if he likes it he should give 3 beavers for that"	Outcome not clear, but customer might also return the item
Borrowed gun, returned it after 5 days	Debt appears canceled, no charges
Acquired gun on credit, returned it after 1 day	Debt canceled, no charges
Bought a shirt at "the carrying place"	Development of debt by absent[e] client accepted
After having been indebted 5½ years, customer gave "satisfaction on the Commissioners"	Duration and transfer of debt
1 cask of rum sent to him, Wendell: "he can reimburse me as he pleases"	Price-setting by customer
Incurred a small debt, promised to come and trade with Wendell	Arranged for in the presence of two native witnesses
Total debt remitted by Wendell(s)	No apparent reason

[e] The transaction was made by using trusted intermediaries, both European and Indian.

TABLE 18. Instances of natives' debts paid by the Wendells

Page	Date: M/Y	Debtor	Name
[28]	6/1705	Cayuga?[a]	Caeijhoekedee or Saenaekeranckhack
[20]	9?/1705	Mahican	WaenEnpaeckes
[20]	9?/1705	Mahican	WaenEnpaeckes
[10]	7/1706	Mahican	Niettewapwae
[60]	2/1707	{Mohawk}[c]	Aeijawassen
[82]	8/1707	Mohawk {from Canada}	Aedekanijhaa
[67]	10/1708	Mohawk {from Canada?}	Sakadereiughthaa
[99]	9/1709	Mahican	Wannapackes

[a] The ? indicates that data have not been conclusively ascertained.
[b] This case has also been reported in Table 15.
[c] Information within brackets { } has been deduced from other entries or different sources.

TABLE 19. Recorded transactions taking place outside the trading center

Page	Date: M/D/Y	Affiliation	Name
[30]	2/4/1704 or?[a] 1706	Mohawk	Wagraseroo's wife's mother
[7]	5/?/1704	Mahican	Naghnekampemet
[22]	5/?/1704	Mohawk	{Catrien}[b], Watcaros's sister
[17]	6/?/1704	{Mahican}	Wassewaecke, the Greyhead
[10]	2/20/1705	{Mahican}	Seeckaet
[25]	{10/25/1706}	Mohawk	Aberham, Cenderijokee
[5]	2/?/1707	Mahican?	?
[7]	2/?/1707	Mahican	Naghnakamet's sister
[17]	5/?/1707	Mahican	Nannalamit
[31]	5/?/1707	Mohawk	Sohoonachqae
[21]	?/1707	Mohawk	Rabecken
[22]	?/1707	Mohawk	{Catrin}, Watcaros's sister
[77]	1/?/1708	{Mohawk}	Canosedeckhaa
[87]	5/4/1708	{Mohawk}	Areiaa
[77]	10/?/1708	{Mohawk}	{Marijae}, Canosedeckhaa's wife
[88]	10/4/1708	{Mohawk}, from Canada?	Dekaquarendightha
[36]	?/1708	{Mohawk}	Arija's mother
[93]	8/24/1709	{Mohawk}	Decaregjaghiaghquaa's son
[96]	3/8/1710	{Mohawk}	Catrin, Watcaroo's sister
[77]	3/8/1710	{Mohawk}	{Marijae}, Canosedeckhaa's wife
[77]	4/6?/1710	{Mohawk}	{Marijae}, Canosedeckhaa's wife

[a] The ? indicates that data have not been conclusively ascertained.

Sex	Type of debt paid by Wendell	Receiver of payment
m	57 quarters; circumstances remain obscure	Johannus Bratt
m	1 beaver	Jonas Douw
m	1 quarter, for riding [him?]	?
m	10 quarters, on a gun left as a security with Anties Moll (Schenectady)[b]	Anties Moll
m	6 martens for a dog, advanced to a soldier for him	A soldier
m	6 quarters, at 1 beaver	Schoo, son of Lavlueer
m	4 heavy beavers	Johannis Becker
m	7 guilders, pig had "walked there on the island"	Andries Jansen

Sex	Type of transaction	Description of locality
f	Paid 3 skipple Indian corn (counted as 3 martens)	In the country
m	Paid 3 beavers.	In the country
f	Paid 1 beaver and 1 *lap*	In the country
m	Paid 1 beaver	Schenectady
m	Bought 1 coarse blanket	In the Mohawk country
m	Bought 1 bag of gunpowder	In the Mohawk country
f	Paid 2 skipple Indian corn	In the country
f	Paid 3 skipple Indian corn	In the country
m	Paid 3 beavers	Saratoga
m	Paid 4 beavers, 1 *lap*, 3 otters	Saratoga
f	Paid 20 skipple Indian corn	In the country
f	Paid 3 martens	In the country
m	Bought 1 cask, rum	In the country
m	An exchange	In the country
f	Bought 1 pair of stockings	In the country
m	Bought 1 nightcap	At the carrying place
f	Paid 3 skipple Indian corn (counted as 3 martens)	In the country
m	1 shirt bought; sent to him	At the carrying place
f	Paid 9 skipple Indian corn	In the country
f	Paid 42 skipple Indian corn	In the country
f	Paid 16 skipple Indian corn	In the country

[b] Information within brackets { } has been deduced from other entries or different sources.

TABLE 20. Occurrences of possibly prominent native individuals

Page	Date: M/Y	Customer	Name or description	Sex
[85]	9/1704	A Mohawk boy	Arent	m
[41]	1/1704?[a]	{Mohawk}[b]	A boy	m
[13]	2/1706	{Mahican?}	Mackseckwant	m
[14]	8/1706	{Mahican}	Nietewapewa	m
[79]	6/1707	?	Awanaaceere	f
[15]	7/1707	Young, Mahican	Heerij	m
[84]	8/1707	Young, "lives in Canada"	TiocaghneeRadeie	m
[84]	8/1707	Young, "lives in Canada"	TiocagneeRadeie	m
[16]	9/1707	Mahican	Maghmaghcees	m
[93]	8/1709	{Mohawk}	Decaregjaghiaghquaa's son	m
[104]	9/1709	Seneca	Osiestout, Sonieno	f
[104]	9/1709	Seneca	Anniethaa	?
[38]	6/1710	Seneca	Aeshaerijkoo	m

[a]The ? indicates that data have not been conclusively ascertained.

[b]Information within brackets { } has been deduced from other entries or different sources.

[c]These cases have also been reported in Table 12.

Prominent individual(s)	Name	Sex	Role/position
Mohawk	Canosedeckhaa	m	He stays at Canosedeckhaa's
{Mohawk}	Arija	m	The boy lives in Arija's house
{Mahican}	Naghnahamett	m	He stays at Naghnahamett's
{Mahican}, ?	Masequant, and Caetsee nacquas	m, ?	The two are witnesses, when an arrangement is made between Wendell and Nietwapewa[c]
?	Tijdedores	m	The woman stays or lives in his house
?	Awanwaghquat	?	The young man "stays with Awanwaghquat's people"
?	Noquaresen	?	The young man stays in Noquaresen's house (see also following case)
Mohawk {, fr. Canada}	Carghiaedsiecoo	m	The young man "belongs to" Carghiaedsiecoo (see also preceding case)
{Mahican}	Nietewakam	m	He stays at Nietewakam's
{Mohawk}	Waghrosraa	m	Wendell sends goods with Jacob d'Schriver, "in the presence of waghrosraa"[c]
?	Waiesaa	?	The woman "stays at Waiesaa"
{Seneca}	Coghcaaradawen	m	The customer stays or lives in his house
? [not certain if "Oriewaes" is a name], Seneca	Oriewaes, and Caienquaragtoo	?, m	The two are witnesses, when Aeshaerijkoo promises to trade with Wendell[c]

TABLE 21. Positive or likely identifications of Indian leaders

Page	Note	Name	Affiliation/position
[2]	19	Maghack	Catskill sachem
[5]	42	Kaloolet	Schaghticoke sachem
[9]	81	Ouwee suckwans	River Indian sachem
[18]	147	Waeleghlauwett	Schaghticoke sachem
[19]	154	Korneles	Mohawk sachem
[20]	159	Kaeijeenquereeko	Mohawk sachem
[24]	187	Roodes	Mohawk sachem
[24]	188	Sohnerowane	Mohawk sachem
[27]	202	Dekarijhondie	Mohawk sachem
[32]	243	Owanije	Mohawk sachem
[35]	260	Tanijijooris	Mohawk sachem
[36]	266	Thackaeijackh	Cayuga sachem
[39]	291	Kanasquiesackhe	Mohawk sachem
[40]	295	Brant	Mohawk sachem
[44]	323	Dekannasoorae	Onondaga leader
[50]	352	Thrghijoores	Mohawk sachem
[52]	361	"Satkatsteghcooe or Aennetsoendeijae"	Oneida sachem
[53]	363	Aewaen[accoo/anoo], "new name" of Dekanesthejendaghqua	Seneca sachem
[56]	390	Orghjaedikhae	Mohawk/Canadian Mohawk sachem
[58]	402	Jisep	Mohawk sachem
[58]	403	Giedeijon	Mohawk sachem
[65]	455	Senjaad'riesen	Canadian Mohawk sachem
[71]	485	DaawienEeckhaa	Seneca sachem
[75]	505	Sander	Mohawk sachem
[83]	553	Ohoonsiewaanens	Onondaga sachem
[94]	604	Kaghtsweghtjoenie	Onondaga or Seneca sachem
[105]	653	Canaghcoonia	Oneida war leader, later sachem
[107]	671	Essaraes	Mohawk sachem
[108]	673	Atsakanhaa	Onondaga sachem

Notes to the Introduction

1. The manuscript collections in the NYSL contain the covers of an additional fur trade account book by Evert Wendell, but the contents have been removed. Acquisition records of the Archives indicate the item was received in that condition. The covers, filled with some notes, are clearly marked in Evert Wendell's handwriting as "E. Wendell's french Savages B[ook]" (*E. Wendell sijn frans Wilden B*[oeck]). The inside of the front cover reads like a family bible: it records Evert's marriage and three births in the family. Even there, one discerns the remains of American Indian names. The inside of the back cover presents a similar picture, as the names and, in this case, the remnants of some actual accounts can be recognized. It includes a pictographic rendering of the debt of Penneghttako, an Indian customer of Evert Wendell (he does not appear in the present manuscript); see Ephraim Wendell Letters, NYSL, SC 9684.

2. The year of Evert Jansz Wendell's birth is derived from a deposition he made before a notary in Albany on July 29, 1675 where he gave his age as "about 60 years"; see *ERA*, 3: 331. For a brief biography of Evert Jansz Wendell, see Van Laer, *Rensselaer Bowier Manuscripts*, 837. For a discussion on Wendell's children and his Emden background, see Van Laer, "Letters to Evert Jansen Wendel," *DSSY*, 4: 1–2. For Wendell's appearance as a defendant in a court case in New Amsterdam, see Van Laer, Scott, and Stryker-Rodda, *Council Minutes*, 184. The exact date of his death has not been established conclusively.

3. For the permission by the patroon's court of October 15, 1648, see Van Laer, *Minutes of the Court of Rensselaerswijck*, 35.

4. For the will of Evert Wendell, Jr. (second generation), see *ERA*, 4: 143–45. Payment was received on June 18, 1702, for the use of the pall for the burial of Evert Wendell. See Hannay, "Burial Records First Dutch Reformed Church Albany," *DSSY*, 8–9: 21. For the third-generation Evert, see Talcott, *New York and New England Families*, 379–80.

5. The other account books in the handwriting of Evert Wendell are cataloged as Ledger, 1708–1750; Ledger, 1711–1738; Ledger, 1717–1749; and Day Book, 1711–1749, NYHS. For the date of this Evert Wendell's burial, see Hannay, "Burial Records First Dutch Reformed Church Albany," *DSSY*, 8–9: 58. Talcott lists the date of his death as May 3, 1750, *New York and New England Families*, 388. For Evert's will and testament, see New York (County) Surrogate's Court, *Abstract of Wills on File*, NYHS, *Collections*, 29: 15–18. It is abstracted in Talcott, *New York and New England Families*, 388–89. Although Armour correctly identified Evert through his mother, he made the erroneous assumption that this Evert Wendell (third generation) began writing the account book in 1695, when he would have been only fourteen years old. He overlooked the different handwriting of Evert's older brother, Harmanus, who filled the earliest section of the manuscript; see Armour, *The Merchants of Albany*, 65. The same, flawed interpretation informs Dunn, *The Mohican World, 1680–1750*, 114.

6. A list of Albany inhabitants, compiled on June 16, 1697, shows that Ariaantje Wendell and three children occupied a dwelling in the city. It did not specify any other adults in the household, nor did it list Hieronimus or Jeronimus Wendell. See *AA*, 9:81.

7. Besides owning a house and lot on one of the thoroughfares in the city, he acquired various tracts of land just outside the city's north gate; see *ERA*, 2: 213–14, 326–27, 368, 478–79. In 1679, he was among a select group of inhabitants who agreed to contribute

funds for repairs to the city ports. His share in the contributions was modest, however, and later that year he was reprimanded by the magistrates for failure to keep the street in front of his house in good repair; see *CMARS*, 2: 396, 446.

8. This sketch of Johannes (1649–1692) is based on Christoph and Christoph, *Books of General Entries of the Colony of New York*, 316, 327, 353; Christoph, *The Leisler Papers*, 23, 52–53, 102, 450, 452; and Talcott, *New York and New England Families*, 379.

9. To trace the several lineages of Wendells, see Talcott, *New York and New England Families*, 376–415. Unlike Pearson, Talcott had the opportunity to consult various documents in the possession of a descendant of the family. This enabled him to reconstruct the family's genealogy with a greater degree of accuracy, see ibid., 376. For Harmanus's profile, see Talcott, *New York and New England Families*, 386–87, 380; and for Hieronimus's and Ariaantje's progeny, see ibid., 380. For the identification of Evert as Hieronimus's son, he is included as such in an abstract from his father's will on April 25, 1690, ibid.

10. For using particular labels for American Indian peoples or nations, I have followed naming practices in *HNAI*, vol. 15.

11. See pages [80] and [93] in the account book.

12. An entry from 1708 lists goods exchanged outside Albany between Areiaa, a Mohawk man, and "brother [Jo]hans." Earlier, this younger brother of Evert and Harmanus was entered simply as "our [Jo]hans." See pages [87] and [78]. Other entries describe the involvement of their older sister Susanna (1676–?) in the Indian trade. See pages [36], [101], and [119]. In addition, starting in 1714 Evert refers several times to the existence of a separate account book kept by Hester, most likely indicating his younger sister of that name; see pages [61], [87], [95], and [107]. The youngest sister, Elsje (1689–?), is the only member of the nuclear family not mentioned in this manuscript. However, her husband Nicolaes/Nicholas Bleecker, is mentioned—see page [107].

13. Bielinski describes the local elite in "How a City Worked," 119–36.

14. For Evert's inclusion in the committee of three assistant aldermen, formed on June 17, see *AA*, 3: 51. Their report, issued ten days later, contained negative judgments on the residence of several important traders; ibid., 52–53.

15. For Evert, see *AA*, 4: 184; 5: 176; 6: 279, 288; 7: 14, 21, 24. Also see the "Indenture of land to the Dutch Church," NYSL, CO 9838. For Harmanus, see *AA*, 4: 144, 167–69; 5: 115, 125, 158–61, 178; 6: 248, 249, 268, 279, 288; 7: 21; 8: 245, 252, 270, 271; 9: 21; Corwin, *Ecclesiastical Records of the State of New York*, 3: 2046–47, 2112; and "Resolutions of the [Albany] Church Council," NYSL, AFM 331.

16. See Norton, *The Fur Trade in Colonial New York*, 100–101. Matson places the sharpest decline in New York's fur trade after the end of Queen Anne's War in 1713, "The 'Hollander Interest,'" 251–68.

17. Harmanus signed a petition to Governor Bellomont in August 1700, in which the petitioners expressed concern over far more extensive matters than the Indian trade alone; see *DRCHNY*, 4: 752–54. His broader activities are more clearly indicated by his contract to deliver provisions of bread, corn, and peas to the colonial troops in 1711; see Armour, *Merchants of Albany*, 97.

18. For the record of Evert's receipt of a license, see "Indenture of land to the Dutch Church," NYSL, CO 9838. His docket book for 1723–1740, and account book 1732–1746 contain legal fees for cases in which he was involved as an attorney. For earlier cases, see *AA*, 6: 182–83, 7: 81–83.

19. As indicated above, Evert's ledgers and daybook are also in the NYHS. Taken together, they cover the period 1708–50 and constitute an indispensable source for the study of commerce on the Upper Hudson.

20. This section is based on Armour, *Merchants of Albany*, 156–57, 166–67. References to Evert's will are in note 5.

21. For discussions of this divisive period, see Gehring, *Fort Orange Court Minutes*,

492, 503–4, 511; Jacobs, *New Netherland,* 212–14; Merwick, *Possessing Albany,* 88–99; Shattuck, *A Civil Society,* 271–92; and Sullivan, *The Punishment of Crime,* 149–58.

22. In a letter from 1648, otherwise undated, Govert Loockermans informed Gilles Verbrugge that trade at the Delaware River was ruined because small traders went to the native villages and paid exorbitant prices for peltries. The situation was no better at Fort Orange, where "brokers" (*mackelaers*) spoiled the trade; Loockermans noted that every house there had "one or 2" brokers, Stuyvesant-Rutherford Papers, 3–3, NYHS.

23. The petition was read on July 5, 1681; see *CMARS,* 3: 143–44.

24. Letter, Jacques Cornelissen van Slyck to Peter Schuyler, December 25, 1689. Apart from Johannes Wendell, Cornelissen and Schuyler were the only other persons listed in this fashion, see "New York council minutes," NYCM, ser. A1894, 36: 17. Also see Christoph, *The Leisler Papers,* 36: 27–29. Where the above leaves room for uncertainty about the proposed locality of the meeting, the reply from Albany's leadership is unambiguous; see "New York council minutes," NYCM, ser. A1894, 36: 18; Christoph, *The Leisler Papers,* 30–32.

25. See *DRCHNY,* 3: 775.

26. For portions of this controversy, see *DRCHNY,* 4: 539–41, 345–47. For the request for assistance from "Everet Wendel Jun.r," see ibid., 541.

27. In June and July 1700, he was present at three diplomatic encounters between the commissioners and Iroquois sachems or their messengers. For June 11, see *LIR,* 176–77; and for June 30–July 3, see *DRCHNY,* 4: 693–96.

28. See Howell and Munsell, *History of the County of Albany,* 41. They, and other sources, give Harmanus's term as beginning in 1728, but documents in the Livingston papers clearly state Harmanus's presence at the meetings of the commissioners from June 22 to December 27, 1727; see Robert Livingston Papers, Indian Affairs, 1666–1727, NYHS, GLC 03107.

29. For this request, see *CCM,* 231.

30. See *AA,* 9: 60.

31. See page [99], and the tally in table 18.

32. See Feister, "Indian-Dutch Relations in the Upper Hudson Valley," 89–113, 98–100, 105–106. Feister concludes that the Wendells were "some of the most frequent sponsors" at Indian baptisms, ibid., 99.

33. For the aunt, Diver/Diewer (1653–1724), daughter of Evert Jansz Wendell, see Pearson, *The First Settlers of Albany County,* 376, 379. For her sponsorships, see Pearson, "Extracts From the Doop-Boek," 72; and Sivertsen, *Turtles, Wolves, and Bears,* 226–28. Involvement of Dutch religious authorities, or individual traders, in Indian participation in Christian rituals was not a new development. Venema reports that individual traders and deacons of the Dutch Reformed Church helped to pay for the funeral of three native men in the last decade of the seventeenth century, *Kinderen van weelde en armoede,* 60. She lists two cases for 1693 and one for 1697. There are indications of additional connections between the deacons and individual Indians, such as a payment by the former to Albany's magistrates in March 1701, for "maintaining Jacob," an Indian boy; ibid., 425n187. It is unclear if this is the same individual as "Jacob the savage" who is listed in Evert's account book (pages [2] and [18]) as trading in 1698 and 1699.

34. See *AA,* 4: 177. In July 1699 Stephanus Groesbeeck (?–bur. July 17, 1744) married Elisabeth Lansing, the sister of Evert's wife Engeltje, see Pearson, *First Settlers of Albany,* 56, 70. For the Oneida's request in 1709 for assistance from Evert Wendell as interpreter also included the presence of Stephanus Groesbeeck, see *CCM,* 231.

35. See Van Nuys, "William Van Nuys Papers," NYHS; and Wendell, Misc. papers, NYHS, June 23, 1717. The second instance includes a statement that Evert is charged for customs in England.

36. On October 14, 1724, Evert sent a considerable amount of peltry to an unidentified agent in London. Placing an order for return goods, Wendell noted that he desired

a specific sort of blue strouds. He concluded by expressing his confidence in his correspondent's expertise, "you know best how the Indian fashion is in our Parts"; see Wendell, Ledger, 1711–1738, NYHS.

37. For Abraham's letter to Evert on April 3, 1721, see Wendell Family Papers, "Wendell, Abraham. Letter to Evert Wendell; 1721," NYPL, item 14. Another example of Evert's exchanges with Abraham Wendell is in the Ledger 1708–1750, NYHS, f. 20. Evert sent beaver furs, beaver coats, and elk hides, for which Abraham sent a return shipment of a sizeable quantity of lead, shot, and woolens. For a multitude of similar accounts with other merchants in New York, see Evert's other ledgers.

38. For the account of Harmanus with Evert dated October 1721, see Wendell, Ledger, 1711–1738, NYHS.

39. For the lists of goods shipped to these destinations between 1717 and 1728, see Wendell Family Papers, "Wendell, Abraham [Legal and business papers] 1714–1731," NYPL, item 33. One of Abraham contacts in Amsterdam was Abraham Engelgraeff. The latter, on December 22, 1717, made a deposition at a notary public in Amsterdam that Abraham Wendell had sent him three casks and two bundles of peltries from New York City, see Schabalje, Notorial Archive.

40. Evert's trade with Boston after 1710 is indicated in his accounts with Andrew Faneuil and John Mico, 1710–1714, see Wendell, Ledger 1711–1738, NYHS. For the invoice from Stephen DeLancey to Evert Wendell (August 4, 1714), which includes beaver furs weighing 87 pounds for Faneuil, see Wendell Correspondence, 1711–1749, NYHS.

41. For the letter from Jacob Wendell to Abraham Wendell (Boston, November 26, 1711), see Wendell Family Papers, 1682–1794, NYPL.

42. For and Evert and associates in Albany (June-September 1713), see Wendell, NYSL, SC 9684. There is no indication that Ephraim ever succeeded in his efforts.

43. In a letter from that city, dated April 2, 1714, Johannes Roseboom, Jr., informed Evert Wendell that he had passed the request to pay Nondaresochte on to Monsieur Cologne. The circumstances and the amount remain unspecified, see Roseboom, Misc. Papers, NYHS, April 2, 1714. In addition, Roseboom informed Wendell that he had heard that the governor would return the seized goods. Nondaresochte may very well be Evert's client ondeRiesaghtoo, described in 1706 as "A Mahican who lives among the Ottawas"; see page [69] for his account that also covered 1707. A Mohawk name for the same individual is also recorded there.

44. See Armour, *Merchants of Albany*, 132 and 150n33.

45. The incident was reported in correspondence from the Commissioners to the provincial council; see Wraxall, *An Abridgement of the Indian Affairs*, lxxiv–v.

46. Historical Society of Pennsylvania, Gratz Collection, Colonial Governors, June 30, 1729, case 2/box 30.

47. Harmanus's accounts (dated October 5) for the deliveries in 1727 are found, together with those from Stephanus Groesbeeck and Myndert Schuyler; see O'Callaghan, *Calendar of Historical Manuscripts*, 1: 499. His commissions from June 1729, and his accounts for three years of deliveries in his official capacity (submitted by his wife Anna Glen, executor of the estate after his death in December 1731); see ibid., 504, 516–17. As late as 1737, an unnamed member of the Wendell family was still active in supplying the garrison; see ibid., 543. This possibly may have been Harmanus's son, Johannes Harmanus Wendell, who settled in Schenectady, as store accounts in his ledger (1741–1744) reveal a large number of deliveries to Oswego; see Wendell, Ledger, 1741–1744, NYSL, SC 12910. Talcott identifies him as official victualler of Oswego, *New York and New England Families*, 386–87.

48. Based on "that with what Mr. Wendel has undertaken," the assembly decided to station two interpreters at Oswego for the winter season, and a doctor for the whole year, see the State of New York, *Colonial Laws of New York*, 2: 551.

49. See the State of New York, *Colonial Laws of New York*, 2:485. Evert received the commissions together with Rutger Bleecker and Ryer Gerritse. The assembly ratified their appointment in the following year and they remained collectors until 1731; ibid., 2: 537. Talcott mistakenly reports that Evert received the commission in 1727, *New York and New England Families*, 388.

50. See Evert Wendell's memorandum of April 28–30, 1708, in Ledger, 1711–1738, NYHS, verso of f. 2. Cowass was a large village of the Cowassucks, a division of the Western Abenakis; see Day, "Western Abenaki," *HNAI*, 15: 159.

51. Evert Wendell's memorandum of January 26, 1714, in Ledger, 1711–1738, verso of f. 2. The Mohawk man had signed the land deed in 1710. In many cases, where land was "given," as Evert called it, this resulted from an Indian's mounting debt to European merchants; it appears that Schaghnerowane is recorded in the account book, see pages [23], [24] (and the note there), and [28].

52. See O'Callaghan, *Calendar of New York Colonial Manuscripts*, 153. For the permission, see *CCM*, 282. This may have related to lands in Mohawk territory, since one of Evert Wendell's ledgers contains an account dated October 1721 for his brother, Harmanus, describing Evert's compensation for going to Mohawk country; see Wendell, Ledger, 1711–1738, NYHS, f. 93. In addition, both Harmanus and Evert were witnesses to the sale of Mahican lands along the Housatonic River in 1730, Dunn, *The Mohican World*, 266–67.

53. See Demos, *The Unredeemed Captive*, 178–79. For thorough discussions of Beverwijck, present day Albany, see Jacobs, *New Netherland*; Merwick, *Possessing Albany*; Shattuck, *A Civil Society*; and Venema, *Beverwijck*.

54. This, for the last several decades at least, has been the common interpretation of that conflict. Recently, Starna and Brandão have critiqued this representation of the Mohawks' motivations and objectives, arguing that it inadequately portrays the conflict as "economic warfare." See Starna and Brandão, "From the Mohawk-Mahican War to the Beaver Wars: Questioning the Pattern," 51: 725–750.

55. For a brief, but insightful overview of the alliance, see Brandão, "The Covenant Chain," 416. For a detailed study, see Jennings, *The Ambiguous Iroquois Empire*. For valuable discussions of principal aspects of this alliance system, see Richter and Merrell, *Beyond the Covenant Chain*.

56. Richter provides an excellent analysis of such dynamics in Iroquoia in *The Ordeal of the Longhouse*.

57. See Starna, "Assessing American Indian-Dutch Studies," 27.

58. Compare GRAPH 1 in the section "trading accounts."

59. For the estimated population in 1686, see Bielinski, "A Middling Sort," 72: 261–90. For 1697, the number is recorded as approximately 714 "regular residents"; see Bielinski, "The New Netherland Dutch," 1–15. For the number of (free) householders around 1700, see Merwick, *Possessing Albany*, 280. For the population data resulting from a province-wide census in, see *DRCHNY*, 3: 905; and Burke, *Mohawk Frontier*, 138. Varying estimates of the population in Beverwijck in 1660–1664 are discussed in Shattuck, *A Civil Society*, 9–10. Shattuck arrives at the conclusion that one thousand or more people lived in the town during those years, ibid., 11; Venema has adopted the same figures, *Beverwijck*, 429.

60. For an early description of the complications in funding construction and maintenance of the fortifications, see Trelease, *Indian Affairs in Colonial New York*, 207. A visitor stated in 1696 that the fort was perfectly located to dominate the land and the river, but he was unimpressed by the town's defenses; see Miller, *New York Considered and Improved*, 122. Rev. Benjamin Wadsworth, who wrote in 1694, would only go so far as to admit that the town was well "scituate[d]" for defense, not expressing an opinion as to if and how that position was taken advantage of. See "Albany in 1694," *DSSY*, 6: 9–12.

David Armour has said that Albany at the outbreak of Queen Anne's War was "virtually defenseless," *Merchants of Albany,* 73. Little changed until the French and Indian War in the 1750s.

61. See Trelease, *Indian Affairs in Colonial New York,* 204–05.

62. For a discussion of the "crafts and trades and the subtle emergence of the middling sort of people[, as] the more representative factor in the development of Albany's community economy," see Bielinski, "Artisans in Colonial Albany," 268–73.

63. See Matson, *Merchants and Empire,* 222.

64. See paragraph 2 of this introduction, and notes 35, 36, 39, and 41, above.

65. Bookseller John E. Scopes & Co. in Albany had offered the manuscript for sale to some of his customers, in a letter from the early 1900's, putting the price at $150. According to a brief article by John Pierce in the Albany newspaper *The Times-Union* of June 14, 1909, an attorney had acquired the manuscript at an auction some years earlier. By the time he wrote his article for the paper's "Letters of the People" section, Pierce held it in his possession. The wording he used to describe it corresponds almost completely to a one-page note on the manuscript by John E. Scopes, that is now also in the case with the item itself. Scopes's letter to his customers, and the newspaper article are in an unmarked folder; see Wendell Family Papers, 1682–1794, NYPL.

66. This occurs on pages [18] and [19], with an entry dating from June or July of 1705.

67. After pages [18], [44], and [54], sections are torn out of the manuscript, although the number of removed pages seems to be limited. In one case it can be determined that only a single leaf has been removed, following page [120].

68. Pages [55] to [74] have smaller dimensions.

69. They are marked as his on the first page, in the same handwriting as the notes themselves.

70. Versteeg also made a few translations of key passages. Among them, the account that provides the title of the present edition, which Versteeg translated as: "for the sake of doing justice to him and myself" (unnumbered page in his notes). His notes are included in the microfilm of the manuscript that is available from the NYHS.

71. Talcott does not give the date of her death, *New York and New England Families,* 389. Burial records date her interment as September 6, 1742. See Hannay, "Burial Records First Dutch Reformed Church Albany," 45.

72. There are many examples of account books that follow the standard layout. For a Dutch manuscript from the same period, that also deals with trade with Indians in the area of Kingston, New York, see Philip John Schuyler Papers, Account Book, 1711–1729, NYPL, reel 30. Another Dutch account book from the same period as the Wendells' manuscript, but detailing transactions with Europeans on the upper Hudson, is that of Joachim Staats, Account Book, 1681–1711, NYSL, SC 15250, microfilm 3635.

73. Also see note 107, below.

74. Although the place or area of residence of the small number of Abenaki Indians cannot be determined, since they may have lived in Canada, the destination of an Indian agent or peddler can be identified as the homelands of the Abenakis. See table 12.

75. Perhaps once a Mahican village, but, following King Phillip's War, inhabited mostly by refugees from various Indian groups in Connecticut and Massachusetts; see Day, *In Search of New England's Native Past,* 132–33, 144.

76. "Mahican is what is referred to by linguists as an n-dialect. The Proto-Eastern Algonquian *r always becomes /n/ in that language. As a result, the Mahican language had no *r*'s or *l*'s in it. Of the Algonquian groups in the area, the names may come from Wappinger, Munsee, Western Abenaki, or Paugussett, but not Mahican" (BR). Merit of this analytical tool has been confirmed by Ives Goddard (pers. comm., May 2004).

77. Historians have observed that the Albany-Montreal trade, by means of native carriers, had become an established commercial liaison during Queen Anne's War; see

Norton, *The Fur Trade in Colonial New York*, 56; and White, *The Middle Ground*, 120. In 1725, two Dutch traders in Albany "estimated that 80 percent of the beaver shipped from New York to Europe was obtained from French smugglers"; White, *The Middle Ground*, 120. Also see Lunn, "The Illegal Fur" Canadian Historical Association, *Report, 1939*.

78. The evaluation of the Wendells' capacities, in this regard, was provided by Gunther Michelson after he had studied my translation of the document, including transcriptions of the Indian names (pers. comm., December 2003 and January 2004).

79. Ibid.

80. All occurrences of this complicating factor are discussed in the annotation to the translation.

81. These individuals appear, in the order in which they are listed in the text above, on pages [12] (she has an additional account on [9]), [69], [82], [68], and again [68] (he has an additional account on [112]).

82. For his account from 1706 (and earlier), see page [63].

83. In the account book, and other documents, the Wendells consistently refer to Indians as *wilden*. "Savages" is the most immediate translation of that term.

84. See page [9].

85. See page [93]. He has not been incorporated in table 1.

86. For the migration of the Tuscaroras from 1713 onwards, and their admittance to the League as the sixth nation in 1722–23, see Landy, "Tuscarora among the Iroquois," *HNAI*, 15: 518–20.

87. For data on Mohawk populations, see Snow, "Mohawk demography, 15: 160–82; and Snow, *Mohawk Valley Archaeology*, 38, 45. For Snow's data on the Senecas, see *The Iroquois*, table 7.1, 110.

88. For the undated entry in which the deceased woman appears, see page [107]; Aghsienjaaeijeei's account is found on page [65]. The third French Indian, Schoeoendees, a young man escorted by a Seneca man, appears in an account on page [59]. Considering the date of the latter's appearance, he may have arrived from the area north of Lake Ontario. The Iroquois had invited several groups of "Farr Indians" to settle and share the hunting grounds there, as part of the agreements in the Treaty of Montreal in 1701. Brandão and Starna argue that that one of the reasons for these native groups to accept the Iroquois' offer was because they hoped to gain better access to the market in Albany; see Brandão and Starna, "The Treaties of 1701," 43: 230–32.

89. Table 1 lists 325–330 identifiable Indian individuals, but since 23 natives were mentioned solely to identify other Indians, the total *n* of active native clients was between 302 and 307.

90. Table 1 includes the total number of male and female Canadian customers (13). The Canadian women appear as Ohonsaioenthaa, Okaajathie, Anna, an unnamed woman, Quanakaraghto, and two unnamed women, on pages [62], [66], [75], [85], [89], [90], and [93].

91. See Gehring and Starna, *A Journey into Mohawk and Oneida Country*, 6. The editors remark: "it is interesting to note the presence of women on the trail without the escort of men and transporting items to trade," and add "perhaps women had always been involved at some level in trade and that their participation has simply gone unreported," 36n48.

92. Gehring, *Fort Orange Court Minutes*, 523. The case was adjourned and the results are not known.

93. See *CMARS*, 3: 502–03. Tryn Claes was the woman who received sixteen and eighteen skipples of Indian corn from two native women, "which was measured for her by an old squaw, for the old squaw was surety for the two squaws who were the owners of the maize."

94. See page [85], last account. One month later, she had goods fetched for her by Sakadereuightha, a Mohawk man with connections to Canada.

95. See page [62], third account. Presumably, the Catholic priest lived and worked in the Montreal area. Her account shows active involvement of a number of additional individuals: Thouwenjouw, a Mohawk man with strong connections to Canada, who accompanied her; her son, Warhosse Rode; and it identifies her son's father, SaadecaeeRehos.

96. See Richter, *Ordeal of the Longhouse*, 23.

97. For a recent description that applies this model, see Mann, "Haudenosaunee (Iroquois) economy," 120–34. Tooker and Bonvillain both described women as remaining within the boundaries of their established spheres of economic influence and control; see Bonvillain, "Iroquoian Women," 6: 47–58; and Tooker, "Women in Iroquois Society," 109–123. This model has recently been described as conservative and one that can be questioned for many American Indian societies; see Bragdon, *Guide to American Indians of the Northeast*, 245, 239–40. Merritt, in discussing native women's economic activities in and around colonial Pennsylvania, notes several active, female traders in the period between the 1720s and the mid-eighteenth century. Merritt concludes, "native women expanded their role as household provider into one of active participant in the Atlantic market economy," *At the Crossroads*, 63–64, 66.

98. See tables 12 and 13 Other special functions or characteristics of customers, as reported in the tables of this introduction, tend to refer to male customers, with the exception of occurrences of gifts to (or special arrangements with) individual clients (table 16, 38.5 percent of the listed individuals were women). Note, however, that two out of the five women appear in a shared arrangement with their husbands.

99. See page [74], first account; the arrangement is also listed on page [115], first account, where the relationship between the women is spelled out more clearly. There, the other Mohawk woman is described as aiewases's wife.

100. See the last entry, in the first account, on page [33].

101. The color green occurs once (1.2 percent), but is not specified as being light or dark. The two cases of yellow appear on pages [87] and [89]; and white is listed on pages [24], [38], [50], [51], [66], [67], [76], [77], [85], [87], [104], [107], [110], and [114].

102. See Axtell, *Beyond* 14925: 136.

103. For the importance of textiles and rum, see Norton, *The Fur Trade in Colonial New York*, 30–32.

104. See page [98], and the note there.

105. The statement by Norton, that "in addition to the main items in the trade, the Indians also purchased large quantities of knives, assorted textiles, ornaments, and wampum" does not apply to the findings from this account book, *The Fur Trade in Colonial New York*, 34.

106. The charter stipulated specifically which "small wares" were to be the domain of smaller traders. These included: knives, looking glasses, tobacco, tobacco boxes, flints, "Steels," wire, bells, thimbles, "Beedes," "Indian Combs" and needles, see *AA*, 8: 211–12.

107. References to the "small book" are on pages [14], [77], [87], and [109]; "Hester's book" is mentioned on pages [61], [87], and [95]; and the "Indian corn book" is on pages [22] and [96]. Somewhat different is a reference to "Hester's small book" on page [107], and a "waste-book" mentioned on page [75].

108. See page [117]: in 1703, Aqueras[e], a male client (probably a Mohawk), had a debt of one "quarter" for "buying meat." This does not specify who he bought the meat from. The ambiguity is also present in the Dutch description; *voor flys te copen* does not indicate whether Aqueras had already bought meat from the Wendells, or if he borrowed the money to purchase meat somewhere else at a later date.

109. Eighteenth-century shipments from the Hudson's Bay Company centers in the Subarctic north present a completely different collection of furs: beavers normally constituted between 80 and 92 percent of the peltry; see Ray, and Freeman, *'Give Us Good Measure,'* table 18, 168–74.

110. For Indians, the use of hops (*Humulus lupulus*) in the brewing of beer was a

post-contact experience. However, hops is a plant species indigenous to both Europe and North America. European varieties were introduced to North America early in the seventeenth century as a garden food and folk medicine, and specifically for use in the flavoring of beer. European varieties escaped and crossbred with the American varieties in many regions. The American species is genetically distinct, and hop pollen has been found in the upper Midwest in lake sediments deposited long before the presence of Europeans in North America. George R. Hamell, Norton G. Miller, and Charles J. Sheviak, pers. comm., September 2004.

111. Indian traders used it to carry personal items; see Gehring, *Fort Orange Court Minutes*, 352n. Around 1644, *notas* were described as "bags that they [Indians] can weave from hemp"; see Megapolensis, "Kort ontwerp van de Mahakuase Indianen in Nieuw-Nederlandt [. . .] beschreven in 't jaer 1644," 48. In Munsee Delaware, a word for "bag" (*sàki:nó:tay*) consists of a Dutch element (*sàk*, or *zak* in modern Dutch) and a native one (*-i:no:tay*, with the same meaning); see Goddard, "Dutch Loanwords in Delaware," 157.

112. The debt is recorded on page [97], and repeated on page [99], when it had been paid.

113. Data from TABLE 2.

114. Carlos and Lewis identified fluctuations in the prices of furs in Europe, and increased French-English competition in the trade with American Indian hunters and trappers as the main causes for such fluctuations in the eighteenth-century Hudson Bay area, "Property Rights and Competition in the Depletion of the Beaver," 131–49. Ray and Freeman also focused on the shift from the monopoly of the English Hudson's Bay Company in the area, to growing competition with the French as the primary cause for increasing price fluctuations, '*Give Us Good Measure*,' 155–62. White observed the same for the Great Lakes area, *The Middle Ground*, 120–22.

115. For this computation, see the first account on page [83], and compare the last account on page [58].

116. See the last account on page [73].

117. For the range of numbers of martens for one beaver, see the third account on page [24], the last accounts on pages [31] and [35], and the fourth account on page [42].

118. See the first account on page [59] and the relevant note, and compare the note with the last account on page [48].

119. For Canosedeckhaa (various spellings), see the only account on [77]; the Mahican couple's shared accounts appear on [13] and [106].

120. For 'Wannepackes' (various spellings), see the main account on page [99], and the only one on page [113]. Another example is the only account on page [111].

121. For an overview of these appearances, see note 232 to the translation.

122. Their roles are summarized in the annotated translation: Arijawaasen note 271; Arijenhotsen note 178; Wagrassero note 223.

123. Her accounts appear on pages [98] and [114]. The first instance contains the remark on her private debt. Most of her debt was crossed out, and her private debt was completely eliminated.

124. For an example of such deferred payments among merchants in New Netherland in 1662; see Jacobs, *New Netherland*, 192. That case involved a debt that had been "outstanding for no fewer than eleven years."

125. For this instance, see the first account on page [80].

126. For cases of indebtedness from "older times," see pages [37], [38], and [59]. "Earlier times" appears on pages [18], [40], [62], and [64]. The earliest occurrence of these descriptions is in an account that probably dates from 1698, the last one is from 1707.

127. His accounts are on pages [54] and [100].

128. See segments [19]–[37] and [38]–[75] in table 11.

129. See segment [76]–[114] in table 11.

130. Another case, on page [64], quoted in "Gifts and special arrangements," below,

is of a different nature: a native customer was welcome to acquire additional merchandise, as long as the new charges were added to the balance of his own account, not his wife's.

131. Gifts and arrangements, ten cases, table 16; leniency in collecting debt, twenty-one cases, table 17, totaling thirty-one. For the three cases of the Wendells' uneasiness with the debt of individual customers, and their request for a security in fifteen cases, see "Unusual circumstances with Indians' debts" above, and table 15, totaling eighteen.

132. The practice in Albany of extending large amounts of credit to Indians may have been documented earlier. Around 1680 (the entry is not dated), a Dutch widow asked for permission from Governor Dongan to move her bakery. She cited her difficult financial position as a reason for the request, claiming that her late husband had extended credit to Indians amounting to between four and five hundred beavers; see Christoph and Christoph, *The Andros Papers*, 438.

133. These cases can be found on ("staying at") pages [20] (twice), [39], [42], [54], [70], [72], [92], [94], [101], [104], and [119] (twice); ("trading at") one of the two cases on page [20], and on pages [9], [50], [68], and [84].

134. Shattuck, *A Civil Society*, ch. 5 and the references cited there, 289–92; Jacobs and Shattuck, "Bevers voor drank / Beavers for Drink," 99.

135. Shattuck, *A Civil Society*, 256, 281, 289.

136. These cases appear on pages [50], [54] (twice; different cases than the ones mentioned in note 133), [71], and [83].

137. Those numbers result from not counting the instance from page [7], and by considering the remark with the case on page [55]. An overview of the instances from table 6, by page number: [2], [5] (two occurrences), [6], [7] (a restated account, from page [5]), [16], [17] (two occurrences), [18] (four occurrences), [22], [31], [34], [36], [38] (two occurrences), [55], [57] (two occurrences), [62] (two occurrences), [64], [71], [75], [79] (two occurrences), [84], [88], [90], [94], [98], [115], [116], and [119].

138. An overview of the instances from table 7, by page number: [5], [6], [9], [17] (two cases), [22], [23], [28], [29], [33], [43], [55], [57], [112], [115], and [116].

139. This holds true for the occurrences on pages [5], [17] (two cases), [22], [55], [57], [115], and [116].

140. That instance occurs on page [57]. See Michelson's note on the woman's name, on page [23].

141. The customers are on pages [19], [24], [42], [48] (a woman), [49], [58], [66], [67], [83], and [112] (two customers, including one woman).

142. An overview of the instances from table 15, by page number: [1], [2] (two occurrences), [3], [10] (two occurrences), [14], [20], [45] (two occurrences), [50], [47], [62], [69], [72], [79], and [100].

143. For a resolution of Albany's Common Council from July 1706, see *AA*, 5:138.

144. All cases are in the handwriting of Evert Wendell.

145. For this instance, see page [42].

146. See page [64].

147. An overview of the instances from table 12, by page number: [8] (two cases), [9], [10], [17], [20], [33], [34], [65], [76] (three cases), [77], [83], [86], [87] (two cases), [92], [97], [98], [103], [107], [116], and [119].

148. See the section "travels by Indians," and table 12. The first total results from including all native customers who may possibly have been Western Indians, or were living among them.

149. The accounts of the French Indian customers are on pages [59] (young man, October 1705), [65] (young man, June 1706), and [107] (woman, undated). It should be noted that the account holder on page [65] is described as a French Indian, "who

lives among the Cayugas." The Ottawa customers appear on pages [9] and [12] (woman, August 1705–July 1707), [68] (man, June 1706), [69] (man, June 1706), and [82] (young man, June 1707). Note that the affiliation of the two account holders on pages [9], [12], and [69] is ambiguous, hence the range listed in table 1.

150. In table 12, these cases are the Mohawks Thotquariesen's wife, in 1706; Aeijewasen's wife's mother, Canosedeckhaa (a man), and Aeijewaesens's wife, all in 1707; the Mohawk couple Aequaenaghthaa (or the small Thickhead) and his wife, possibly from Canada, in 1708; the Mohawk couple Thotquariesen and his wife, the Mohawk men Arija and Caaheghtsiedawee, also in 1708; the Seneca man Josquassoo (or Annosktoo), also in 1708; three Seneca women (Schadseeaaee, Ossenant, and Dekaeont), all in 1709; and the Mohawk Daniell, in 1710.

151. The more ambiguous case occurred in February 1708 when Aequaenaghthaa (or the small Thickhead) and his wife took twenty-five "small *tonties* with them to sell for [Evert's] account." A number of elements in their accounts strongly suggest they lived in Canada, and other individuals mentioned in their account had strong liaisons there. The instance is on page [65] in the manuscript, and listed in table 12.

152. This, and the other four cases, are in table 12: the Mahican man Nannalamit in 1696; the Catskill man Schewas quawas, in 1701; the unnamed Mohawk woman bringing rum to the Oneidas, in 1703; the (likely) Mahican man Niettewapwae in 1704; and the Mohawk woman, described as Thotquariesen's wife, in 1708. Thotquariesen's wife is the only individual appearing in both categories, in a total of three cases.

153. For additional comments on these cases, see the discussion in table 12.

154. See *LIR*, 196; Richter, *Ordeal of the Longhouse*, 210, 215, 223. Richter states that the 1704 group had been "led" by the Mahicans and Mohawks, ibid., 223.

155. See Richter, *Ordeal of the Longhouse*, 223–24.

156. According to at least one analysis, Mahican and other Algonquian groups had begun to explore and settle in areas to the west from the Hudson valley as early as the 1660's, some of them eventually merging with the Miami Indians; see Brasser, *Riding on the Frontier's Crest*, 24–25.

157. A trip by Nietewakam (a Mahican man) to an undisclosed destination in September 1705 can perhaps be added, see entries on pages [8] and [20]. Also, the Wendells traded in Albany with three American Indians, two of whom they described as French (including a man, who lived among the Cayugas); these cases are dated October 1705 and June 1706 (the second one exhibiting the Cayuga connection), see entries on pages [59], [65], and [107] (undated).

158. These included an account for a young Ottawa man, see page [82], and one for a Mohawk man, who had arrived in Albany "by way of Ottawa," see table 12 (both from 1707). As noted before, the account of the individual with a multi-facetted identity from Detroit extended into 1710.

159. A French official in Montreal reported in 1737 that Indians involved in this trade earned ten to twelve percent of the value of the goods they transported; see Lunn, "The Illegal Fur Trade out of New France, 1713–60," 62–63.

160. An overview of the instances from table 17, by page number: [6], [8], [13], [14], [17], [25], [29], [38], [41], [42], [47], [49], [58], [60], [74], [76], [80], [92], [93], [94], and [101].

161. See the account of Canossedeckha, a Mohawk man, in July 1701 on page [45].

162. Three such cases appear: see page [23], Arijenhotsen's daughter, a Mohawk woman, in July 1701; page [49], the Mohawk man mentioned in the text, Watjandondie-ijo, in June 1702; and page [38], an unnamed Mohawk woman, on an undisclosed date.

163. Three such cases appear: see page [59], ToeWistToewee, a Seneca woman, in May 1707; page [84], Sajacaawecha, a Mohawk man, living in Canada, in July 1707; and page [108], for the instance mentioned in the text, dated September 1709.

164. An overview of the instances from table 18 by page number: [10], [20] (twice), [28], [60], [67], [82], and [99].

165. The only appearances of English currency are on the last pages of the manuscript, and they all relate to dealings with European merchants: see pages [118] through [120]. On page [120], Harmanus listed the value of goods in Dutch guilders, but used the symbol for the English pound in the tally.

166. See for instance, the accounts of the Mahicans Naghnaekamett on page [13], and Wannanpackes on page [113].

167. See Philip John Schuyler Papers, Account Book, 1711–1729, NYPL, reel 30.

168. See Carothers, *Fractional Money*, 26–27; and Mossman, *Money of the American Colonies and Confederation*, 57. McCusker, pers. comm., August 2002.

169. See Nettles, *The Money*, 205.

170. This currency has been characterized as "the premier coin of the Atlantic world in the seventeenth and eighteenth centuries"; see McCusker, *Money and Exchange*, 7. A bill of sale in 1651, from New Amsterdam in New Netherland, required payment in pieces of eight reals, and an inventory of the same year and place lists pieces of eight and quarter pieces of eight (the original reads *quaerties van achten*); see Peña, *Wampum*, 52. The British Board of Trade, in a proclamation of June 18, 1704, attempted to regulate the value of pieces of eight "at which [the] Piece is to pass in Plantations." It listed five types of pieces of eight, to which was added: "All Halves, *Quarters*, and Lesser Pieces are to Pass in Proportion to the above Rates" (emphasis added); see Brock, *The Currency of the American Colonies*, 134–6.

171. The three cases are: the last line of page [14], dated April 1708; and twice in one account on page [97], dated May and June 1709. That value has also been reported for Albany in the third quarter of the seventeenth-century; see Venema, *Deacons' Accounts, 1652–1674*, xix, and various accounts in that translation.

172. The "quarters" from this manuscript have not been identified. Their value excludes the possibility that they were equivalent to smaller Spanish coins, like the *cuarto, cuartillo*, and one that North American colonists sometimes referred to as pistereens.

173. An overview of the twenty-one instances from table 19 by page number: [5], [7] (twice), [10], [17] (twice), [21], [22] (twice), [25], [30], [31], [36], [77] (four times), [87], [88], [93], and [96].

174. See page [74]. It refers to an account with an unnamed Mohawk woman, probably in June 1707.

175. See Wendell, Ledger, 1711–1738, NYHS, f. 93. The journey was to be financed also by Nicolaes Schuyler and cousin Abraham Wendell. For the connection with a petition for a grant of some two thousand acres, see section 2 ("contacts and interactions between Indians and the Wendells") of this introduction.

176. See *DRCHNY*, 4: 741.

177. Ibid.

178. See *LIR*, 229.

179. For one of the more recent publications that describe this quality, see Parmenter, "The Significance of the 'Illegal Fur Trade' to the Eighteenth-Century Iroquois," 40–7.

180. The description appears with the first account on page [89]. It must be noted that the account has a caption stating "Canada an Oneida," possibly identifying the man as an Oneida. In addition, a man who can (almost certainly) be identified from other entries as a Mohawk (d'canjadereghtoo) was reported in February 1709 as having a Cayuga wife, see page [98].

181. For the Seneca man, his brother Decakedoorens and his father Sajacaawecha' see the combined entries on pages [74], [84], and [91], and the accompanying notes.

182. He appears in the first account on page [69]. The Mohawk name was listed as OnderRiesaghtoo, and possibly also as SoowaJaghCoo (the latter name was crossed out).

183. See page [68].

184. His dual residence and new name were reported in May 1707 see the first account on page [78]. His father appears on page [84], where he is described as a Mohawk, living in Canada (July 1707). A third, and final, case of an individual with a new name is described farther below in this paragraph (see naming practices).

185. This has been identified as, most likely referring to, Shawnee, see the two accounts on page [1], and the accompanying notes.

186. They are on: page [16], a Mahican boy, usually lives at the Catskill, September 1707; page [38], a Seneca woman, lives in Cayuga, 1704; page [39], a similar case; a woman, Seneca by birth, lives in Cayuga, 1704; page [54], a Seneca man, lives in Canada, among the Mohawks, September 1702; page [65], a French Indian man, lives among the Cayugas, June 1706; page [71], a Seneca man, lives in Cayuga, April 1708; page [100], a Seneca man, lives in Cayuga, September 1709; and page [103], a Mohawk man, lives in Seneca country, September 1709. As derived from the accounts of his wife's son and a woman, another Seneca man must be added: he lived among the Cayugas. See the account of Catquerhoo, on page [54] and the note there, dated June 1705. This excludes the case of a Mahican man, Sesecaet/Seeckaet (various spellings), who was recorded in February 1704/5 as trading with Harmanus in Mohawk country, see page [10]. Although he clearly has connections with some Mohawk individuals, there are no indications that he also resided among them.

187. The instance, dated August 1705, occurs on page [9]. While the woman may have migrated to the area inhabited by the Ottawas, Harmanus (the account is in his handwriting) could not make up his mind on how to refer to the woman.

188. They are: page [47], a young [male] Cayuga, described in 1702 as *swartaghge* (blackish); page [56], a Seneca woman, living among the Cayugas, *swart* (black) in 1704; page [89], an old woman from Canada, *swart*, in 1707; and page [119] a Mohawk woman, *swartigh* (blackish), for the period 1698–1702.

189. They are on: page [2], a woman, no affiliation (probably Mahican), *blanck*, in 1704; page [20], an Oneida woman, *blank*, in 1700; page [36], a Mohawk woman, *blanck*, in 1704; page [56], a Seneca woman, *blanck*, in 1705; page [58], a Seneca woman, *blanck*, again in 1705; page [90], a young Canadian [male], *blank*, in 1708; page [101], the same woman as page [36], *blanck*, in 1709; and [119], again the same woman as page [36], *blanck*, probably in 1704.

190. For that case, dated January 1710, see the note with Hendereck on page [10].

191. There is, for instance, no indication that the "black" customers were in any way related to, or derived from, the group of Indians sometimes referred to by Dutch and Swedish colonists as "Black Minquas." During the first half of the seventeenth century, the terms "White" and "Black Minquas" were applied to various Iroquoian groups, probably including the Susquehannocks and the Eries, "Black" perhaps referring to a large mark on the chest of male members of the group(s). Thus in two letters from 1648, Governor Loockermans described Indian customers at the Delaware River as *swarte wilden* (black savages); see Stuyvesant-Rutherford Papers, NYHS, 3–3, 465, 3–6. Abstracted and summarized documents relating to New Netherland contain a description of trade with American Indians in an area on or in the vicinity of the Delaware Bay. Their territory was labeled, in 1657, as the *lant der Minquas*, also *de Minquaesen lant* (land of the Minquas, Minquaes country); see New Netherland papers, "Abstract of papers from New Netherland, which arrived on the ship De Beever," Bontemantel Collection, NYPL. The terms appear to have become virtually extinct by the second half of that century. See Jennings, "Susquehannock," *HNAI*, 15: 362–68; White, "Erie," *HNAI*, 15: 412–17; and Hunter, "History of the Ohio Valley," *HNAI*, 15: 588.

192. During my research, up to April 2005, I have located only one case of an Indian in the seventeenth-century Northeast who was described in terms suggesting non-Indian descent by way of his/her complexion. In the 1660s and 1670s Tuspaquin,

a sachem of New England Wampanoags (an Algonquian group, also referred to as Po-kanoket), was referred to in various land deeds as "the Black Sachem" of Namassakett, and some small lakes were referred to as "the Black Sachem's Ponds"; see Bangs, *Indian Deeds*, 122, 127, 321–23. Indians in general were sometimes referred to as "Black," as in 1698 when a militia troop in Maine was described as consisting of "both Black and White" men; Norton, *In the Devil's Snare*, 59. For the mid-1700s and later, references to Indians' aberrant complexions occur more often. Sivertsen, mentions a "whitish Indian" man, sachem of the Tiononderoge Mohawks in the 1750s (he was also known, Sivertsen states, as "White Hans"), *Turtles, Wolves, and Bears*, 178, table 7–3B, 87. Hamell reports a number of cases of "Black Indians," (pers. comm., May 2004.) Among them "(Captain) Sun Fish," said in 1767 to have been living "as a free Negro" among the Senecas for fifteen years, references to this individual continue to appear until about 1800. At least one of the references also places his brother, Duck (English) or So-wak (Seneca), in the area around 1800. From the Sir William Johnson Papers, Hamell also reports on Samuel Tony, an escaped slave from Maryland, and Sherlock, a drummer at Fort Niagara. Hart has noted the appearance of a Cayuga headman, identified in the 1750s as "The Negro"; see "Black 'Go-Betweens.'" 111. A slightly earlier instance dates back to 1744, when "the Seneca chief Tachanuntie, or the Black Prince" was said to have participated in a meeting in Pennsylvania. The English claimed that Tachanuntie (according to Hamell, actually an Onondaga name, spelled in various ways in the document) was "either begotten on an Indian woman by a Negro, or by an Indian chief on some Negro woman"; see Marshe, "Journal of the Treaty Held with the Six Nations," 8: 179–80. The appellation of "Black Prince" also may have come from his extensive tattooing, rather than mixed African ancestry; "Sketches of Onondagas of Note," Beauchamp Papers, American Philosophical Society, Microfilm 643, p. 43.

193. A similar situation occurs with the description of a "Negro boy," below, whose Indian owner stated that she would sell him.

194. The entries are dated from 1705 to May of 1706.

195. The couple maintained both shared accounts and separate ones, see pages [20], [97], [99], [112], and [113]. The account, stating her proprietary relationship to the boy is on page [97], her statement dates from May of 1709. As mentioned in the annotation, they cover the period between September 1705 and May 1718.

196. See *AA*, 4: 213.

197. As indicated in a note on page [41], with the appearance of Dekanijaderegh-koe, Evert Wendell's other account books contain clear evidence that he acted (at least once) in this fashion. A note on the inside of the front cover of Evert's Day Book states that on January 6, of 1723/4, he had paid a large amount of goods "to Canjadereghto a Caghnawake [Caughnawaga] for that he surrendered a Negro boy which he had Taken in Vergenya [Virginia]." Evert was later repaid for this effort by the commissioners for Indian affairs in Albany, who seem to have ordered the attempt to liberate the boy; see Wendell, Day Book, 1717–1749, NYHS.

198. For cases in the records providing evidence of runaway slaves suspected of living among Indians, see *DRCHNY*, 5: 637–38, 674–76, 796, 965; ibid., 7: 732; and Sullivan, et al., *The Papers of Sir William Johnson*, 1: 43, 5: 32. The earliest case is from September 1721.

199. The earliest documented case is quoted in Hart, "Black 'Go-Betweens,'" 99. Hart cites a reference to a newspaper advertisement from 1679, which indicated that the escaped slave Jacob (speaking "Good English, Dutch, good Mohawk and Mohegan") could be staying in "Indian or Christian territory"; see Hodges and Brown, *"Pretends to Be Free,"* 79. Hodges also presents the same case, *Root and Branch*, 52.

200. See accounts on pages [5] and [6] for her own trading, and pages [7], [12], [105], and [106] for accounts of a Mahican man, married to her, her son (on whose account she also appears), and her sister's son.

201. Her direct kin and her sister's son are explicitly described, or listed as, Mahican.

202. For "our Susanna's" Indian woman, see the account on page [36]; the more neutral expressions of her relationship to the native woman are on pages [101] and [119]. The cross-reference within the manuscript from her account is on page [101], which refers to the one on page [36] that establishes the identity of the woman in these cases.

203. See accounts of Kacksaaweede on page [73], dated 1706 to May 1707, and Kaghtsweghtjoeni' on page [94], dated November 1710.

204. See Kawashima, "Indian Servitude in the Northeast," *HNAI*, 4: 404–06; Hodges, *Root and Branch*, 37. Hart adds that other legislative actions included references to Indian enslavement in 1715 and 1717, "Black 'Go-Betweens,'" 99n20.

205. Based on all New York City wills between 1664 and 1775, one historian tallied 182 cases of slaves being specified in testaments, but did not report occurrences of American Indian slaves; see Narrett, *Inheritance and Family Life*, 186–87. In at least two cases, however, it seems very plausible that Indians were among the slaves, listed as property. Besides bequeathing several "Negro" slaves, Sarah Roelofse stipulated "my Indian, named Ande" was to go to her daughter, see "Will of Sarah Roelofse, New York City, July 29, 1692," *Abstract of Wills on File*, NYHS, *Collections*, 25: 225–26. Thomas Swan, of Suffolk County, enumerated his twelve slaves, to be distributed among his children, to which the Pelletreau remarked that "some of them [the slaves] were Indians," though he provides no specifications (ibid., April 23, 1704, 413, clarification added).

206. Scott, "The Slave Insurrection in New York in 1712," 43–74, quoted in Nash, *The Urban Crucible*, 69, also see 256n8.

207. An ordinance dated March 17, 1723/4, prohibited any congregation of more than three "negro or Indian slaves," and stipulated that they were not to carry any weapons; another ordinance dated November 10, 1726, repeated these limitations. See *AA*, 8: 296; ibid., 9: 15–16.

208. These exports occurred notably after the Tuscarora and Yamasee Wars; see Gallay, *The Indian Slave Trade*.

209. Evert's will, for instance, stated that he left "all [his] Negroes" to his son Abraham (see note 5). For evidence of Evert Wendell obtaining slaves of African descent, see Schenectady County Historical Society, *Newsletter*, 38, nr. 3–4. It states that in November 1721, Evert Wendell purchased a "Negroe child, aged between four and five years Called Siera" from Johannis Halenbeck and his wife for seventeen pounds and six shillings.

210. Jacobs mentions two cases only: one of an Indian child (1 *wilt kint*) in the inventory of an estate in 1641, and a young Indian girl (*klijn wildinnetie*) in the 1680s, *New Netherland*, 398–99. One seventeenth-century account of New Netherland claims that this was a reasonably common practice; Van der Donck, *Beschryvinge van Nieuw-Nederlant*, 77–78.

211. See Lauber, *Indian Slavery in Colonial*, 112–13, 144–45, 290–92.

212. Ibid., 293. Kawashima also discusses two additional forms of Indian labor that natives delivered to colonists: apprenticeship and employment for wages, "Indian Servitude in the Northeast," 404–06. Recently, the various of ways in which young American Indians in eighteenth-century New England were forced into a situation described as "pauper apprenticeship" have been presented by Herndon and Sekatau, "Colonizing the Children," 137–73. Again, the specifics of the occurrences here do not permit us to conclude that they pertained to any of these categories.

213. Instances where the Wendells inserted a remark on their clients' tattoos are on pages [1] (twice), [65], and [68]. On pages [47], [50], [51], [57], [68] (a different case than the one mentioned in the preceding sentence), and [79], the lack of a tattoo is listed as a distinguishing feature. All cases refer to male traders and are limited to, from east to west, Onondaga (2 instances), Cayuga (4), and Seneca (3), except for the one male Shawnee on page [1].

214. Such cases are on pages [52], [57] (a different case than the one mentioned in the preceding note), [68] (a different case than the two mentioned in the preceding note), [70], and (very likely) [104]. Again, all are men, and in this group they are, from east to west: one Cayuga, three Senecas, and one Ottawa. This brings the total from the previous note to Onondaga (2 instances), Cayuga (5), Seneca (6), and Ottawa (1) (again except the one male Shawnee, on page [1]). See PLATES X, VIII, VI, V, and XIII, in the order as they are listed above.

215. Women would have applied paint, and other less permanent means of ornamentation. For a good overview of the practice of tattooing by American Indians, see Hodge, *Handbook of Indians North of Mexico*, 2: 699–701.

216. For example, portraits of the "Four Kings" (Mohawk and Mahican/River Indians' emissaries visiting London in 1710) have been frequently reproduced, mostly accompanied by enlargements showing (often enhanced) facial tattoos. See Brasser "Mahican," *HNAI*, 15: 201–12; Fenton, "Northern Iroquoian Culture Patterns," *HNAI*, 15: 310–11; and Fenton and Tooker, "Mohawk," *HNAI*, 15: 474.

217. This is the instance on page [47].

218. Five cases were left unspecified. Hamell submits that, possibly, "there was a certain minimum calendar or social age when tattooing became appropriate [. . .] sometime after the youth had his vision quest and was introduced to his guardian spirit. [. . .] Perhaps this was also coincident with the youth's adoption of his adult name" (pers. comm., March 2004).

219. This is the second instance on page [51], dated June 1702.

220. See PLATES XII, IX, and VII, in the order as they are listed in the text. The account on page [1] may also show a second mark, but the text and drawings are inconclusive in this regard.

221. They appear in accounts on pages [76] (a gun), and [95] (a pistol).

222. For these cases, see "native ethnic fluidity."

223. This occurs on page [53].

224. The Seneca man's case dates from July 1699, see page [41]. The other ten instances are: Tijoom/Rochkaeuw, a Mahican man, in the "register," repeated in account on page [14]; Tarahakeene/tasoonihasse, a Mohawk man, page [19]; Dekanoghtijeere/kanigraekeijijoode, a Mohawk man, page [20]; Caeijhoekedee/Saenaekeranckhack, a Cayuga man, page [28]; Aeniadiero/Tackkoniackha, a Mohawk man, page [44]; Satkatsteghcooe/Aennetsoendeijae, an Oneida man, page [52]; oghquesen/Canaghkwase, a Mohawk man, page [61]; Canandaa/oendack, an Oneida man, page [64]; Quanakaraghto/SeakRiesjies, a Canadian woman, page [89]; and Soeiae/Osseraecoe a Cayuga man, page [100].

225. The five cases are: Roetsieijoo/Dekaweeijeendigtachkoo, a Mohawk (?) woman, page [34] (possibly, the first name is a reference to a locality); Caijassee/Canissoe, a Seneca man, page [54] (the two names appear to be variations of one name); Sackkoonoeoenie/Sadkoodquathaa, a Seneca man, page [55] (possibly, the names refer to two brothers); TiocaghneeRadeie/Caanondaa, a man living in Canada, page [84] (possibly, the second name is a reference to a locality); and Osiestout/Sonienone, a Seneca woman, page [104] (possibly, the second name was a correction of the first version). Even in these cases, the general pattern is confirmed: most instances deal with men (although the tendency is less pronounced here, as two out of five concern women).

226. The first appears on page [54], with three names; the second string of three names can be found in an account on page [57], and is partially repeated on page [92]. One historian has hinted at the possibility of a native individual having more than two names, but did not document it; see Demos, *The Unredeemed Captive*, 159.

227. The name Sam can be found on pages [10] and [11], and Aberham on page [25]. Hottentot is an Oneida man, see page [72]. Considerably more given names of European

origins are scattered throughout the manuscript, but they are not used alongside native names (e.g. Hendrick, Cees, Korneles, Brant, Adam, Jan, Marija, Catrin).

228. See page [46], and the note there.

229. John Demos reported descriptions of naming practices in Caughnawaga, but based them on general observations from eighteenth-century French Catholic missionaries, *The Unredeemed Captive*, 141.

230. The adoptees appear on pages [76] and [105].

231. The possible adoptees appear on pages [9] and [84]. The latter instance has also been incorporated in table 20.

232. Identical situations arise when analyzing additional types of relations between relatives, described in European terms as in-laws: men's wife's sisters occur five times; their wife's brothers, twice; their wife's daughter, once. In addition, sons of women's sisters (nephews) appear twice, and a daughter of a woman's sister (niece) once. Again, *none* of such descriptions were used with men in the same position as those occupied by women in any of the situations described here and in the relevant paragraph of the introduction.

233. See "native ethnic fluidity."

234. These cases appear on pages [74], [83], and [55]. They all occurred between 1707 and 1708.

235. See the case on page [96]. The entry was dated 1708/9.

236. See the case on page [107]. The entry was dated September 1710.

237. See pages [41] and [86]: the first instance is dated October 1703, and the latter seems to be from October 1710.

238. These descriptions appear on page [41], the last account, and page [83]: the first one seems to be from a date before July 1700, and the second is from June 1707 or earlier. In the first case, the use of the more cordial, perhaps even respectable, term brother-in-law may be a reflection of the relatively high degree of intimacy regarding each other's lives and undertakings, developed between this individual and the Wendells. The note in the edited translation shows that, apart from other exchanges recorded in this manuscript, their liaison continued to exist for at least two more decades.

239. See the discussion regarding the term *aensoet*, in the last account on page [57]. The instance is dated September 1705.

240. He appears as Naghnacamet on page [101], but also as Naghnekampenit in the "register," and additionally as Naghnahamet, Naghnaekmet, Naghnekampemet, and Naghnaekamett.

241. See accounts and notes on pages [5], [6], [13], and [106] for trading by the woman, described as "our female savage"; and pages [3], [7], [12], [105], and [106] for accounts of the Mahican man, "married to" her, her son (on whose account she also appears), her sister, her sister's husband, and her sister's son. The sister of the Mahican man also traded on her own account, and that of her brother, see page [7].

242. One of the names that was reported as a witness, in 1710, is (perhaps) not a personal name. See the last instance in table 20, and the note on page [38]. An overview of the instances from table 20, by page number: [13], [14], [15], [16], [38], [41], [79], [84] (two occurrences), [85], [93], and [104] (two occurrences).

243. See the notes on pages [30], [8], [98], and [38], and the references there.

244. See page [98].

245. They are all Senecas: an unnamed woman on page [55], an unnamed man on page [75], a woman called Cawasthaa on page [83], and a man called Cawesaet on page [93]. Also see the note at the instance on page [55].

246. She appears in the third account on page [11]. For the only other instance, see page [65].

247. The following twelve works mention Wendell's account book: Armour, *Merchants of Albany*, ch. 4–8, esp. 65–67; Demos, *The Unredeemed Captive*, 133–34, 278–79n43, 279n45; Dunn, *The Mohican World, 1680–1750*, 122; Ezzo, "Female Status and the Life Cycle," 140; Foley, "The Mohicans: Alcohol and the Fur Trade," 137; Grumet, "Sunksquaws, Shamans, and Tradeswomen," 57; Matson, "'Damned Scoundrels' and 'Libertisme of Trade,'" 389–418; Norton, *The Fur Trade in Colonial New York*, 28–30, 35–38, 65–67, 86–87; Richter, *Ordeal of the Longhouse*, 382n28; Sivertsen, *Turtles, Wolves, and Bears*, 10, 275n21; Sullivan, *The Punishment of Crime in Colonial New York*, 311n152; and Tooker, "The League of the Iroquois: Its History, Politics, and Ritual," *HNAI*, 15: 431. Only Armour, Dunn, and Norton offer more detailed analyses. The status and activities of the Wendell family has also received little attention in the literature. Three exceptions are: Bielinski, "How a City Worked," 249–83; Alice P. Kenney, "Dutch Patricians in Colonial Albany," 249–83; and Matson "The 'Hollander Interest,'" 251–68. Feister, "Indian-Dutch Relations," indicated the potential for a survey of the Wendells and their interactions with American Indians.

248. See Norton, *The Fur Trade in Colonial New York*, 28n4; Grumet, "Sunksquaws, Shamans, and Tradeswomen," 57; and Ezzo, "Female Status and the Life Cycle," 140. It should be noted that, in the same article, Grumet also urged scholars to consider differences between ideals and realities when deliberating static native economic arrangements separated into gendered compartments.

249. For a discussion of the relevant literature, see the notes in the section "trading accounts."

250. The statement is from Ramsey, "'Something Cloudy in Their Looks,'" 55. The need for analyses at the micro-level, to complement macro-economic studies, has been described by Pickering, "Articulation of the Lakota Mode of Production," 57–69.

251. For a general study of the subject, see White, *The Roots of Dependency*. Braund has described this process among the Creeks in the eighteenth-century, *Deerskins and Duffels*, 136–37.

252. That sachem was named Caloolet. He appears in the account book as kaloolit in the "register," and as Kaloolet on page [6] in an entry from 1697. For his lament, and the observation that some Indian groups had moved away to Vermont because of their arrears and the abuse by traders from Albany; see Dunn, *The Mohicans and Their Land*, 155–57.

253. See Richter, *Ordeal of the Longhouse*, 86–87. He adds that one century later the transition to a complete reliance on European goods was virtually complete, ibid., 268–69.

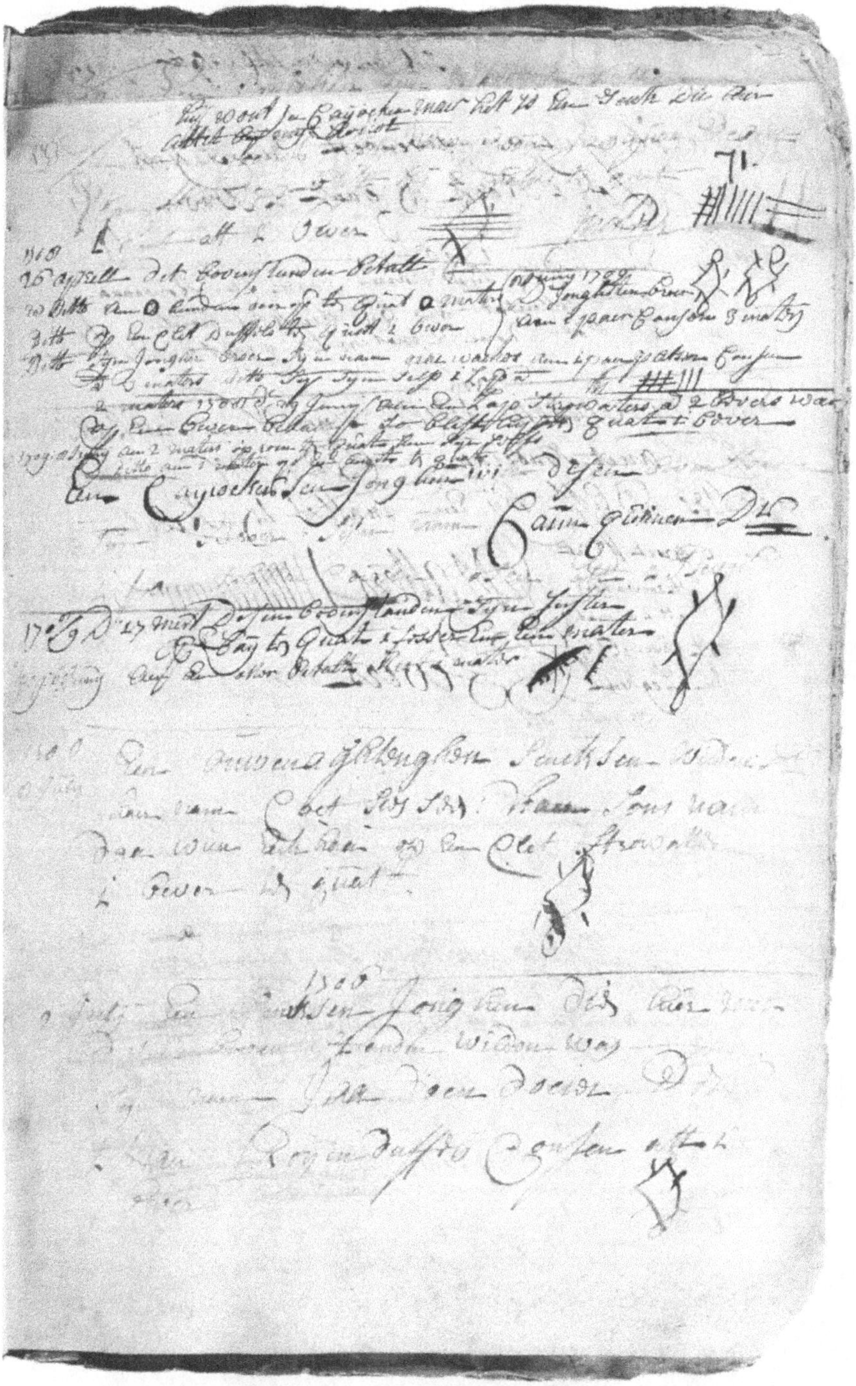

PLATE I. Sample page [71]. A layout of the accounts showing vertical marks for counting smaller animals, pictographs of beavers, and one of a fisher and an otter (considerably smaller) in the center of the page. Written in the hand of Evert Wendell.

Source: New-York Historical Society

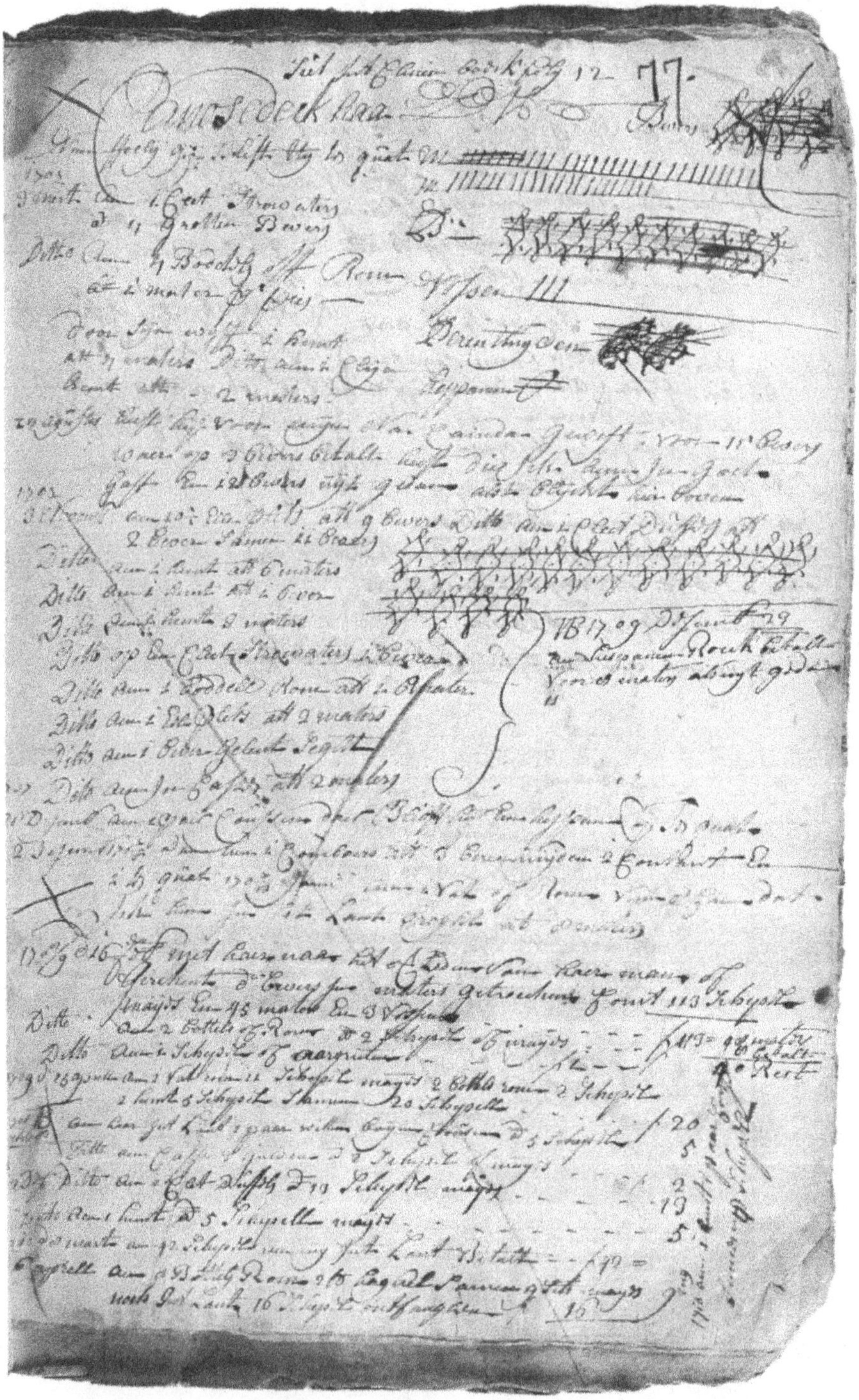

PLATE II. Sample page [77]. Pictographs of two bearskins, which are crossed out. Untypically, the page is devoted entirely to the account of a single person—Canosedeckhaa, a Mohawk, one of the Wendells' most important customers.
Source: New-York Historical Society

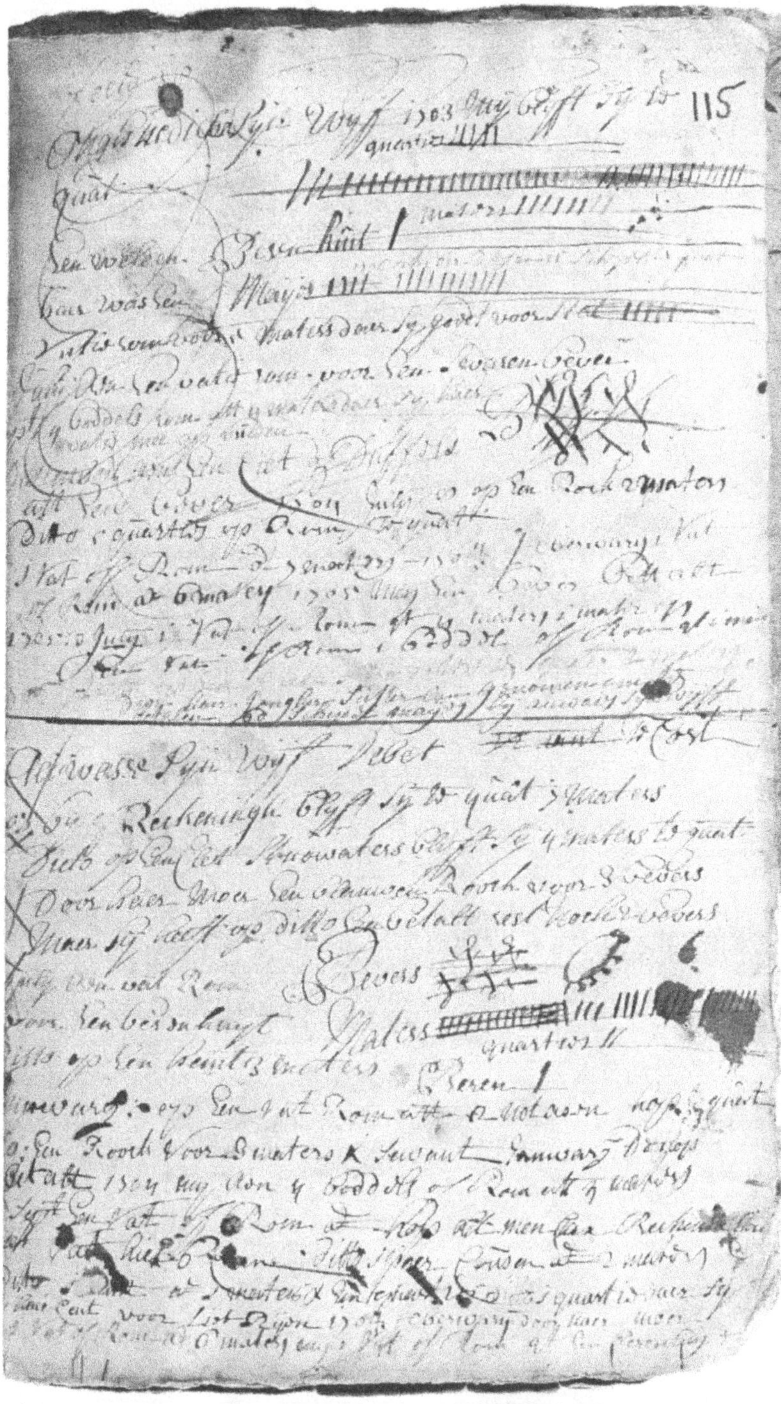

PLATE III. Sample page [115]. An example of one of the more disorderly pages from the account book. The handwriting is mostly Harmanus's; however, Evert's is in the middle and at bottom of page. The accounts are of two Mohawk women, identified by their husbands' names: Onghnedicha and Aeijwasee.
Source: New-York Historical Society

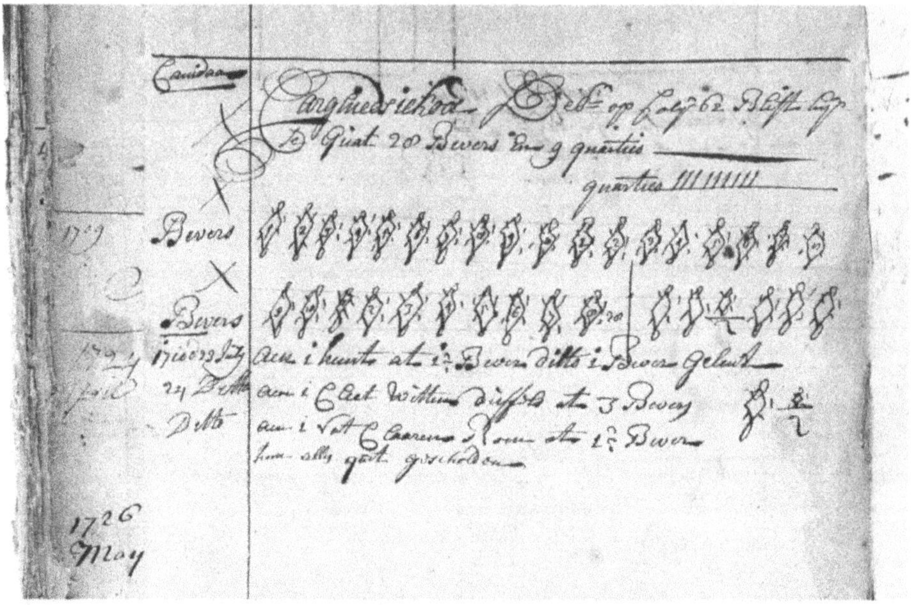

PLATE IV. Details of page [110]. The only instance where Evert Wendell numbered the pictographs of the beaver furs that an Indian customer owed him. The customer was Carghiedsiekooe— a Mohawk man who (most likely) lived in Canada.
Source: New-York Historical Society

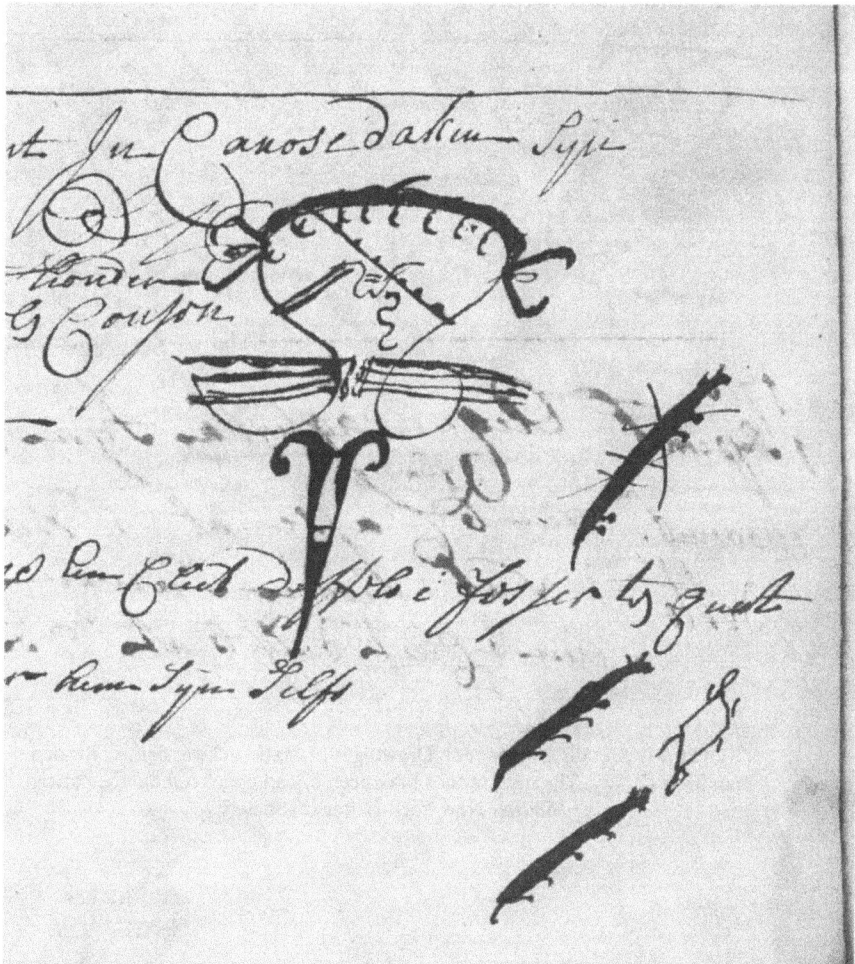

PLATE V. Details of page [70]. Drawing of TannaEedsie, described by Evert Wendell as "a young Seneca" with tattoos. The neck tattoos have been folded open to show the pattern. The pictographs are of three fishers and one beaver.
Source: New-York Historical Society

PLATE VI. Details of page [68]. Drawing is of Mackkockwassien, a tattooed man from Ottawa. The neck tattoos have been folded open to show the pattern. *Source:* New-York Historical Society

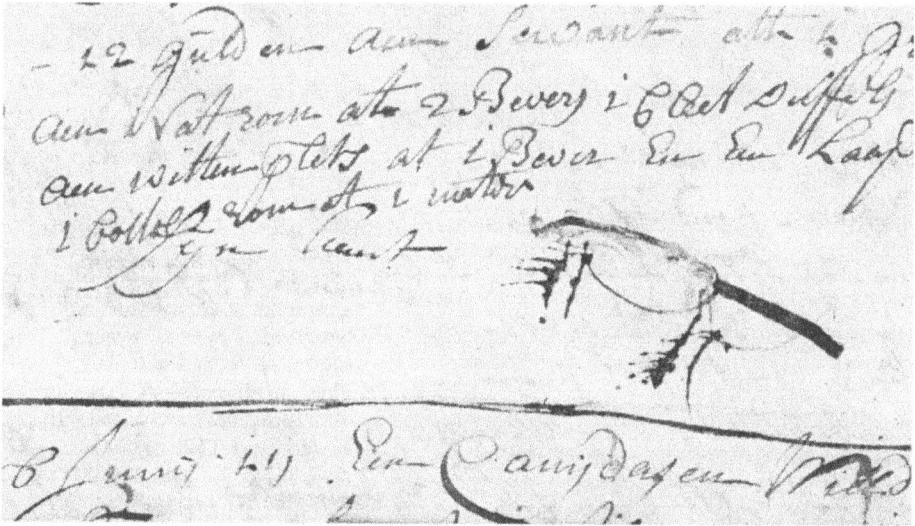

PLATE VII. Details of page [66]. Drawing is a symbol placed in the account of DeCanjaeDeReghtToo, a Mohawk man with evident connections to Canada. *Sijn hant* (his hand) is written to the left of the symbol.
Source: New-York Historical Society

PLATE VIII (above). Details of page [57]. Sketches are from an account of Aennaedsoenes, described by Evert as "a young Cayuga." Also, an additional individual (probably a relative of Aennaedsoenes), is depicted with a hairdress and tattoos on the neck, at the side and towards the top of the natives' heads. Again, the tattoos in the neck have been folded out.
Source: New-York Historical Society

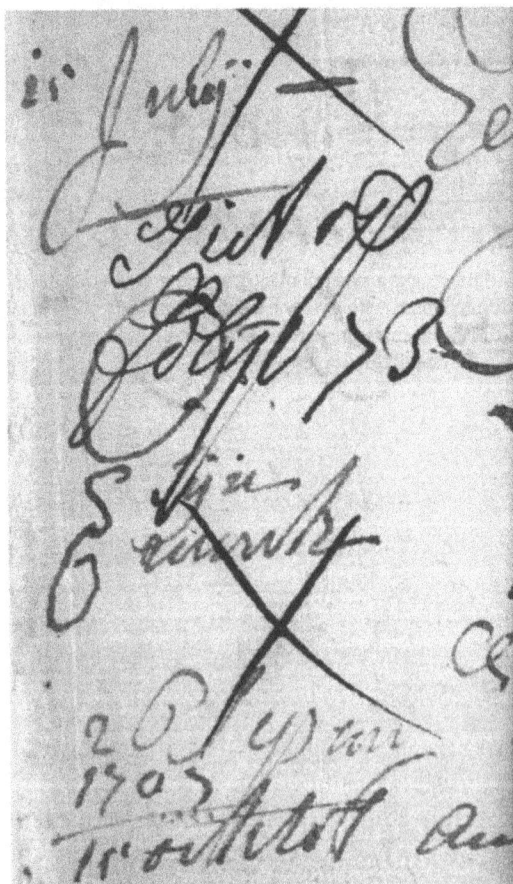

PLATE IX (left). Details of page [57]. From the account of Josquassoe or Tennessocthaa, a young Seneca. The Indian client had placed a mark at the left side of the page, probably to confirm a transaction or the total value of his debt at a given time. To the right of it, it reads *sijn merck* (his mark). It appears to consist of the oval shape and the snake-like swirl just below it. The large cross, to the right of the mark, is unrelated.
Source: New-York Historical Society

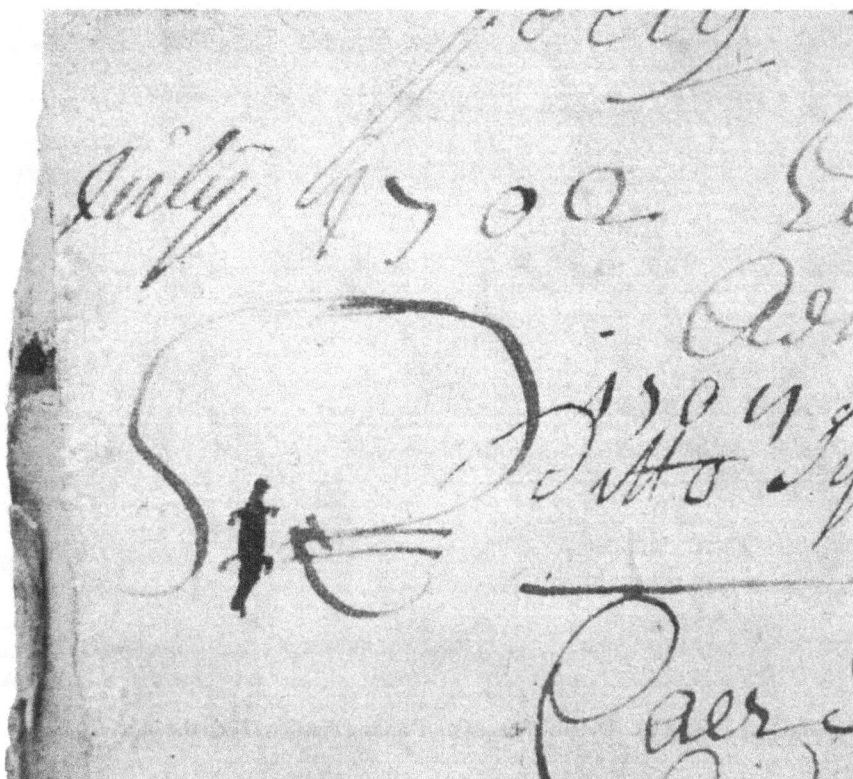

PLATE X. Details of page [52]. From the account of the male Seneca customer Conowaroo. The drawing is a sketch showing the client's tattoos on his neck. To the right two lines have been folded out.
Source: New-York Historical Society

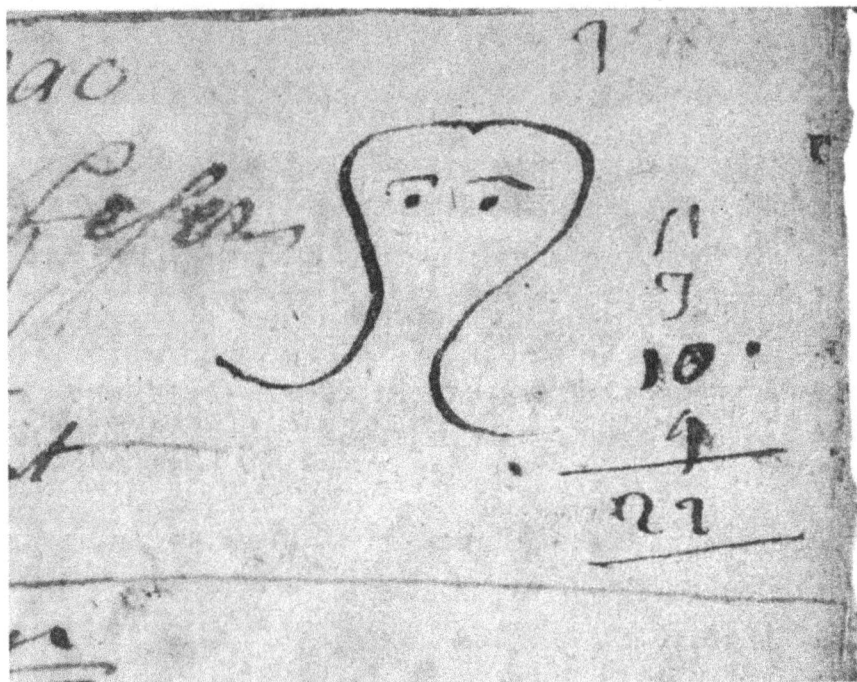

PLATE XI. Details of page [51]. Drawing may have been the start
of a sketch of Soghsiecoowao's head or face.
Source: New-York Historical Society

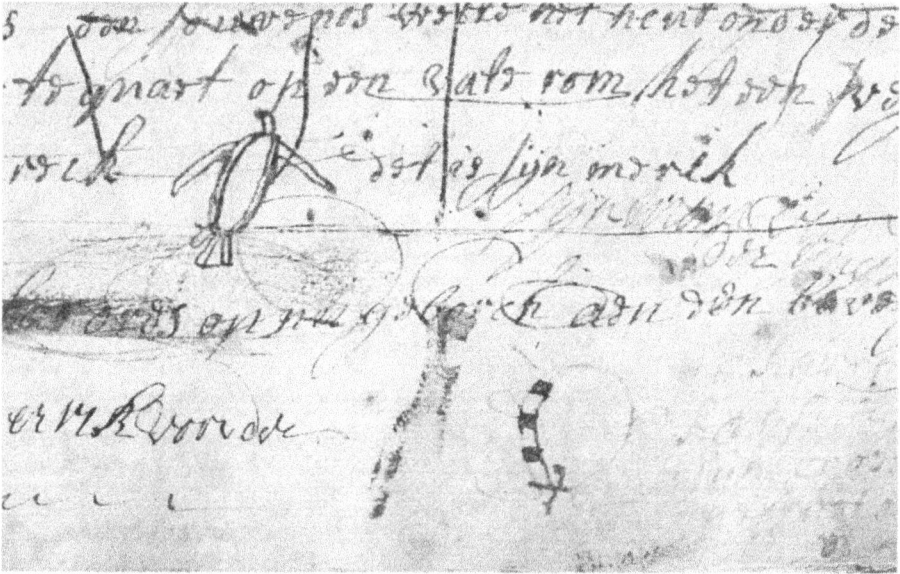

PLATE XII. Details of page [1]. Drawings in the account of Tankarores/ tackkarores. Shows the man's mark (a turtle, probably a clan symbol), and a rough sketch of an individual's head with a tattooed band along the side of it. To the right of the turtle it reads *det is sijn merck* (this is his mark). It is not clear from the text or the images whether the cross at the bottom of the tattooed band is part of the tattoo, or another mark of the customer.
Source: New-York Historical Society

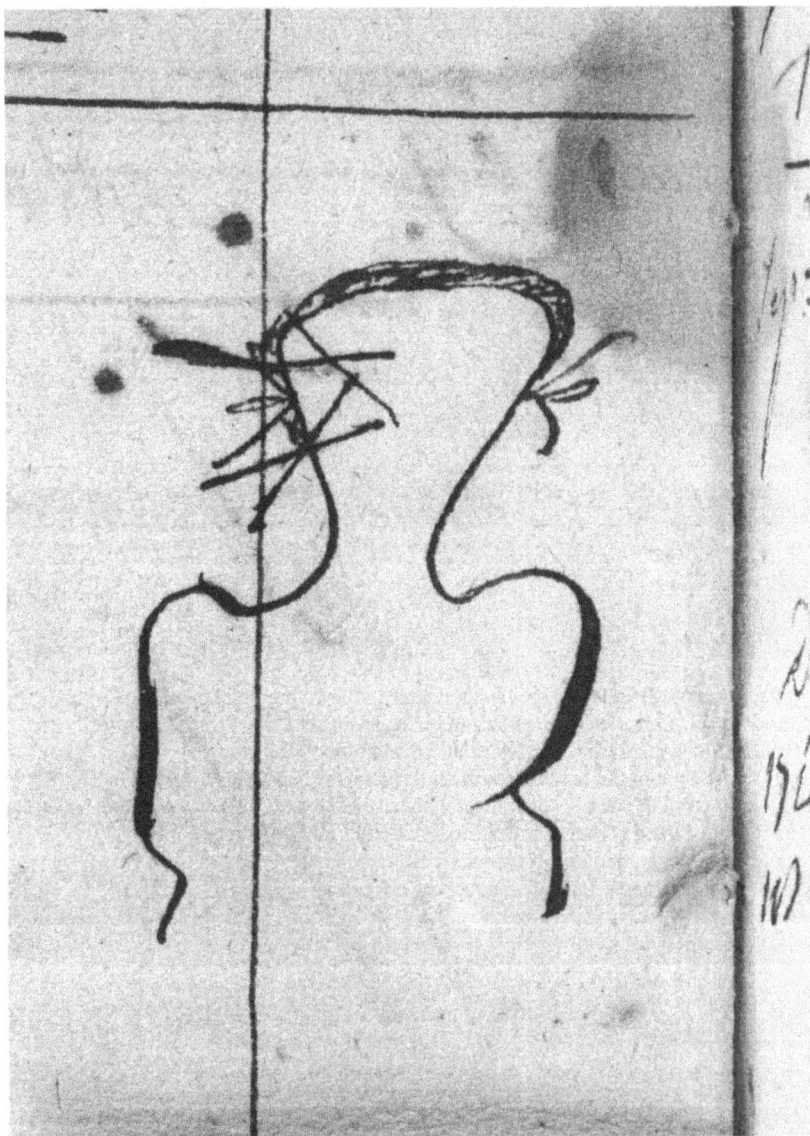

PLATE XIII. Sketch on page [104]. Drawing is of the head, hairdress, and possibly some facial markings of Canowaacightuea, a Seneca man.
Source: New-York Historical Society

Evert Wendell's

Account Book, 1695–1726, of Trade with Indians

Annotated Translation,
Dutch–English

Page Numbers of the Wendell Manuscript

THE ACCOUNT BOOK has some gaps, and the Wendells attributed the same page numbers to several (usually consecutive) pages. The table below is intended to assist readers in accessing the manuscript.

Ascribed page number, [ ]	Page number in manuscript
——	Front cover, outside
——	Front cover, inside
[1]	1
[2]	—— (verso)
[3]–[12]	1–10
[13]	—— (recto)
[14]–[15]	11–12
[16]–[17]	8–9
[18]	—— (verso)
[19]–[40]	1–22
[41]	—— (recto)
[42]	22 (verso)
[43]–[44]	22–23
[45]	—— (recto)
[46]	15
[47]–[48]	18–19
[49]	19 (recto)
[50]	19 (verso)
[51]–[54]	19–22
[55]–[56]	38–39
[57]–[76]	39–58
[77]	—— (recto)
[78]–[83]	60–65
[84]–[99]	65–80
[100]	80 (verso)
[101]	80
[102]–[105]	81–84
[106]–[114]	86–94
[115]–[119]	38–42
[120]	—— (verso)
[121]	Back cover, inside

Editorial Method

The layout of the manuscript's pages has been retained as much as possible. This also applies to accounts where parts of a page have been left empty. These spaces may mark instances where the Wendells anticipated additional trade with Indian customers.

[text]	remarks between brackets reflect editorial comments on, for instance, the lay-out of the original text. On occasion, the brackets contain additions to the original text.
[text?]	where the original text is difficult to read, illegible, or illogical in its given context. Text with a question mark between the brackets reflects an editorial suggestion.
[text = cr]	text, preceding the =, has been crossed out.
Text	direct transcriptions of Dutch, English, or Indian words or sentences.
∗text∗	indicates text that is written in the margins of the page. If the location is not given, the text is located in the left margin.
[xb drawn, xcr]	to visually record the total debt of an Indian trader, the Wendells made drawings (or small vertical marks) in the right side of a page. When a customer redeemed all or part of the debt, the corresponding number of drawings or marks was crossed out. The information between the brackets reflects the number of drawn animals, and those that have been crossed out.
[xmk(s), xcr]	The information between the brackets reflects the number of marks, and those that have been crossed out.

Abbreviations, between brackets [ ] in the tallies (translation/transcription):

[b/b] = beaver
[B/B] = bear
[e/e] = elk
[l/l] = lap, see the glossary
[f/v] or [f] = fisher
[m/m] = marten (may also refer to weasel)
[o/o] = otter
[r/h] = raccoon

X (\)	By placing an X to the left of an account, the Wendells recorded that a customer had satisfied some (or all) of the

debt recorded. Also see the following entry. Sometimes, a slash was used.

[account cr]   Besides placing an X in an account , the Wendells sometimes crossed out an entire account, indicating that the debt had been paid. In order to not to complicate reading those accounts, crossed out accounts are rendered here without the markings, but with the remark between brackets.

½, ¼   Throughout the account book, ¹/₁ was used to indicate what is clearly ½. It has been replaced with ½. Entries with ¼ have been maintained.

Glossary

Anker   Dutch liquid measure, equivalent to 10.128 gallons.

Baize   a coarse woolen textile, often with a long nap.

Can / kan   Dutch liquid measure, equivalent to one quart.

Draegbant   carrying strap, or carrying belt.

Drieling   also 3ling, drije lingh, and drijelingh. A portion of an entire pelt.

Duffel   a coarse or thick woolen cloth.

Ell   a standard Dutch linear measurement, used primarily for measuring cloth. Roughly equivalent to 68 centimeters, or 27 inches.

f   florijn, see guilder.

Gelijt   see oplijen.

Gemp   also gimp and gijmp. A textile in which the threads are encapsulated by another material. In Europe, silk was applied to cover the thread. Often used to hem the edges of a blanket, for decoration and reinforcement.

Guilder   monetary unit of the Dutch Republic, consisting of 20 stivers.

Haelmes   a type of knife used to scrape the surface of wood, freshly skinned hides and furs, and leather.

Houwer   a short, broad sword; falchion.

Karpoes	also *karpoets* or *kapoets*. Dutch word with several meanings, all related to some form of head gear. It may specifically refer to caps.
Kno / cnoo	canoe.
Lap	plural: *lappen*. Literally, a "cutting" or "remnant piece." The Wendells used this term (also spelled *laep* and *laap*) to describe both textiles and furs. Where the first meaning is obviously intended, it has been translated as "piece [of cloth]." Since precise information regarding the size of a *lap* of peltry is lacking, the word has been maintained in the translation.
Notas	Indian (probably Algonquian) name for a pouch or bag.
Oplijen	*opleggen*, of which *oplijen* may be derived, in commercial exchanges is "to raise" or "to lay onto/on top" (a price, for instance). It also has two other, contradicting meanings: to charge interest, or to pay off a debt. Both meanings can be applicable to the usages in the account book.
Plets	a coarse woolen textile.
Quarter	*quartije(s)*, *quaertije(s)*, *quartie(s)* or *quarttie(s)*. A monetary unit or a form of currency with a value of 1½ Dutch guilders. It may also denote or represent the value of one-quarter of a Spanish piece-of-eight.
Sijven/schijven	wampum.
Singerlin[g]	a type of fabric. Linen or hemp strap, coat belt.
Skipple	*schepel* in Dutch. A dry measure equivalent to 0.764 English bushels.
Stiver	one-twentieth part of one guilder.
Tonties	also *tonies*, *toniets* or *tonieties*. Literally, a small keg or cask. Specific usage in the account book remains undetermined.
Vlenningh	also *vlengh*. A type of textile, possibly flannel.
Voeteling	also *foeteling*. The foot of a stocking or a heavy, strong sock. Usage in the account book suggests it may also refer to a specific kind of textile.
Vret	modern Dutch: *fret*. A small gimlet or awl with screwthread at the lower end.

Translation

[Front cover, outside.
Bears a large sign in the shape of an inverted *A*, with a crooked cross bar. Its form suggests a variation on the capital *W*. The Wendells may have used this sign to mark their peltry before shipment. Furthermore, the cover contains some notes and quick scribbles, but they are faded and illegible.]

[Front cover, inside.
A listing of undetermined origin and purpose:]

> A camisole
> 3 [skeins?] stitching silk
> 2 [skeins?] sewing silk
> 3 skeins of yarn
> ½ dozen buttons
> 1 piece of buckram
>
> _____
>
> 12 ells of fabric
> 13 ells of lining
> 90 silk strings
> 2 skeins of stitching silk
> 1 piece of buckram
> 3 skeins of yarn

> Thirty lb
>
> lb now *voorttrodart*[1]

Savages Book [followed by faded words, reconstructed as:
[Ca?]*stor* and *baize.*]

R R [both inverted]

folio 1

Anno 1699, June 20, Debit. [Delivered] a small cask of rum for a
beaver to a Shawnee[2] named tackkarores who stays with the Onondagas
[In addition,] 3 bottles of rum for 2 martens

1700 To 1 Onondaga boy, owes 1 beaver on a gun
his name [is] Decoo

	NB [Paid?[3]] in the book	6	[unclear
	[computation?:]	99/009	scribble]
		9	

X tannaRachqua
A young Cayuga savage, with an *ackdes*[4] tattooed on his chin.
Debit, a beaver for a pair of baize stockings[.] In addition,
X a fisher for a small shirt
1700 June[,] he has paid an elkskin

> *I have receiued your Letter bij Joh[annes] Doo and*
> *perceieivd [sic]*[5] [1b drawn, cr. Pertains to preceding account]

That Jan van Allen has paid the above and as follows, that we, the
undersigned, acknowledge together[6]

---

for my account
for for then her name [is] karehadee[7] and her husband's name
[. . . = cr] Tanngh   To a female Mohawk savage a small
[*den mana*[e/c]*qua* = cr]   cask of rum for a beaver
                              [She] has put down[8] 6 [units of] wampum
[d. . 1699 . . . = cr]
klop
          [account cr = paid]

1700
keijhokeseren, a Cayuga with one eye, [owes] a beaver on a small cask
of rum
See on folio 17 for his newly extended credit
See on folio 17, where he is transferred[9]

An old female savage lives on *Metstaeharae*[10] with the Lame hand[11]
[. Owes] 1 marten on a pair of duffel stockings
From us another marten   m[artens]   [2mks, cr]

[——————————————————————————————]

Tankarores[12], a Shawnee savage who stays among the Onondagas
owes an otter on a small cask of rum[. He] has a bird tattooed
X on his head   [Drawing of turtle]   this is his mark[13]

                                          his name further *ij* [. . . ?]
[Tackkarores = cr] Credit extended anew for a beaver
His mark for this[14]
[Drawing of head, and probable tattoo along the side of the head[15]]
[Next to drawing, lower right hand corner:]   sakayenasqua
                                                     katsedeniet[i?]e
                                                     his brother
                                                     .*rste*[o?]*tor.k.e.* .[16]

——[2]——

[This page is divided into two parts. On the left, a list of names with references
to folio numbers. On the right, some accounts, apparently connected to entries
on the last pages of the book.
First, the names:]

A register of the
Mahican[17] savages

Jan the savage folio - - - - - - - 1	Nooseewalamit folio - - - - - - - 8
His wife folio - - - - - - - - - - - 1	Jacop the savage - - - - - - - - - 10
His wife's sister folio - - - - - - - 2	mackenant folio - - - - - - - - - - 3
A female savage who she escorted	Netewakam f[olio] - - - - - - - - 7
Nemamet's wife folio - - - - - - - 3	Wanckpaee owes 1 piece of
Jan Seeps folio - - - - - - - - - - - 3	meat for baize[18]
Walitgaes folio - - - - - - - - - - 4	Naghnekampenit folio - - - - - 5
His brother Malsik folio - - - - 4	Pamolet folio - - - - - - - - - - - - 1
Sicktock folio - - - - - - - - - - - 5	Sesecaet f[olio] - - - - - - - - - - 8
Naernis folio - - - - - - - - - - - 5	Naghnaehamet [X]
Awannighqaet folio - - - - - - - 6	his sister f[olio] - - - - - - - - - - 5
Naeckaepen folio - - - - - - - - - 6	his wife's son - - - - - - - - f 5–f 3
Tijoom or Rochkaeuw folio - - 7	Herij f[olio] - - - - - - - - - - - - 12
Awans folio - - - - - - - - - - - - 7	
kaloolit folio - - - - - - - - - - - 8	

Nannaelaemit who was escorted
by the Greyhead - - - - - - - - 9
the Greyhead is called
Wassewaencke folio - - - - - - - 9

[At X, between the list and the
accounts, two names are inserted,
in a drawn box. Their function
here remains unclear: Maghack[19]
Secqaet[20]]

[Second, the accounts at the right side of the page:]
The wife of Cees[21] the savage Debit
1704 July 12 skipple Indian corn
X at [12mks]   guilders
3 bottles of rum at 9 guilders   f 9
X 1 coat at 16 guilders - - - - - - - - - - - - - f 16
August 1 cask of rum at - - - - - - - - - - - - f 16

_____

Wamosie[22] Debit for 1 blanket of
duffel at 34 guilders
        [account cr = paid]

_____

X [H]er sister, who she escorted,
X 2 bottles of rum at f 6

───────────────── 1704 ─────────────────

September 3, kahaeckan or kaeghakan's
X wife Ceuwanwaas Debit
10 *can* of rum at 2 skipple
X Indian corn   Indian corn   [30mks]
his wife Ceuwanwaas skipple 30
X A piece of strouds at 9 skipple 39
1 bottle of rum

───────────────── 1704 ─────────────────

Wamossij a female Mahican savage
X Debit [for] a red duffel blanket
X at 34 guilders, on which she has put
down a security, received 13 skipple

───────────────── 1704 ─────────────────

Cees the savage Debit
X in the back of the book 23 guilders[23]
August 19, 4 bottles of rum
X at 3 guilders each, 12 guilders
[guilders] [35mks, 26cr]
X He had put down a blanket here [as security]

which I bought from him on August 28[24]

———————————————— 1704 ————————————————— August 30

[See] across[25]
Schekquae's sister, a white female savage[26],
X 3 ells of baize for 2 pigs.[27] One of
3 years old and one c[uu?].[28] [And] 2
X bottles of rum and a shirt which is on
her brother's account[,] the pig
[has] to be delivered in one month
X 1 pair of stroud stockings

——— [3] ———

folio 1 Mahican page[,] March 12[,] 1698
        1698 Paid on this account 3 beavers and 1 otter and 2 martens
        Jan the savage[29] Debit at balancing of the account 8 beavers
        and 14 martens 1 otter 2 deerskins
        [Credit extended] anew: 3 bottles of rum for 3 martens,
        also 2 bottles of rum for 2 martens[,] 1 bar of lead [for]
        1 marten
1700 for a shirt 12 guilders and for a small shirt 5 guilders
ditto, a duffel blanket for 20 guilders, also a bottle of rum
        3 guilders

1703/4 the son of Jan's wife, his name [is] Waskaemp,[30]
        from his mother's time a shirt for 2 martens
        A blue coat at   M[artens] [8mks]
        a beaver[.] A duffel   B[eavers] [2b drawn]
        blanket at one beaver and
        2 martens, a pair of stockings
        for 2 martens[.] January a bottle of rum at a marten
D[itt]o: A big knife at a marten[,] but then I must give him a
        quarter

        March 12, 1698   she is also again listed above
        Balanced accounts with Jan's wife, she remains indebted
        54 guilders [in] wampum
        [Credit extended] anew, 12 guilders on a shirt, also
        owes one skipple of Indian corn, also a bottle rum for a
        marten, also a small shirt [for] 5 guilders, also 2

bottles of rum [for] 2 martens.
1699 in addition a [blue duffel = cr] blue coat for a beaver
[1700 in addition[,] a beaver for baize = cr]
1700 in addition owes 5 skipple Indian corn on a duffel blanket
ditto also 5 skipple Indian corn for a shirt, together makes
10 skipple
1702 [owes] 2 martens on a pair of stockings, also 1 bottle rum [for]
1 marten

Paemoelt[31] Debit[,] rum at 5 quarters, for which he puts down his
        blanket but it is old[.] 1704 July him [has] again given
        a new blanket and [we are] even[32]

—— [4] ——

1695 Ditto   folio 2

1698 One beaver paid on this account
The sister of Jan's wife [owes] one beaver and 2 martens for a duffel
blanket [, also] owes 6 guilders on a small coat Also, a debt of 6
deerskins remained Also owes 2 skipple Indian corn Also owes 12
martens Also 5 skipple Indian corn [for] a shirt
Also a cask of rum for 1 beaver Also 2 bottles of rum [for] 2
mar[tens] Also 2 quarters [for] 1 marten Also 2 guilders for rum
Still owes 6 skipple Indian corn on a knife and a quarter Also 2
bottles and one pint of rum for 3 martens Also 1 marten for 2
quarters Also 4 martens for a pair of stockings and a bottle of rum
In addition owes 2 guilders Also 4 martens for a shirt Also a marten
on a bottle of rum Also 12 guilders on a small coat
[Also 12 guilders on a shirt = cr] A pair of stockings for 4
guilders
[Also a beaver for strouds[.] still 4 quarters short = cr]
[Also to her husband 2 bottles of rum for 2 martens[,]
also 1 marten for 2 quarters Also 1 marten for a bottle of rum = cr]
1699 ditto 9 guilders and 10 stivers in money [and] a shirt for 4
martens [Her husband on a knife and a *vret* for 1 marten = cr]
1700
[a beaver for a duffel blanket = cr] Also on a shirt 5 guilders Also on
a pair of stockings one marten
       [account cr = paid]

1697 She for another female savage
a beaver on a duffel blanket[.] For another savage,
a beaver and 2 martens on a duffel blanket[.] For another savage[33], a
beaver and a *lap* on a duffel blanket
Also 6 hands[34] of duffel and a shirt, together a beaver

———————————————————— 1704 ————————————————————

The sister of Jan's wife who is listed above[.]
1704 October[,] 1 pair of stockings at 5 martens: 1 marten on 1
bottle of rum
She is listed on folio 1[35]   M[artens] [18mks]
1707, May 5
Had another female savage fetch 4 shirts[,] 1 of which [she] has paid
and three to be paid at the first occasion when she returns from
Sarghtoke[36]
Amounts to 12 martens
        [account cr = paid]

—————— [5] ——————

folio 3   1698
Another female savage[,] who was escorted by our young female savage[37]
[,] Neemam[et's][38]
wife[39][,] remains indebted 7 skipple Indian corn and 16 guilders in
wampum Also for rum and lead 3 martens Also
for 3 *kan* rum 15 guilders Also a half skipple Indian corn [for] 3
guilders

1700 July
Jan's wife['s sister[40]] at balancing of accounts, she remains
indebted 53 martens [blot] beavers and
8 skipple Indian corn and 4 deerskins

1700 her husband[,] half an ell of baize [for] 4 guilders
1701 In addition [she sent] her sister's son[41] to fetch
        1½ bar of lead
1701 in the month of March also 4 martens on 1 shirt
in the month of May also 3 shirts for 3½ martens each,
        makes 10½ martens And[,] in addition[,] ditto 1 small
        shirt for 1 marten[,] amounts to   - - -   11½ mar[tens]
ditto An additional 3 martens for *plets*
1701: June 27, 6 martens paid

1697   [5b drawn]   [martens?] [4mks]
Jan Seeps a bottle of rum [for] 1 marten[,] 3 *kan* cider 1 marten[,] 1
marten in copperwire Also 3 bottles of rum [for]
3 martens Also 6 bottles of rum[,] 6 martens[.] Kaloolet a bottle of
rum for which he[42] is guarantor[,] he also 2 quarters Also 9 bottles
of rum [for] 9 martens Also a cask of rum [for] a beaver Also a small
coat for 3 martens [and] 1 marten in flintstones

1701, July 18   Mackanant[43] debit for
        1 small cask of rum 1 elkskin[, he] promises to
        bring this elkskin in 20 days[44]

1704/5 February A female savage who was escorted by Naghnaekmet[45][,]
[and] from whom I received the piece of meat on *Nutkathaa*[46], remains
indebted on a pair of stockings   M[artens]   [2mks, 1cr]
1707 February received 2 skipple Indian corn from her in the country[47]

———[6]———

1697[,] August 16[,] Mahican page
folio 4
Walitgaes[48] debit 7 guilders for cider [to?] the one he escorted [and]
for whom he is guarantor For 19 guilders in paint and knives: he
[himself] also a bottle of rum [for] a marten Also 2 bottles of rum
[for] 2 martens Also a shirt 3 martens Also a cask of rum [for] a
beaver Also carried away 2 small empty casks [for] 2 martens
1699 he paid a beaver on this
ditto 1 marten in paint
1700 in copperwire for 2 martens[,] a bar of lead for a marten
ditto one marten for a small looking glass[,] in paint for 1 marten
together 5 martens

1704/5[,] March 1 the son of our young female savage   Debit
1 skipple Indian corn @ 1 marten [1mk] 1705 June paid[,] so that [we]
are even

1697 His brother Malsik[49] Debit 1 marten for a bottle of rum
Also a cask of rum for a beaver[,] a tobacco-box [for] 1 marten[,] ½

beaver in rum

Also a small box of paint [for] 1 marten Also 2 *kan* cider [for] a
marten Also in cider for a marten Also 2 *kan* rum [for] 12 guilders
Also a small cask of rum [for] a beaver

———————————————— 1704 ————————————————

X Retsert[50] the savage Debit
X a raccoon[51] for lead: June a *houwer*
X for 2 beavers[,] together 2 beavers and 1 marten
ditto 2 strings of beads [for]
2 raccoons[,] together 3 raccoons
D[itt]o in good beer 1 raccoon   B[eavers]   [3b drawn, cr]
X D[itt]o in good beer 1 raccoon   raccoon   [7mks, cr]
D[itt]o in beer 1 raccoon
in beer 1 raccoon Ditto in good beer a beaver
17010[52] [*sic*] January he has given me a satisfaction on the
commissioners[53] for 30 guilders for the balance of the preceding
[account][54]
        [account cr = paid]

————[7]————

folio 5   1697[,]   September 2[,]   Mahican

            1698 a beaver paid on this [account]
Sicktock[55] 3 bottles of rum [for] 3 martens Also a duffel blanket
[for] a beaver and 3 martens

———————————————————————————————————

        See folio 80
Naghnekampemet[56][,] who is married to our female savage[,]
Debit   1703 in January
X A pair of *plets* stockings for a beaver
D[itt]o A half worn-out blanket at 2 beavers[,] amounts to 3 beavers
1704 May he paid me in the country   Beavers   [3b drawn, cr]
1704 October 1 cask of rum @ 1 bar of lead and a knife[,] together 7
martens   m[artens]   [28mks, cr]
1704/5 January [To] his sister a pair of stockings @ 4 martens
                                             m[artens]   [4mks, cr]
His sister has paid 4 martens[,] as has been credited
February[,] 2 lb. gunpowder @ 3 martens[,] 1 pair of stockings @ 4
martens
1705 9: August
2 skipple Indian corn [and?] 3 [lb.?] shot @ 2 martens[,] 1 shirt @ 2

martens
2 lb. tobacco @ 1 marten[,] 1 *can* of rum @ 1 marten
1 marten indebted on 1 bottle of rum Also indebted on 1 bottle [of rum?] 1 marten
      [account cr = paid]

Naernis[57] Debit[,]   3 martens for 3 knives Also a *draegbant* [for] 2 martens Also 1 marten on a pair of *hansijoes*[58] shoes[.] Another pair of shoes[,] 1 marten Also a small cask of rum [,] a beaver Also a beaver [for] gunpowder Also a *haelmes* for an otter Also a small cask of rum for a beaver Also a tobacco-box for 4 guilders[.] Paid on this [account] an otter and 2 *lappen* and 1 fisher[:] the 2 *lappen* [credited] as 2 martens[,] the fisher as 6 guilders
1698 Remains indebted for 3 beavers and 6 martens
                [3b drawn] [6mks]

Naghnakamet's sister Debit
1704/5 February *plets* stockings @ 2 martens
April 2 martens for rum   See folio 3 where the female savage is listed who she escorted here[59]   [martens]   [5mks, 2cr]
1707 Feb[ruary] [has] paid 3 skipple Indian corn in the country[.]
3 martens remain

—— [8] ——

1697 Mahican page   folio 6
                               folio 7

folio 7
Awaannaghqat[60] Debit 3 martens for 3 bottles of rum
Also a small coat for 4 martens and a piece of meat

———————— 1701 ————————

See on folio 8[61]
June 24, A young *Catschelse*[62] savage Debit
His name Schewas quawas[63]: the female savage who was with him
Tack kaiwee[64][,] he went to the Ottawas[65]
a pair of stockings for a large beaver
Ditto a shirt for a large beaver
D[itt]o 10 *can* of rum @   B[eavers]   [7b drawn, 2cr]
2 beavers ditto an axe   raccoons [7mks, 4cr]
for a large raccoon ditto a kettle for a beaver
A piece of strouds and a bottle of rum and the above mentioned axe

together [for] a beaver
in beer for 2 raccoons 1 bottle of rum[:] when he was away he had
ordered to give a bottle of rum [for] 1 raccoon
28 Ditto sent Niettewapwaee[66] with a harpoon for him when he was
already in *Scheneghtenda*[67] [for] 1 raccoon[.] His sister[68] 1 shirt for
1 large beaver[.] August[, owes] 2 raccoons [on] 2 screws and 1
trigger-guard for his gun

1697 September 2
      1698 He paid on this [account] 1 beaver [and] his
         wife paid 1[,] together 2 beavers
Naeckapen[69] Debit for 3 quarters Also a bottle of rum [for] a marten
Also a small cask of rum for a beaver Also a bottle of rum [for] a
marten [H]is wife a duffel blanket for a beaver and a *lap*[.] 1700 has
paid a beaver
1702 Paid [to the amount] of 1 beaver Remains indebted [for] 3
quarters and 2 martens

--------------------- 1704 ---------------------

June the Greyhead's[70] wife Debit
1 cask of rum at 5 martens   M[artens] [5mks]

1705 September 10 A female savage who went with Nietewaekam[71][,]
X her name is Segh nae waes quae[72] Debit
X [on] 1 large beaver indebted on 4 *can* of rum   [1b drawn, cr]
X 1706 paid

—— [9] ——

  1697 Mahican page
       folio 7
[S/he is] called tijoom or rochkauw[73] Debit on a bottle of rum[,] a
marten Also a small looking glass for 2 martens Also 3 martens for
wampum Also a bottle of rum [for] 1 marten

1703 July 16 Nietewakam debit
when he went to the Ottawas[74][,] 2 beavers for a small cask [of rum?]
X but it was pure[75] [also] a pair of stockings for a beaver
X [Also] 4 heavy bars of lead [for] a beaver[,] together 4 beavers
August 29, 4 beavers paid which   [7b drawn, 4cr]
closes all our accounts

Septem[ber] 9[,] on 1 French *cnoo*[76] indebted for 6 beavers
September 9[,] 2 lb. gunpowder at a large   [6b drawn, cr]
beaver[,] for which Gerret[77] will trouble himself that he will pay
[one] of 2 lb.
10 ditt[o] 2 beavers [indebted] [for] 1 coat

1697 August 16
Awans[78] debit on a *haelmes* and a *karepoes* and a pair of stockings[,]
together [for] a beaver and an otter Also a ½ beaver in rum

1705 August 21
X A female Mahican savage her name [is]
Waelekeiet[79][.] She traded at old Blecker's[80]
X A female Ottawa savage[,] she said that [she] will return
in the spring   [1b drawn, cr]
1706 June has been paid

1703 Caeiewamp a young boy who
Ouwee suckwans has always h[a]d[81]
paint for a marten   m[artens] [4mks]
ditto on a shell for 3 martens

1705 September 10
Nietewakam Debit   anew
2 lb. gunpowder [for] 1 beaver   [5b drawn, cr]
Ditto [on] 1 coat remain 2 beavers
Ditto he must pay 2 beavers for aettesoghkamen[82] on 1 cask of rum
[sold for] 1 beaver and 1 *lap* [,] together 2 beavers[.] Also
atesoghkamen himself is guarantor for that
1708 August he has paid

——[10]——

1697 Mahican page
                              folio 8
Kaloolet[83] Debit   3 martens on 3 bottles of rum

See ffolio [*sic*] 11 on a minus page[84]

Niettewapwae[85] Debit   when he went
to the Ottawas[86] a gun for 5 large beavers
ditto the carting of his goods and his
sister's and his wife's goods to *Scheneghtende*[87]
[for] one large beaver   Beavers   [10b drawn]
Ditto a large shirt for a large beaver
ditto a large woodcutter's knife to make *papegaie*[88] with[,] for a
large beaver
1706 June sold his belt [which] was 145 black [wampum beads] long and
wide 10 long with 61 white places on it[,] each place 36 small white
[wampum beads].[89] 1706 July 1 cask of rum at 1 beaver and 10 quarters
paid on his gun that I have redeemed[90] from Anties Moll[91]

―――――――――――――――――――

1698 Nooseewalamit[92] Debit
8 bottles of rum for 8 martens

✱See across✱
February 20, Seeckaet[93] Debit in the
Mohawk country on a coarse blanket 5 martens   [11mks]
23 ditto sent with Hendereck[94] the savage 2 bars of lead to him at 1
marten [,] 1 lb. gunpowder @ 2 martens [and] 2½ lb. small[95] shot at 2
martens[.] Amounts to 4 martens and everything 10[96] [martens]
✱1705 May✱
His wife's mother[97] 1 duffel blanket at 2 beavers   [2b drawn]
and 1 marten on stockings   ✱03✱
                                                            ✱f 03✱
                                                        ✱:30 guilders✱[98]

✱1706 May✱
his wife's brother is called Sam or
Cattelaemet[99] [, on] 2 lb. gunpowder [he] owes 2 martens
2 bars of lead [for] 1 marten[,] together 3 martens   [3mks]
in the same house an English savage[100] with red
hair[:] 1 lb. gunpowder and 2 bars of lead together   [3mks]
also [for] 2 knife [*sic*] a debt [of] 3 quarters   quarters [3mks]
Sep[t]em[ber] 29[,] 1 spring on his gunlock[,] 1 marten[, for] Sekat
himself
13 Oct[ober] Sam 1 duffel blanket indebted 30 guilders to wit   - -   f 30
ditto Sam 1 bottle of rum indebted 3 guilders to wit   - - - - f 03
ditto Sam 1 bottle of rum indebted 3 guilders   - - - - f 03

f[olio] 9
1704/5 February 20
Seec kaet Debit his received merchandise is listed across from here
             [so] that he remains indebted M[artens]   [11mks]
1707 July 8 Has paid 3 beavers at 8 martens Still remaining 3 martens

1708 June 22 Secatt's wife D[ebit]
on 8 *can* of rum @ 2 beavers   [2b drawn]
His own mother on 3 lb. gunpowder @ 6 martens   [6mks]

         Seec katt's wife's mother[,] an old[,] small female savage
1705 May on 1 duffel blanket indebted 2 beavers
         [2b drawn, cr]
         D[itt]o on a pair of stockings 1 marten   m[arten] [1mk]
         2 beavers paid by her daughter's son[101]

Sam's account follows here below D[ebit]
1 lb. gunpowder at 10 guilders[,] 6 flintstones at 1 guild[er]
2 bottles of rum at 3 guild[ers] - 1 bar of lead at 2 guilders

———————————— 1705 ————————————

Ditto his wife's brother Sam or Cattelnalemet[102] Deb[i]t
1707 Janu[ary] 1 bottle of rum at 3 guilders   Martens [3mks]
         1 lb. gunpowder indebted 2 martens   [20mks]
         2 bars of lead indebted 1 marten
September 19 1 spring on his gunlock indebted 1 marten or a
         bottle of rum[,] Sekatt had the spring
ditto 1 duffel blanket indebted 30 guilders[,] the debt
                                        amounts to   f 30 =
d[itt]o 1 bottle of rum indebted 3 guilders   f 03
d[itt]o 1 bottle of rum 3 guilders   f 03
         guilders f [72mks discernable, 30cr]   f 42
∗1705/6 Janu[ary] 22∗
8 deerskins paid at 24 lb. @ 1 guilder p[e]r lb. and
1 cat @ 5 guilders[,] together 29 guilders -
ditto 1 reed cane[103] indebted 3 guilders Debit
ditto 2 bottles of rum at 6 guilders
ditto 2 pair of stockings indebted 24 guilders[,] 1 half quarter in
money [and for] 1 knife indebted 3 g[uilders]

Ditto in the same house an English savage with red hair[104] Deb[it]
1 lb. gunpowder and 2 bars of lead together 3 martens   [3mks]
d[itt]o 2 knives indebted 3 quarters   [5mks]
January
23 d[itt]o 1 knife indebted 2 quarters[,] his name peckwanck

———— [12] ————

[folio] 10   1706 a female savage[,] her name Malkiet[,][105] Debit
June 18 1 red stroud blanket C[illegible] [at] 4 heavy
            beavers   [6b drawn, 4cr]
            [the blanket] was easily 2½
            ells long[.] [she] lives among the Ottawas [and] promises
            to come here to trade
1707 July 19 1 duffel blanket at 2 large beavers and [she] has paid
            the 4 beavers above[,] so that 2 beavers are due to me

———————— 1707 ————————

Our young female savage's son[,] his name
osaawaawans[106] Deb[it]
2 lb. gunpowder and 2 bars of lead[,] together   f 24: =
1 duffel blanket at 2 beavers   [2b drawn, cr]
Janu[ary] 22 1 lb. gunpowder at 10 guilders   - - - - - -   f 10
2 bars of lead at 4 guilders   - - - - - -   f 04
2 knives at 2 guilders p[e]r piece   - - - - - -   f 04
June 2 beavers paid
1708 July 30 for 1 piece of strouds at 10 guil[ders] - - - - -   f 10
October 20 for a shirt at a bearskin[,] fetched by his mother
                                                  [1B drawn]
1708/9 January for 1 beaver in gunpowder and 2 martens in lead
            [1b drawn]   m[artens] [2mks]

———— [13] ————

                        His[107] wife 2 skipple Indian corn
                        [indebted for] 1 shirt[.]
Naghnaekamett[108] D[ebit] guilders   [9mks, rest unclear and cr]
                        [guilders 4mks, cr]
on folio 5 is his received merchandise[.] Remains indebted to
the sum of 24 martens   [42mks, 14cr]

Novemb[er] 9 by his wife in gunpowder and lead[,] together 2 martens

[1705?] Decem[ber] 11 his wife's son borrowed a gun to hunt with

1705/6 February 13 2 bottles of rum indebted 2 martens

ditto balanced the account, 23 martens due to me

16 ditto Anew 3 lb. gunpowder indebted 6 martens [On] 2 bars of lead
indebted 1 marten

and 1 shirt for his child indebted 1 2[109] martens

June 16 received by his wife's son 3 pieces [of] beaver at

4 lb.[,] credit 8 martens for that

Ditt[o] 1 *lap* [paid as] 1 marten, together 9 martens

13 ocktob[er] his wife [fetched] 2 lb. gunpowder @ 9 guild[ers] p[e]r

lb. and 8 guilders indebted on a duffel blanket ditto 2 bars of lead

at 3 guilders[.] This gunpowder and the 2 bars of lead are listed

across [from here] on the boy's account

1707 Octob[er]

1 blue duffel blanket at 2 beaverskins	[2b drawn]

1708 Apr[il] 1

fetched by Maqseequant[110] 2 lb. shot at 1 marten 2 lb. tobacco @ 1

marten and 1 lb. gunpowder @ 2 martens and 2 lb. lead at 1 marten[,]

together 5 martens[, as] listed above

ditto received from him 5 shaggy deerskins [that]

weighed 27 lb. at 1 guilder per lb.[,] amounts to Cr[edit]	f 26

guild[er]s They were brought here by Abraham Groet[111]

1708/9 March his wife indebted 3 martens on a pair of stockings

1705/6 February 16 Mackseckwant[112][,] who stays at Naghnahamett's[113][,]

Debit indebted 1 marten for 1 skipple of Indian corn	[1mk]

———————————— 1708 ————————————

June 11 An *Anakonkersen*[114] savage[,] his name Temaghquant Deb[it]		
D[itto] 2 pairs of *plets* stockings @ 1 beaver		
D[itto] 1 cask of rum @ 1 beaver		
Dit[to] 1 tobacco-box @ 1 knife together 1 beaver	[5b drawn]	
Dit[t]o 2 shirt[s] @ 1 beaver, amounts to		
Dit[t]o 1 bottle of rum @ 3 guild[ers]	- - - - - -	f 3
Dit[t]o his wife 2 casks of rum @ 1 beaver		

———— [14] ————

Nietewapewa[115] on folio 8 Debit

10 beavers		[11b drawn, cr]
[1706?] August 1 bottle of rum at 3 guilders	- - -	f 3:00
ditto 1 bottle of rum at 3 guilders	- - -	f 3:00
ditto 1 bottle of rum at 3 guilders	- - -	f 3:00

ditto 1 bottle of rum at 3 guilders   - - -   f 3:00
Agreed with [him] to deduct three beavers for his belt which he has
put down with me,[116] as I have done and to charge 1 beaver for the
above 4 bottles of rum[,]
so that 9 beavers still remain due   127
to me[,] this ditto 1706 August 15   <u>15</u>
                                                                 142

16 ditto 1 bottle of rum at 3 guild[ers]   - - -   f 3–
18 ditto 1 bottle of rum at 3 guilders   - - -   f 3–
        so we are even in all and everything[,]
        we have satisfied for the above account with
        his gun that he has [put down] here and
        his belt in the presence of
        Masequant and Caetsee nacquas[117]

———————————————   ————————————————

X A Mahican boy[,] the son of Joswaa[118] from *hghketock*[119][,] or his
wife's son Debit
✳across✳[120]
X on his received merchandise[,] noted in the small book, he remains
indebted 50 guilders and 1 beaver - f50   [1b drawn]
1707/8 February 2 bought from him 56 guilders worth of furs
after which he remains indebted 38 guilders[,] as follows
1 duffel blanket at   30 =
1 shirt 18 guil[ders] - - - f 18
1 p[ai]r stockings - - - - f 18   See across
tobacco - - - - - - - - - - f 6
in lead - - - - - - - - - - - f 4
2 lb. gunpowder - - - - - <u>f 18</u>
                 f 94 totals 94 remains due to me f 38 = 0 –
                            <u>56</u>
                          f 38
April 13 paid 3 quarters totals 4 guil[ders] - 10 stivers   - - - - -
Cr[edit]   f 4:10

———— [15] ————

f[olio] 12

1707 July 1
        A Mahican who stays with Awanwaghquat's people[121]
        his name Heerij[122] D[ebi]t
        1 pair of stockings at 1 large beaver   [1b drawn]

─────────────── 1707 ───────────────

July 1 An *Annaaconkeer*[123][,] his name [is] Pleessewee
    1 pair of stockings at 1 beaver   [1b drawn]
    he is a young fellow [with a] handsome stature
    July 18 2 bottles of rum at 2 martens   [2mks]

─────────────── 1707 ───────────────

July 1 A young *Aennaacoonkeersen* savage D[ebi]t
    his name Jan[124] Leeweeweett[125]
    pair of stockings at 1 beaver   [2b drawn]
    Ditto 1 piece [of cloth] at 1 beaver
    It is a savage with a small stature

─────────────── 1708 ───────────────

    Josewa his wife's son[126][,] from across[,] remains indebted
    f 83-10 and 1 beaver   [1b drawn]
Apr[il] 15 2 lb. lead at 1 guild[er] 10 stivers p[e]r lb.
                      totals - - f 3 = 0
June 9 on a shirt remained indebted 9 guil[ders]   totals - - f 6
24 ditto paid 1 skin @ 6 guil[ders]
ditto on a shirt remained indebted 4 guil[ders] totals - - - - f 4
ditto 1 *can* of rum @ 3 guilders   - - - - f 3
ditto the small cask that contained the rum 3 guil[ders] - - - - f 3
                                          f 96:10
August 11 1 piece [of cloth] @ 12 guild[ers]   - - - - f 12
17010 [*sic*]
January 4 1 lb. gunpowder @ 6 guil[ders] still indebted - - - - f 6
1710 ditto 1 lb. shot @ 1 guil[der] 10 stivers   - - - - f 1:10
February 24 1 shirt @ 15 guilders   - - - - f 15
May 5 paid 1 beaver at 12 guil[ders]   - - - - f 12

                    127[127]

─── [16] ───

f[olio] 8   See folio 81
A Mahican boy who usually lives in *Cattskill*
his name Sanhaquisquaas[128] d[ebi]t
As you can see above[, he] remains indebted 5 beavers [and] 3
raccoons [for] his received merchandise
                    [5b drawn] raccoons [3mks]
Since then _____
1707 Septemb[er] 7 1 pair of stockings at 18 guilders   - - - - f 18 =

ditto 1 lb. gunpowder at 9 guilders   - - - - -   "[9 =, cr]

a bar of lead at   - - - - -   " 2

1708 June 14 paid a bearskin at 2 beavers as has been credited

Decemb[er] [paid] 18 lb. deerskins at 1 guil[der] p[e]r lb.

[for which he] had a lb. gunpowder and was paid 9 guilders

1709 April 26 on 1 shirt remained indebted 8 guil[ders]   - - - - -   8

ditto 1 piece of strouds @ 14 guild[ers]   - - - - -   14

May 5 4 *can* beer @ 2 guild[ers]   - - - - -   2

ditto 4 *can* beer @ 2 guild[ers]   - - - - -   2

      X A young savage[,] who was escorted by the

      X above [Indian]129[,] has but one eye d[ebi]t

      X 1 lb. gunpowder at 9 guilders   - - - - -   f 9

1708 June 7 he has paid [in?] otter so that we are even

✱1709 June 7✱

X the above has a beavercoat here on which he remains indebted

X 5 guil[ders] and the rest must give him when he returns130

[Account] settled

——————————————— 1707 ———————————————

Septemb[er] 29 A Mahican young savage[, he] stays at

Nietewakam's131[,]

his name magh-maghcees132[,] a handsome young savage D[eb]it

      2 duffel blankets at 2 large beavers   [5b drawn, 2cr]

Ditto 1 pair of stockings at 1 beaver

Ditto 1 piece [of cloth] at 2 martens   Martens [6mks]

Ditto 1 cask of rum at 2 beavers

Ditto 2 quarters in specie at 1 marten

Octob[er] 1 bottle of rum at 1 marten

Dit[t]o in tobacco at 1 marten

——— [17] ———

1696   Mahican page

Folio 9

Nannalamit133 who went with the Greyhead134 to

*Annaekonccoo*135[,] debit 2½ beavers in wampum Also a pair of duffel

stockings and 2 bottles of rum[,] together 5 martens 1707 May[,]

received 3 beavers from him in *Sareghtoken*136 which have been credited

      1707 August 1 bottle of rum at 1 marten

Jnijt[137] 1 balanced account with the Greyhead
As the following account shows he remains indebted[,]
as he himself admits

Martens	[16mks]
Beavers	[3b drawn]
L[ap]	[1 small b drawn]

1695/6
Wassewaecke the Greyhead debit [for] pipes 2 beavers
A kettle for a beaver Also a pair of stockings for 3 martens Also 4
bottles of rum 4 martens Also 2 small boxes of paint 2 martens Also
Also [sic] for another savage who he escorted
[, and] for whom he is guarantor[,] pipes [for] a beaver
See above for his account[138]*
Also a small axe and a small bunch of copperwire[,] together 3
martens Also a pair of duffel stockings 3 martens: Also a savage who
he escorted and [for] whom he is guarantor
shells for a beaver also a knife and 10 flintstones for a marten: He
[himself] a piece [of cloth] for his wife at 1 beaver Also a beaver
in quarters Also a cask rum [for] a beaver Also a bottle of rum for a
marten
he remains indebted for 6 beavers [and] 11 martens
also 2 beavers and 6 martens for other savages
1703/4 : 1 bottle of rum at a ma[rten]

      [6b drawn, cr] [martens] [12mks, cr]
      [2b drawn, cr] [martens] [6mks, cr]

[1704?] June 4 in *Seghneghtende*[139] he [has] paid me a beaver for
another savage, which has been credited[140]

                      131[141]

——— [18] ———

1698 Actober [sic] 7
1699 paid on this [account] a fisher
           [which has been credited] as 2 martens
Jacob[142] the savage Debit
A small looking glass for 2 martens
Also 2 buckles for him and [the one] who he escorted

Together 2 martens	marten	[1 circle drawn]

Also 1 bottle of rum [for] a marten and ribbon [for] a marten
together 2 martens

X 1705 June 5 She[143] remains indebted to me for the sum of
X 24 guilders in   [24mks]
X and 12 skipple Indian corn   [22mks]
13 Ditto 2 bottles of rum indebted 4 skipple Indian corn
Ditto 1 bottle of rum indebted 2 skipple [Indian corn]
   A female savage who she escorted[144] 2 bottles
   of rum @ 4 skipple of Indian corn   [4mks, wiped]
June 1 bottle of rum indebted 2 skipple [Indian corn]
ditt[o] 1 bottle of rum indebted 2 skipple [Indian corn]

———————————— [thin line] ————————————————

X June   aet Taemanemee 2 bottles [of rum?] at 4 skipple
[Indian corn]   [4mks]

dit[to] A female savage who she[145] escorted Debit   her name
Seghstawaesqua[146]
1 shirt indebted 2 skipple Indian corn   [2mks]

1705 June Waeleghlauwett[147]'s wife[, who] plants at Cornele[ ]
X Schuijlers[148] Debit 1 bottle of rum indebted [empty]
1 cask of rum indebted 6 skipple Indian corn

Ditto A female savage who she[149] escorted   debit
X 3 bottles of rum indebted 6 skipple Indian corn   [10mks]
Also 3 quarters from earlier [times][150] her name Sou waes [she is]
a *Cattckeles*[151] savage
June 1 bottle of rum indebted 2 skipple Indian corn
ditto 1 bottle of rum indebted 2 skipple [Indian corn]

1705 June A female savage Aeu Segh quauwa Debit
[she] plants on the island[. for] 1 bottle of rum indebted
1 skipple   [2mks]

1705 June Nooses[152][,] sister of the above female savage
X For 2 bottles of rum indebted 4 skipple [Indian corn]
1 bottle of rum indebted 2 skipple [Indian corn]
        Indian corn [6mks]

[Introduction of new system of bookkeeping: at right margin, three columns are drawn. Entitled from left to right; B(eaver), M(arten) and O(tter), although sometimes other peltries are listed in the last column.]
[Beginning of Mohawk section]

1697 February 18
Folio 1   Mohawk page

he has paid[153]

	B	M	O
1697 Tarahakeene or tasoonihasse Debit at the balancing of the account he remains indebted 1 otter	0	0	1
his sister with the pearl on the eye remains indebted 4 martens[,] 3 [of which] for duffel	0	4	0

The mother of Korneles[154] the savage on a shirt for 6 skipple Indian corn 1701 July 18 her son Corneles for a small cask of rum 1 marten	0	1

1701
X July 12 Sander[155] the savage debit on a piece of strouds
X stipulated [that he will] bring an elkskin[, that I]
deduct the piece [of the cloth] thereof [and] will give [him]
merchandise for the remainder

X He has[= carries] a bill with him[,] indebted in total
X beavers [5mks] otters [1mk] martens [11mks]
Search further on folio 23[156]
X put down 2 wampum belts on [this]

	B	M	O
1696/7 Mohawk Kanossoodickhae[157] Debit			
X On a bottle of rum 1 marten also a [marten] in beads	0	2	
On a coarse blanket 2 beavers	2		
A small bag of gunpowder for an otter	0	0	1
On a shirt 3 martens[,] 2 bars of lead for 2 martens	0	5	
X A small bag of gunpowder for 1 beaver	1	0	0

1698 paid on this [account] 1 beaver 1 marten[,] also credited the
account with a beaver[,] deducted from a coat
X Remains indebted 1 beaver 6 martens 1 otter   1 6 1
paid on this [account] 5 martens
1699 X also for a small shirt 1 marten   0 1
di[tt]o also for a large shirt 6 martens   0 6
di[tt]o also for a piece [of cloth] for 3 skipple Indian corn
satisfied[,] Canossedeckha [has] satisfied the above

1700
X credit extended anew for 2 pairs of shoes[,] one of 4 martens   0 4
and one of 2 martens[,] together 6 martens   0 6
dit[t]o also 1 duffel blanket for 1 beaver and 1 otter   1 0 1
1700 X 6 October on a duffel blanket 1 beaver and 4   1 4
martens also on 2 pairs of stroud stockings 2 beavers   2
also a bag of gunpowder for a beaver   1
together, as listed above, 5 beavers 1 otter and
10 martens also 1 bottle of rum [for] 1 marten   0 1
transported to folio 23[158]

——[20]——

1697 November 21   Mohawk page
Folio 2

1697
X Kaeijeenquereeko[159] Debit
·X A small bag of gunpowder for an otter   0 0 1

1700 Debit[,] a female Oneida savage[,] [she is] a white savage
[who] stays at Claes Luijckessen's[160], and to whom she is indebted[.]
bought here on credit [:] 2 martens on a small cask of rum and 2
martens on a shirt[,] together 4 martens   0 4
1705 May paid 2 martens[,] 2 martens remain outstanding
ditto 1 shirt indebted 4 martens   Martens [8mks, 6cr]
it was a large shirt[,] she must come here to trade
her husband is called Thehotsooen[161][,] he stays
at Cuijler's[162] Ditto paid 4 martens[,] 2 martens remain
outstanding

[thin line; pertains to following account]
Martens [10mks] Beavers [2b drawn] *Lap* [1 small b drawn]
fishers [3mks] otters [1mk]

1691/2[163] Mohawk
1697 paid on this [account] 2 beavers

[6b drawn, 4cr] [fishers] [3mks]
[martens] [10mks] [1 0 drawn]
[*lap*] [1smaller b drawn, cr?]

1696 Dekanoghtijeere or kanigraekeijijoode[164] Debit
At balancing of the accounts [he] remains indebted

5 beavers	5
10 martens	– 10
3 fishers	0 0 3
1 otter and a *lap*	

1705 Sep[tember] 10 A young Mahican savage Debit
his name [is] WaenEnpaeckes[165][,] [he] went with Metewackam[166]
1 duffel blanket indebted 2 beaver
1 pair of stockings indebted 1 beaver B[eavers] [14b drawn, cr]
1 shirt indebted 1 beaver raccoons [4 circles, cr]
4 lb. gunpowder indebted 2 beavers[,] 4 bars of lead [and] 1 a piece
of cloth, together 1 beaver
also 1 bar of lead and 1 knife and gunpowder[,] together
3 beavers with those 2 beavers
1 axe and 2 bottles of rum[,] together 1 beaver
[he] has redeemed his belt [for?]
1 beaver[,] I have the belt as a security[167]
[repairs to?] his gun and 1 harpoon[,] together 2 raccoons
for rum indebted 3 beavers[,] 1 guilder in money [and?]
1 raccoon
paid 1 quarter for riding [him,?] indebted 1 raccoon
paid 1 beaver for him to Jonas Douw[168]
     See folio 78

——— [21] ———

1697 ditto Mohawk page
Folio 3
X Touwenijouw[169]'s wife Debit
X A pair of stockings [at] 4 martens 0 0 4

Rabecken[170] the female savage Debit

December 27 10 *can* of rum at 10 martens[,] it was
pure rum   Martens [10mks, 2cr]
1704/5 April 1 1 marten paid[,] 9 martens still remaining
June paid 1 marten 1707 received 20 skipple Indian corn in the
country[,] so that we are even

[thin line, belongs to the following account]
1700 June 5 [I] have balanced [account]with him[, he paid] 11 beavers
1700 and 2 beavers in balls[171][,] together 13 beavers[,] remain 12
beavers and 3 martens and 4 otters
remains indebted 21 beavers All computed at 6 martens to a beaver and
so on

1697 February 18

	b	m	o
Kahonckhae[172][,] at the balancing of the accounts he remains			
indebted 2 beavers[,] a *lap*[,] an otter[,] 2 fishers[,]	2	0	1
1 mink[,] 3 raccoons[,] 16 martens[,] together	0	19	0
anew 1 bottle of rum [for] 1 marten [and?] 1 quarter	0	1	
Also a beaver in strouds and gunpowder	1		
Also a beaver in duffel[,] and one for strouds	2	0	0
Also for a piece of strouds[,] 4 martens	0	4	0
Also a black coat for 4 beavers	4	0	0
Also a small bag of gunpowder[,] for a beaver	1	0	0
Also a pair of shoes [for] a beaver[,] 3 bars of lead			
[for] 3 mar[tens]	1	3	0
Also a pair of stockings [for] 2 martens[,] 1 bottle of			
rum [for] 1 marten	0	3	0
Also a blanket of strouds [for] 2 beavers	2	0	0
Also a bottle of rum [for] 1 marten[173]	0	1	0
paid on this [account] 1 beaver			
1698 Also a pair of duffel stockings for 5 martens	0	5	
Also a bag of gunpowder for a beaver	1	0	
Also a duffel blanket for 2 beavers	2	0	
Also in lead for 2 martens[,] a small axe and a quarter			
together 4 martens	0	4	
1699 paid on this [acccount] 7 beavers			
1700 also 3 bars of lead [for] 3 martens	0	3	

1697 ditto   Mohawk page
Folio 4

1697 [Johoonoch = cr] Dekaeijedoennis   [Debit]
a duffel blanket for a beaver   1 0 0

——————————————————— 1704 ———————————————————

Sept[ember] Watcaros['s] sister[174][,] who is listed below[,]
1 duffel blanket
ditto 1 shirt[,] together 19 skipple Indian corn [17mks, cr]
          A female savage who she escorted[,] 2 skipple [Indian corn]

28 October 1706 indebted for a duffel blanket at 8 martens

✱See the Indian corn book✱
1702 3 June balanced accounts with Watcaros['s] sister
remains indebted 1 elkskin
and 1 otter and 2 martens   elk [1e drawn,
X [otter] [1 0 drawn]   marten [14mks, cr]   with antlers, cr]
     b[eaver] [1b drawn]
X Also on a shirt[,] 3 martens
September borrowed 1 deerskin[[,] or otherwise she must give 3
martens if she does not return the deerskin
ditto A pair of stroud stockings for 1 beaver
1703 ditto a marten in gunpowder
1704 May in the country [she] has given 1 beaver and 1 *lap* to me[,]
as has been credited
1707 3 martens received from her in the country[,] as has been
credited

✱1697✱
X Watkaroos['] sister at the balancing of the accounts remains
indebted [for] 1 beaver and 11 martens   1 11 0
X The female savage who she escorted[,] for whom she is guarantor[,]
a *karpoes* [for] 4 martens   0 4
X Also a shirt [for] 4 martens   0 4
1699 For a pair of stroud stockings[,] a beaver   1
X Also indebted on a shirt[,] a marten   1
paid on this [account] 3 martens[.] 1700 indebted on a   1
duffel blanket[,] a beaver and 12 beaverballs[175][.]
1699 a bag of gunpowder for an otter   0 0 1

1700 November remained indebted 2 skipple Indian corn
on a duffel blanket
1701 January 10 also 2 beavers [paid] on a blanket of
strouds [, she still] owes 5 martens   0 5
ditto also on a pair of stroud stockings[,] a beaver
or 5 martens   1
1701 10 July also 1 elkskin [for] an ell of strouds
and 1 shirt[,] to be paid when the Indian corn is ripe[176]

——[23]——

1697 ditto   Mohawk page
Folio 5

                                    See folio 62   [1b drawn, cr]
X Karighijaetsijkoo[177] [Debit]   a small coat for 2 martens   0 2 0

See further on folio 16[,] the following [account]
is listed there also

1701 Janu[a]ry 15 Debit   Arijenhotsen[178]
1 duffel blanket for 8 martens[,] she has paid 4 martens in cash
X and he must still pay 4: ditto also on
a small cask of rum a marten[,] amounts to 5 martens   0 5
1701 X in the month of July she paid 4 martens [but]
denied [the debt of] 1 marten[,][179] so that it remains open   0 1
X ditto credit extended for 2 martens on 2 duffel blankets   0 2

                    [martens?] [47mks. 20cr]
                    [beavers]   [10b drawn, 6cr]
                                [1 0 drawn, cr]

                                                                      b m bear
Sagnirroowanne[180] Debit   [at the] balancing of the accounts [he]
remains indebted a beaver[,] 1 bearskin [and] 2 martens   1 2 1
anew a duffel blanket for a beaver   1 0 0
Also 2 shirts [for] 1 beaver[,] 2 shirts [for] 6 martens   1 6 0
Also 8 quarters [for] 4 martens[,] 2 beavers for strouds   2 4 0
Also 5 bottles of rum [for] 5 martens[,] also 2 martens
                                                       for *gimp*   0 7 0
Also a duffel blanket [for] 1 beaver[,] 3 bottles of rum
                                             [for] 3 martens   1 3 0

His wife[181][,] a *karpoes* [for] 4 martens   0 4 –
kanaetsakigto[182][,] for whom he is guarantor[,] a pair of
duffel stockings [for] 2 martens[,] also a duffel blanket
                                         [for] 1 beaver   1 2 0
Also a duffel blanket [for] 1 beaver[,] remains indebted
                              1 marten on a cask of rum   1 1 0
Also a shirt for an otter   0 0 1
Sagnirroowane 3 bottles of rum [for] 3 martens[,]
                              2 quarters [for 1 marten?]   0 4 –
Also a shirt for a child [for] 1 marten[,] also a piece of
baize [for] 2 martens [and] a pair of duffel stockings
                              4 m[artens,] together   0 7 –
also in rum 1 beaver[,] indebted on a blue coat 1 beaver   2 0 –
also a marten for the mending of [the] gunlock also 1 mar[ten]   2
        He is also listed on folio 6[183]

——[24]——

1697 Dit[t]o   Mohawk page
Folio 6

A female savage [named] kanijokoghoo a cask of rum   b m
for a beaver   1 –
1698 Also 3 martens indebted on a cask of rum   0 3

1704 Saequanekarij[184] [his = wiped] account from folio 13
[for] his received merchandise
He remains indebted 2 beavers[,] 1 bearskin [and] 11 martens
                              B[eavers] [3b drawn, cr]
Sept[ember] A bag of gunpowder for a beaver   Bearskin [1B drawn, cr]
ditto a pair of stockings at 6 martens   m[artens] [18mks, cr]
fetched by his wife[185]   quarters   [1mk, cr][186]
ditto 1 bar of lead at 1 marten

1708/9 January his wife has accepted to pay 20 skipple Indian
corn[,] for which I have crossed out the account

1697 Roodes's[187] daughter 4 bottles of rum   b m
for 4 martens   0 4

1699 September 3 Debit   for 1   F[isher]
\ Sohnerowane[188] a duffel blanket for   1 2 0
a beaver and 2 martens[,] also a small cask of rum   1 0 0
X for a beaver[.] Especially for his wife[189][,] a white
X piece of *vlenningh* for 1 marten and a fisher   0 1 1
1700 also for a marten in paint   0 1
1701 January a shirt for 5 martens or
5 skipple of Indian corn
X September 8 Paid 7 beavers[,] a debt remains [for]
27 martens[,] as the bill shows which he [carries]
X with him[.] his wife is still indebted
X for 5 martens and a 1 [sic] fisher
1703 July for a [empty]
                    See on folio 27[190]

——[25]——

                    1697 dit[t]o   Oneida page
                        Folio 7   b m
1697 Dekanijieendan[191] a blue coat   *lap*
for a beaver and a ½ beaver   1 0 1

————————————— 1704 —————————————

Sept[ember] A Mohawk boy Debit
He is Caienkeriekoo[192]'s brother[,] his name is
in Dutch Aberham[193] and in the savage [language] Cenderijokee[194][.]
2 bars of lead @ 1 marten Ditto 1 piece [of cloth] @ 3 martens
Ditto a quarter[,] together amounts to   quarters   [1mk, cr]
1705 December 14
paid 1 *lap* of a beaver[, still]
indebted 2 martens December 18[,] 2 bottles   M[artens] [6mks, cr]
of rum indebted 2 martens So that I still   B[ear]   [1B drawn]
have 4 martens coming to me
Octo[ber] 25
On 1 bag of gunpowder at 1 a [sic] large bearskin[,] which I let him
have in the Mohawk country[195] since he was very destitute[196]

1697 Jassijdassijkoo 2 martens for 2 bars of lead   0 2 0
Also 2 pair of duffel stockings for 5 martens   0 5 0
Also indebted 2 martens on a small cask of rum   0 2 0
Also 3 martens indebted on a duffel blanket   0 3 0

Paid on this [account] 1 beaver and 2 martens which	10
have been credited as 8 martens, remains	8
	2
——	*lap*
anew a small looking glass for a	0 0 1
3*li*[n]*gh* also for a marten in *gemp*	0 1
Remains indebted 3 martens and a 3*lingh*	
1704 he has paid me a *drije lingh*	Martens [3mks]
Remain 3 martens[197]	Beavers [1b drawn, cr]

—— [26] ——

1697 Ditto   Mohawk page
Folio 8   b m f

1697 Dekarowe[198] Debit at the balancing of the accounts [he/she]	
remained indebted 11 martens and a fisher	0 11 1
1697 anew a blue coat [at] 2 beavers	2
On a duffel blanket 1 beaver and 2 martens	1 2 0
On 2 knives 1 marten[,] on *gimp* 1 marten[,] together	0 2 0
1702 paid an elkskin[,]	beavers [3b drawn]
credited as 12 martens	Martens [16mks, 12cr]
	fisher [1mk]

[account cr = paid]

1697 Swathose[199]'s brother and Satsoorij[200] [Debit]
a cask of rum for 6 martens also
a bottle of rum [at] 1 marten[,] together 7 martens   0 7 0
Swathose has paid for his brother

———————————— 1704/5 ————————————

Feb[ruary] 23 Hendereck the savage
1½ lb. shot at 1 marten   [marten] [1mk]

[remainder of the page is empty]

1697 Dit[t]o   Mohawk page
Folio 9
1699 he paid[,] but remains indebted
in all for an otter and 7 martens
[1b drawn, cr] [martens[201]] [32mks] [1 o drawn]

Dekarijhondie[202] 1 cask of rum [at] 5 martens		0 5 0
Also a shirt [at] 3 martens[,] also a shirt [at] 3 martens[,]	together	6 0
Also [for] a beaver in gunpowder		1 0 0
Also a bottle of rum and a quarter[,] together		0 1 0
Also a pair of stroud stockings for 4 martens		0 4 0
Also indebted a marten on a shirt		0 1 0
Also 2 shirts [at] 8 martens		0 8 0
Also 1 shirt [at] 4 martens		0 4 0
paid on this [account] a *lap* for 2 martens		
Also for Kakoensijwaecke[203] indebted for 2 martens[204]		0 2 0
1698 paid on this [account] a beaver and 10 martens		
dit[t]o credit extended anew for a ½ beaver on strouds		
[and a] ½ beaver for *gimp*		1
A duffel blanket for 1 beaver[,] 1 bag of gunpowder		otter
[at] 1 otter		1 0 1
also a fisher in *gijmp* paid by his sister[205]		fisher
		1

[account cr = paid]

See on folio 58[206]

anew on a shirt for 5 martens	0 5 0
also a small shirt for 2 martens	0 2 0
also for a quarter and paint[,] together	0 1 0
a pair of baize stockings [at] 2 martens	0 2
also a shirt for a fisher	0 0 1 f

1700 all of the above paid by his sister[,] Marija[207]
[account cr = paid]

--- 1704 ---

See on folio 58[208]
The month of June Caenoseedeckhae[209] Debit
At the balaning of the accounts, [he] remains indebted 10 beavers and
36 martens and 16 quarters[.] everything computed in quarters comes
to a total [of] 244 quarters[210]

Sept[ember] remained 3 martens indebted

on a shirt	bears	[1B drawn, cr]
Now a pair of stockings	B[eavers]	[10b drawn, cr]
[at] 3 foxes	Martens	[47mks discernable, cr]
1705 A cask of rum	quarters	[34mks, cr]
at 1 bearskin	foxes	[3mks, cr]

August 4 1½ lb. gunpowder [at] 3 martens and a quarter
ditto 1½ bottle of rum [at] 1 marten
Sept[ember] 9 on 1½ lb. [indebted] 3 martens[,] 2 bars of lead
[indebted] 1 marten
December 1 small coat [at] 5 martens[.] ditto 1 hat [at] 12 martens
[He] paid with his scout-money[211][,] Remains indebted 13 martens[,] 10
beavers [,] 1 bearskin [and] 3 foxes

——[28]——

1697 Dit[t]o   Mohawk[212] page
Folio 10   b m –

1697 Saghnirroowane[213]'s brother Ogwasserooa Debit

2 shirts for 6 martens	0 6 0
A cask of rum for 1 beaver	1 0 0
A duffel blanket for a beaver and	1 0 0
[For a = cr] 2 martens	2

1700 [account] satisfied[,] except for 2 martens
1703 [he] has paid me for all and everything

1704 Caeijhoekedee[214] or Saenaekeranckhack Debit from folio 23[215]
November 17 1 red pipe[216] at 3 beavers

ditto we have ge[mac?]t[217] for a	B[eavers]	[4b drawn]
beaver[.] ditto his wife	m[artens]	[9mks]

1½ ell *plets* at 6 martens
1704/5 January 2 quarters [and] ditto 2 bottles of rum[,] together 3
martens
1705 June 18 he has [instructed?] me to [word(s) omitted?]
the above debt at Johannus Bradt[218]
57 quarters for the above listed debt[219]

1697 Sahorackwaghte[220][,] a boy[,] 4 martens indebted

on a coat	0 4 0
Also 5 martens for rum	0 5 0

Dekarijhondie[221] is guarantor for this
Paid on this [account] 3 martens[,] remains indebted   6
for 6 martens[.] also 1 marten paid[,] remain still 5   5
paid on this [account] another 2 martens[, 3] martens   3
still remain

─── [29] ───

1697 Dit[t]o   Mohawk page
See on folio 19[222]   Folio 11   b m –

See on folio 19 for the following account   f bear
Wagrassero[223] Debit at the balancing of the account[,]   25 0 0
[he] remains indebted 25 beavers[,] 2 fishers[,]   2 1
a bearskin[,] 4 skipple Indian corn calculated as
6 martens[,] and so on
1698 Paid on this [account] 3 beavers
[Credit extended] anew[,] 1 bottle of rum [for] 1 marten
[and] 1 marten indebted on a shirt   2
1698 Also a duffel blanket for a beaver
and an otter   1 0 1
Also a pair of stockings for an otter   0 0 1
Also a bottle of rum for a skipple
        [line inserted:]
    1701 also in gunpowder 1 lb. and 1 half[,] makes 3 martens   3
Indian corn[.] Also a shirt for 4 skipple
Indian corn[.] 1699 25 February 1 marten indebted on a piece of
strouds[.] 1700 paid 2 *drielingen*[,] calculated as 5 martens[,]
brought here by Griet[224]
1701 12 August on 1 piece of strouds[,] it is up to him what he wants
to give for it

────────────────────────────

1697/8 Dit[t]o his mother[225] Debit A cask of rum   b m bear
for a bearskin[,] also a shirt [for] 3 marten   0 3 1
Also 2 small casks of rum [for] 2 beavers   2 0 0
Also indebted 2 martens on a cask of rum   0 2 0
Also a small shirt for 2 martens   0 2 0
kadareonichtha[226][,] for whom she is guarantor[,]
1 beaver on a cask of rum   1 0 0
She [herself] also a of duffel blanket [for] a beaver   1 0 0
Also 4 skipple Indian corn on a shirt[,] fetched by Wagrasero[.] a
beaver paid on this [account.]
＊Paid＊

1698 28 April also had 1 beaver in wampum[227][,] very heavy

                                            - - - - [1, cr]

Also for wampum a *lap* or 2 martens   - - - - [2, cr]
Remains indebted 2 martens on wampum   0 2
1699 on a piece [of cloth] for herself[,] a 1 [sic] beaver   1 0
doti[228] [sic] remained indebted 1 bearskin and also for
4 skipple Indian corn[.] She has paid 1 skipple
                See on folio 12 for this received [merchandise]

—— [30] ——

            1697 Dit[t]o   Mohawk page
              Folio 12   b m –

1697 Wagraseroo['s] wife's mother[229] a cask of rum
      for a beaver   1 0 0
      Also a shirt for 2 martens   0 2 0
      Also a knife and a quarter[,] together 1 marten   0 1 0
1698 Also indebted 5 martens for rum   0 5 0
1705/4 [sic][230] 4 February paid in the country
      3 skipple Indian corn for 3 martens[231]

———————————————————————————— [thin line]

Arija the savage[232]'s wife 3 skipple Indian corn for
3 small children's shirts   transported to Folio 23[233]

———————————————————————————— [thin line]

Balanced accounts with arija the savage[,] and copied his
account briefly on page folio 15

1700 paid [to the amount of] 10 martens and a beaver

———————————————————————————————————————

✳paid on this [account] 10 martens✳   [6b drawn, 5cr]
✳see further on folio 23[234]✳   [martens] [31mks, 10cr]
                        b[eavers]:8   m[arten s]:19
1697 dit[t]o Arije the savage remains indebted at the   b m
balancing of the accounts 4 beavers and 30 martens   4 30 0
1698 A shirt for a beaver   1 0 0
dit[t]o A hand of duffel for 1 marten   1
1699 a small bag of gunpowder[,] 1 beaver   1
[His wife a cask of rum for 4 martens[,] his wife paid [this?] = cr]
for him also a small bag of gunpowder[,] a beaver   1
paid on this [account] 4 beavers [and] 1 otter

1699 also a duffel blanket for a beaver [and] an otter		1 1 ott
also a bag of gunpowder for a beaver		1
1699 his mother fetched a piece [of cloth] for an otter		0 0 1
1700 at the balancing of the accounts he remains indebted		
4 beavers and 15 martens and an otter 1700 August credit extended		
anew[,] wampum for a beaver[,] also a	- - - -	1
duffel blanket for one and a half beaver		
1700 together 3 beavers		3
1700 also a bag of gunpowder for a beaver[,] together		
4 beavers		1
also 2 bars of lead for 2 martens		2
also 1 bar of lead		1
remains B[eavers]		8

——— [31] ———

1698 8 January   Mohawk page
Folio 13   b m –

1698 Sohoonachqae[235][,] indebted at balancing of the accounts		2 14
[Credit extended] anew a beaver for gunpowder		1 1
X [and] a marten for shot[,] also a shirt for 3 martens		3
X also 2 quarters for a marten		0 1
also a cask of rum for a beaver		1 0
See folio 66		
also a marten for a small box of paint		0 1
his wife fetched gunpowder for an otter [and] a		
X small axe for a *lap*[,] together a beaver		1
1699 paid on this [account] 2 beavers		5 20
1707 May received from him in *Sareghtoken*[236]		8
4 beavers[,] 3 *lappen* [and] 1 otter[.] I have		12
still 12 martens coming	[5b drawn, cr]	
	[martens]	[12mks]
	M[artens]	[20mks]

X See on folio 6[,] where the following
    is listed briefly

X Saequarij Debit his received merchandise follows hereunder
        as is evident   [2b drawn]   [1B drawn]
                    quarters [1mk] m[artens] [11mks]
1703/4 4 January [fetched] by a boy [,] a cask
X of rum[,] on which he remained indebted 2 martens

1704 27 May [fetched] by his wife[237] a bag of gunpowder
for a bearskin[,] ditto a bar of lead at 1 quarter
July 1 bottle of rum at 1 marten

1698 A Mohawk who he[238] escorted [on] 8 January
       [his name is] Saqaenakarie[239] Debit
       A pair of stroud stockings and
X 2 bars of lead for a beaver   1 [cr]
X Also a shirt for 3 martens   3 [cr]
       Also a cask of rum for a beaver   1 [cr]
X Also a shirt fetched by another savage   4 [cr]
                           paid these
                           13 martens
                           X [13mks, cr]
1700 paid on this [account] 2 beavers[,] brought by his
X mother [.] 7 martens remain
       1702 4 January also for a cask of rum for 5 martens   5 [cr]
X also a pair of stockings for 3 martens   3 [cr]
       All together [amounts to] 15 marten   15 [cr]

1702 3 June paid 2 skins to be credited as 13 martens
X remains indebted 2 beavers and 2 martens   [2b drawn, cr]
1702 6 Ju[n]e also a shirt for 4 martens   [martens] [8mks, cr]
X A bottle of rum for a marten
       See above for him [[240]]   [2b drawn, cr]

——[32]——

1697 dit[to]   Mohawk page
Folio 14

See folio 19[,] there he is [listed]   b m L[ap]

       Below on this page he is [listed] as well
1697 Watijandandieijoo[241] at the balancing of the
       accounts he remains indebted 2 beavers[,]   2 10 1
       10 martens [and] 1 *lap*
       the same day[,] 1 shirt for 3 m[artens]   0 3 0
dit[t]o 6 martens for rum[,] also a cask of rum for
                              a beaver   1 6 0
       also a pair of duffel stockings 3 martens   0 3 0

also indebted on a duffel blanket a *3ling*	0	0	1
1 gun at 2 beavers	2	0	0
Also 1 cask of rum 1 beaver. 1 bar of lead 1 marten	1	2	0

On a shirt 4 martens[,] indebted 1 marten on a pair
of stockings — 0 5 0

Another shirt 4 martens[,] 3 martens [indebted on]
1 pair of stockings — 0 7 0

Also a beaver in gunpowder[,] 1 beaver in lead — 2 0 0

Also a cask of rum for a beaver — 1 0 0

1698 Duffel for a beaver [and] 1 bottle of rum for — 1 2 0
    2 quarters — 9 38 2

1699 6 May paid 5 beavers[,] remains indebted — 3[242]
    39 martens [and] 2 *lappen* — 6 38 2
    remains indebted   [11b drawn, 7cr]   4 beavers
    2 *lappen*   [2 small b dr]   43 martens   [48mks]

1698 his wife a hand of duffel for a marten — 1

1699 dit[t]o he 2 duffel blankets for 4 beavers
    also 5 martens for a small cask of rum[,] together [?, cr]

1697 dit[t]o Owanije[243] at the balancing of the accounts he remains
    indebted 3 beavers [and] 39 martens — 3 29 0
        [3b drawn] [29mks]

1699 25 February Wagrasseroo[244] fetched
    a shirt for 4 martens and a marten in tobacco — 5[245]
    A small bag of gunpowder for 1 beaver — 1

    Paid on this [account] 3 martens[246]

1703 Sep[t]ember a bar of lead at half [a] marten

1701 February Watjandondieioo Debit
    a shirt for 4 martens[,] also gunpowder for 2 martens[,]
    also a piece [of cloth] for 4 martens[,] also 1 [marten]
    on a tobacco box[,] together comes to 12 martens.
    Promises to pay 2 large beavers for that. — 2
    See folio 19[,] where this is listed briefly

—— [33] ——

Folio 15 1697 dit[t]o Mohawk page — b m [?]

See folio 23[247][,] this is listed briefly there

1702 10 October a kettle   [martens?] [14mks]
          for 10 martens[248]   [martens] [10mks]
          The Limping female savage[249] remains indebted
          at the balancing of the accounts   6 martens   0 6 0
          [Credit extended] anew a bottle of rum [for] 1 marten   0 1 0
          Also a cask of rum for 5 martens   0 5 0
          for another female savage[,] for whom she is   12
          guarantor[,] on this small cask of rum 2 martens paid   2
          She [herself] also paid 2 martens, together   2 8
          [Credit extended] anew quarters for a marten   1
          also a bottle of rum for a marten   1
          also a shirt for 4 martens   4
1700 remains one guilder indebted on a bottle of rum   1
          also indebted for a bearskin   1bear
1700 also a deerskin for a beaver   1
dit[t]o credit given on a French *kno* for 8 beavers
          with which she went to Canada   8
1701 she has paid 2 beavers
          ditto to her husband who she brought from
          Canada[,] 1 small cask of rum 1 [marten] and also
          1 shirt for 3 martens   3
                                          [below this 3, a blotted 1 = paid?]

          See folio 43
1697 dit[t]o Kanadakonckoo[250] [,] a limping Mohawk
X Debit 2 shirts [at] 6 martens [3 martens paid = cr]   0 3 0
X Also 4 bottles of rum [at] 4 martens   0 4 0
1698 paid on this [account] 3 martens, 7 remain   7
X Credit extended 2 martens on a cask of rum   2
1703 May [he] has paid 6 martens, 2 remain
          ditto His wife indebted   his daughter   m[artens] [2mks]
          on a small cask of rum   M[artens] [?mks, ?cr]
          a marten[,] ditto indebted   [3B drawn, 1cr]
          a marten on a shirt[,]   wife   M[artens] [15mks, 1cr]
          ditto a shirt for 4 martens
          [it was fetched?] by the woman[,] but it concerns them
          both[.] 1704 a marten indebted on a shirt[,] ditt[o] a
          bearskin and 2 martens on an 8-*can* cask of rum [and] a
          marten on a shirt[.] Together 3 martens
1704/5 February his daughter 1 man[']s piece[251] at 2 martens[,] ditto
          a blue duffel blanket @ 2 large bearskins
May 31 1705 paid a bearskin and 3 martens [, on] 1 pair of
          stockings indebted 4 martens
June 21 indebted on a cask of rum 1 marten

1697 dit[t]o Mohawk page
Folio 16   b m

her daughter [listed] below
A female savage[,] Roetsieijoo[252] or Dekaweeijeendigtachkoo[253][,]
    remains indebted 10 martens   0 10
    [Credit extended] anew 2 martens on 2 bottles of rum   0 2
    Also 2 martens for baize   0 2
    Also [a] bottle of rum [at] 1 marten and
    1 marten in beads   – 2
    Also a bottle of rum [at] 1 marten   – 1
    Paid on this [account] 7 skipple Indian corn
1698 Credit extended anew rum [at] a marten   1
X 2 bottles of rum [at] 2 martens   2
1699 A bottle of rum for a skipple Indian corn
dit[t]o Given credit 4 martens for rum on 2 occasions   4
X A female savage who she escorted[,] a bearskin for rum
    Also a small cask of rum[,] a [skipple = cr] skipple Indian
    corn   remains   1
1705 4 June at the balancing of the accounts she remains [15cr]
    indebted for 15 martens
    dit[t]o also on *plets* 1 marten[,] 15 martens paid
    remains   [1cr]

1697 karigijagrachquee[254]'s sister Debit
    A child's shirt for 1 marten   0 1 0
    Also 2 bottles of rum [at] 2 martens   0 2 –

X anoo [*sic*] 1699 Rapecke[255] a bottle of rum for a marten   [1cr]
———————————————————————— [thin line]

Rotsie[256]'s daughter debit 3 martens
1701 28 August[,] when [she/they went?[257]] to Canada[,]
a pair of stockings for 2 martens[,] comes to   5
together [6mks, 4cr] martens
She and her daughter remain indebted 2 martens[258]

Folio 17 1697 dit[t]o Mohawk page b m

See folio 22

[Kanadakonckoo[259], cr] paid on this [account] 6 martens 35
                 paid again 2 martens
Tanijijooris[260] Debit a small coat [2] 5 martens – 5 0
Also a pair of small stockings [at] 1 marten 0 1 0
Also a shirt [at] 4 martens[,] also 1 quarter 0 4 ½
1698 2 martens indebted on strouds 0 2
Also a shirt for 4 martens
Also a small shirt for 1 marten
1699 also a shirt for 4 martens 0 4
1700 also a shirt for 4 martens[,] fetched by his wife 0 4
1700 20 June balanced accounts with him and his wife[.]
he remains indebted 3 martens and his wife 2 martens
1701 25 January[,] gave him and his wife a shirt on the
condition that if they come to trade here she must buy
[merchandise to the value of] 10 or 9 or 8 beavers[,]
and if not she must pay it[,] or if she goes to trade at
another [merchant,] she must give a heavy beaver 1

1697 Sasijijan[261] Debit on a duffel blanket[,]
    a beaver and a marten 1 1 0
dit[t]o also a shirt for 4 martens 0 4 0
also a shirt [for] 4 martens 0 4 0
paid on this [account] 2 beavers[,] 1 of which
has been credited as 4 martens
remains indebted 5 martens

folio 18 1697 dit[t]o [hend = cr] Mohawk page
               Folio 18

X Hendrick the savage indebted 1 marten on
X a piece [of cloth] paid 0 1

Arija[262]'s mother from folio 11[263]
remains indebted   B[eavers]   [5b drawn]
26 September A boy's shirt   Bearskin   [2B drawn]
for Waghrosra's   Martens   [8mks, cr]
wife's son[264][.]   *Laep*   [1mk]
She has bought it   1707/8 Paid 3 *schepel* Indian corn in the country[267][,]
herself for a beaver   has been credited one beaver at 3 martens[268]
which was not very good[,]
so that she has to give a
beaver for that again[.] 16 December a cask of rum
for a heavy beaver
1704 May she has paid 2 beavers in wampum
1704 May the boy has paid 3 martens[,] 1 marten remains
1704: 18 May sent to me by a female Mahican savage[265] 2 *lappen*
1707 29 April because Thackaeijackh[266] [asked for?] 1 cask of rum at 1
beaver to send now

1698 dit[t]o [An] Onondaga boy[,] his name is
     kanaedeijorhae[269] a pair of shoes for an otter   1

1706 11 Sept[ember]
A female Oneida savage who was escorted by the female savage listed below[,]
1 small cask of rum at 6 martens [and] 1 [marten] on a small cask of rum[,]
together 7 martens   [7mks]

-------------------------------- 1704 --------------------------------

See folio 80
X Our Susanna['s][270] female savage[,] it is a white,
     young female savage[,] Debit a shirt for   together 14
X 5 martens[,] [when she pays, I] must give her
     a quarter
1705: 20 April she has paid[,] so that we are even
                                                     M[artens]   [22mks, cr]
                                                     Martens   [10mks, 3cr]

---

5 October indebted on a duffel blanket 7 martens
X to be paid in the winter[.] ditto [on] 1 shirt indebted
X 2 martens: 19 January 2 martens paid[,] 7 martens remain
1706 9 February [for] gunpowder[,] fetched by arijawaasen[271][,]
     indebted 3 martens[.] 1706 April paid 7 martens Remains [empty]
24 May 4 *can* of rum at 4 martens[,] together 7 martens[.]
                                                     4 martens paid

10 Septemb[er] a duffel blanket @ 6 martens[,] ditto 1 shirt

@ 4 martens

2 bars of lead @ 1 marten[.] 1708[,] June she paid 7 martens
1709 October 1 pair of stockings at 1 beaver as payment for a
beavercoat that is in the country

1 C[272]

——— [37] ———

Swathosse[273]'s wife a piece [of cloth] for 10 hands of
wampum or 2 martens   0 2 0
paid on this [account] 1 marten

———————————————— 1704 ————————————————

A female Seneca savage[274][,] her son's name
Nansendaghqua[,] a kettle at
X an otter See folio 38
X His wife's mother is called kadaroonichthae[275]
Debit 1 beaver in wampum   1

———————————————— 1704 ————————————————

July A female Seneca savage[,] her son's name
Thathaecenie[,] Debit on a coat a large beaver
Ditto 1 shirt @ 1 large raccoon   B[eaver] [1b drawn]
1704 June 8 her son[,] who is called [empty]   raccoon   [1r drawn]

[Sara[276] the savage Deb[i]t from older times 6 martens   0 [6][277]
[Credit extended] anew a pair of duffel stockings
for a beaver   0 [4]
1699 A duffel blanket for a beaver   [1]
also a pair of stroud stockings for a beaver   [1]
also indebted a skipple of Indian corn on *plets*   [1]
[whole account = cr, followed by one that is almost identical:]

Sara the savage Deb[i]t from older times 6 martens   6
Credit extended anew a pair of duffel stockings
for a beaver   0 4
1699 A duffel blanket for a beaver   1
also a pair of stroud stockings   1 1
also indebted a skipple of Indian corn on *plets*

1702 June paid an elkskin[,] credited as
1 beaver   b[eavers]   [2b drawn, cr]

                                                  M[artens]   [10mks]

——— [38] ———

folio 20   1698 dit[t]o   b m f

A Seneca[,] Aeshaerijkoo[278][,] Debit
a pair of stockings for a fisher   0 0 1

_____

And oriewaes[279] was / Canosedaken[280] / July 1710 he has promised to
present when he promised[281]   come and trade here[,] in the
                                        presence of Caienquaragtoo[282]

_____

1704 June A Seneca boy[,] his name Aennossockte[283][,] Debit
          indebted on a cask of rum 3 raccoons   raccoons   [3mks]
          His wife indebted on a pair of   raccoon   [1mk]
          duffel stockings a raccoon   bears   [1B drawn]
          His mother a kettle for   raccoons   [3mks]
          3 raccoons
1710 13 July
          1 pair of white *plets* stockings @ 1 bearskin

——————————————————— 1704 ———————————————————

          A female Seneca savage [who] lives in Cayuga Debit
          her name [is] Oskeea[284][.] She was here with Cattquierhoe[285]
          a cask of rum @ [1] beaver   [1b drawn]
Ditto a female savage who she escorted
          1 shirt @ 2 raccoons   [2r drawn]

_____

          Jannetije[286]'s wife[,] Marij Debit
          a shirt for 5 skipple Indian corn   0 5
          also a skipple indebted from older times   – 1
          paid on this [account] 1 skipple[,] 5 remain[.]
          satisfied[,] except for 3 martens which she denied

[remainder of page is empty]

folio 21   1697   b m

Sahoorackwachte's mother[287] debit
a bottle rum for a marten   0 1
    [account cr = paid]

———————————————————— 1704 ————————————————————

June A female Seneca savage Debit
[she] lives in *Saront*[288][,] her name is Taehegecoose
a pair of duffel stockings for
an otter   otter [2mks, 1cr]
1706: 16 August paid 1 otter Ditto 1 pair of stockings at 1 otter
her teeth are placed strangely in the mouth

———————————————————— 1704 ————————————————————

A female Cayuga savage [,] around 40 years old[,]
somewhat pockmarked Debit
on a duffel blanket a large beaver   [1b drawn]
she lives in Cayuga but she is Seneca by birth
She usually stays[289] at uncle Evert's[290]

1698 18 May balanced accounts with Kanasquiesackhe[291]   b m f
    [he] remains indebted 3 fishers   0 0 3
    2 *lappen* [or] 7 martens[,] calculated as 1 beaver   1–7
    [account cr = paid]
                                                      [thin line]
1699 Credit extended again to Kanasquiesackhe[,]
    quarters for a beaver[,] credit also extended for
                              3 quarters   1 [292]
      and for 3½ quarters[,] together   1 [ ]
1699 Again 8 quarters for a beaver   1
dit[to] 1 bottle of rum and 2½ quarters   – 1 ½
      2 duffel blankets for 4 beavers   4
      also a small cask of rum for a beaver   1
      also a pair of stockings for a beaver   1
      also a pair of small stockings and a small shirt[,]
      together a fisher   1
      also a bottle of rum for a marten   1
      also a man's shirt for a beaver   1
      also a quarter and a small looking glass for a quarter[,]
      together   1

also a large looking glass for a fisher   1
also a knife for a marten[293]   1
        [account cr = paid]
        [At #s, some amount blotted away]

—— [40] ——

folio 22	1698 7 September Mohawk	b m –

Kanaequathoo[294] a blue coat		2 0
also a shirt [at] 1 beaver		1
also a pair of stockings [at] 5 martens		5
also in lead for a marten		1
also a bottle of rum for 1 marten		1
1704 May[,] he has paid	B[eavers]	[3b drawn, cr]
fully, so that we are	M[artens]	[7mks, cr]
completely even	————	

———————————— [thin line] ————————————

1704 October: 1½ ell of duffel at 7 martens   Martens   [7mks]

——————————————————————————————————

    1699 A female Mohawk savage[,]   b m
short and heavy[, she] is called
Ickheijaedoodeeka [.] Indebted from earlier times
10 martens[,] and now again a cask of rum   10
for 5 [martens = cr] skipple Indian corn

——————————— 1704 ———————————

October Brant[295]'s wife Debit
2 bottles of rum at 2 martens
1707 May paid [to the amount of] a fisher
2 martens remain   Martens   [4mks, 2cr]

[no folio #]   1699 female Mohawk[296] savage   b m
                  With an eye filled with pockmarks Debit
                  A shirt and for rum[,] together 12 martens   12

See folio 57
         Debit[,] a boy who lives in the house of
         Arija the savage[297][,] his name is
X Thaeckenyackhaee[298][.] Fetched by
X the mother of Arya a [shirt . . . . = wiped]
X bag of gunpowder and lead[,] together 1 beaver
X and a marten
24 January a pair of   M[artens] [28mks]
     plets stockings   B[eaver]   [1b drawn]
     at 2 martens
1704 May a marten in gunpowder
Sept[ember] gunpowder for 3 martens and lead for 1 marten[,]
     together 4 [martens]
1704 Decem[ber]
indebted on a duffel blanket 3 martens[,] ditto 1 piece [of cloth] at
2 martens
ditto 1 pair of stockings at 4 martens and 1 quarter
1705/6: 18 February indebted on a duffel blanket 3 martens[,] ditto
on a shirt 3 martens [and] for
     gunpowder and lead 2 martens
     1 piece of strouds at 2 martens [and] on a shirt 1 marten

---

1699 4 July Debit
X A Seneca [named] Tannassecha[299] or Kawessat
     a small cask of rum for a beaver   1 .
X See folio 73, [where] this has been transported

     1700 20 July debit dewannighrijeie[300][,] a boy who stays in
     Canada[,] credit extended for a beaver in   1
     quarters also a beaver for a pair of stroud stockings   1
1703 Ockt[ober] a beaver paid by his brother-in-law
     Dekanijadereghkoe[301][, who] said that he would give me the
     other one in this coming spring
                         B[eavers] [2b drawn, 1cr]

Anoo [*sic*] 1699   folio 22   b m l[*ap*]

	b	m	l[ap]
Dekanasquijesackha[302] Debit[,] credit extended for			
a beaver and a *lap* on a duffel blanket	1	0	1
also a pair of stockings for 4 martens		4	
also axes and beaver scrapers for a beaver	1		
also a bag of gunpowder for a beaver	1		
also a shirt for 4 martens	0	4	
also a small cask of rum for a beaver	1		
also 2 bottles of rum for 2 martens[303]	0	2	
[account cr = paid]			

———————————————— [thin line] ————————————————

See folio 18

	b	m	
1700 July Dekanasquiesackha[304] debit[,] credit			
extended anew[,] a shirt for a beaver also a			
pair of stockings [at] 1 beav[er]	2	0	
a small cask of rum for [a] beaver	1		
dit[t]o 1 stroud blanket [and] a duffel			
blanket[,] together	4	0	1
also as an old debt 2 beavers	2		
also 5 beavers for a gun, also 1 beaver in gunpowder	6		
		fish[er]	
also a pair of stockings [at] a fisher	0	0	1
also a shirt for a beaver	1		
also a small cask of rum [at] a beaver	1		
He must not be charged for what follows[,]			
he has 1 [*sic*] promised a gift for it[305][.] Nor does he carry			
it with him on his bill			
Also a deerskin [at] 2 martens:	0	2	
: 1701 for a small cask of rum [at a beaver]	1		
1700 in rum 11 bottles and 3 quarters[,]			
together 12[306] martens	0	13	
dit[t]o also 5 bottles of rum [at] 5 martens[,] also for			
2 martens in tobacco	0	7	

————————————————————————————————

	b	m	
His [nephew/cousin][307][,]a boy who stays with Uncle Evert's[308]			
X Desochenjoda a pair of buckles and buttons	0	2	
1700 July[,] the above mentioned paid			

———————————————— [thin line] ————————————————

	b	m	
1700 credit extended anew a pair of shoes for 4			
martens or a beaver 1703 July[,] he has paid a	0	4	

small beaver[,] credited as 2 martens[,] remain
2 martens

A[d?]owa[309]

---

	f
also for a young savage who lives in *kanende*[310]	
credit extended on a clock for a fisher	0 0 1
also 2 martens in *gempt*	0 2

—— [43] ——

folio 22   Anoo [*sic*] 1699 28 August   b m f

Debit Sasian[311] the savage[,] a bag of gunpowder for	1
a beaver[,] also a small cask of rum for a beaver	1
[and] a shirt for a beaver	1
also a bar of lead for a [beaver = cr] marten	0 1
also 2 martens for *plets*	0 2
1700 [credit] to his wife[,] 1 pair of duffel stockings	0 0 1
He himself has paid on this [account] 2 *lappen* and	
a beaver	

1703 Ceijenquerij cooe[312] Debit
A bottle of rum at a marten   [1b drawn]
If he does not return the bottle[,] [then he must]
give another bottle[313]   M[artens]   [3mks]
1706 28 February 1 bottle of rum [at] 1 marten
1 March 3 bars of lead and gunpowder[,] together a beaver

X Dekaniha[314]

X anno 1699 Debit[,] credit extended for 2 shirts
for 8 martens   0 8
1703 Sept[ember]
A shirt for a beaver   Martens   [10mks, 5cr]
fetched [at] mother['s][315]   B[eaver]   [1b drawn]
X when I was not at home [and] 2 bars of lead at a marten
[H]e has also received[,] on the same ditto as when he
X took the shirt on credit[,] a bottle of rum at a marten

1704 January paid an elkskin[,] credited as 5 martens
See further on folio 16[316]

———————————— [thin line] ————————————

1701 in the month of May
   Cresteia's wife[317][,] a female Oneida savage in the company
   of the wife of arija the savage[318][,] a shirt for 3 martens
   If she does not pay for it, then Arija's wife is
   guarantor   0 3
                                      M[artens]   [3mks]

——— [44] ———

folio 23   Anno 1699 2 October Debit Mohawk   b m ott

   Kahonck[319] a piece of strouds for 2 beavers   2 0
   also a duffel blanket for a beaver and an otter   1 0 1
   also a stroud blanket for 3 beavers   3 0 0
   also 2 bags of gunpowder for 2 beavers   2 0 0
   also for lead an otter   0 0 1
   also on a shirt[,] an otter   0 0 1
   also 2 bars of lead for 2 martens   0 2
   [H]e said that he was fetching a bag of gunpowder and
   2 bars of lead for a boy[,] whose name is Aeniadiero or
   Tackkoniackha[320][.] Also a knife for a marten   0 1 0
1700 13 beavers paid[,] 12 beavers and 4 otters
      and 3 martens remain
1707/8 26 January
   Indebted 2 martens on   B[eavers]   [13b drawn]
   a duffel blanket   otters   [4mks]
Dit[t]o 1 bag of gunpowder   Martens   [5mks]
   at 1 beaver and 1 piece   quarters   [1mk]
   of lead at 1 qu[arter]

——

1700 28 September an old Cayuga savage
\   with a moustache at his mouth[,] is named
         thoghtachcoo[321]: 8 bars of lead for a beaver   1
\   dit[t]o his wife[,] a savage [who] has no teeth
\   in [the] upper [part of] her mouth
         a blue coat for a beaver[,] together 2 beavers   1
         1701 paid[,] the above is paid

——————————————————————————————————   [thin line]

Credit extended anew [to] Sochtaghcoo[322]
2 beavers on a coat[,] she has paid 1 beaver

[2b drawn, cr]

1704 July[,] she has paid 1 beaver[.] Remains 1 beaver
August he himself a shirt at fisher   [1f drawn]

Febru[ary] 1703/4 Dekannasoorae[323] Debit
        indebted 2 martens on strouds
        Paid   M[artens] [2mks, cr]

—— [45] ——

[no folio #][324]   1701 14 February Debit   b m f

        See folio 43
X A young savage[,] his name [is] oghquese or Canaghquese[325][,]
        a shirt at 4 martens and a truss of copperwire[,]
X together makes 5 martens or a beaver
        also 3 martens for 1 pair of stockings[,] makes   o 8 o
1702 June also 4 martens on 1 pair of stroud stockings[,]
        also a shirt for 3 martens[,] also 1 marten for
X beads[,] together comes   o 8 o
X He has put down a gun here,[326] I have bought the gun
1703 May he has paid an elkskin[,] for which 4 martens
        have been credited   quarters   [1mk]
ditto a bag of gunpowder   M[artens] [33mks, 4cr]
        for a beaver   B[eaver] [1b drawn]
X 4 bars of lead at
        2 martens   See on ffolio [sic] 43
        1 bottle of rum at 1 marten
[October he has put down a gun here, cr] ditto given
X on credit a pair of *plets* stockings for [empty] martens
ditto a shirt for 4 martens
Novemb[e]r indebted on a shirt for 2 martens ditto on a small
        cask of rum indebted 1 marten[.] 1705 July 1 quarter in
        money: November indebted 1 marten on 1 shirt

1700 again Canossedeckha[327] debit   otter
X 6 Ocktober [sic] 2 pairs of shoes[,] 1 pair for himself
        and 1 pair for his child[,] together 6 martens   o 6
ditto 1 duffel blanket for a beaver and [an] otter   1 o 1
X 1 duffel blanket for 1 beaver and 4 martens   1 4

ditto 2 pairs of stroud stockings [at] 2 beavers   2
X 1 bag of gunpowder for 1 beaver[,] makes   1
          also a bottle of rum for 1 marten[,] makes[328]   0   1
1701 13 July paid [to the amount of] an otter[,]
          ditto credit extended for a small cask of rum. It
          is up to me to decide what I want to have for it when he comes
          to pay
[[he has?]   torn] put down two hands of wampum belts[,] so
[[when he?]   torn] pays then he must have them returned again
[[also?]   torn] a shirt for 1 marten   0   1
[torn] quarters indebted on a coat   0   1
[torn] also 1 pair of stroud
[[stockings at?] torn] 5 martens   0   5
[[a date]   torn] paid the above
[[except for?]   torn] 3 martens[,] check on folio 19

——[46]——

Folio 15   1701 June   b m ott

1701 8 June credit extended to an old Seneca
          a pair of duffel stockings for 1 otter   0 – 1
          his name [is] Aeadoonijont

1703 July A female Cayuga savage[,] her sister's
          name is Thaghijoenij[.] She had no name[329]
          indebted 1 otter   otter [1 0 drawn]

X 1701 arija the savage[330] indebted   debit   [on] folio 23[331]
          his wife
          it is briefly listed across from here
          At the balancing of all the accounts he remains
X indebted 2 beavers and 19 martens   2 19
1701 12 July 1 duffel blanket and 1 bag of

gunpowder[,] together makes 1 elkskin[,]
which must be a large one
1701 27 December also 1 duffel blanket
X and a piece of strouds[,] together for an elk
    skin[.] [O]ne can deduce accurately how heavy [the
    skin] must weigh[.] Also 2 martens in lead   2
1702 2 June
    also 2 quarters for 1 marten[,] so that [[he remains
                                          indebted?]   torn]
X 2 elkskins and 20 martens and [[2 beavers?]   torn]
    for a quarter[.] Also a bottle of ru[[m?]   torn]
    July also for 5 quarters[,] dit[t]o a [[bag of?]   torn]
    gunpowder 1 beaver[,] also 1 bar of lead [[1?]   torn]
X marten[.] December duffel for 4 [[martens/beavers?]   torn]
    also on a cask of rum 1 marten[.] A bag [[of gunpowder
                                          at 1?]   torn]
    heavy beaver [and?] a quarter _____ [torn]

———— [47] ————

folio 18   1702 in the month of April
A young Cayuga savage, [he is] a blackish savage[332] [and]
not yet tattooed on his face
his [name is] Aijadatha[,] indebted on a gun 1 fisher   1
Also indebted 1 marten on a shirt[.] 1703 September 18
his mother brought a gun[,] which I have had repaired
for him without any charge
1704 August he has paid
20 Ditto he remained [indebted] a large beaver on a duffel blanket
        his brother['s account] is [listed] below[333]
21 Ditto 1 piece [of cloth] for an otter   B[eaver]   [1b drawn]
                                                      [otter]   [1 0 drawn]

————————————— 1704 —————————————

Ditto his brother [is] listed above Debit
a large beaver on a duffel blanket
his name [is] Canoeawee   [1b drawn]

1702 May Dekansquiesackha[334] Debit
Wrote out his account briefly[,] he paid this 1 ditto
X 9 beavers[,] remains indebted 10 beavers and 24 martens
and 2 fishers   10 24 2
16 July a shirt for a beaver and   b[eavers]   [15b drawn]

| a bag of gunpowder for a beaver[,] | Martens | [27mks] |
| amounts to 2 beavers | fishers | [2mks] |

a bag of gunpowder for a beaver[,]
amounts to 2 beavers
August 1 duffel blanket for 2 beavers
also a beaver on a pair of stockings
On 1 harpoon and an axe[,] amounts to
[1?] mar[ten?][,] but then I must give him a quarter
1719 25 May 1 small cask of rum at 7 skipple Indian
corn for his wife
        Dit[t]o for himself 1 lb. of gunpowder at 2 martens

——[48]——

F[olio] 19   In albany anno 1701 Debit

	b	m
Dekansquesackha[335]'s wife Deb[i]t		
1702 13 May 2 casks of rum[,] 5 martens per cask[,]		
together	0	10
ditto for *gemp* 1 marten[,] together comes 11 martens	0	1
ditto on 1 pair of stockings[,] 2 martens	0	2
December a shirt for 4 skipple Indian corn[,] or		
otherwise martens		
ditto baize for 3 martens		3

b[eavers] [empty]
m[artens] [16mks]

1704 June
See folio 9[,] Canosedeckha[336] Debit also [listed] below and across

Beavers [14b drawn, cr]	Bearskin	[1B drawn, cr]
quarters 242	m[artens]	[57mks, cr]
2	quarters	[16mks, cr]
together 244		

1702 July
    Ceghnae[,] a Cayuga boy[,] Debit
    A pair of stockings for 1 fisher

1704 29 Febru[ary]
    he is [listed] across   B[eavers] [4b drawn]
    Canosedeckhae Debit   Marten[s] [19mks, 9cr]
    A stroud blanket at 4 large beavers
    Ditto a kettle at 6 martens

ditto a marten for shot[,] the strouds was 2 ells and 3
fourths long
and there was 2 pounds of shot
1704 May[,] he has paid 6 martens[,] which have been
credited as 4 [martens?] July a cask of rum at 22 quarters
ditto she has her bill with her[,] [which] amounts to
242 quarters
1 bottle of rum at 2 quarters

1702 July a female Cayuga savage [her] name [is]
CaewenenDaghque

		fisher	raccoon
and her husband's name [is] Aennestoodde[337]			
a pair of stockings for 1 fisher and a raccoon		1	1
[,] they were *plets* stockings			

1703 Decemb[er]
X Canosedeckhae's wife Marijae[338]
for two boys[,] their names Arent[339] and
Hendereck[340][,] Arent has a coat for 6 martens
X and Henderek has a coat and a pair of stockings
X together 8 martens

X Hendereck has paid his 8 martens	Martens	[8mks, cr]
1706 1 January [for] Arent 1 coat	Martens	[15mks, cr]

at 9 martens[,] together 15 martens[.] paid[.] see folio 66

——[49]——

folio 19 June Albany anno: 1701

1702 18 June

Watjandondieijo[341] Debit	B[eavers]	[4b drawn, cr]
wrote out his account briefly	L[appen]	[2l drawn, cr]
on folio 14[,] [where] his received	M[artens]	[48mks, 43cr]
merchandise is listed[,] remains		

indebted 4 beavers and 2 *lappen* and 48 martens
See on [folio] 32[342]

he has with him his bill in the same		
fashion[,] therefore[,] if you give him	*these are not*[343]	
credit [,] so demand his bill and note	*on his account*	
it thereon as well[,] or he will deny it	*[martens?] [14mks]*	
1702 this he has not on his account	quarters	[2mks, cr]

On a pair of baize stockings and 2

bottles of rum[,] makes together 4 martens
16 October on a [sic] 2½ quarters[,] makes 1 marten
[and] half a quarter ditto gunpowder for 2 martens[,] makes   0
1703 January gunpowder for 2 martens
ditto a shirt for a marten
March[,] 2 quarters for a marten 1703/4 January 1 bar of lead
at a quarter An axe at a marten[,] 1 quarter @ [empty]
the above bar of lead a quarter[,] together a marten
          [whole account cr = paid]

See for him also across
1702 5 July again   B[eavers]   [10b drawn, cr]
Canosedeckha[344]   M[artens]   [32mks, 24cr]
he has paid 4 beavers and 15 martens[,]   M[artens]   [7mks]
remains indebted for 1 b[ea]ver [and] 3 martens
ditto 1 coat for 6 martens and 2 strings of beads
for 2 martens[,] together makes   0 8
3 October 1 duffel blanket [at] 1 beaver

                                                    bearskin   [2B drawn, cr]
5 October 1 blue coat for 3 beavers   quarters   [1mk]
ditt[o] 1 gun borrowed 1703 January he returned the gun
1703 May a shirt for a bearskin[,] she says that he is in the country
to bring it immediately
26 May he has paid me the bearskin
ditto a bottle of rum which he fetched for his wife[,] he said that
his wife was ill July 2 small coats at 4 martens [and]
gunpowder [at] 1 marten
1703/4
Two shirts for a bearskin
Sept[e]mb[er]
Adooho[345] fetched a bottle of rum for a marten
2 December indebted on a duffel blanket a beaver and a marten
ditto 2 bars of lead for a marten
24 ditto indebted on a pair of stroud stockings 1 marten
25 ditto indebted on a shirt 3 martens[,] ditto a half bottle of rum
8 January [1704?] a coat from my body which I had been wearing
at 2 beavers
13 ditto his wife fetched 1 cask of rum at 8 martens[,] when he
went as a scout[346]

—— [50] ——

folio 19   In new Albany[347] anno 1701

                    who trades here
1702 July a young Cayuga savage
Not tattooed[,] his name [is] Dekarowade[348]
Debit an otter for a pair of baize stockings   [1 0 drawn]
1709 June 13 A large shirt at 1 large beaver   [1b drawn]

Aerijenhotens[349]'s daughter Debit
1 pair of white baize stockings for 4 martens
1704 January 5 martens or a large   quarters   [12mks, 8cr]
beaver on a duffel blanket   m[artens]   [17mks, 8cr]
ditto a quarter in money[,] on the condition that
if she comes here to trade that she will have it for free[.]
ditto a quarter in money[,] ditto a bottle of rum at 2 quarters[.]
March 4 a shirt for her boy [at] 5 quarters
She did not bring the shirt with her[.] Remain 3 qua[rters]
1704 Paid a beaver[,] calculated as 3 martens[,] as has been credited
November 2 quarters at 1 marten 1706 September she and her husband
together 2 bottles and a small cask of rum[,] together 7 martens

---

1701 CaghEnjockendase[350] Debit[,] on folio 18 he is indebted for
11 martens
1702 July a beaver for a pair   Martens   [14mks]
of stroud stockings[,]   beavers   [2b drawn]
and a bag of gunpowder
for a beaver[,] 2 bars of lead for a marten
also 1 piece [of cloth] for 2 beavers

———————————————— 1703 ————————————————

September Thrghijoores[351] Debit
indebted for a duffel blanket and
a small cask of rum[,] 3 martens   M[artens]   [4mks, 2cr]
which I gave him for a gun[352]
1704 August 2 bars of lead @ 1 marten
27 December paid 1 fisher, [remains] indebted 2 martens

folio 19   In Albany Anno 1701

N:B November 1708[,] On a white duffel blanket [empty]
lb. deerskins to be paid   [2b drawn, cr]

X 1702 June Waghrosra[353] transported from folio 11
where his delivered merchandise is listed[,] he has paid this ditto 4
elkskins which have been credited as 4 beavers
See folio 76
and 2 martens[,] so that ditto he remains indebted
X 19 beavers and 7 martens and 2 otters and 1 bearskin
and 2 fishers[.] 1703 also a bag of gunpowder for a beaver
                   B[eavers] [21b drawn]   Martens [21mks]21
16 December indebted on a stroud blanket 5 martens
1703/4 January 11: A beaver for what he buys   quarters [1mk]
gunpowder[,] he must give me a large   otters [2mks]
beaver in return   bearskin [1mk]
1704 1 marten for gunpowder   `   fishers [2mks]
1705: 9 October indebted 2 beavers on 1 duffel blanket
                       B[eavers] [2mks]
1706 4 Novemb[er] 2 duffel blankets at 6 martens[,] to be paid at the
first opportunity[.] 1707 June 2 martens for shot and 1 bar of lead
ditto 1 shirt at 2 martens for another female savage
1707 July 1 quarter in money[.] 15 Septemb[er] 1 bar of lead
at 1 marten

1702 A Seneca boy[,] his name [is] Soghsiecoowao[,]   5
July a pair of baize stockings for a fisher   [***[354]]   3
[Fetched] by his mother an axe for 2 fishers   10
2 June 1706 [on a duffel blanket at 1 beaver indebted = cr]   4
        Dead   22[355]

X 1707/8 Waghrosraa's son Aedam[356] D[ebi]t
X 12 January [fetched] by his father 1 red duffel blanket at
5 martens
X 1708 26 April 3 martens paid by his father[.] Remain 2 martens
11 August 3 martens for 1 shirt
       fetched for him by his mother 1 small coat @ 10 martens
1711 January 1 pair of stockings @ 4 martens
                     M[artens] [22mks, 3cr]

1702 June a Seneca[,] he is not tattooed but he has
2 moustaches at his mouth[,] his name [is] ThghThoras[357]
1 pair of baize stockings for a fisher   fish[er]   [2mks]
1705 June 2 indebted on a blue duffel   [1b drawn]
blanket for 1 beaver   [1 circle drawn]
1706 June 4 1 pair of children's stockings at 1 raccoon
18 August 1 piece of strouds at 1 Fisher

——[52]——

folio 20   in Albany debtor

July 1702 A Seneca[,] his name [is] Conowaroo[,] debit
a baize coat for a beaver   [1b drawn, cr]
1704 Sept[ember] he has paid this beaver   [1 circle drawn]
ditto he remains indebted a deerskin on a duffel blanket
[at left of last 3 lines,
outline of human head
drawn, with tattoo[358]]

CaerReghcondeyae Debit [A] Seneca
a bottle of rum @ a marten   M[artens] [5mks, 1cr]
this marten he has paid[.] Ditto 1 pair of *plets*
stockings[,] indebted 4 martens

1702 July A Cayuga with a piece missing from his nose[,]
it is a sedate[359] savage[,] debit
A pair of baize stockings for 1 fisher
his name [is] Canossora   [1f drawn]

———————— 1704 ————————

May: Soghquedekoee[360][,] credit extended anew[,] a bottle of rum
[at] a marten[.] ditto a bottle at a marten
ditto 1 bottle of rum at 1 marten   Martens   [3mks]

Sooquedacoo[,] an Oneida boy[,] debit
1702 July 1 pair of stockings for a marten and a
shirt for 2 martens[,] together makes 3 martens   [3mks, cr]
1704 May, he has paid the above

_____

1704 May[,] an Oneida Satkatsteghcooe[361] or Aennetsoendeijae[,]
X Debit a marten on a pair of stroud stockings
X 1706 [paid] all and everything[,] [so that we are] even
                                                         M[arten]   [1mk, cr]

———— [53] ————

folio 21   [herstwa?]

1702 July[,] a young Cayuga savage[,] debit[,] his name
[is] Caghkiewassee[,] a pair of baize stockings
for an otter[.] ditto 2 strings of beads
for a 3lenck

———————————————— 1704 ————————————————

August 20 [A] female Cayuga savage[,] debit
her name[,] or her father's name [is] Sedewaserot[362]
a beaver indebted on a duffel blanket   [1b drawn]

_____

1702 28 July[,] a Seneca[,] debit
his name [is] Dekanesthejendaghqua[363][.]   Martens   [1mk]
a raccoon indebted on a coat[.] Paid[.] His new name
[is] Aewaen[accoo/anoo?] His wife a red duffel blanket
at 2 beavers[.]   1710 Sep[tember] 1 pistol at 3 beavers
1707: 19 July 1 piece [of cloth] at 1 beaver and for rum 1 marten
1708 4 Septemb[er] his son and his brother have been here to buy a
gun on credit at 4 beavers
                                          [1b drawn] [4b drawn, cr]
His brother's name is Okade[364][,] as on folio 38   [6b drawn]

_____

1702 28 July[,] a Seneca boy[,] his name [is]   [1b drawn]
Thannoqua[.] a bag of gunpowder for a beaver

———————————————— 1704 ————————————————

August[,] a female Seneca savage[,] her name [is] Ohonsenowae[,]
Debit a shirt for an otter [1 0 drawn, cr] paid

154 ‡ *Account Book, 1695–1726, of Trade with Indians*

1709 4 Septemb[er] 2 martens indebted on a cask of rum

martens [2mks]

Ditt[o] a piece of lead @ 1 otter[,] to wit   [1 0 drawn]

1702 18 July A young Seneca savage[,]
his name [is] Eienoo[.] indebted 1 beaver
on a pair of stockings   [1mk]

————————— 1704 —————

August[,] A female Cayuga savage[,] Debit
her [inserted: husband's] name [is] Canawaede[.]
a kettle [for] a *drijelingh*   [1*drieling* drawn][365]
Ditto a pair of duffel stockings at 1 fisher   [1f drawn]

—— [54] ——

folio 22   Debtor

1702 July[,] A Seneca boy[,] his name [is] Caijassee or Canissoe
A piece [of cloth] for a *lap*[,] he stayed at [h?]ans's[366]
when I extended this credit to him   [1b drawn]

See on folio 46
X A female Seneca savage[367][,] Debit
X [She is] Aeriedonquaes[368]'s sister[,] a coat for 3 raccoons
1705 25 Septemb[er] 1 large deerskin   raccoons [3mks]
indebted on 1 pair duffel stockings   [1 circle drawn]

See on folio 46
1702 9 September Debit[,] has 2 names[369][:] Onissonda
or Aeredonquas[370]
or Thanawase[,] a Seneca [who] lives in Canada[371]
X among the Mohawks[.] promises to come to trade here[.]
X 2 strings of beads for 2 martens   [2mks, cr]
X if he does not come to trade he looses 1 large beaver[,]
X but if he does come to trade here[,] I loose a shirt
and a pair of stockings[372]
1704 May a pair of duffel stockings for a beaver
ditto a coat and a shirt[,] together 2 large beavers
ditto a coat for a heavy beaver   B[eavers] [4b drawn, cr]

Thanijores[373][,] the lame savage[,] Debit
at the balancing of the accounts remains indebted
3 martens   M[artens]   [8s+ 4mks]
1702 September a duffel blankets for 2 beavers
ditto 1 pair of stockings for 3 martens
ditto for 1 marten in baize   beavers   [3b drawn]
ditto 1 shirt for 1 marten
his wife a shirt on condition
See on folio 17 for the condition
1703 July Thotquerijese[374]['s] brother fetched a pair
of stroud stockings [for] 1 beaver

1705 June 25
Catquerhoo[375] Debit / his wife's son folio 80[376]
At the balancing of the accounts remains indebted
1 beaver[,] as is listed across [from here]   [2b drawn]
Ditto a duffel blanket at 1 bearskin
his [blot]*ij*[377] owes this bearskin   [1B drawn]
1709 15 Septemb[er] indebted 1 fisher on a cask of rum
ditto 1 piece of strouds @ 1 fisher[,] together   [2mks]
2 fishers[.] 1710 4 July indebted 1 beaver or bearskin on a stroud
blanket

——[55]——

folio 38   Albany debit 1705

[above the title of the folio:]
NB 1710 June 3 raccoons indebted on a small coat

1704 a female Seneca savage[378] who stays here[,] she has a scar
on her head from a cut   Debit
her son's name [is] Sendaghqua[.] a kettle at an otter - - -
          [1 o drawn]
1705 June[,] her son debit[,] owes 1 fisher for
1 looking glass _____   [1f drawn]
And her other son is called Nansendaghquee[379]   [2b drawn]
1708: 16 August a female savage[380][,] 2 raccoons on 1 duffel blanket
                                                 raccoons   [2r drawn]
10 July 1 cask of rum at 1 large beaver
1708: 16 August 1 red duffel blanket at 1 beaver and 1 otter   [1 o drawn]

the other son's name [is] Sackkoonoeoenie and the other
Sadkoodquathaa[381]   raccoons   [3 circles]

———————————————————— 1705 ————————————————————

paid
A female Seneca savage who stays here[382][,] she is a big[383] female
savage[.] She is somewhat pockmarked[.] Debit
her [inserted: husband's] name [is] Oekaedee[384][.] a fisher indebted
on a coat [1f drawn][.] ditoo[= ditto] a female savage who stays here
with her[385][,] 1 fisher indebted on a cask of rum[.] she is called
Sackhoowa [1f drawn] [, and] lives in *Saront*[386][.] her husband's name
[is] SoeckquenEndaghquee
1706 August[,] a female savage who [she escorted?] here[387] 1708 4
Sep[tembe]r he himself a gun at 4 beavers[.] his wife is dead[,] he
was here this ditto with Caghquena's son when he bought the gun on
credit and said that Caghquena was also a guarantor for this
                                                      [4b drawn, cr]

———————————————————— 1705 ————————————————————

June : 13 A young Onondaga savage[,] debit
his name [is] Teiekaeweehaa [,] [indebted] for 2 martens on a pair of
stroud stockings[.] ditto 1 pair of blue *foetelinger* stockings for 3
martens[,] together 5 martens   [5mks, cr]
1708:
13 June he has paid 5 martens[,] as has been credited
anew
Ditto 1 bag of gunpowder at 1 beaver   [1b drawn]
Ditto 1 duffel blanket at 1 fisher[,] remains indebted 1 fisher
                                                      [1mk]
Ditto 1 piece of strouds at 1 marten   [1mk]

——— [56] ———

folio 39   Anno 1705 June 13

X An Onondaga boy Debit
His name [is] Oranij[388][,] 3 martens indebted on
X a pair of stroud stockings
Ditt[o] 1 pair of blue *voettlingen* stockings
X at 3 martens   [11mks, cr]
18 May paid 2 martens[,] 4 martens remain
X Ditto a cask of rum at 2 martens and 1 pair of stroud
X stockings at 3 martens[,] together 5 martens -
paid 3 June 1707   See folio 61

A female Seneca savage [who] lives in *Caenaederhaa*[389][,] [she is a]
black savage[.] She was here with Catquierhoo[390][,] her name [is]
Osheea[391][.]
Debit 1 beaver on a cask of rum   [1b drawn]   martens   [1mk]
1705 July on 1 pair of stockings indebted 1 marten and 1 raccoon
                                       raccoon   [1mk, cr]
1708 paid the amount of 1 raccoon

1704 A female Seneca savage who was here with the above [,]
Debit[,] her name [is] Souenijaesie[.] on a shirt indebted 2 raccoons
                                     raccoons   [2mks]

A white female Seneca savage[,] debit
her husband's name [is] Orghjaedikhae[392][,] she
bartered with Uncle Evert's wife[393] when they bought on credit
1 cask of rum at a beaver   [1b drawn]

—— [57] ——

[folio] 39
July 1705 A young Onondaga savage[,]   Debit[,]
his name [is] Canmincoodee[.] 1 beaver indebted on
1 pair of *plets* stockings   [1b drawn]
       Ditto 2 martens indebted on 1 piece of strouds   martens   [2mks]

         His name [is] Josquassoe
✳See folio 73[394]✳
✳His mark [395]✳
X   15 July A young Seneca[,] his name [is] Tennessocthaa[396] [,]
Debit[,] he has not been tattooed[,] his teeth protrude somewhat in
his mouth[,] lives in *Canosedacken*[397] [and] bartered with Abberham
Cuijler[398]
X   6 martens indebted on 1 pair of stockings   martens   [6mks]
26 Sep[t]em[ber] 1 fisher indebted on 1 piece of strouds
                             [1f drawn]   [followed by:] or: Anadeias
1707   15 October for 1 beaver indebted on 1 duffel blanket
X   Ditto 1 small duffel coat at 1 beaver and a *lap*

Ditto 1 stroud blanket at 4 beavers[,] for which [he] puts down a
hand [of wampum] belt   [7b drawn, 3cr]
                                          Lap   [1 small b drawn]
Ditto a big[399] savage who he escorted Debit for one dotted shirt at 1
beaver
Ditto the above mentioned[,] [him]self for 1 red duffel blanket at 2
beavers

———————————— 1705 ————————————

24 July An old Cayuga with one eye[,] his name [is]
Thein deaes Debit one marten on a shirt   martens   [1mk]

———————————— 1705 ————————————

Septem[ber] A young Cayuga[,] Debit[.] His name [is]
Aennaedsoenes[400][.] 3 martens indebted on 1 piece of strouds
1 marten indebted on a shirt   martens   [7mks, 6cr]
he is a short, heavy savage
d[itt]o for 2½ ells of *gemp* indebted 1 marten   marten   [1mk]
His *aensoet*[401] who he escorted is called Radewackeree[,]
2½ ells of *gemp* [at] 1 marten for which he is guarantor
✳1707 8 October✳
d[itt]o for having his brother's[402] gunlock repaired at 2 martens

[this account contains two sketches of a person's head and neck,
showing their hairdress and tattoos.][403]

———— [58] ————

[folio] 40
1705 August 13 Jisep[404][,] Debit[,] on 1 bottle of rum
indebted 1 marten   M[arten] [1mk]

———————————— 1705 ————————————

13 August Giedeijon[405] the savage[,] debit[,]
on 1 bottle of rum indebted 1 marten   [1mk, cr]
24 May[,] paid so that we are even

———————————— 1705 ————————————

October[,] a white female savage [who] lives in *Saront*[406][,]her
name [is] Caienjawie[,] Debit[,]
her son's name [is] Sooquentssoowaa[407][.] on ¼ ell of duffel
indebted 1 deerskin
she is a gaunt savage[.] she bartered here when she bought on credit

1703/4
See folio 65
1705 X   a young Mohawk[,] Debit[.] his name is Caheghetsiedauw[408]
[, he is] the son of the female savage who was killed here on the
mountain
See on folio 65
See folio 27[409][,] where he remains indebted for 21 martens and a gun
X which he has borrowed[,] and if it pleased him he should give
X 3 beavers for that or otherwise [return] the gun
2 October on gunpowder 3 martens [indebted]

[40 his account = cr]

d[itt]o 2 bars of lead for 1 marten	martens	[41mks, cr]
X 3 ditto 2 quarters for 1 marten	martens	[22mks, cr]
Beavers 3 = = or the gun	quarters	[7mks, cr]

He carries a bill with him for 32 martens and the gun
X ditto on 1 pair of duffel stockings indebted 2 martens
[, which] are included in his bill
X 5 Febru[ary] 1705/6 has paid 3 beavers[,] at 9 martens
9 ditto [fetched] by aeijawassen[410] 1 knife for 1 marten
Since he [had] his bill[411]
X 1706 June 1 pair of stroud stockings at 4 martens[.] Ditto 1 knife
and 1 bar [of] lead at a marten[,] which he does not carry on his
bill
19 August 1 piece [of cloth] at 1 marten[.] 1 mink and 1 quarter
together for 1 marten
X 16 Septemb[er] on 2 quarters at 1 marten which is not included in
his bill
X Ditto 1 bottle of rum for 1 marten which is not included in his
bill
_____ Since the bill for 53 martens[.]
24 June 1707 paid 6 martens as have been credited Di[t]to 1 bottle
rum at 1 marten[.] June 4 quarters at a pair of buckles [and] 1
bottle of rum
X All in all, calculated in beavers, I still have coming to me 16
beavers and 2 mar[tens] which I have to select of 2 lb[412]
June 1 pair of stockings at 1 beaver
on a gun 1 beaver   [18b drawn]

[folio] 41
1705 August 4
[*dek* .... = wiped] Caeinderonkee[413] and Taijenoekee[414][,] Debit
accepted to pay me for their brother half [of his debt,]

the half amounts to 14 martens	m[artens]	[14mks]
and a bearskin[,] which they must	bearskin	[1B drawn]

pay at the first opportunity
for their brother Aeshentheree[415]

The wife of Aeshentheree[,] the Greyhead's son[,]
Debit 4 martens indebted on a stroud blanket
[and] on duffel 1 marten   [5mks]

1707 May 13
A female Seneca savage [who] lives in *Canendedaerhaa*[,][416] her
name [is] ToeWistToewee D[ebi]t owes 1 fisher on a small coat
and from older times [owes] a raccoon[,] which she admits herself[417]

Arijenhotsen[418] Debit[,] on folio 16[419] is his delivered merchandise
listed[,] [for which] he remains indebted   martens   [10mks, 4cr]
                                                 Indian corn   [1mk]
1706 June 12 he himself paid 4 martens[,] still 4 remaining
October his wife 2 martens indebted on a duffel blanket
Ditto[420]

——————— 1705 ———————

A Seneca who very much resembles Catsedeneiont[,] his name
        [is] Oquenjonquas D[ebi]t[,] he was here with orghiaedecka[421][,]
X he lives in *Caweke*[422]: 1 fisher indebted on 1 pair of red
X duffel stockings[.]   paid   [1f drawn]   1706 19 September

——————— 170[5?] ———————

X Ditt[o] A French boy[,] who he escorted[,] his name
[is] Schoeoendees[423] : 1 deerskin indebted on a duffel blanket
X paid   [1circle drawn]

[folio] 42

Aeijawassen[424] Deb[it] from folio 28[425][,] where his delivered merchandise is
listed[,] remains indebted   Beavers   [3b drawn]

1705 30 October

4 martens indebted on 1 pair of stockings

4 martens indebted on 2 lb. gunpowder   elk   [1e drawn]

                            martens 91[,]

1 February 1707

1 marten indebted on 2 knives   quarters   [4mks]

1 marten indebted on 2 bars of lead   Martens   [91mks, 19 set apart]

d[itt]o 4 martens on [a] small cask of rum

1706:9 February on 1 knife indebted 1 bar of lead

indebted 1 marten[,] together [empty]

4 June 2 quarters[.] ditto for tobacco at 1 marten

19 August 1 pair of stroud stockings [fetched] by Caheghtsiede[426]

at 4 martens =1707 the first of February[,] he admitted to be

indebted for 91 martens[.] a shirt for him at 4 martens[,]

for tobacco at 1 marten[.] a dog at 6 martens which I have advanced

to a soldier for him[427] _____

he admits to those 91 martens which are marked above[,] in addition I

find his debt in the book[.] when he pays those [I will] return to

him the value of 19 martens[,] to do justice to him and myself[.] on

the first day of February Anno 1707 _____

[For goods] after this confession[,] the martens will be marked below

24 August 1 piece of strouds at 2 martens

ditto 1 lb. gunpowder at 3 martens   martens   [7mks]

1708 23 March 2 pieces of lead fetched by a female savage[,] she is

Aetsenhaa's[428] wife[,] at 1 marten

[remainder of this page is empty]

[folio] 43
Cannadekonka[429] Debit on folio 15
his delivered merchandise is listed[,] remains indebted

his daughter	Martens	[20mks, 4cr]
1706:18 August 1 duffel blanket	bearskins	[2B drawn]

1706:18 August 1 duffel blanket
     at 2 beavers
1707/8 19 Feb[ruary] his daughter

indebted 1 beaver and 2 martens	daughter [martens]	[2mks]
on a duffel blanket	Beavers	[3b drawn]

1708/9 9 January his wife indebted 4 martens on a duffel blanket
15 May paid 1 elkskin at 4 martens[,] as has been credited

———————————— 1701 ————————————

A Mohawk[,] his name [is] oghquesen or Canaghkwase[430][,]
Debit from folio 23[431] remains indebted on delivered merchandise for a
total of 27 martens and a beaver and a quarter

1708 June paid 2 beavers[,]	martens	[39mks, 4cr]
as has been credited	quarters	[1mk]
13 July 1 beaver indebted on 1 fine shirt		
ditto 1 small looking glass at 2 martens	Beavers	[4b drawn, 1cr]

1708 October 28 1 lb. gunpowder at 2 martens
1709 August 2 martens indebted on 1 shirt
1709/10 Feb[ruary] 1 marten indebted on 1 pair of stroud stockings
20 ditto 1 shirt at 4 martens[.] ditto for repairs to his gun 1
marten

1718 October 5 bottles of rum at 5 martens	[8mks]

1719 9 March 1 pair of *plets* stockings at 2 martens
Nb last year 1 duffel blanket at 2 martens[.]
See Hester's book[432]

62

See folio 87
[folio] 44
WaghRosraa's wife's son Danijell[433]
X 14 Dece[mber] Debit from earlier times 1 marten indebted[,]

for 1 shirt indebted 4 martens	martens	[24mks, cr]

Ditto 3 martens indebted on 1 pair of duffel stockings
1706 April 12 5 martens paid by Waghrosraa[,] 3 martens remaining
                See folio 87

X 18 June 1 pair of red duffel stockings at 3 martens
ditto 1 cask of rum at 6 martens
1708 23 June 1 shirt at 4 martens[,] [fetched] by the father
X 1709 5 July 1 piece of strouds at 2 martens[,] to wit [:] on his[434]
Steptember [sic] 1 bar of lead at 1 marten | 17010 [sic] January 1
                                    shirt at [empty] martens[,]
                                    that [I?] had given to his
                                    father for the pistol[435]

1706 July A female Canadian savage[,] her name [is]
Ohonsaioenthaa[436]
Debit on pair of stockings at 1 beaver   [1b drawn]

                                                           14 fathoms[437]

A female Mohawk savage from Canada[438][,] her husband's name [is]
Tharencoo[.] She was here with Thouwenjouw[439][,] she is a pockmarked
savage[,] with greetings from the priest
Debit A[nn]o 1705 27 Decemb[er]
on 1 pair of red duffel stockings indebted 2 martens
on 9 bars of lead indebted 3 martens[,] together amounts to
5 martens   [9mks, cr]
her son's name [is] Warhosse Rode[440][,] a young fellow who she
eacorted
29 January the boy indebted 3 martens on a coat
His father's name [is] SaadecaeeRehos[441][.] ditto 1 marten indebted on
1 axe[.] has put down an axe[442]
M[ar]ch she has the axe again
May she has paid three beavers and a *lap*[,] so that we are even

---

see folio 62
1706 May 9 [credit extended] anew[.] 4 bottles of rum at 4 martens
X Ditto an old female savage who she escorted - she is an Oneida
savage -   Martens   [12mks, cr]
[she is] thehoghtaghqueesren[443]'s sister[,] 1 pair of duffels
stockings
X at 3 martens[.] 1706 May[,] her mother 1 pair of stockings
at 1 beaver   M[artens]   [3mks, cr] [1b drawn]
Ditto for her a shirt at 4 martens[,] and 2 quarters paid to
Jelles van Voorst[444] for driving[.] the boy is called
WaerhoesRoodee[.] Together 9 martens
1706 July fetched by an old female savage[445][,] 1 piece of strouds at
3 martens[.]

And given for her son for free a piece of strouds[.]
the boy and his mother have paid everything

—— [63] ——

[folio] 45
Jan or Aedewackhaa[,] a Frenchman
who lives in Mohawk country[,][446] Debit
His delivered merchandise is listed on folio 34[447][,] for which he
remains indebted 6 martens   martens   [11mks, cr]
1705/6 February 7: 1 marten indebted on 1 pair of *plets* stockings
7 Ditto on 2 bars of lead indebted their value in beaverballs[448]
d[itt]o October borrowed my carbine and took it with him[,] promised
to pay me the sum of
5 beavers for this   B[eavers]   [5b drawn, cr]
Ditto a duffel blanket at 2 bearskins   [2B drawn, cr]
Ditto a stock for his gun @ 4 martens
paid. Except a gun that he has borrowed and 2 bearskins

1708 Adam[449][,] Waghrosraa's son de[bit]   martens   [22mks, 3cr]
12 January his father fetched 1 red duffel blanket at 5 martens

                                                                [5mks]

26 April his father paid 3 martens
11 August 1 shirt at 3 martens
        his mother fetched 1 coat for him at 10 martens
1710 January 1 pair of stockings at 4 martens[,] to wit together
m[artens] 19
1714 27 September balanced accounts[,] remains indebted
        5 beavers and 24 martens   [5b drawn]

—— [64] ——

[folio] 46
1706 May 25 A young Oneida [,] his name [is]
Canandaa or oendack[450][,] Debit
on a pair of stroud stockings for 1 marten   [1mk]

——————————————— 1706 ———————————————

A young Seneca[,] his name [is] Aedonquas[451][,] he usually lives in
Canada [,] Debit

1706: June 4: 1 pair of stroud stockings at 1 beaver
and a marten   b[eavers] [2b drawn]
ditto 1 shirt at 1 beaver
Ditto 1 knife at 1 raccoon
1709: 30: August: 2 ells of *singerlin* at 2 otters
NB not for his wife[.] although he   martens [5mks]
insisted that he would get it on her
account I did not want him to   raccoon [1r drawn]
proceed like that[,] so that he has   otters   [2mks]
it on his own account[452]
1710 22 August 1 cask of rum @ 4 martens[,] to wit [empty]

——————————————— 1706 ———————————————

8 June Aeraedonquas's sister[453] D[ebi]t
from earlier times 3 raccoons   raccoon [3mks]
1 pair of stockings at a deerskin   [1 circle drawn]
Ditto 1 female savage who she escorted[454][,]
1 pair of stockings at 1 fisher   [1f drawn]

—— [65] ——

47
1706 June 8
Te ottquiee[,] a young Seneca D[ebi]t
[he] has a snake [tattooed] on his right cheek
he is a small savage[,] 1 pair of red duffel
stockings at 1 beaver   [1b drawn]
1 raccoon indebted on a pair of stockings   [1 circle drawn]

——————————————— 1706 ———————————————

8 June AghsienjaaEijeei[455][,] he is a young French
savage who lives among the Cayugas
Debit 1 pair of stockings at 1 beaver   [1b drawn]

——————————————— 1706 ———————————————

9 June Aequaenaghthaa[456] or the small Thickhead[,] Debit
See folio 51
he and his wife[,] 1 red duffel blanket at 2 large beavers[,]
promises to come here to trade   B[eavers] [2b drawn, cr]
7 Jan[uary] his wife [fetched] 1 small   beavers   [8mks, cr]
cask of rum at 4 marters[.] ditto supplied   martens [4mks, cr]
her with 1 skipple Indian corn[,]   [8b drawn, cr]
½ skipple peas[,] 1½ quarters in money [and] 1 bottle of rum[,] if

she and he do not come here to trade[,]
they must pay for it ___ 1707 June she has paid
[credit extended] anew 1707 24 July D[ebi]t   [7b drawn, cr]
he and his wife
1 cask of rum at 1 beaver   quarters   [1mk]
Ditto 1 pair of green *plets* stockings at 1 beaver
Ditto 1 pair of *voetenlingen* stockings at 1 beaver
Ditto 1 pair of blue *plets* stockings at 1 beaver[,] they all need to
be large beavers
Ditto 1 quarter in specie
1707 October Senjaad'riesen[457] [fetched] a blue duffel blanket at 2
large beavers ___ 1707/8 Febru[ary] sent 25 small *tonties*[458] with them
to sell for my account[,] for which they must deliver 8 beavers
ditto 1 shirt at 1 beaver
1708 4 July she has returned the *tonies*[.] Ditto fully satisfied

—— [66] ——

[folio] 48
DeCanjaeDeReghtToo[459] D[ebi]t
1703 Octo[be]r 1 pair of *plets* stockings at 1 beaver
1706: 12 June 1 cask of rum at 2 beavers
         1 piece of strouds at 2 martens   [16b drawn]
         3 bottles of rum at 3 martens[,] 4 quarters at
         2 martens[,] 1 marten indebted on a   *lap*   [1 small b drawn]
         duffel blanket[,] together 8 martens[,]
         for which he is charged 2 beavers
         1 shirt at 1 beaver   martens   [1mk]
         1 duffel blanket at 2 beavers
         1 shirt which he gave to Sakadereiughthaa[460]'s son[,]
         at 1 beaver[.] he carries his bill with him [for] 9 beavers[.]
         2 quarters together a beaver[,] so that he must give 9 large
         beavers[461]
13 July 12 guilders in wampum at 1 large beaver
1710 November a cask of rum at 2 beavers[,] 1 duffel blanket at 2
         beavers
Ditto for white *plets* at 1 beaver and a *lap*[.] 1 beaver in lead [and]
1 bottle of rum at 1 marten
         His hand [sketch of animal, possibly a beaver or a deer[462]]

1708 June a female Canadian savage[,] her
name [is] OkaajatHie[.]
1 beaver indebted on a belt   [1b drawn]

[folio] 49

Sakadereiughthaa[463] Deb[it]

1706 12 June 1 blanket of blue strouds at 4 heavy
 blanket beavers   [15b drawn, cr]
 1 blue duffel blanket at 2 large beavers
 18 *can* pure rum at 6 large beavers
 1 deerskin at 1 large beaver
 1 pair of baize stockings at [empty = 1 beaver] together 14
 beavers[.][464] For which he carries a proper bill with him

1706 25 June 1 piece of strouds and 2 quarters[,] together 1 beaver
 This beaver is not included in his bill[465]

1708 4 October he has paid 15 beavers

Debit anew

1708 4 October 1 duffel blanket at 2 beavers
Ditto 2 duffel blanket at 4 beavers   [33b drawn]
Ditto 1 gun at 5 beavers
Ditto [I] paid 4 heavy beavers to Johannis Becker[466]
 1 duffel blanket at 2 beavers
 8 quarters in money at 1 beaver
 8 quarters in money at 1 beaver
 1 pair of stockings [and] 2 shirts[,] together 2 beavers
Ditto for 1 lb. gunpowder and also lead[,] together 1 beaver
8 Decemb[er] Carghiaedsiecoo[467] 1 piece [of cloth] at 1 beaver[,]
small   quarters [14mks]

1708/9
11 January 2 casks of rum at 3 beavers
 ditto 2 beavers in gunpowder[.]
 ditto 1 beaver in lead
 ditto 1 beaver in lead
 di[t]to 2 beavers in beads
 ditto in money 12 quarters
1710 24 July 1 pair of white stockings at 1 beaver
Ditto 2 quarters in money at 2 qu[arters] *oplijen*[468]
23 August 1 cask of rum at[469] 1 pair of shoes[,]
together 3 beavers

[folio] 50
        See further on folio 53
1706 June 16 A Cayuga savage Debit
his name [is] Nacoeghnajasquei[470]
1 pair of duffel stockings at 1 fisher   [1f drawn, cr]
he is tattooed on his face[.] paid 1707 January

1706 June a young Onondaga Debit
✳See folio 92✳
has been prisoner of the *Tweghtteghen*[.][471]
Can barely speak Onondaga [,] he is not tattooed[.]
he was here with the Ottawa savages[, and] he traded
at uncle Evert's wife[472] when he bought here on credit
a small cask of rum [at] 1 beaver
His name [is] d'waddierhoe[473]
Ditto a gun at 3 beavers   B[eavers]   [10b drawn, cr]
1708 15 June 1 cask of rum [at] 1 bearskin
Ditto 1 cask of rum @ 1 bearskin[,] to wit   [2B drawn, cr?[474]]
1 duffel blanket @ 2 beavers ――― 1 gun [at] 3 beavers
                  1 bag of gunpowder [at] 1 beaver
        [account cr = paid]

1706 June 19 An Ottawa savage[,] about forty years old[,]
his name [is] Mackkockwassien[475] Debit
1 pair of stroud stockings at 1 large beaver
he must come to trade here   [1b drawn]

    [Most human, appealing drawing of an Indian in the book[476]]

[folio] 51
1706 A Mahican who lives among the Ottawas
his name [is] [SoowaJaghCoo = cr] and in the Mohawk language
Maghcoes[477] or onderRiesaghtoo[478] Debit
rum at 1 beaver   [4b drawn]
1 red duffel blanket at 3 beavers[.] 1 piece of strouds at 1 otter
                      otters   [1 o drawn]
1706 July 1 quarter   quarters   [1mk]

─────────── 1706 ───────────

A young Cayuga his name [is] HanNaaRoncoo
12 October 1 pair of duffel stockings at 1 deerskin
has put down a gun[479]   [1 circle drawn]

─────────────────────────────

✳1710 1 September✳
Aequanaghtka[480]'s wife De[bit]
6 [inserted: quarters] in specie at 1 beaver
1 Novemb[er] 1 cask of rum [at 1 beaver][,] together[ ] 2 beavers
Ditto 1 duffel blanket at 2 beavers   [4b drawn]

─────[70]─────

[folio] 52
        A Mahican from below[481]
1706: 25 June his name [is] Aekoetts D[ebi]t

                                                         [16b drawn]
        raccoons   [3 circles drawn]
1 duffel blanket at 2 beavers - - - - .02
16 *can* pure rum at - - - - - - - - - - .07
1 piece of strouds and 1 axe - - - - .01
1 pair of stockings at - - - - - - - - - .01
2 rolls tobacco at 4 beavers - - - - - .04
1 shirt at 1 beaver - - - - - - - - - - - .01
                B[eavers] -16- and 3 raccoons

─────────── 1706 ───────────

13 August a young Seneca who lives in *Canosedaken*
        his name [is] TannaEedsie D[ebi]t
        he usually stays at Nieckas Blecker's[482]
        1 pair of blue duffels stockings
        at 1 fisher or an otter
1708 [he has] paid the fisher
24 July [credit extended] anew[,] his wife 1 fisher indebted
        on a duffel blanket
        Ditto 1 shirt at 1 beaver

Ditto 1 pair of stockings at 1 fisher[,] for himself

[1b drawn]

[3f drawn, 1cr]

[Most elaborate drawing in the account book[483]]

—— [71] ——

[folio] 53

A Cayuga[,] his name [is] Coenjaesquaa Debit
he lives in Cayuga but he is a Seneca who
always stays with me[484]
from folio 23[485] he remains indebted 2 martens
1 shirt at 1 beaver   [1b drawn, cr]   martens [9mks, 4cr]
1708 26 April [he has] paid the above   [2b drawn]
28 ditto 2[later changed to 0] martens indebted on
2[later changed to 0] shirts
8 June 1709 The youngest brother 3 martens indebted on 1 pair of
stockings
Ditto 1 beaver indebted on a duffel blanket
Ditto his younger brother[,] his name [is] oiaewaekos[,] 1 pair of
plets stockings at 3 martens[.] ditto he himself 1 piece [of
cloth] at 2 martens
1708 29 June a piece of strouds at 2 beavers[,] on which
[he] paid a beaver so that he remains indebted for 1
beaver
1709: 8 June he himself 2 martens indebted for rum
ditto 1 marten indebted for a shirt

A young Cayuga savage[,] the brother of the above[,]
his name [is] Caunquienen D[ebi]t
1 pair of *plets* stockings at 1 beaver   [1b drawn]

1708/9 17 March the sister of the above
1 fisher and an otter indebted on baize   [1f drawn]

[1 o drawn, cr]

1709: 6 June paid to the amount of an otter[,] 1 marten remains

1706 8 July A female Seneca savage [,] somewhat old[486][,] D[ebi]t
her name [is] Coetsiessee: her son's name [is]
daawienEeckhaa[487][,] 1 beaver indebted on a
stroud blanket   [1b drawn]

———————————————— 1706 ————————————————

9 July A Seneca boy who was escorted by the above female savage[,]
    his name [is] Jaadoendoeiee De[bi]t
    1 pair red duffel stockings at 1 beaver   [1b drawn]

——— [72] ———

[folio] 54
1706 July 25 Awenoett[,] a Seneca[,] De[bi]t
X 1 beaver indebted on 1 coat   [1b drawn]
———————————————— 1706 ————————————————

August An Oneida[,] his name [is] SoghseeRowanna[488]
    or Hottentot[,][489] who stays at Niecklas's[490]
    2 martens indebted on [a] cask of rum   M[artens] [2mks]
———————————————— 1706 ————————————————

An Oneida savage[,] his name [is] Sattkattstoghka[491]
or anetsondeian De[bi]t
9 August[,] he remains indebted for a marten
Dit[t]o 1 large stroud blanket at 16 martens

                                           Martens   [17mks, cr]
he put down 35 pipes[492]   Beavers   [empty]
    1707 May 16 his wife has paid everything

———————————————— 11706 [sic] ————————————————

15 October a French Mohawk[,] his name [is] Aedecaijijkaa[,]
correctly said aedecanijhaa[493] De[bi]t
1 cask of rum at 3 beavers
Ditto 1 blue duffel blanket at 2 beavers   [7b drawn, cr]
Ditto 2 pairs of large stroud stockings at 2 large beavers
    and 2 martens   martens   [2mks, cr]
Ditto 1 coarse blanket at 4 beavers
    together makes 11 beavers[494]   [6b drawn, cr]
16 [October?] 1 cask of rum at 2 beaver[s]
1707 all and everything paid[,] so that we are even
    See folio 64

[folio] 55
OnighRadieha[495] Debit on folio 40   quarters   [1mk]
he remains indebted   Indian corn [1mk]
1705 25 September 3 martens indebted   Beavers   [6b drawn]
        for gunpowder   Elk   [1e drawn]
                                               Bearskins   [1B drawn]
                                               Martens   [25mks]
Di[tt]o has given 1 mink for repairs to his gunlock[,]
        indebted to give another marten
        ditto 1 [marten?] indebted on 3 bars of lead
24 Novemb[er] an old female savage fetched 1 lb. gunpowder
        and 3 bars of lead[,] together 4 martens[.]
        her name [is] Osienoghqua
10 August on a shirt remained indebted   [empty, followed by one
                                               quarter of a page of
                                               unused space]

————————————— 1706 —————————————

An Oneida of Stevanes Groesbeeck[496] Debit
his name [is] Kacksaaweede
a 6 *can* cask of rum at 6 martens   Martens   [6mks, 3cr]
1707 17 May received from him 1 beaver of 1¼ lb
was [credited as] 2½ martens

[folio] 56
Aeijewases[497]'s wife Debit from across[498]
X 1 August she remains indebted   martens   [23mks, cr]
2 ditto 10 quarters indebted   Beavers   [2b drawn, cr]
X on 5 bottles of rum   Bearskins   [1B drawn, cr]
ditto X 2 quarters indebted on 1 shirt   quarters   [14mks, cr]
                                              Indian corn [8mks, cr]
                                              Hops   [5 small circles, 2cr]
                                              Deerskins   [1circle, cr]

6 *can* of rum[,] for which hops is to be given as payment[.]
the number of pounds may be established at that moment
1705 2 Oct[ober] 2 skipple Indian corn indebted on 1 shirt
X 28 March 1 marten indebted on a stroud blanket
ditto 5 skipple Indian corn indebted on 1 large shirt
1706 19 August [for] her son[,] 1 small coat at 4 ma[rt]ens

                                                       [4mks, cr]

1706 13 Octob[er] 2 martens indebted on 1 shirt
Ditto 4 bottles of rum at 1 skipple
1707 January [fetched] by Caheghtsiede[499] 1 small cask of rum @ hops [empty]
X 9 June 1 marten indebted on a shirt
Ditto 1 piece of *plets* at 1 large beavers
ditto 1 piece [of cloth] at 1 large deerskin
X 16 July paid to the amount of 1 large beaver and 1 deerskin
ditto 1 cask of rum at 1 deerskin
      See further on folio 67 [where] this has been transported

Gave her 1 red duffel blanket at 60 skipple Indian corn[,] to be
brought to *Schaneght*[edee][500]
from oneghriedhaa[501]'s deceased wife which her sister owed me[502] - - - -
she has kept the blanket and must pay me in Indian corn

————————————— 1706 —————————————

15 Octob[er] An old Onondaga[, who] lives in *Chaghnaawakee*[,][503] his
name [is] Suckckughoieghtie[504] Debit
2 quarters at 1 *lap*   L[ap]   [3 small b drawn, cr]
Ditto 2 quarters at 1 *lap*
Ditto 1 shirt at 1 beaver   Beavers [10b drawn, cr]
1 pair of stroud stockings at 1 beaver and 1 *lap*
Ditto 1 cask of rum at 2 beavers
1708 22 May paid

————————————— 170[6?] —————————————

     See folio 72
Annahriesaa[505][,] A young Seneca savage debit[,] his name [is]
TaenNaahariesie who now lives in Canada
17 Octob[er] 1 stroud blanket at 4 beavers
1 shirt at 1 beaver[,] together 7[506] beavers   [7b drawn, cr]
1½ ells of *plets* at 1 beaver
paid

[folio] 57
A boy's mother debit
His name [is] Sander[507], who lives in *Canaaschore*[508]
1 shirt @ 4 martens[,] to wit   m[artens]   [4mks]

[one quarter of a page of unused space]

———————————————— 1706 ————————————————

X A Mahican who was escorted by Cattenarockes[509][,]
X his name [is] Sanpatijs D[ebi]t 1 beaver on a gun
        Paid [so that we are] even

———————————————— 1706 ————————————————

A Mohawk[,] his name [is] Thackenijackhaa[510]
his delivered merchandise is listed on folio 22[,] for which he remains
indebted 25 martens and a beaver   M[artens]   [36mks]
5 January 1 shirt @ 5 martens   Beavers   [1b drawn, cr]
ditto 1 piece [of cloth] at 2 martens
on a shirt 1 marten[.] 1707 June paid to the amount of 1 beaver
1707 15 Octob[er] for gunpowder and repairs to his gunlock[,]
together 4 martens

Anna[511] 1 female savage who lives in Canada De[bi]t
1 pair of stockings at 1 beaver   [1b drawn]
Also gave some merchandise with her on credit[,] as one can see in
the waste-book

ff[olio] [*sic*] 58
                    See farther below
A Mohawk Thotquariesen[512] and his wife D[ebi]t
he is listed on folio 19[513] [and remains indebted]   M[artens]   [7mks, cr]
                                                        Indian corn [3mks, cr]
1707 Janu[ary] 1 stroud blanket @ 4 martens indebted
His wife [is indebted] on folio 19   martens   [13mks, cr]

Ditto 2 quarters @ 1 marten

Anno 1706 May paid 2 beavers

Ditto [for] him and her 1 piece [of cloth] at 2 martens[.] ditto 2
bottles of rum @ 2 martens[.] 14 Septemb[er] she [fetched] a bottle
of rum at 1 marten

15 Septem[ber] 1 harpoon and 1 quarter[,] together 1 marten[.]
1 stroud blanket given with his wife to sell on my account[,] and [I]
have paid her 1 cask of rum for that[,] and then she must give me 8
beavers   [8b drawn, cr][514]

1708 9 March 6 quarters in specie at 3 skipple Indian corn which must
be delivered here at home[515]

Ditto 2 pairs of *plets* stockings at 4 martens each pair

Ditto 2 shirts at 4 martens each pair[,][516] together 16 martens[.] or
she can return the merchandise[,] that will also be accepted[.][517] the
female savage has this _____   [martens]   [31mks, cr]

1708 20 [March?] 2 shirts and 2 pair of stockings fetched by
Attsenhaa's[518] wife on the same[519]

See below

————————————— 1707 —————————————

A prisoner who has been given to Areijenhotsen[520][,]
his name [is] Thaijadoores[521] D[ebi]t

Janu[ary] 1 quarter in specie and a knife[,] together 1 marten

Septem[ber] 1 gun borrowed by Totquaresen for which he must give 3
beavers if he likes it[522] ___ 1708 14 June borrowed for the amount of 1
marten ___ 1709 9 July 1 marten indebted on a pair of stockings

Gun	[1 gun drawn, cr]
[martens]	[10mks]
quarters	[3mks]

1710 9 Feb[ruary] 1 piece [of cloth] at 2 martens [and] 1 knife @ 1
marten[,] together 3 martens

2 lb. of shot @ 1 marten[,] together makes 6 martens[523]

1710 22 August string at 3 quarters

30 November 2 martens indebted on 1 pair of stockings

30 November 1 piece [of cloth] at 2 martens

Thotquariesen and his wife Deb[i]t[.] See above

31 April also 1 pair of stockings @ 4 martens
to sell[524]

M[artens]	[23mks, 2cr]
deer	[1 circle drawn]

1708 13 June the female savage 3 guil[ders] [and] 10 st[i]vers
in specie @ 1 marten

1708 ditto 4 quarters in specie @

Ditto 1 piece [of cloth] @ 2 martens

Indian corn	[9mks, 6cr]
[quarters]	[6mks]
beavers	[8b drawn, 1 cr]
Martens	[36mks, 30cr]

Ditto 1 kettle @ 2 beavers[,] to wit 2 beavers   [2b drawn, cr]
                        kettle taken out on credit again
Septemb[er] he himself 2 bottles of rum @ 2 martens
Ditto she 6 bottles of rum @ 6 skipple Indian corn
Ditto 2 quarters in specie
Ditto 1 shirt [@] 1 skipple Indian corn / 17010 [sic] January 1 shirt
[@] 1 marten[.] 1710 Feb[ruary] paid 3 guil[ders] in wampum
1710 [both of] them 3 martens indebted for a cask of rum
Ditto she 1 large deerskin indebted for a cask of rum
Octob[er] she [is indebted] for 2 martens on an ell of white *plets*
        her son paid 2 martens

—— [77] ——

[no folio #]   See folio 12 in the small book
X Canosedeckhaa[525] D[ebi]t
on folio 9 remains indebted

Beavers	[4b drawn, cr]
M[artens]	[42mks, 7cr]
B[eavers]	[10b drawn, cr]
Foxes	[3mks]
Bearskins	[2B drawn, cr]
raccoon	[1 circle drawn, cr]

1707 3 March 1 stroud blanket
@ 4 large beavers
Ditto 4 bottles of rum @ 1 marten each
[fetched] by his wife 1 shirt
@ 4 martens[.] Di[t]to 1 small
shirt at 2 martens
24 August he went to Canada for me for 15 beavers[,] for which he
[has been] paid 3 beavers which I gave him in merchandise[.] And has
been credited 12 beavers[,] as appears above
1707 3 Novem[ber]
10½ ells of *plets* at 9 beavers[.] Ditto 1 duffel blanket at 2
beavers[,] together 11 beavers   [16b drawn, cr]
Ditto 1 shirt at 6 martens
Ditto 1 shirt at 1 beaver   NB 1709 December 23
Ditto 1 shirt [at] 3 martens   paid [a] raccoon
Ditto a duffel blanket [at] 1 beaver   coat for 8 martens
Ditto 1 bottle of rum at bmarten [sic]   as has been credited
Ditto 1 ell of *plets* at 2 martens
Ditto borrowed the amount of 1 beaver[,] to wit
Ditto in specie at 2 martens[526]
1707 18 Decemb[er]
1 pair of stockings on which he remains indebted a raccoon
22 Decemb[er] 1707/8 1 coarse blanket @ 3 bearskins[,] of which he
paid 2 and remains indebted 1
X 1707/8 Janu[ary] 1 cask of rum of 8 *can* which I delivered to him in
the country at 8 martens

1708/9 16 Feb[ruary] balanced accounts with her after the death of
her husband[,] the beavers calculated in martens makes 113 skipple
Indian corn and 45 martens and 3 foxes - - - - - - - - - .113 = 48 martens
Ditto 2 bottles of rum @ 2 skipple Indian corn   8 paid
Ditto 1 skipple of grits [at] - - - - - - - - - - - - - - - - - .1   40 remain
1709 15 April 1 cask of rum [for] 11 skipple Indian corn[,]
2 bottles of rum [at] 2 skipple [Indian corn][,] 1 shirt [at]
5 skipple [Indian corn][,] together 20 skipple   - - - - - - .20
1708 NB Ocktob[er] [sic]
to her in the country 1 pair of white baize stockings
@ 5 skipple [Indian corn]   5
Ditto 3 guilders in specie @ 2 skipple Indian corn   - - - - - - - . 2
23 Dec[ember] Ditto 1 duffel blanket @ 13
skipple Indian corn   - - - - - - - 13
Ditto 1 shirt @ 5 skipple Indian corn   - - - - - - - 5
1710 8 March [she] paid me 42 skipple in the country - - - - - - - .42
6 April 8 bottles of rum [and] 2 lb. shot[,] together
9 skipple Indian corn   9
in addition[,] received 16 skipple in the country   - - - - - - - .16
               (added vertically, in lower right hand corner:)
1710 May 1 shirt [and] 1 pair of stockings[,]
together 8 skipple[527]
      [account cr = paid]

—— [78] ——

[folio] 60
1707 May 23 A Mohawk who lives [both] in Canada
           and in Seneca country[,] his name [is] Decakedoorens[528]
           and his new name is Canaghquajeese[529] Deb[i]t
           1 red duffel blanket at 2 large beavers
           1 pair of blue *plets* stockings at 1 beaver
           1 piece [of cloth] at 1 beaver[,] together 4 beavers
           27 July 1 gun at 5 beavers[,] to wit   [22b drawn]
Ditto 1 large blanket blue duffel at 2 large beavers
27 ditto 1 pair of stockings at 1 beaver
Ditto 1 shirt at 1 beaver
Ditto 1 cask of rum at 3 beavers
Ditto our Hans's[530] old coat at 1 beaver
Ditto in specie and 1 knife[,] together 1 beaver
Ditto 1 cask of rum at 1 beaver[531]
1710 4 Novemb[er] gunpowder and lead[,] together 2 beavers

[remainder empty: half a page]

—— [79] ——

f[olio] 61
An Onondaga[,] his name [is] Oranij[532] D[ebi]t
[1707[533]] 3 June 1 stroud blanket at 4 large beavers   [4b drawn]

A female savage who was escorted by the above Onondaga[,]
her name [is] Awanaaceere[,] [she lives] in the house
of tijedores[534]
1707
3 June 1 beaver indebted on a blue duffel blanket
Dit[t]o 1 pair of duffels stockings at a beaver   [2b drawn]

A young Onondaga[,] his name [is] SecquaRiesera[s?]
who was escorted by the above mentioned [Indian][535]
1707
4 June a pair of *plets* stockings at 1 beaver   [1b drawn]

A young Onondaga[,] not tattooed[,]
his name [is] Cananouwejaae[536] De[bi]t
1707
4 June 1 beaver [indebted on] a piece of strouds   [3b drawn]
1709/10 18 January 1 blue duffel blanket @ 2 large beavers
Ditto 1 marten for paint   martens   [2mks]
has put down a gun[537]

—— [80] ——

[folio] 62
          See folio 90[538][,] where the following is transported
X   A Mohawk from Canada and his wife
His name or her son's name [is] Waerhosradee[539]
1707 3 June D[ebi]t
Paid 5 beavers for her to brother Manes[,][540] since she does not know any
better but that Manes must have them
Ditto the father Johana[541]   [16b drawn, cr]
X   1 blue duffel blanket at 2 large beavers
Ditto on a blanket of strouds 1 beaver at indebted [sic]
Ditt[o] a blanket of red strouds at 4 heavy beavers
A beaver from older times[,] which he owed father[542]
X   Dit[t]o a cask of rum at 1 large beaver
Dit[t]o 1 pair of stockings at 1 large beaver   quarters [9mks, cr]
Dit[t]o 2 quarters at [empty]
1707 26 July he and his wife have paid 16 beavers
                                                      [27b drawn, 25?cr]

Since then[,] new D[ebi]t
8 Octob[er] 2 *dollers*[543] in specie at 2 beavers
Dit[t]o [1] pair of stockings at 2 beavers
Dit[t]o 2 large blue coats at 8 beavers
Dit[t]o 1 coarse blanket at 4 beavers
a cask of rum at 2 beavers
Dit[t]o 1 pair of stockings at 1 beaver
Dit[t]o 1 cask of rum at 2 beavers[,] together 21 beavers
1708 15 August for 4 quarters in specie
                                [At the right of previous 10 lines:]
                                1708: August 3 quarters [at = cr]
                                ditto 6 quarters for 1 beaver*sij*[544]
                                8 Decemb[er] 1 duffel blanket [at] 2 beavers
                                1 cask of rum [at] 2 beaver[s] [it was] pure rum
                                1 bag of gunpowder [at] 1 beaver

23 June A Canadian savage[,] his name [is]
SasseNowanense[545] D[ebi]t
3 beavers indebted on a Christian's coat   [3b drawn, cr]
1708 paid 2 beavers[,] 1 beaver remains[.] 1710 paid

———— [81] ————

f[olio] 63
A young Onondaga[,] his name [is] Sacknawedie[546] Deb[i]t
1 shirt at 1 beaver   [1b drawn]

A Seneca who lives in *Canadedaerhoo*[,] his name [is]
SoenNaacentsees [.]
his wife 1 blue duffel blanket at 1 fisher   [1f drawn]
1710 20 Septemb[er]
1 otter indebted on a blue duffel blanket   [1 o drawn]

A Mohawk[,] his name [is] ThowaaHodieshenthoo[.]
22 June
he is a savage who came here this dit[t]o by way of the Ottawas[.]
[I] have arranged with him for 6 beavers that he must come and trade
here[.] if he does not come to trade here then he must pay me 6
beavers[.] Dit[t]o sold him on credit ___
1 hat at 1 beaver   [9b drawn][547]
4 bars of lead @ 1 beaver
2 looking glasses at 1 beaver

———— [82] ————

f[olio] 64
A Mohawk from Canada[,] his name [is] Aedekanijhaa[548]
1707 7 June
1 stroud blanket at 4 large beavers

1 blue duffel blanket at 2½ beavers
Ditto 1 cask of rum at 2 beavers
Dit[t]o [1] blue duffel blanket at 2½ beaver[s]   [24b drawn, cr]
dit[t]o 1 shirt at 1 beaver   quarter   [1mk]
21 August 1 gun at 4 large beavers
ditto 6 quarters that I paid for him to the son of Lavlueer[,][549]
named Schoo - - - at 1 beaver
1707/8 15 Feb[ruary] 7 ells *plets* at 6 beavers
Ditto *plets*, 2 quarters and 1 small box of paint[.] Together 1 beaver
1708 24 May he has paid me for the above
                    See further on folio 69

An Ottawa savage who speaks Mohawk[,] he is a young savage[,] his
name [is] Hanaenpamet D[ebi]t
1707 22 June 2 bottles of rum at 2 martens   [martens] [4mks]
Dit[t]o 1 pair of stroud stockings @ 1 beaver and 1 marten
and 2 bags gunpowder at 1 beaver   [3b drawn]
4 bars of lead at 1 beaver
Dit[t]o 1 bottle of rum at [1] marten

                    [remainder of page is empty]

——[83]——

folio 65

1707   See folio 91
A Mohawk[,] his name [is] Caaheghtsiedawee[550] D[ebi]t
X his delivered merchandise is listed on folio 40 [,] for which he
remains indebted 18 beavers and 2 martens   [43b drawn, cr]
For which he carries a bill with him   martens   [11mks]
the 18 beavers must weigh 36 lb. because they have all been converted
into 4 martens [each][,] as one can see on folio 40
His present wife is the daughter of Tanenjores's[551] wife
24 June 1 cask of rum at 4 martens   [martens] [9mks]

14 Septemb[er] 2 rolls of tobacco at 2 beavers

Ditto 9 beavers in pipes and *toniets*[,] together 11 beavers

Ditto 1 pair of stockings for a boy at 2 martens

Ditto in specie and lead and paint[,] together 1 beaver

Ditto 1 axe at 1 marten

Ditto 1 bottle of rum at 1 marten[.][552] ditto borrowed a gun for
aetsenhaa[553]

And 1 a [*sic*] pair of stockings and 1 knife and others[554]

1708 4 March 1 lb. gunpowder at 2 martens[.] He carries a bill with
him[,] dated 4 March 1708[.] Remains indebted 30 beavers and
5 martens[,] as above

9 July by going to Canada he has earned 14 beavers from me

14 ditto indebted on 1 duffel blanket at 1 beaver

Ditto 1 deerskin at 1 beaver[.] August 28 1 cask of rum @ 1 beaver[.]

Ditto 1 bottle at 1 marten[.] 18 May 1709 remained indebted on 1 cask
of rum @ 1 beaver and 2 martens[.] 1710 Feb[ruary] 2 lb. of shot at 1
marten[.] 1710 May 1 shirt @ 1 beaver [and] 1 stroud blanket[,]
together 5 beavers

──────────────── 1707 ────────────────

A female Onondaga savage[,] her deceased husband's name [was]
Ohoonsiewaanens[555] D[ebi]t

1 July 1 beaver indebted on a pair of gray stockings   [1b drawn]

──────────────── 1707 ────────────────

A female Seneca savage who lives in *Saront*[,] she stays here[.] she
is a big[556] female savage

her son's name [is] Aewendoocee and hers is Cawasthaa D[ebi]t

19 July 1 cask of rum at 1 beaver   [1b drawn]

──── [84] ────

f[olio] 65

Praise the Lord   D[ebi]t   Albany 22 July Anno 1707

A Mohawk who lives in Canada[,] his name is Sajacaawecha[557][.]
He is d'Cackkeedooren's[558] father

1707 22 July

3 beavers indebted on a coat   [4b drawn, cr]

Ditto 1 beaver and 1 otter indebted on

a blanket of red strouds   otters [1 o drawn, cr]

N:B To the best of my knowledge[,] he has paid

One can ask himself

Annahariese is his new name

The younger son of the above
his name [is] Sacksareeij D[ebi]t   or Annahriese[559]
July 23 Ditto 2 quarters in specie   quarters   [3mks]
24 Ditto 1 small coat at 2 beavers   beavers   [5b drawn]
ditto 1 quarters [*sic*] in specie
1710 18 Novemb[er] 3 ells *plets* at 3 beavers

A young savage who lives in Canada[,] his name [is]
TiocaghneeRadeie D[ebi]t   or Caanondaa[560]
3 August 1 blue duffel blanket at 2 beavers
Ditto 1 pair of stockings at 1 beaver   [3b drawn]
he belongs to Carghiaedsiecoo[561]
Carghiaedsiecoo also escorted him
but he trades at Uncle Hans[562]
he stays in the house of Noquaresen[563]

———— [85] ————

folio 66
Praise the Lord   D[ebi]t   in Albany 27 August Anno 1707

A female Canadian savage[,] her husband's name
[is] JeoWoondaaquieree D[ebi]t
a coarse blanket at 3 large beavers[,] and he has promised to come
here to trade   [3b drawn, cr]   1708 June 25 paid

A boy who stays at Canosedeckhaa's[,]
his name [is] Arent[564] D[ebi]t
15 Sept[ember] Repairs to his gun at 1 marten
ditto gunpowder at 1 marten   martens   [2mks]

Johonnaghquaa D[ebi]t   from another page[,] on folio 13[565]
remains indebted 12 martens   [12mks]
1707 8 Octob[er]
1 blue duffel blanket at
2 large beavers[,] to wit   [6b drawn]
1708 15 August
his wife 1 deerskin at 1 beaver
NB October 1 cask of rum which had not been deducted from her
[account] when she brought the pack of beavers for me from Canada
Ditto to his wife 1 pair of white stockings at 1 beaver
1708/9 11 Jan[ua]ry
fetched by Sakadereuightha[566]
for 1 beaver in gunpowder and 2 martens in lead

—— [86] ——

folio 67   1707
    A young Mohawk who lives in Canadaa[,] his name [is]
    SoeHaahies[567][,] he is married to Senjaad'riesen's daughter[568]
    Deb[it]
8 Octob[er] 1 cask of pure rum at 3 beavers[,] to wit
27 Ditto 1 duffel blanket at 2 beavers   [7b drawn]
Ditto 8 quarters in specie @ 1 beaver
    [he] has picked up another blue duffel blanket [and] said
    that it was for Aquanaghthaa[569]'s wife[.] but [he] has not
    given it to her[,] so that he must pay for it
    aquanaghthaa has paid   [2b drawn, cr]
1708 2 Septemb[er] 1 deerskin at 1 beaver

    The wife of Canghcuasen the elder[570] Debit
8 Octob[er] 1 shirt at 1 beaver   [2b drawn, cr]
    Ditto 1 pair of stockings at 1 beaver
    1708: 29 June paid

27 October A young Mohawk Canadian savage[,] his name
    [is] Oghsiknoendoo[571] D[ebi]t
      2 ells of silk ribbon at 1 beaver
Ditto red *plets* at 1 beaver   [11b drawn]
Ditto 1 small cup at 1 quarter   quarter   [6mks]
Dit[t]o 1 pair of blue stockings at 1 beaver
1708 24 June 1 blue duffel blanket @ @ [*sic*] 2 beavers
2 Septemb[er] Sohasie[572] fetched 1 duffel blanket at 2 beavers
1710 22 Feb[ruary] 2 blue duffel blankets at 2 beavers each
23 Ditto 1 small looking glass @ 5 quarters as above

✴See folio 78 for the mother✴
Aeijewaesens[573]'s wife D[ebi]t   her delivered merchandise is listed on
folio 56 for which she remains indebted   martens [33mks]
31 Octob[er] sent 10 ells of red *plets*   bearskin [1B drawn]
with her to sell for me at 6 pairs of   quarters [14mks, 4cr]
stockings[,] for which she must bring   beavers [3b drawn, 1cr]
martens from this winter   hops   [2 circles drawn]
Ditto 1 red duffel blanket at 2 beavers   hops   [3 circles drawn]
1708 13 May she has satisfied the [debt for] the stockings and paid 1
elkskin @ 4 martens or a beaver[,] as has been credited
Her mother 1 shirt at 2 martens   [2mks]
Dit[t]o 1 *notas* of hops at [empty][574]
1710 Feb[ruary] 1 cask of rum at 4 martens
1710 a 6 *can* cask of rum @ 2 *notasse* of hops[,]
to wit [empty]

──────[87]──────

f[olio] 68
Areiaa the savage D[ebi]t   his delivered merchandise is listed on
folio 33[575] for which he remains indebted 6 beavers[,] 31 martens and
2 quarters
1708 26 April [I] have sent with him   Beavers [7b drawn, 5cr]
to the country to sell on my account[:]   martens [36mks]
10 ¼ ells of *plets*[,] to wit 8 pairs   quarters [2mks]
of stockings[,] 7 shirts [at] 3 martens each[,]
3 bags of gunpowder at 6 lb. - - - he can satisfy [me] with merchandise
for all that he does not sell
4 May from brother Hans[576] 2 pairs of white *plets* stockings in the

country[,] for which he returned 2 of the 7 shirts[.]
so that the old amount stays with him

this is the merchandise		[3b drawn, 2cr]
which he carries with	[martens]	[70mks]
him to sell - - - - -		

1708 23 June 2 beavers
  1 *lap*
  17 martens
  1 fisher: 30 ditto he has returned the merchandise
30 Ditto 1 yellow piece of *plets* @ 3 martens as above
9 July 1 bottle of pure rum at 1 marten
21 ditto 1 marten indebted on 1 small coat
1710 24 Septemb[er] 1 deerskin at 1 beaver[,] which he had received
conditionally when he went to Ca[n]ada with my merchandise that
he has returned

  Albany 11 August 1714
  Balanced accounts with Arijae[577][,] he remains
  indebted in this book and Hester's book[,] together
  5 beavers and 43 martens and 2 quarters
    [7b drawn, 4cr]
    [martens]   [43mks]
    quarters   [2mks]
  This does not include the debt in Indian corn

he himself [fetched] 1 cask of rum at 2 beavers
Dit[t]o 1 bottle of rum and the bottle[,] together 1 marten
1718 Febru[ary] [a?] cask of rum at 7 skipple Indian corn
Dit[t]o his wife [indebted] 3 skipple [Indian corn] on 1 pair of
 stockings
  paid 1 duffel blanket _____ 1719 June he himself
  [fetched] a blue duffel blanket at [empty]
  1719/20 January Transported all to a small book

—— [88] ——

folio 69
Aedekanihaa[578] who lives in Ca[n]ada D[ebi]t _____ 15 [beavers]
1708 25 May

1 blanket of red strouds @ 4 heavy beavers		
1 duffel blanket @ 2 beavers		[16b drawn, 1cr]
2½ ells of red *plets* @ 2 beavers[,]		
7 ells blue *plets* @ 7 beavers together 15 beavers		

Dekaquarendightha[579][,] a young savage who was escorted by
Oghseaknoendoo[580] D[ebi]t
24 June a piece of *plets* @ 2 ells @ 1 beaver each ell[,]
     to wit 2 beavers
1708 4 Octob[er] @ 1 gun indebted on 1 duffel blanket
     dit[t]o 1 beaver [indebted] on a stroud blanket   [10b drawn]
Ditto 1 shirt @ 1 beaver
Ditto 1 [coarse blanket = cr] at 4 beavers
Ditto at the carrying place[581] my nightcap at 1 beaver

[remainder of page is empty]

——— [89] ———

f[olio] 70   Canada[,] an Oneida
Decannoessoekee[582][,] a young Mohawk who lives in Canada and has an
Oneida woman as his wife Deb[it]
1707 29 June 3 large beavers indebted on a coat from my body
Ditto 1 duffel blanket @ 2 beavers
a piece of baize @ 2 beavers   [9b drawn]
30 Ditto 1 piece of yellow *vlengh* @ 1 beaver

A female Canadian savage[,] her name [is] Quanakaraghto[583]
she is an old black savage ——— De[bi]t[,] SeakRiesjies [is her]
second name

1 July 1 blue duffel blanket @ 2 large beavers
Ditto 1 large beaver [indebted] on 1 kettle   [4b drawn]
Ditto 1 beaver indebted on 1 stroud blanket
Ditto 1 *lap* indebted on 1 shirt   - - - -   [1 small b drawn]

[remainder of page is empty]

——[90]——

               In Albany Praise the Lord D[ebi]t

———————————— 1708 ————————————

Ashareiake[584][,] a young Canadian savage[,] white[585] D[ebi]t
30 June 8 lb. of lead @ 1 beaver[, he] promises to come to trade here
Ditto 1 duffel blanket @ 2 beavers   [9b drawn]
Ditto 1 shirt @ 1 beaver
1710 Sept[ember] Ditto 1 large coat at 5 beavers

———————————— 1708 ————————————

A female Canadian savage who was escorted by Carghiaedsiekoo[586][,]
her child is called D'caiendanharij[587] D[ebi]t
1 beaver indebted on a stroud blanket   [1b drawn]
Ditto 2 quarters in specie   [2mks]

[remainder of page is empty]

folio 72   In Albany Praise the Lord D[ebi]t

————————————— 1708 —————————————

A young Cayuga savage[,] his name [is]
Aedeniehaes[588] D[ebi]t
3 Septemb[er] 1 beaver indebted on 1 blue duffel blanket
Ditto 1 beaver indebted on 1 duffel blanket   [3b drawn]
Ditto 1 pair of stockings @ 1 beaver

                        [empty space]

————————————— 1708 —————————————

Annahariesen[589] D[ebi]t[,]   he is a Seneca who used to live in Canada
but now lives in Seneca country again
8 July a small coat for his child at 2 beavers
Ditto 1 duffel blanket at 2 beavers[,] to wit   [14b drawn, 3cr]
Ditto 1 blanket of cloth at 4 large beavers
Ditto 1 duffel blanket at 3 fishers[,] to wit   [3mks]
Ditto 1 axe @ 1 beaver
Ditto 1 gun @ 3 beavers
13 Ditto he has sent the gun back[590]

                [remainder of page is empty]

f[olio] 73   In Albany Praise the Lord D[ebi]t

————————————— 17[0]8 —————————————

A Seneca from folio 39 [,] his name [is] Josquassoo or annosktoo[591]
D[ebi]t this ditto remains indebted 4 large beavers and

1 *lap* and 6 martens   B[eavers] [9b drawn, 1cr]
1708 9 August 2 martens [indebted] on 1 pair of stockings
                                                      Lap   [1 small b drawn, cr]
Dit[t]o 2 martens [indebted] on 1 pair of stockings
                                                      martens   [14mks]
Ditto 1 delicate shirt @ 1 beaver [and] 1 marten
Septemb[er] Ditt[o] [he] borrowed 1 raccoon[592]   [1r drawn]
Ditto [I] gave 19 *tonties* with him to sell for me
@ 9½ beaver   [9½mks, 1cr]
Ditto 1 cask of rum [of] 5 gallons @ 3 beavers fisher   [1f drawn]
Ditto 1 piece [of cloth] @ 1 fisher   beavers   [2mks, cr]
Ditt[o] 1 small coat @ 1 beaver
1710 March 30 [have] received from a female savage as payment for the
tonties 1 beaver[,] 1 bearskin   bearskins [8mks]
and 2 deerskins @ 1½ beaver for which he has been credited as his
account shows[.]
[Sent] by ditto female savage[593] 1 cask of rum of 8 *can* for which he
can reimburse me as he pleases[,]
to wit 2 beavers / 1710 9 June 3 casks of rum @ 5 bearskins[.]
Dit[t]o 1 duffel blanket @ 2 bearskins
Ditto 1 pair of stockings @ 1 bearskin[,] together 8 bearskins
30 August
3 martens or 1 bearskin indebted on 1 duffel blanket

A Cayuga with a piece of his nose missing[,] his name [is]
Caienkaroenkee D[ebi]t[,] [he] usually stays at Blecker's[594]
1708 August 1 beaver indebted on a duffel blanket
Ditto 1 pair of stockings @ 1 beaver   [2b drawn]

[remainder of page is empty]

——[93]——

[folio] 74   In Albany Praise the Lord D[ebi]t

———————————— 1708 ————————————

A boy[,] called Decaregjaghiaghquaa's[595] son [*sic*][,] D[ebi]t

1709 24 August 1 bottle of rum @ 1 marten   [5mks]
brother Manes[596] sent for a shirt from the carrying place[597][,] then
sent to him by Jacob d'Schriver[598] @ 4 martens[,] in the presence of
waghrosraa[599][.]

[empty space]

———————————————— 1708 ————————————————

A big[600] Seneca whose name [is] Cawesaet[601] D[ebi]t
12 August 1 piece of strouds at 1 otter   [1 o drawn]
Ditto 1 small blue coat at 1 beaver   [1b drawn]

1710 22 Novemb[er] Canada
Sanakaresen's wife D[ebi]t
1 duffel blanket at 2 beavers   [10b drawn]
1 stroud blanket at 6 beavers
1 piece [of] cord[602] at 2 beavers

[remainder of page is empty]

———— [94] ————

folio 75
A Mohawk who lives in Ca[n]ada[,] his name [is]
D'waerhoeseeRaguqu[a?][603]
A female savage who stays at Abraham Cuyler's[604] is his mother D[ebi]t
1708: 11 Septemb[er]
1 gun at 4 large beavers   [6b drawn, 4cr]
Ditto 1 cask of rum at 2 beavers[.] has returned the gun
Also 10 lb. beaver indebted on a piece of strouds[,]
to wit 10 lb.

1710 22 Novemb[er] A young Onondaga savage who lives in *Canada*[,]
he is the savage of Joh[annes] Lansingh[.][605]

his brother [is] Schaikjoewiesen and he is called Kaghtsweghtjoenie[606]

D[ebi]t

1 pair of stockings at 1 beaver	[4b drawn]
1 duffel blanket at 2 beavers	
1 piece [of cloth] at 1 beaver	

A Cayuga who remains indebted for the merchandise on folio 16[607][,] 1
beaver[,] 2 fishers [and] 4 martens[.]

His name [is] Aedewanienoo			[3b drawn]
1708 Novemb[er] 8 1 pair of stockings @ 1 fisher	fishers		[4mks]
Dit[t]o 1 large shirt at 1 large beaver	martens		[11mks]
Dit[t]o 1 pair of duffel stockings @ 1 fisher			

For a boy who he escorted

1709 18 July ¼ ell of strouds @ 2 martens
Ditto 1 piece [of cloth] @ 2 martens
18 Septemb[er] 1 ell red *plets* @ 1 beaver of a pound
22 Ditto 1 pair of duffel stockings @ 3 martens

[remainder of page is empty]

——[95]——

folio 76	In Albany D[ebi]t

———— 1708 ————

Waghrosraa[608] D[ebi]t[,] remains indebted from folio 19 for his delivered

merchandise 25 beavers	[27b drawn, 7cr]
24 martens	[24mks]
2 otters	[2mks]
1 bearskin	[1B drawn]
2 fishers	[2mks]
1708/9 1 March paid 7 beavers	
1709/ 18 Septemb[er] 1 shirt for a pistol	[rough sketch
Ditto 1 duffel blanket @ 2 beavers	of a pistol]

1714 24 Septemb[er] transported from Hester's small book
1 marten on a shirt   [23mks]
1 duffel blanket at 2 beavers   [4b drawn]
1 marten on a shirt
2 quarters in specie [at] 1 marten
4 martens indebted on a duffel blanket
1 pair of stockings [at] 5 martens
4 martens for gunpowder and lead
1 duffel blanket at 2 beavers
1 shirt at a bag of hops or 4 martens [1 blotted away][,] as has been
credited[609]
1718 Septemb[er] 1 duffel blanket and 1 pair of stockings[,]
together 6 lb. dressed deerskins   [6mks]
1719 February 1 shirt [and] 1 small cask of rum at to wit 6 martens
1719 December 2 bars of lead at 1 marten

[remainder of page is empty]

——[96]——

[folio] 77
                        Transported to the Indian corn book on folio 11
X Watcaroo's sister[610] Catrin D[ebi]t
1708/9 Balanced accounts for all and everything [and] she remains indebted
20 skipple Indian corn that she pays for her last husband Saquanakaij
                                                           Indian corn   [27mks]
1709 26 May rum @ 5 skipple Indian corn
29 June 2 skipple Indian corn indebted on a small coat
29 Novemb[er] 1 blue duffel blanket @ 15 skipple Indian corn
                                                           Indian corn   [20mks, 14cr]
1710 8 March received 9 skipple [Indian corn] in the country
                                                           9 -   [blot]
_____

[empty space]

A Mohawk[,] his name [is] Atsenhaa[611] D[ebi]t
1708/9 3 March a bag of gunpowder @ 1 beaver   [5b drawn, cr]
Ditto 1 shirt [at] 1 beaver
Ditto 2 quarters in specie at 1 marten   [6mks, cr]
1709/10 3 January 1 duffel blanket @ 2 large beavers
21 February 1 bag of gunpowder @ 1 beaver
Ditto lead for 1 marten[.] ditto 1 knife @ 1 quarter   [2mks, cr]
Ditto 1 bottle of rum @ 1 marten[.] ditto 1 bottle of rum @ 1 marten
22 Ditto 1 axe @ 2 martens[,] to wit *op d' lijen* 2 martens
1710 20 May 1 pair of stockings @ 1 beaver   [2b drawn]
30 ditto 1 [bag] gunpowder for a beaver
Dit[t]o 1 piece [of cloth] @ 3 martens   martens [5mks]
1 bar of lead [and] paint for 1 quarter[,] together 1 marten

———— [97] ————

folio 78

See on folio 80

A Mahican[,] his name [is] WaenEnpackes[612][,] remains indebted on
X folio 2 [for] 8½ beaver   [8b and 1 small b drawn, cr]
1708/9 11 January 1 duffel blanket @ 30 guil[ders]
X ditto 1 lb. gunpowder @ 9 guil[ders][,] together   - - - - f 39 =
1709: 12 April had repairs done to his wife's axe
[at] 3 guil[ders]   f 3 =
X ditto 1 cask of rum @ 6 *can* @ 4 guil[ders] each *can* and
[3 guilders for the] cask   f 27 =
17 ditto paid to the amount of 29 martens[,] as has been credited
[for] 8 beavers
19 ditto 1 bottle of rum at 3 guil[ders][,] to wit together   f 3 =
11 May for having repairs made to her scythe @ 1 guil[der] [and]
10 st[i]vers   - - - - f 1 = 10
Ditto 1 duffel blanket for her @ 33 guil[ders] [and] 10 st[i]vers
Ditto she has paid 2 bearskins[,] so that she at this ditto remains
indebted at the balancing of the accounts [for] 30 guil[ders]   f 30 =
She says that she has a Negro boy who she will sell this coming
June[613]
the male savage 1 *can* of rum @   - - - - - - - - - - [f] 4
13 May: for 6 quarters in specie to he himself[,] to wit   - - - - f 9

on payment of 2 pigs[614] that he must deliver to me this fall

11 June 1 quarter in specie	- - - - [f]	1 = 10
Ditto for him[,] 4 [*sic*] *can* of beer @ 2 guil[ders]	f	2
16 June 16 guilders indebted on a stroud blanket		16

———————————————— D[ebi]t ————————————————

A female savage[,] Aeijewasen[615]'s wife's mother, an old female savage,
D[ebi]t on folio 67 she remains indebted 2 martens and a *notas*
of hops
1707 17 April 3 small casks of rum[,] on which she remained
10 martens indebted

Ditto 5 men's shirts and 1 small	33	
shirt[,] together 21 martens	martens	[33mks, 28cr]

she had to sell the shirts @ 4 martens each or a heavy beaver[,]
she can satisfy [the account] with the shirts

[remainder of page is empty]

———— [98] ————

[folio] 79
A female Cayuga savage[,] who wanted to cut my twigs with the axe[616][,]
her son's name [is] Eghnidaa

1708/9 17 Feb[ruary] remained indebted for 2 martens on a stroud blanket	[2mks]
Ditto 1 beaver indebted on a duffel blanket	[3b drawn]
Ditto 1 coat for her son [at] 2 large beavers	

———————————————— 1708/9 ————————————————

17 Feb[ruary]
A female Cayuga savage[,] d'canjadereghtoo's wife[617][,] who was
escorted by the above mentioned female savage

1 cask of rum 2 beavers indebted on a duffel blanket[618]	[2b drawn]
Ditto 2 martens [indebted] on a cask of rum	[2mks]
Ditto borrowed 1 raccoon[619]	[1mk]

See folio 94 [,] where this has been transported

———————————————— 1709 ————————————————

[A] female Seneca savage[, is called] Schadseeaaee[620][,] her father's
name [is] Ceghcaareedawee[621][,] the highest sachem of the Seneca
country _____ Deb[it]
9 August half an *anker* of rum at 4 beavers and 2 *tonieties*
X for 5 beavers[,] together 9 beavers   [9b drawn, cr]
Her front teeth are somewhat sooted[,]
[she is] a stout female savage
1709 29 August
she has paid the 9 beavers and fully satisfied [the account]
29 August 1 pair of stroud stockings @ 1 large beaver
30 Ditto 1 cask of rum @ of 8 *can* @ 2 bearskins and an otter
X because selling rum was prohibited then[622]
X ditto 1 duffel blanket @ 2 beavers   bearskin   [2B drawn, cr]
ditto 1 beaver for 1 pair of [stockings[623]]
ditto 1 shell @ 1 beaver   otters   [1mk]
X Ditto 70 small *tonties* to sell   beavers   [5b drawn, cr]
for me @ 20 beavers   beavers   [20mks, cr]
                                    besides the private debt

          [Entered in the lower right corner:]
          1710 25 August a new agreement on the *tonties*[,]
          [I] have again extended credit to her for them as a private debt
                                                  [10b drawn, cr]

[Below that:]
See folio 94   1710 25 August paid 4 bearskins[,] 1 deerskin
                 [and] 2 elkskins[,] together 6 beavers
                 as has been credited

——— [99] ———

folio 80
Aeiathaa[624][,] a young Cayuga Deb[it]
1709
16 June 1 beaver indebted on a duffel blanket[,] to wit
Ditto 1 beaver [indebted] on a stroud blanket[,] to wit

                                                  [2b drawn]

[empty space]

See below on folio 93

His wife is listed below
Wannapackes[625] a Mahican D[ebi]t remains indebted on folio 78[626]
      74 guil[ders] [and] 10 st[i]vers[,] as may be checked   f 74 = [627]
June
18 ditto 1 small coat @ 20 guil[ders][,] to wit   20 =
20 ditto 1 bottle of rum [@] 3 guil[ders][.] Ditto
      another bottle [@] 3 guil[ders]   6
Dit[t]o kept the bottle @ 1 guilder [and] 10 st[i]vers   1 = 10
1709 September   107 = 10
3 Ditto paid 2 pigs[628] @ 80 guilders
ditto paid 7 guilders for him to Andries Jansen[629] because the
      pig had walked there on the island   73[630]
      Remains to be paid   34 = 10
Ditto 3 guilder[s] [and] 15 st[i]vers in specie   3 = 15
20 Octob[er] a deer[,] to wit I bought the meat from   38 = 05
      him @ 20 guil[ders][,] so that he remains indebted   20
      on this date for the sum of 18 guilders[631]   18 = 5
23 Decemb[er] 24 guil[ders] indebted on a handbelt[632]   24 =
Ditto 6 guilders in specie   6 =
Ditto 1½ ells duffel @ 12 guil[ders] each ell   18 =
Ditto 1 large shirt @ 15 guilders   15 =
1710 June 18
1 raccoon[633] @ 3 guil[ders][,] to wit   3 =
29 ditto 3 *can* of rum @ 4 guil[ders] each *can*[,]
      fetched by his wife[,] to wit   12 =
15 July 2 *can* of rum [fetched] by himself @ 8 guil[ders]   8 =
ditto 1 *can* of rum @ 4 guil[ders]   4 =
                                 108 =

the wife of the above
1709 18 June his wife remains indebted on the same account on folio
78 for 30 guilders[,] to wit   30 =
24 June 1 shirt [@] 7 guilders[,] to wit   7 =
Novemb[er] 1½ ells of *plets* @ 7 guil[ders] each ell   10 = 10
                                47 = 10

See folio 93

[folio] 80

A Cayuga[,] to wit a Seneca who lives in Cayuga

———————————————————— 1709 ————————————————————

18 Septemb[er] the son of Cattquierhoo[634]'s wife is called /
Caghneghtjakoo[635] Deb[it]
1 pair of stroud stockings @ 2 fishers   [2mks]

——

A Cayuga D[ebi]t
1709 18 Septemb[er]
X He is annaedsoenes's brother[,] a gaunt savage
his name [is] / Soeiae / or Osseraecoe[636]
X 1 duffel blanket @ 1 large beaver   [1b drawn, cr]

——

A young Cayuga
Sasiendes D[ebi]t
X 1709 18 Septemb[er]
1 duffel blanket @ large beavers   [3b drawn]
X Ditto 1 pair of stroud stockings
@ 1 large beaver and 2 martens   martens   [2mks]
X He put down[637] his bracelet which he must redeem in the spring[,]
otherwise I can sell it

[folio] 80

1709   Mohawk *Canadeohare*[638] - 1709

—————————————————   —————————————————

3 Octob[er] A female savage who stays at our Susan's[,][639]
[she is] a fair, white savage
she remains indebted for the delivered merchandise on folio 18
7 martens

Ditto [I paid] anew for the value of a pair of stockings for a
beavercoat that she has in the country[.] [I] must pay the remainder
to her when she brings the coat

Ditto 1 small cask of rum | martens [14mks, 10cr]
@ 4 martens[,] to wit | beavers [1b drawn, cr]
1715 May she has paid 1 beaver at 2 martens

[empty space]

[A] Mahican[,] Naghnacamet[640]
1709 remains indebted for the delivered beavers
merchandise on folio 5 martens [14mks]
14 martens otters
Ditto 1 duffel blanket @ 30 guilders f 30 =

[remainder of page is empty]

——[102]——

folio 81 In Albany Debtors

——— 1709 ———

1709 Sahaquesquass[641][,] a Mahican		f
remains indebted on folio 8 2 beavers and		
45 guilders in specie[,] to wit	[2b drawn, 1cr]	45 =
23 June 5 guilders indebted on 1 shirt		5 =
Ditto 5 guil[ders] indebted on 1 pair of stockings		5 =
Ditto for silver money from mother [at] 1 guilder		1 =
23 Decemb[er] paid 1 beaver[,] as has been credited		
1710 18 May 1 shirt @ 15 guilders		15 =
12 July 10 guild[ers] indebted on 2 pairs of blue stockings[,]		
to wit blue stockings		9 = 10[642]
1712/3 Janu[ary] 25 paid in skins for 48 guild[ers]		

| + + + + | + + + | | |[643] – [1b drawn]

[remainder of this page is empty]

—— [103] ——

[folio] 82   [A] Mohawk who lives in Seneca country

Saakadesendee[644] D[ebi]t
1709 1 Septemb[er]
1 beaver indebted on 2 stroud blankets   [3b drawn]
Ditto 1 bag of gunpowder @ 1 beaver
Ditto 1 pair of stockings @ 1 beaver
[I/one] must query him in person [to determine] how much more he
owes[,] for it is not listed[645]

[empty space]

Ossenant[,] a female savage D[ebi]t   Seneca   beavers
1709 1 Septemb[er]
41 *tonieties* to sell on my account for 10 beavers[,]
to wit   10
1710 4 April
1 cask of rum @ 1 beaver[,] to wit   [2b drawn]

15 May 1 cask of rum @ 1 beaver
Ditto 1 bottle of rum @ 1 marten   [1mk]

Dekaeont[,] a female savage   Seneca
1709 1 Septemb[er]
70 *tonieties* to sell for my account
at 13[646] beavers[,] to wit   13
Ditto 1 otter indebted on a small coat[,] to wit   [1 0 drawn]

[remainder of page is empty]

——[104]——

folio 83   [A] Seneca in *Canosedaken*[647]   D[ebi]t 1709

Canowaacightuea Deb[it]
1709 2 Septemb[er]   [outlines of a sketch][648]
X 1 beaver indebted on a coat from my body[,]
[it was] a French coat   Beavers   [1b drawn]
Ditto 1 pair of stroud stockings   otters   [1 0 drawn]
X at 1 large beaver and 1 marten   martens   [1mk]
[has been] paid

A female Onondaga savage
1709 Septemb[er]
Jawaaneehae D[ebi]t 1 shirt @ 3 martens   [5mks]
1710 30 March
1 cask of rum @ 2 martens
Ditto 1 shirt @ 1 large beaver   [1b drawn]

Anniethaa D[ebi]t in the house of Coghcaaradawen⁶⁴⁹
[she?] stays at Joh[annes] Rosebom's⁶⁵⁰
Seneca
1709 Septemb[er]
2 pairs of white baize stockings @ 2 large beavers   [2b drawn]

Sonieno: stays at Waiesaa⁶⁵¹

Osiestout D[ebi]t 1 Seneca[,] correctly said Sonienone
*Saront*⁶⁵²
1709 9 Septemb[er]
2 martens indebted on 1 cask of rum   marten[s] [2mks]
1 pair of stockings [for?⁶⁵³] her son @ 1 beaver
1710 June paid this beaver   [2b drawn, 1cr]
Ditto 1 shirt @ 1 beaver
Ditto 1 piece [of cloth] @ 1 otter   [1 0 drawn]

—— [105] ——

folio 84
          A Seneca who lives in *Canosedaken* 1709 10 Septemb[er]

Canossaase⁶⁵⁴ D[ebi]t
Sep[tembe]r
1 red duffel blanket @ 1 large beaver   [1b drawn]
Ditto 1 otter indebted on 1 cask of rum   otter   [1 0 drawn]
1710 18 August
1 marten indebted on a casks of rum   [1mk]

A Cayuga[,] AnniesSadde D[ebi]t
1709 15 Septemb[er]
1 pair of stockings @ 1 beaver   [1b drawn]

An Oneida[,] Orghiakeuwaghkaa[,] he is an adopted brother
of Canaghcoonia[655] D[ebi]t
1709 21 Octob[er]
1 pair of stroud stockings @ 5 martens   [5mks]
Ditto 1 lb. of gunpowder @ 1 fisher   [1mk]

A Mahican boy[,] OsSaawaawaens[656][,] he is the son of our female
savage D[ebi]t
1709 24 Octob[er]
1 duffel blanket @ 30 guilders   - - - - - - - f 30
2 lb. of gunpowder @ 9 guilders each lb   - - - - - - - f 18
1710 24 Feb[ruary]
paint for 1 marten[,] gunpowder for 2 martens[,]
together 3 martens   [3mks]
[empty] lb. of gunpowder @ 9 guilders each lb[,]
to wit f [empty]

——[106]——

Naghnakamet[658]'s wife D[ebi]t
balanced all accounts with her so that she remains indebted to me on
this di[tto] 50 martens and 5 beavers
24 Octob[er]
Ditto 1 bottle of rum [at] 1 marten   martens   [50mks]
                                                 Martens   [1mk]
                                                 Beavers   [5b drawn]

[One-third of the page is empty]

1709 A Mahican[,] he is the son of our female savage's sister[,]
who[659] she has with Jan the savage[660][,] a boy D[ebi]t
1 pair of stockings @ 4 martens   [4mks]

Rabeeke the female[661] savage D[ebi]t
1724 April
1 small cask of rum for 7 skipple Indian corn

Kanosquisaekhe's[662] wife D[ebi]t
1 small cask of rum for 6 skipple Indian corn

Knosquisackje's wife Debit
1726 May
1 shirt for 6 skipple Indian corn

Cornelis's wife Debit   Aria's son[663]
1 small cask and 1 bottle of rum for 8 skipple Indian corn

——[107]——

folio 87   In Albany D[ebit]   January 1: 1709/10

Daniell[664] a Mohawk[,] who is the son of Waghrosraa's wife[.]
Transported from folio 44 where he remains indebted for delivered
merchandise 23 martens[,] to wit
1709/10 January   martens [32mks, 20cr]
2 guilders in specie
21 Feb[ruary] Ditto 1 shirt @ 4 martens
Ditto 2 small shirts @ 2 martens each[,] to wit 4 martens
Ditto 2 lb. shot @ 1 marten
Ditto 1 bag of gunpowder @ 1 beaver   [1b drawn, cr]
1710 18 May paid the value of 1 beaver and 20 martens
19 Ditto 1 shirt @ 4 martens   martens [12mks]
Ditto 1 shirt @ 4 martens   martens [10mks]
20 Ditto 1 pair of stockings @ 4 martens   [1b drawn]
7 Septemb[er] his stepfather[665] [fetched] 1 pair of white stockings
@ 4 martens
Ditto 1 pair of stockings at 1 beaver[,] which was given to him as
payment when he proceeded to Canada with my merchandise

Octob[er] 1 pair of stroud stockings at 5 martens
[and] 1 bottle of rum [at] 1 m[arten]
1714 27 September transported here from Hester's small book[,]
28 martens and 14 skipple Indian corn

	martens	[28mks]
	Indian corn	[14mks]

Areja[666] paid 20 skipple Indian corn to Niecolaes Schuijler[667]
for Arjantie Wendell[668] from the female savages
by the French female savage[669][,] who has died[:] 3[,] remain 2
& by Rabeckha[670]   4 skipple
by Catrien[671]   5 skipple
by Cannasqusakje[672]   5 skipple
by Essaraes's wife[673]   3 skipple
paid for the female savages   20 skipple

——[108]——

[folio] 88[674]

An Onondaga 1709/10 January D[ebi]t

NasaeDekee[,] he is a young savage[,] Atsakanhaa[675] is his father
17010 [sic] 18 June
1 beaver indebted on 1 blue duffel blanket[,] to wit

[1b drawn, cr] paid

[empty space]

--- 1710 ---

[A] Mahican D[ebi]t - f

MassenantSeet D[ebi]t
20 Feb[ruary]
2 lb. of gunpowder [at] 10 guild[ers]
                [each pound] ------- f 20
3 lb. shot [at] 1 guil[der] each lb ---------- " 4:10   --- f 33:10
1 knife @ 3 guild[ers] ----------------- " 3
2 bars of lead @ --------------------- " 6
1 small coat @ 6 martens   [6mks]

1 pair of stockings[,] 2 ells [long]
@ 9 guild[ers] each ell[,] 18 guil[ders]   f 18
                                                                            ――――――
                                                                            f 51:10

[remainder of page is empty]

―――[109]―――

[folio] 89

                        In Albany D[ebi]t   guilders

――

[A] Mahican
Correlaer[676] the savage remains indebted   himself
from the small book 48 guilders   f 48 =
his wife D[ebi]t   the female savage
by transport[,] she remains indebted
in the small book   f 69"00"

[empty space]

――

                        A female Mohawk savage
Tanawaneke[677]'s wife D[ebi]t
1710 6 April
1 shirt @ 1 beaver   [2b drawn]
Ditto 1 pair of stockings @ 1 beaver

[remainder of page is empty]

[folio] 90
An Oneida   In Albany   9 June 1710

SiekaghquaRere D[ebi]t
1 cask of rum at 4 martens   [6mks]
Ditto his wife's son[,] he is called Onnakaeree D[ebi]t
1 shirt @ 2 martens[,] to wit

[empty space]

Canada
X Carghiedsiekooe[678] D[ebi]t remains indebted on folio 62
28 beavers and 9 quarters   quarters [9mks]
X Beavers   [28 numbered[679] b drawn]
X Beavers   [5½b drawn]
1710 23 July
1 shirt at 1½ beaver[.] ditto borrowed 1 beaver[680]
24 Ditto 1 white duffel blanket at 3 beavers
Ditto 1 cask of pure rum at 1½ beaver   [1½b drawn]
      [I, or we, have] remitted his whole debt

[folio] 91
            In New Albany[681] Deb[it] 1710

1710 June
Caheghtsiede[682] D[ebi]t on folio 65 [.] there he remains indebted
12 beavers and 11 martens[,] and 9 martens for his wife
as one can see there
                  Beavers   [12b drawn, 3cr]
                  Martens   [11mks]
                  for his wife[,] martens [9mks]

[remainder of the page is empty]

———[112]———

folio 92

Albany   28 June 1710   D[ebi]t

Dewadierhoe[683] who lives in *Thussighrondie*[684]
Ditto 2½ stroud blanket @ 10 heavy beavers
See below[,   for an account]
for which he is a guarantor   [16b drawn]
Ditto 1 duffel blanket at 2 beavers
Ditto 1 stroud blanket @ 4 beavers
    1 pair stroud stockings @ 1 bearskin
                                         bearskin [2B drawn][685]
    [account cr = paid]

[empty space][686]

1710 June[.] A savage[,] who was escorted by the above [Indian]
    who is also a guarantor for him[,] his name [is]
    hoedsewerke[687] in Dutch[.] A raccoon *gelijt*   [1mk]
    D[ebi]t
    2 ells of strouds @ 3 beavers   [4b drawn, cr]
Ditto 1 beaver indebted on a duffel blanket
    [account cr = paid]

1718 May 18 Wanapakes[688] D[ebi]t   xxxxxxxxxxx//////[689]

balanced all accounts[,] old and new[,] and he remains indebted
126 guild[ers][,] for which he himself also carries a bill
Dite [sic] also [balanced accounts] with his wife[,]
who remains indebted 127 guild[ers][,]
for which she also has a bill - - - - together   f 253
                                              xxxxxxxxxxx///////

——[113]——

folio 93

In Albany D[ebi]t 1710

Wannanpackes D[ebi]t[,] his wife below this[690]
Before this[,] on folio 80 [,] his delivered merchandise for which he
remains indebted the sum of f 108 guilders[,]
                                              to wit " 108"
1710 28 August
1 guilder in specie - - - - -   " 001"
7 Septemb[er]
1 gun at 1½ fat deer of this fall
Ditto for repairs to the lock of his gun   "   2"
                                                      f 111

1711 May 8 paid 25 guild[ers] on this [account]   " 25
                                        Remains f 86
                  Paid 4 skipple Indian corn for   " 12
                                        Remains f 74
1713 May 17 paid 43 guilders   " 43
                                        Remains " 31
1714 5 lb. beaver paid at f 6 [each] lb   " 30
                                        Remains f   1

          [account cr = paid]

Wannanpackes[,] from above[,] his wife Deb[it]
The delivered merchandise is listed before this on folio 80
She remains indebted the sum of f 47 guild[ers] [and]
                                  10 st[i]vers f 47"10

1710 24 Septemb[er]
2½ ells of *plets* at 8 gui[lders] each ell   " 20
10 Novemb[er] ¼ ell of duffel [and] 1 quarter[,] together   "   5"10
                                                                      f 73

8 skipple Indian corn paid on this [account]
                                          [at] f3 each skipple   " 24
                                                     Remains   " 49
1713 May 17 she pays 9 guilders   "   9
                                                     Remains   " 40
          1 pair of stockings @   12
          [account cr = paid]

————[114]————

1710 / folio 94   In Albany   [A] young Cayuga savage
_____

5 August
Soekajonthaa's brother[,] Carrahoedee Deb[it]
1 pair of white *plets* stockings at 1 bearskin   [1B drawn]

               ·   [empty space]

_____   _____

a female Seneca savage
Cahenquathaa[691][,] she is Caghqueriedawee[692]'s daughter D[ebi]t
She remains indebted on folio 79[693] / 11 beavers [and] 1 otter
1710 25 Augus[t]
ditto 3 casks of rum at 2 bearskins   Beavers   [11b drawn]
and 2 beavers   otters   [1mk]
Ditto 1 duffel blanket at 2 bearskin[s]   Beavers   [2b drawn]
                                           bearskin[s] [4B drawn]
Ditto lead @ 1 parchskin[694]   parchmentskin [1 drawn?, blot]

               [remainder of page is empty][695]

folio 38 [*sic*]
Onghnedicha's[696] wife[,] May 1703 she remains
indebted

	quarters	[5mks]
	M[artens]	[40mks, cr]
	Martens	[8mks]
A female savage	Bearskin	[1mk, cr?]
[who she escorted]	1706 October these 15 skipple indebted	
a small	Indian corn	[15mks, 4cr]

cask of rum for 5 martens[,] for whom she is guarantor   [5mks, cr]
4 July a small cask of rum for a heavy beaver
Sept[ember] 4 bottles of rum at 4 martens with which she filled her
small cask   B[eavers]   [2b drawn, 1cr]
December a duffel blanket at a beaver
1704 July 8 2 martens [indebted] on a coat
ditto 5 quarters indebted on rum
1 cask of rum @ 7 martens
1704/5 February 1 cask of rum @ 6 martens[.] 1705 May paid a beaver
1705 3 July 4 martens indebted on 1 cask of rum[.] 1 marten
[indebted] on a cask of rum[.] 1 ma[rt]en [indebted] on 1 bottle of
rum
1706 July 2 martens indebted on a stroud blanket
her younger sister has accepted to pay 60 skipple Indian corn by
aiewase's wife[697]
        [account cr = paid]

X Aeijwasee's wife Debit   [12 hands short = cr]
1703 at the balancing of the accounts remains indebted 7 martens
X *dieto* [*sic*] she remains indebted 4 martens on a stroud blanket
X a blue coat [fetched] by her mother for 3 beavers
But on ditto she paid one [beaver][,] 2 beavers still remain

X July a cask of	Beavers [2b drawn, cr] [1B drawn]
rum for a bearskin	Martens [34mks, 15cr]
[D]itto 3 martens on a shirt	quarters [2mks]
	Bears [1mk]

[Ja]nuary: 2 *notasse* of hops indebted on a cask of rum
d[itt]o: a coat for 3 martens in wampum
January[,] the hops has been paid
1704 May 4 bottles of rum at 3 martens
Sept[ember] a cask of rum @ hops [empty][,] as one can calculate

the cask contained 6 *can*[.] ditto 1 pair of stockings @ 2 martens
[d]it[t]o 1 shirt @ 1 marten and a quarter
ditto 1 quarter for which she had her child ride[698] 1704/5 February
her mother [fetched] 1 cask of rum @ 6 martens
May indebted a bearskin on 1 cask of rum

—— [116] ——

folio 39   Debtor in Albany
Aeijewasee[699]'s wife[,] she is a short female savage
1701 17 July extended credit to a female savage[,]
her husband's name [is] Aeijwasee
X she remains indebted at the balancing of the accounts
14 martens and 2 skipple Indian corn
the same ditto[,] 1 shirt for a bearskin
28 December also indebted 1 marten on a cask of rum

1703 March a shirt for a beaver	bearskin	[1B drawn, cr]
D[itt]o: a cask of rum for 6 martens	beavers	[3b drawn, 1cr]
[the savage[700]] who she escorted	martens	[21mks, cr]
also a cask of rum for 5 martens[,] for		
which she is guarantor	martens	[5mks, cr]

her husband remained 2 beavers indebted on a blue coat
Paid a shirt[701]

[. . . . = wiped] Oogeroyoke's daughter[,] a young female savage
who is Cendeijughquae's wife[702]
1703 30 Decemb[er]

| an ell of duffel at | Martens | [5mks] |

1701 [Aeijewase's wife   debit[,] at the balancing of the accounts = cr]
remains indebted 7 martens
1702 30 May 4 martens indebted on 1 stroud blanket

---

30 December his mother fetched a coat for 3 beavers
on ditto she gave one [beaver] and her daughter must give 2 in the

| spring | B[eavers] | [3b drawn, cr] |

Onoghredieha[703]'s wife debit
she remains indebted at the balancing of the accounts

| 7 martens on a stroud blanket | M[artens] | [11mks] |

[and] 4 martens[,] together makes

1701 28 December Onogradieha himself
X 4 ells of *plets* to make a coat with
for a large elkskin: ditto has also paid
a marten on 1 pair of stroud stockings
1703 May
one elkskin remaining: 4 July when he went to Canada with
Aquerase[704][,] a pair of stockings for 9 guil[ders]
when he returned a coarse blanket for 1 beaver
and 2 martens

——[117]——

f[olio] 40
1702 the sister of Aeijewasee[705]'s wife Deb[it]
3 martens indebted on a stroud blanket   [3mks, 2cr]
1704 paid 2 martens[.] 1 marten remains

A pair of *plets* stockings [at] 4 martens
ditt[o] a knife at 1 quarter
1703 August
Aqueras[706] Debit 4 martens indebted on a pair of stroud stockings
Ditto a quarter for buying meat[707]   M[artens] [13mks, 4cr]
a quarter in *gem*[p][,] together a marten   quarters   [1mk]
1 bottle of rum at 1 marten
1704 May his mother paid 4 martens for his wife
20 Septemb[er] a bottle of rum for a marten
Ditto a bottle of rum at a marten
ditto 2 bottles of rum at 2 martens
————————————————— [thin line] ——————————————

Ragel[708] the female savage Debit 1703 : 15 April
2 kettles for 6 martens or the value of 6 martens[,]
but then I must give her 1 quarter
the two [kettles] weighed 2½ lb[,] if she would bring other things
then one can calculate [their value]
June she has paid [so that] we are even

See folio 55
1701 28 December OnoghRediehae[709] Debit   quarters   [1mk]
4 ells of *plets* for a large elkskin   elkskin   [1e drawn]

1703 August a coarse blanket for a beaver and 2 martens
[d]itto 4 bars of lead [at] 2 martens   bearskin   [1B drawn]
[di]tto 4 bottles of rum   beavers   [6b drawn]
[at] 4 martens[.] rum for [1] quarters [*sic*]⁷¹⁰   martens   [16mks]
paid[.] ditt[o] gunpowder for   quarters   [1mk]
2 martens[.] 1704/5 February 1 beaver indebted on 1 stroud blanket
9 August 1 duffel blanket for a bearskin and 2 martens
ditt[o] a shirt for 4 martens
ditto 2 bars of lead at a marten
[d]itto 1 bag of gunpowder @ a beaver[,]
2 bars of lead [at] a marten
[O]ctober a beaver indebted on a duffel blanket [di]tto 1 bag of
gunpowder @ 1 beaver[.] ditto 2 bars of lead @ 1 marten
[di]tto 1 pair of stockings @ 3 martens[.] Ditto 1 bar of lead [at] 1
quarter

—— [118] ——

folio 41

Memorial
1698 17 April Me and Uncle Hans⁷¹¹ together bought at
Barboores⁷¹² 1 piece of strouds for 11 lb   lb - s - d
and 2 pieces of white goods
[at] 26 shilling each piece[,] together   # 13 -12
1 piece of duffel for 6 [shillings] and 3 pennies
each yard[,] makes 44 yards long[,]
makes in money 13 lb [and] 16 *schelng*⁷¹³   # 13 -16 - –
                                         27 - 8

For myself[,] besides this[,] 112 lb of lead   lb - s - d
for 26 *shelnghen*⁷¹⁴   # 1 - 6
For which I put down 128 lb beavers
at his house for the merchandise until the price
of beavers improves

Corneles [the] savage Deb[i]t [A] Mahican

——————————————————————— ———————————————————————

Cees⁷¹⁵ the savage Debit 3 *can* of rum @ 4 guilders[,]
3 bottles [and] 1 bottle[,] together makes 24 guilders[.]
3 guilders for a bottle of rum[,] makes 27 guilders[.]
received 11 guilders[,] 16 [guilders] remain
At the balancing of the accounts he remains indebted 20 guilders
[and] 3 gui[lders]

dit[to] a [empty]

Me and Uncle Hans[716] together had 3 pieces of duffel from
Abram de Pijst[er?][717] for 6 *scheln*[718] the yard

X Sonyowaene[719] or the bold [or naughty] boy[720] Debit
X 1703/4 29 Febr[uary] a bottle of rum at 2 quarters
Paid

X Aederijhoores[721] or Flatfoot[722] Debit 1704: 29 February
X a wide comb[723] at 2 quarters[,] [which he has] paid the first of
March[,] so that we are even

1704 July 9 Cees[724] the savage remains indebted at the balancing
of the accounts 20 guilders[.] ditto a bottle of rum
@ 3 guilders[,] makes f 23 = 00 =

The one package contains 38 lb for me[,] and among the beavers that
are with Jan[,] 32 lb is [for me][,] makes   38
                                                              32
                                                              70

1703 30 December ooghreijocken's daughter[, who is]
Cendeiughquae's wife[725] and lives in the upper castle[726]
a piece of duffel at 5 martens: Martens [5mks]

		Rabecke[727] the female savage must give 6 skipple
		Indian corn
H [. . . . ?]	27	
	11	
	16	

——— [119] ———

f[olio] 42   1698 ditto thirty lb current
                                money of this[728]
I[,] Harman[u]s Wendell[729] received of this merchandise

                                                      lb - s - d
½ piece of duffel for 6 s[hilling] each yard   # 6 - 10 - 0

X 50 lb gunpowder for 3 lb [and] 10 s[hilling]   #   3 - 10 - 0
112 lb lead for 26 shil[ling]   1 - 6 - 0
½ piece of baize for 3-3 pen[nie]s the yard

                                                10 yards long   1   12
            [this account lightly cr]   12   18

    [Page is filled with small computations and scribbles on left and right side]

                    warm Transport
                    Warm transport
                 hem harm De[bi]t   [G?]antz
          har harm Harmanes   Transport
                    Wendel
                harmanus Wendel
                         Harmanis
                         Wendel Debit for
                         3 *can* of pure rum

1698 9 May in addition for me 4 small shirts for 9 guild[ers]
         each[,] together 18 shilling   / - 18
         [entry cr = paid]

Rum   Rum   For the goods to Jan Ca[de/ele?]
B
Eevert Wendel   H   Harmanis
Rum Rum 24 - 18   Wendell is my name
Rum   13 - 10   Jeroninus
            11 - 8   A
                          Evert Wendel   28 - 11 - 7
                              Evert Wendel
            Eevert Wendel   Evert Jeronis Wendel

X A female savage from the farthest castle[730] Debit
1703 January 8: she stays at Johannis Rosebom's[.][731]
She is a blackish female savage
X a three-*can*'s cask of rum at 4 martens
and she must return the cask[,] or otherwise 5 marte[ns]
She went to Oneida to sell the rum
1704 May she has paid

A white female savage from the upper castle[732]
X she stays at our Suschan's[733] Debit
X [cask = cr] rum for 4 martens   1704 June paid

X Area's wife Groetie [I?] must have from her
25 skipple Indian corn[.] the small old female savage[734]
who was escorted by her must give 10 skipple Indian corn

—— [120] ——

[This is the last page of the book; 121 is inside of back cover. Page 120 is filled with small scribbles and notes. Also, it appears that lines were written over each other. Transcribed only what remains legible.]

[First, two items written across each other:]
[1st]
That Joohanus
van Allen[735] Debit
to me Evert Wendel old[736] and of Marija van Thrijght[737]
van Alenijnen
Clas Luyckesen[738] debit
for 3 *can* of rum
[2nd]
Wierom Cast the child
in Albanij 1703 Ictober [*sic*] 3
Aerijen hotse[739]'s daughter Debit
a duffel blanket for a bearskin
Also a small cask of rum for a *notas* [of] hops
        [inverted line:]
        We underwrit[ten] that we

D[itt]o Canoseedickhae[740]'s wife
Debit a bottle of rum
for 1 marten fetched by Adohoo[741]

D[itt]o Dekaenijhae[742] Debit 2 bars of lead [at] 1 mart[en]

[related to 2nd entry?:]
S[e]ptember [13?] my husband
did arrive [or: arrived well?] and the [*sta*?]
                                Jaebroer
                                    JaeBrer.

[Then, a second set of intertwined writings:]
[1]   *Johannis Schuijler*[743] *Meijer Esqr of de sitie*
                        of Albanij to the schrijef[744] *constabels*
                        x oder her maijstis ofesers crijester cueen[745]
                              4 ells at 3 guilders each ell   £   12:00[746]
                              8 *can* of rum at 3 guilders each   £   24:00
                                                                        £   24:00

                     [1?] January 15 ell ell [*sic*] black crepe
                              at 3 guilders [and] 10 stivers   £   52:10
                              24 ells of strouds fetched by
                              Your Honor's sister
                              at 18 guilders each ell   £ 332:00
                     18 Febr[uary] 16 ell cloth[747] at 4 guilders
                              [and] 10 sti[vers] each ell   £   72:[...]
                                     mistakes excepted   492
                                     Cr[edit] Evert Wendel

[2] [Sunday?] 9 May [I/we] have
settled and agreed
with Jan de Doo[748]

[Interspersed within previous two, another:]
Johannis Doo[749] Debit 1703
            that Joh:
December
        D[itto?]
Wijender Reijten
that Jan C . . .

[At various points following remarks inserted:]
- thirty lb current money of this [province]
- anno 1704 thirty
- Wijender Rijeten
- that Joh Clasd

[Page ends with remnant of contract, involving Jan and Pieter Douw:]
So we have recognized that
              as the truth[,]
              without craft or guile

wandert
and so on   We[,] undersigned[,] acknowledge to have agreed with
    Jae br   each other in the way and manner as follows[,]
                 namely so do acknowledge
                 Jan to have bought and Pieter Doo[750] to have
                 sold the aforementioned Jan Doo[751]'s ho[use]
                 and lot situated in the Joncker street

and that for the sum of one hundred and fifty
pounds current money of this province[752]
[Diagonally, at the left side of the contract, but cr:]
my house is included therein[753]

——[121]——

[Inside of back cover. Page filled with small number of computations, meaning
unclear.]

[[On top of page:] Soghsweedes a Mohawk
                            [set of numbers, inverted]   536
                                                                      3618
                                                            with the
                                                                 m
                                                            with th' the

[Vertically, along left side of page:]
                    Jaakaajansoo[754]

[A list of twenty-eight Dutch names is placed vertically along the bottom of the
page. Its meaning remains unclear,[755] but members of many of Albany's most
established families are included. The list predates 1708, and is probably from
1704–05; see notes with Johannes Schuyler, Jackob (Jacob[us]) Schuyler, and
[C]oen Rat (Coenraet) Ten Eyck. Transcribed what was legible. No dates, no
signatures or marks; all individuals are men.]

Johannes Schuijler[756]
Claes Luijckesen[757]
Melgert Van der Po[e]l[758]
Niecklas Blecker[759]
Evert Wendell[760]
Joh[annes] Vinhagel[761]
[D]erck Van Der Hijden[762]
Joh[annes] Lansingh[763]
Eysack Lans[i]ngh[764]
Anthony Coster[765]
Jackop Schuijler[766]
Gosen Van Schaijek[767]
Wellem Van Hallen[768]
Harmen Rijckman[769]
Barent Stats[770]
Anthonij Van Schaijek Juny.r[771]
Anthonij Van Schaijk[772]

Jackop Visser[773]
Hendereck ffroman[774]
Wouter Kwackenbos[775]
[Wouter ffroman = cr][776]
Pietter Winen[777]
Joh[annes] Wendel[778]
[Da]niel Cettelum[779]
Pieter Bronck[780]
[C]orneles Van Den Bergh[781]
[C]oen Rat Ten Eyck[782]   Constabell
Robert Lievenston[783]

[Outside, back cover]
[Only remaining legible word is *Welden* [= savages].]

End of Manuscript

Notes to the
Translation

1. The meaning of this term remains unclear.

2. Wendell lists the affiliation of this individual as *sounos*, and *souwenos* farther down the same page. He is the only individual from this account book identified in such fashion. He has been incorporated as the only (likely) Shawnee individual in TABLE 1 of the introduction. Tackkarores reappears farther down the same page as Tankarores.

3. This word is hard to decipher. My closest approximation is B[et?]ta[n/lt?], which resembles *betalt*, a word the Wendells used at times to mean *betaald* (paid).

4. *Ackdes* may be a rendering of the Dutch word for lizard (*hagedis*) (J. B. den Besten, pers. comm., April 2004). Another instance where the Wendells inserted a remark on their clients' tattoo (a bird) is farther down this page. Also see page [65] (a snake), and page [68] (unspecified). On pages [47], [50], [51], [57], [68] (a different case than the one mentioned in the preceding sentence), and [79], the lack of a tattoo is listed as a distinguishing feature. All cases refer to men, and are limited to Onondaga, Cayuga, and Seneca men (except for the Shawnee, farther down this page). See the introduction.

5. Perhaps continued in the next account.

6. The two Dutch individuals and their contract, of which a fragment of the introductory sentence is listed here, are repeated on the last page of the account book, page [121]. Jan/Johannes van Alen was the youngest son of Pieter, one of two brothers with that surname who first settled in Albany. Johannes died in 1750; see Pearson, *First Settlers of Albany*, 112.

7. "Karehade in 'modern' Mohawk is karenhate' or 'a tree is there'" (GM).

8. This is the first of seventeen cases where native customers left an item (or items) as a security against a debt. For an overview and brief discussion of these cases, see the introduction (and TABLE 15).

9. No folio 17 has been located.

10. From the context, this name may refer to an Indian settlement within the area where the Wendells positioned their commercial activities. Due to the diverse ethnicity of the various clients on this first page, it is difficult to determine which Indian group or subdivision Metstaeharae belongs to. It is possibly a reference to the nominally Mohawk village Eskahare in the Schoharie Valley, approximately twenty-four miles south of Tiononderoge (often referred to as the lower castle). Snow describes this locality in the Schoharie Valley as the Bohringer site, inhabited from 1713 (or before) to around 1773, *Mohawk Valley Archaeology*, 471–72, 481–83. The woman has been incorporated in TABLE 1 of the introduction, as of unknown origins.

11. Wendell used this to indicate a person. It could be a nickname or alias.

12. Second *a* inserted. For the same individual in a different account, see note 3 on the same page.

13. Evidently, the Shawnee drew a turtle. See PLATE XII. A note card by William C. Sturtevant and T. J. Brasser with a photograph of this mark describes it as "sketch of a bird"; see Wendell, Account book with Sketches, NAA, Photo Lot 81R.

14. Immediately below this statement there are some scribbles which may have been an attempt to write a name. More likely, "mark" refers to a cross-like symbol at the bottom of the page. See PLATE XII.

15. See PLATE XII. A notecard dated January 1966, by Sturtevant and Brasser concerning a photograph of this sketch, describes it as "apparently show[ing a] facial tattoo and hairdress," ibid.

16. "This is a truncated form of Mohawk 'othore'ke', or 'north.' This does not seem to be a personal name" (GM).

17. All names in this "register" have corresponding accounts in the first pages of this account book, with the exception of Wanckpaee. Applying a basic linguistic distinction (BR), described in the section "traders" of the introduction, it becomes apparent that the Wendells (in this case, Harmanus) used Mahican as a generic term for a number of Algonquian-speaking groups. Mahican names cannot have an *r* or an *l* in them, of which there are several in the "register." Thus, it is very unlikely that, for instance, Walitgaes and his brother Malsik were Mahican.

18. No page number listed. Neither this individual, nor the debt, have been located in this account book.

19. This may be "Maghah, alias Magtsaput upper sachem of the Katskill," see the note with Naernis on page [7]. He does not appear in the account book as actively maintaining an account with the Wendells.

20. It seems likely that this is the same individual as listed in the "register" as Sesecaet, and who appears quite prominently in the account book. He is also listed as Seeckaet and Secatt on pages [10] and [11].

21. In Dutch, Cees/Kees was (and is) a common derivation of Cornelus, Cornelis, and Cornelius. Other accounts with the name Cees appear on page [118], and they are also dated July of 1704. An additional account, in August 1704, of Cees (but not his wife) is farther down this page. It is not likely that he is the same as Korneles, Cornelis, and Corneles, whose wife also trades on an account on page [106]; but if he is the same as Tanawaneke (which is possible), his Mohawk wife appears on page [109] (see the notes there). With the same stipulation regarding Cees/Corneles, his mother can be added: she shared a small account with him on page [19]. Since this Cees, mentioned in two accounts on this page, and the one in one of the accounts on page [118] are cross-referenced, and appear in a Mahican environment, he has been counted as a Mahican individual in TABLE 1 of the introduction. This does not apply to Korneles (page [19]), Cornelis (page [106]), and Tanawaneke (page [109]); they have been incorporated as one Mohawk individual.

22. Wamosie reappears as Wamossij farther down page [2], in 1704.

23. On page [118] accounts of Corneles and Cees do appear, dated July of 1704. The total debt in the last account is twenty-three guilders. Consequently, this account on page [2] must be of a later date since it is dated August 1704. It is unlikely that the appearances of a Corneles and /or his wife on pages [19] and [106], and Tawanake on page [109], refer to the same person, since these occur in a Mohawk context. There are no other elements to link the Mahican Cees to the Mohawk Corneles. See the note with Corneles on page [19].

24. Twenty-six vertical marks have been crossed out, suggesting this was the price at which Wendell bought the blanket.

25. No corresponding account has been located.

26. In eight cases, the Wendells described native customers as "white" (*blanck*; once *blank*). For a listing and discussion, see the introduction.

27. The Dutch reads *varcken* (modern Dutch, *varken*), "pig" or "hog." Other than this case in 1704, the other occurrence of pigs are found on page [97] (repeated on page [99]), and can be dated to 1709. In both this and the later case, the accounts relate to Mahican individuals (probably in this case, and more clearly in the second), and the swine are listed as the natives' debt.

28. The word specifying the type of pig or hog is hard to decipher. My first transcrip-

tion was *cnuu*, which has no retrievable significance. Janny Venema points out that it can also be read as *cuu* (pers. comm., February 2004). A *keu*, for pig, has several meanings in Dutch: pig, young pig, and female pig. In various regions in the Netherlands, it was used predominantly to indicate a young pig. Combined with the requirement in the entry, that the other pig must be three years old, the latter appears to be an appropriate interpretation.

29. He is listed in the "register" as Jan *de Willt*, and (if it concerns the same individual) is mentioned with the same name on page [106]. The latter entry occurred in 1709, a much later date. He is not the same individual as Jan Seeps in the "register," and on page [5]. Records show several other Mahican/Schaghticoke individuals with the given name Jan (e.g., Jan de Backer, Jan Coneel); see Dunn, *The Mohicans and their Land*, 316. His wife's son, Waskaemp, has his own accounts. He has one immediately below this one, of a later date, and another on page [5] dated 1701; the wife's account follows that of her son. Her sister's account is on page [4], and the latter's husband's on page [5]. He is also mentioned in his wife's account on page [4].

30. The name Waskaemp does not occur elsewhere, but it is likely that he has a small additional account on page [106], and that he fetched goods for his aunt (his mother's sister) in 1701 (on page [5]).

31. Listed as Pamolet in the "register." The *l*'s in both versions of the name make it unlikely that he was Mahican (BR).

32. The entry seems illogical in its exact transcribed form and translation. It is likely that Harmanus Wendell made a mistake, and intended to record that the customer had replaced his surety, an old blanket, with a new blanket. One arrives at that conclusion by changing the word him (*hem* in the manuscript.) into he (*hij*). For a similar case, see the note on page [16].

33. The three women in this account have been incorporated into TABLE 1 of the introduction, as of unknown origins.

34. A "hand" was a common length measurement in the commercial exchanges between Europeans and Indians. Measuring around four inches, it was applied to both native products, like strung wampum, and European trade goods. For other cases in this account book, see pages [30], [32], [37], [57], [115], and possibly [99].

35. No such occurrence has been located.

36. Sarghtoke, or Sareghtoken as it is referred to in accounts on two other occasions, was a common early name for the area surrounding present-day Saratoga, New York. Various other ways of spelling the name of this locality can be found in contemporary documents. The Wendells developed significant interests in the area. Johannes, son of Evert Jansz Wendell, participated in the acquisition of land there in July 1683 from Mohawk and Mahican headmen. See *ERA*, 2: 195–97; and Horn, "Saratoga County," 1354–57. In his will dated November 20, 1691, Johannes left his part of the land called Sarachtoge to his son Abraham; see Talcott, *Genealogical Notes of New York*, 379. The account book shows that in May 1707, Evert Wendell made commercial transactions in that area. Two clients are described as Mahican, and the origins of the third can be established as Mohawk. See the occurrences on pages [17] and [31]. Entries that mention this locality are in Evert's hand.

37. Additional references to "our female savage" are on pages [6], [7], [12], [105], and [106]. "Our Susanna's female savage" is mentioned on page [36]. Male "savages of" Stephanus Groesbeeck and Johannes Lansing are described on pages [73], and [94], respectively. Also see the introduction.

38. The page is somewhat torn at the right side. The name has been reconstructed from the information in the "register."

39. She is listed in the "register" as Nemamet's wife.

40. This specification of the relationship was inserted later.

41. This is most likely Waskaemp, see the note on page [3]. He is probably also referred to on page [106].

42. Since the rum for Jan Seeps was given to Kaloolet, the latter must have offered some assurances to Wendell. In addition, Kaloolet then took some merchandise with a value of two quarters. Jan Seeps and Kaloolet appear in the "register." For an account of the latter's, see page [10]. The two *l*'s in his name make it unlikely that Kaloolit was Mahican (BR). Other evidence links him to Schaghticoke. On June 30, 1699, the sachem Callolet brought a message to Albany from the Schaghticoke Indians who had recently moved to Vermont; see *DRCHNY*, 4: 575–76. Earlier that year, he had explained that a group from Schaghticoke had spent the winter at Lake Champlain because they could not pay their debt to traders in Albany, and their corn and clothes were being taken away. In July of 1708, Caloolett and four other joint owners confirmed previous land sales by Mahicans, to the Van Rensselaers, on the east side of the Hudson River. Another one of the joint owners was another Schaghticoke sachem, Waniglawett. He appears here, and as Waeleghlauwett on page [18] (see the note there). See Dunn, *The Mohicans and Their Land*, 155–57, 306.

43. He is listed in the "register" as Mackenant. The name is phonetically close to Mackseckwant/Masequant (and variations), who appears on pages [13] and [14] (see the note on page [13]), but he is not the same individual.

44. There is no record of a payment by Mackanant/Mackenant.

45. He is listed in the "register" as Naghnaehamet, although it refers to his sister and his wife's son. He appears, with his relatives, on pages [7], [13], [101], and [106]. Although the "register" gives a separate listing for Naghnekampenit, the reference from pages [7]–[101] excludes the possibility that they were two different individuals. Taken together, the accounts span the period between 1703 (no month) and October 1709. He may be the same individual as Naghnakanet, who sold land (with others) east of Kinderhook in 1733; see Dunn, *The Mohicans and Their Land*, 322.

46. No information regarding this settlement has been located. Since it is listed in a section of the account book almost completely devoted to dealings with Mahican traders, it is very likely that it refers to a village of those Indians.

47. The first of a total twenty-two instances where Indians purchased goods on credit outside of Albany, or paid (part of) their debts there. For an overview of these cases and a brief discussion, see the introduction and TABLE 19.

48. See the note for his brother Malsik. Walitgaes is possibly the same individual as Wallingas, who appears on the roll call of Abraham Schuyler's company of scouts, March 3, 1702/3. He had been in service since at least November 21, 1702. See Hastings, *Second Annual Report of the State Historian*, 477.

49. The brother of Walitgaes, both here and in the "register." The *l*'s in the brothers' names makes it unlikely that they were Mahicans (BR).

50. Possibly, a Dutchified rendering of the English name Richard.

51. The Dutch text reads *hespan* (also spelled *hespaen* in this manuscript), a loanword from the Munsee language. See Goddard, "Dutch Loanwords in Delaware," 158.

52. Originally, the entry gave 1709, but the 9 was changed into 10.

53. Here, Wendell wrote *commiesenaers* which may have two meanings. The most obvious supposition would be that this is a Dutch rendering of the office of commissioners for Indian affairs. This would coincide with the particular context in which the term is applied. However, it appears more likely that Wendell refers to Albany's magistrates. The term was widely used among Dutch residents, usually intended to describe the town's judiciary authorities. One historian of early New York has observed that the court in Albany "remained Dutch in its composition and language" for a considerable period of time after the English conquest; see Jacobs, *New Netherland*, 184.

54. The meaning of this passage remains obscure. The Dutch reads:

[. . .] *heeft hij mij een adeegwasie [ge]geven op d'*
commiesenaers van 30 gulden voor dut belans van
d' boven standen (addition to the verb *geven* [to give] is mine).

It appears that the native customer had arranged that Wendell could call on the town's magistrates to collect the balance.

55. He is also in the "register," with the same name.

56. He also appears in the "register," and on pages [5], [13], [101], and [106]. See the note on page [5]. Page [101] is folio 80 in this account.

57. Although listed as a Mahican in the "register," the *r* in his name makes it unlikely that this is a correct description (BR). A deposition by Indians from August 1709 relating to land at Coxsackie, New York, mentions an individual by the name of Narmoes, who had recently died. Phonetically, there is a resemblance with this Naernis, and the account occurs before that individual's documented death. He was mentioned among the six native owners, besides "Maghah, alias Magtsaput upper sachem of the Katskill," who had sold the land there in 1672; see Van Rensselaer, NYHS, August 22, 1709. This may be the same individual, which would locate him in the Catskill area. He has been counted as possibly being a Catskill Indian in TABLE 1.

58. The term appears only once in this account book, but is fairly common in documents of the time. It refers to types of merchandise, and housing accommodation for Indians. In an account of the Livingston's with Willemtje Schermerhoorn, covering 1698–99, they are charged by Schermerhoorn for sewing *hansijoos* shirts; see Livingston Papers, 1637–1771, Gilder Lehrman Collection, GLC 03107. An undated listing of an auction's returns in Albany (probably held in or around 1667) states that Barent de Smit acquired a set of *hansjoos juweelen* (or *hanjoos* jewelry) at the value of five-and-a-half Dutch guilders; see Venema, *Beverwijck: A Dutch Village on the American Frontier*, 78. Around Albany, small houses that Indian visitors used were sometimes called *hansioos/hanschoos/hanshoos* houses during the second half of the seventeenth-century; see *ERA*, 1: 319; 2: 105–06, 187, 261.

59. Naghnakamet's sister may also have been a guarantor for the other woman she escorted. While her own debt amounts to four martens, the account has a deficit of five martens. Presumably, the other Indian woman traded for one marten on the account of Naghnakamet's sister. This remains unclear, however, since the escorted woman is listed with a debt of her own of one marten on page [5] (last account). Both women paid part of their debt in the country in February 1707. Page [5] is folio 3 in this account.

60. He also appears as Awannighqaet in the "register," and on page [15] as Awanwaghquat. The latter account in July 1707 suggests he exercised some form of authority.

61. While there are several pages that are numbered 8, see page [16].

62. The Catskill area, or the Indians residing there. For a similar usage, see page [18].

63. The internal references here, and on page [16], leave little doubt that this individual appears also on page [16] as Sanhaquisquaas (see the note there), and on page [102] as Sahaquesquass. Note that his sister also trades on this account, see below. The relationship between the Wendells and this Catskill Indian was still apparent in June 1713; a letter in Evert's handwriting identifies Sahaquesquas as messenger between Wendell, Johannes Bleecker, and Johannes Visscher in Albany, and Ephraim Wendell in Montreal. For the letter of correspondence (dated June 25, 1713) between Ephraim in Montreal and Evert and company, see NYSL, ser. 9684. Excluding the reference to Maghack on page [2], and the possible reference to the Catskill individual Naermoes (see the note with the account of Naernis on page [7]), three (possibly four) Catskill customers can identified in the accounts. Besides Schewas quawas, they is Tack kaiwee and (or who is also) the sister of Schewas quawas in this account, and Sou waes' on page [18]. The accounts cover May 1701, May 1705, and May 1706 to January 1713.

64. She possibly reappears farther down in this account, as his sister.

65. Or the area where the Ottawas resided.

66. He also appears on pages [10] and [14]. Together, the occurrences cover the period from June 1701 to August 1706. There seems to be little doubt that he is the same individual as itawapewa, listed among the Schagkok [Schaghticoke] Indians as a member of Abraham Schuyler's company of scouts in March of 1702/3; see Hastings, *Second Annual Report,* 477. He had been in service since at least November 21, 1702. From the combined entries and accounts, it becomes evident that this individual had connections to the Catskill area and Schenectady, and that he went to the Ottawas in May 1704. Also see the note with Nietewaekam, below.

67. Schenectady, New York. Other references to the locality can be found on pages [10], [17], and [74]. Only one of these four instances refers to a commercial transaction with a Mohawk trader, the others deal with a client from the Catskill and two Mahican traders. For a detailed discussion of the largely illegal role of Schenectady in the early fur trade, see Burke, *Mohawk Frontier* chaps. 3, 6.

68. Since it remains a strong possibility that she is the same as Tack kaiwee in the same account, their appearances have been incorporated in TABLE 1 of the introduction as representing one Catskill individual.

69. He is listed in the "register" as Naeckaepen.

70. For a note on the Greyhead, see page [17].

71. N(i)etewa(e)kam occurs regularly in the account book: in the "register"; here; twice on page [9]; on pages [16] and [20]—in the latter case as Metewackam. Together these instances cover the period between July 1703 and August 1708. The woman's trip linked to Nietewakam's account, for the same day, is on page [9]. Since he escorted several individuals to the Wendells, acted as a guarantor, an individual was reported as staying at his place, and he went with a party to the Ottawas, it appears that he occupied a position with some status or acted as mediator or both. He may be the same as the River Indians' warrior or principal chief Eetowacamo, who accompanied Major Peter Schuyler on his expedition against the French and their Indian allies, defeating a major war party at La Prairie between June and August 1691; see DRCHNY, 3: 803. "This is the same individual as the Mahican (or River Indian) chief, referred to as Metewacom/Etowaucum/Etow Oh Koam, or Nicholas, fl. 1690–1720" (GM). He was one of the "Four Kings" to visit England in 1710; see Sivertsen, *Turtles, Wolves, and Bears,* 64–67.

72. It is likely that she is the same individual as listed on page [18], where her name is listed (earlier: in June 1705) as Seghstawaesqua.

73. The same combination of names appears in the "register." The *r* in this person's name makes it unlikely that he or she was Mahican (BR).

74. Or their area of residence.

75. Harmanus Wendell probably added this remark to justify the relatively high price of the small cask of rum.

76. The term here, *cnoo,* reappears as *kno* on page [33], again with the addition "French," where its value is listed, in 1700, as eight beavers. In both cases, the Indian customers purchased the canoe on credit, before traveling considerable distances: here to "the Ottawas," and on page [33] to Canada.

77. If this is an individual of European origins, he is one of the few in the account book who remains unidentified. Evert had no relatives named Gerrit, and no particular commercial or other liaison has been established with an individual of this name. It is also possible, however, that Wendell refers to an American Indian with that given, Dutch name. He has not been incorporated in TABLE 1 of the introduction.

78. He is listed with the same name in the "register." Noting the relatively early date in the time range covered in this account book, he may be the same individual who was mentioned at the sale of three pieces of land on the east side of the Hudson on June 15,

1680. The three Indians who sold the land were described as "having authority from a certain Indian named Awannis who has an interest therein," see *ERA*, 2: 84.

79. She is most likely the same woman as Malkiet, on page [12]. The accounts complement each other perfectly, and both contain a reference to Ottawa. Together, the occurrences cover the period August 1705 to July 1707. The *l* in both names makes it unlikely that she was Mahican (BR). As the account for Malkiet on page [12] also lists her as living among the Ottawas, she has been incorporated as an Ottawa individual in TABLE 1 of the introduction.

80. Jan Jansen Bleecker (ca. 1641–1732), the first settler of this family. He was among the most prominent citizens of Albany when the city received its charter in 1686. He served as alderman then, and later as recorder, justice of the peace, and mayor. See Pearson, *The First Settlers of Albany*, 19; Reynolds, *Hudson-Mohawk Genealogical and Family Memoirs*, 1: 128–29. In addition, he was among the commissioners for Indian affairs in 1690, with Evert Wendell's uncle Johannes; see *AA*, 1: 277. Later, this influential position was also occupied by several of his sons: Rutger, Johannes, Jr., and Nicholas. The latter is also mentioned in the accounts, see page [70], and possibly page [72].

81. The original wording of the verb is hard to read, my transcription is: *die Ouwee suckwans altit geh[a?]t heeft*. Although it is difficult to think of another possible reconstruction, note that the translation is not absolute. Perhaps Wendell's remark signifies that Ouweesuckwans had once adopted the boy. If correctly interpreted here, Wendell's remark that Ouwee suckwans had always had the little boy, this possibly indicates that he held a position of some status in society. There is an intriguing possibility that he is Sackquans or Suchquans, a River Indian sachem, who was mentioned in August 15, 1702 (close to the date of this entry) as relaying the last wish of the "late sachem Minichque" to Governor Cornbury; see *DRCHNY*, 4: 997. In that case, the Ouwee-segment in his name may be a somewhat corrupted entry for *ouwe* (*oude* in modern Dutch: old, or senior) suckwans. The specific way in which the name is entered in the account does allow that possibility, because it consists of two unconnected segments.

82. Aettesoghkamen (one line below this: Atesoghkamen) is the same individual who was mentioned in October 1703 with his brother Sokam /Sokaem, as exercising a claim on land at Westenhook that had been sold to four people from Albany. His name is recorded there as Attamaghkamin and Akamaagkamin; see Dunn, *The Mohicans and Their Land*, 304, 313. He also may be included in the list of Indian scouts in Abraham Schuyler's company on March 3, 1702/3, as atsegh (illegible) a Schagkok (Schaghticoke) Indian; see Hastings, *Second Annual Report*, 477. He had been in service since, at least, November 21, 1702.

83. This Schaghticoke sachem also appears on page [5], and a note with information is provided there. Both the appearance on page [5], and the account here relate to 1697.

84. See page [14], a cross-reference there confirms the connection. In both instances, the minus aspect of the account is constituted by the Mahican selling a wampum belt to Wendell, the value of which is detracted from his debt.

85. He also appears on pages [8] and [14], and see the note on page [8].

86. Or the Ottawas' area of residence.

87. Schenectady. This is a significant indication of the existence of Indian entrepreneurs who bought substantial quantities of trade goods and consequently attempted to enter the market, either as agents for the Wendells or on their own account. This entry strongly suggests that Niettewapwae and his family participated in such activities, since they send goods away from the core area of Mahican habitation. Possibly, the items that were transported to Schenectady for him and his family were used during the same journey. For other occurrences of Schenectady, see pages [8] (and the note there), [17] and [74].

88. *Papegaai*, the literal translation is "parrot," and plural is used here. *Papegaai* was used by the Dutch to describe the wooden target in the shape of a bird, placed on a pole

or in a tree, used in arrow-shooting competitions. See Jacobs, *New Netherland,* 371, 470; and Venema, *Beverwijck,* 110–11. Merwick also described its occurrence in Albany in the 1650s, *Possessing Albany,* 79n30. She has noted that some decades after the English conquest, Indians were the only ones still recorded as performing these competitions, ibid., 168.

89. This description of Niettewapwae's wampum belt is somewhat flawed: it is impossible that it contained sixty-one white figures with thirty-six white beads each. It does make sense, however, if the sixty-one in the text is substituted with sixteen. If each white figure consisted of and area of six by six white beads (to arrive at the described thirty-six beads per white area), it would leave sixteen areas and three vertical rows of black beads (between the sixteen white figures, and at the end or beginning of the belt), and one vertical row of single black beads at the beginning or end of the belt ([16 × 6 = 96] + [16 × 3 = 48] + [1 × 1] = 145 vertical rows). An entry in his account on page [14] shows that Evert Wendell credited him with three beavers for this belt.

90. The first of the seven cases where the Wendells paid the debt of a native customer to a European person. For an overview, and a brief discussion, see the introduction.

91. Niettewapwae's connections to Schenectady are confirmed by this relationship with Anties Moll. Pearson states that Anties Mol married Caleb Beck in New York City on November 2, 1705 (or 1703). The correct date must have been the earlier one, since Beck had settled in Schenectady as an innkeeper in 1703, and the couple had their first child (Anna) baptized there on October 7, 1704. See Pearson, *Contributions for the Genealogies of the Descendants,* 10–11; and ibid., "Extracts From the Doop-Boek," 315.

92. The *l* in this individual's name makes it unlikely that he was Mahican (BR). He is possibly Nosewigh Kanett, who sold (with an Indian woman, Manuwepen) two islands in the Hudson River, north of Albany, to Jeremias van Rensselaer in 1663; see Dunn, *The Mohicans and Their Land,* 285–86.

93. This Mahican man (with a number of Mohawk liaisons) is listed as Sesecaet in the "register," and also on page [11]. The latter is the page across from this one. His name is listed in a variety of ways: Secqaet, Secatt, Seeckaet, and Sekat. His wife, his mother, his mother-in-law, his brother-in-law (Sam, or Cattelaemet/Cattelnalemet), and what appears to be his wife's son, also occur in these accounts. Together, they span the period between February 1705 and July 1707.

94. A Hendereck also appears in this account book on pages [26] and [36], and an entry for Taijenoekee on page [59] may refer to the same individual. Compare this with an additional entry on page [48] (and the note there) clearly referring to a different, younger Hendereck. In January of 1714 Evert Wendell made a payment in merchandise to "Henderick *de wilt*," with a total value of almost fifty-five Dutch guilders, related to a transfer of land by the Mohawk Schaghnerowane (see the notes on pages [23] and [24]) to Evert, Harmanus, and Abraham Cuyler; see Evert Wendell, Ledger, 1711–1738, NYHS. "Esares *de wilt*" received a similar payment, and DeCaghnawadighko *de Swart wilt* (the Black savage) a smaller one.

95. The original gives *kl* only, an abbreviation for *klein* (small).

96. It seems that Wendell first entered a total debt of nine martens, and later changed it to ten.

97. The additional element of description, *moer* (mother), was inserted.

98. These figures in the right margin also appear at the lower part of this account, and (in a different sequence) in the second to last account on the next page.

99. Cattelaemet also appears on the next page, [11], as Sam and as Cattelnalemet. The *l* in this individual's native name makes it unlikely that he was Mahican (BR). From the accounts, connections can be made with the Mohawk country, and an English Indian who was perhaps an Abenaki Indian. Sam appears to be the English name for this individual. The accounts span the period between May 1706 and January 1707.

100. The specific origins of this individual remain undetermined, both here and on

the only other occurrence of this customer on page [11], where he is identified with the name Peckwanck. He is the only client described as an English Indian, and has been incorporated, as such, in TABLE 1 of the introduction. It is interesting to note that the transaction took place in a house in the Mohawk country, and that the instance is clearly connected to individuals with Mahican or Schaghticoke affiliations.

101. While this remark is somewhat ambiguous, it seems Wendell intended to note that the debt was partially redeemed by the woman's grandson, the child of Sececaet and his wife, the wife being the old, small woman's daughter.

102. He appears on page [10] as Cattelaemet and as Sam, see the corresponding note.

103. Literally *riet stoc*[*k?*] (last letter is difficult to read, but *k* is the only plausible addition), would translate into "reed stick." Considering the price, about equal to the value of one marten fur, it is likely that this is a reference to a particular type of cane. Also known in Dutch as a *rotting*, it was presented to an Onondaga sachem by the French governor in 1687; see *LIR*, 143. For various ritual and ceremonial usages of canes and sticks among Indians in the Northeast, see Fenton, "The Roll Call of the Iroquois Chiefs."

104. The tally in this account is the same, up to the second entry, as the one for this individual on page [10]. The account here has an additional entry for January of 1706 or 1707.

105. She is (almost) certainly the same individual as Waelekeiet on page [9]. If they are the same person, she did not live up to this second pledge to return in the coming spring (like she did previously in August 1705)—or the account book contains no record thereof.

106. This young Mahican also has an account on page [105]. Together these instances span between January 1707 and February 1710.

107. Refers to Naghnaekamett.

108. He also appears in the "register," and on pages [5], [7], [101], and [106]. See the note on page [5]. Page [7] is folio 5 in this account. His wife is active on shared accounts, both here and on page [106].

109. The debt for this small shirt is not specified. Both the one and the two were maintained in the account, although the use of the plural martens suggests the latter value.

110. Maqseequant, written Mackseckwant a few lines below, may be the same as Masequant on page [14], listed as one of two witnesses in an arrangement between Wendell and Nietwewapwae in August of 1706. See the note there.

111. Abraham Symonse Groot was a child of one of the first settlers of Schenectady, Symon Symonse Groot. Abraham's second wife was Hester (Harmense) Visscher, and at the time of their marriage in 1699 he resided in Schenectady. See Pearson, *First Settlers of Albany*, 57; and Pearson, *First Settlers of Schenectady*, 81. Between 1715 and 1725, Evert often used Abraham's services to cart goods between Albany and Schenectady; see Evert Wendell, Ledger 1711–1738, NYHS. The two men must have developed a more profound relationship. One year after the date of this entry, Evert was sponsor at the baptism of Cornelis, son of Abraham and Hester; see *Records of the Reformed Dutch Church of Albany*, 2: 54.

112. See the note, immediately preceding the previous one.

113. See the note for this individual on page [5].

114. On page [15] this identification of an Abenaki Indian appears as *Annaaconkeer* and *Aennaacoonkeer*. On page [17] a region, locality, or territory is indicated as *Annaekonccoo*. For several synonyms for Eastern Abenaki Indians, that closely correspond to Wendell's usages, see Snow, "Eastern Abenaki," *HNAI*, 15: 147. A report on the conference between Mohawk sachems and two Albany leaders in August 26, 1702, presents the term *onnagongue* as referring to Abenakis in general, as did a letter from Peter

Schuyler to New Englander Fitz-John Winthrop on April 24, 1704, referring to the "On-nagongquees or Eastern Indians"; see *LIR*, 184, 184n2. The account book contains three accounts of Abenaki individuals. Temaghquant's account also lists his wife as trading on his account, and TABLE 1 of the introduction lists four individual Abenaki customers. Altogether, the accounts appear only in June of 1708 (here), and in July of the preceding year (on page [15]).

115. He also appears on pages [8] and [10], also see the note on page [8]. Page [10] is folio 8 in this account.

116. As a security against the debt. The belt also occurs in an entry in this customer's account on page [10]. See the note there.

117. Masequant and Caetsee nacquas were evidently witnesses to this arrangement. The latter does not reappear in the account book, and no additional information on this individual has been located. The first individual may be identical to Mackseckwant (or Maqseequant), mentioned on page [13] in 1706 and 1708. He is not the same as Mack-enant in the "register" with an account in July 1701, or on page [5] where the name is listed as Mackanant.

118. He is also listed on page [15], as Josewa. Together, the accounts cover from February 1708 to May 1710. The entry suggests an English name, Joshua, but no additional information on this individual has been located.

119. The construction here is ambiguous, as it remains unclear whether *hghketock* identifies a person or a locality, but comparison with the description used on page [15] ("son of Josewa's wife") renders the present translation as the most logical one. In this form, *hghketock* is an area or locality where the customer's father and/or mother resided.

120. There, a "son of Josewa's wife" is listed.

121. The description of Awanwaghquat indicates that he may have had a position of some status. He also appears with a small account on page [8], from 1697, but the account book contains no evidence to support that interpretation.

122. The *r* in the individual's name makes it unlikely that he was Mahican (BR). Although his name is written Herij, he is also listed (as a Mahican) in the "register." An Indian man (probably Munsee) named Herij is recorded in the account book of an Indian trader in Ulster County, New York, as going to a locality called Namesinck in or around May 1725. He traveled with the Munsee man Sander; see Philip John Schuyler Papers, Account Book, 1711–1729, NYPL, reel 30.

123. For an identification of this as Abenaki, see page [13] and the note there.

124. Difficult to reconstruct: perhaps *Jaa*.

125. Difficult to reconstruct: perhaps *Zeeweeweett*.

126. See also note with Joswaa, on page [14].

127. This figure appears to be detached from other information on the page. Perhaps it is a remnant of a previous or later page numbering; see the bottom of page [17].

128. While there is no account "above" for this individual, as referred to in the next line, an account on the preceding page with a young, male *Catschelse* (Catskill) customer has exactly this amount of remaining debt. The young man's name is listed there as Schewas quawas, and there seems to be little doubt that he is the same individual. The present Sanhaquisquaas also appears as Sahaquesquass on page [102], a page listed as folio 81 in this account. The cross-reference there confirms the connection. For a note on the appearance of Sahaquesquass in communications between Montreal and Albany, see the note on page [8]. Assuming all instances refer to the same individual, the accounts span the period between May 1701 and January 1713.

129. As this young, male customer was introduced by an individual identified as a Catskill Indian, his appearance has been incorporated into TABLE 1 of the introduction, as being of a client of that area.

130. The entry in its present form remains ambiguous. It is possible that Wendell

intended to record that Sanhaquisquaas had delivered, or left behind, a beaver coat, leaving a debt of five guilders. One arrives at that construction by changing the word him (*hem* in the manuscript) into he (*hij*). For a similar case of the interchangeable use of he and him, also concerning a surety and leading to the same ambiguity, see note 32 on page [3].

131. N(i)etewa(e/c)kam/Metewackam occurs regularly in the account book, see the note on page [8].

132. While he developed a reasonably substantial account, this individual does not seem to reappear in the account book. It is very unlikely that he is the same individual as the Mahican Maghcoes, with two additional Mohawk names, on page [69].

133. The *l* in this individual's name makes it unlikely that he was Mahican (BR), although he and the Greyhead (or Wassewaencke/Wassewaecke) are both listed as Mahican in the "register," where his name is listed as Nannaelamit. The direction of his trading expedition with the Greyhead is significant. Nannalamit/Nannaelamit may be the same individual as Mamatamitt, a witness at the sale of land at the Housatonic River in February 1685. See Dunn, *The Mohicans and Their Land*, 320.

134. The Greyhead, or Wassewaencke/Wassewaecke, appears in the "register," and farther down on page [17]; his wife has a personal account on page [8]; his sons appear on page [59], as does the wife of one of them. Together, the accounts span the period between 1695/6 and January 1705. He may very well be the same as Waesamaek, witness at the sale of land at Schaghticoke to the City of Albany, in February 1707. See Dunn, *The Mohicans and Their Land*, 305, 332.

135. *Annaekonccoo* refers to the Abenaki Indians, or the area they inhabited, see the note on page [13]. From the information contained in the trade book, it remains unclear whether the Mahican agents visited either the Eastern or Western Abenakis. In June 1707 and July 1708 Wendell also dealt directly with three Abenaki men—plus the wife of one of them. These instances are further detailed on pages [13] and [15]. Some Abenaki subdivisions maintained contacts with the Iroquois, and a number of them settled in Schaghticoke, at the confluence of the Hoosick and Hudson Rivers. For an overview of Abenaki history, see Snow, "Eastern Abenaki," *HNAI*, 15: 137–47; and Day, "Western Abenaki," *HNAI*, 15: 148–59.

136. For a discussion of this locality, see the note on page [4]. It is also mentioned on page [31].

137. *Jnijt* is most likely a mistake for *Junij* (June).

138. This clearly refers to Nannalamit, in the preceding account. His name is listed as Nannaelamit in the "register."

139. Schenectady.

140. This reveals that guarantors were (at times) held personally responsible for payments on the accounts of the introduced. This is also illustrated by the fact that the Wendells sometimes recorded debts of the introduced customer on the account of the escorters.

141. There is no apparent meaning to this number.

142. He is listed in the "register" as Jacop. He may possibly be the same as Cobus, as both Jacob/Jacop and Cobus are diminutive renderings of Jacobus. This man's Indian name was listed as Kachketowaa and Kachtowaa, when he sold land at the Catskill in 1678 and 1686. A Jacobus Cohquahegameek/Coocheecomeek was mentioned in 1737, selling land at the Housatonic River in Massachusetts to John Stoddard. He was described as being "formerly of Menanoke or the island in the Hudson below Albany [Moesimus Island]," see Dunn, *The Mohicans and Their Land*, 315–16, 309. It cannot be ascertained if this is the same individual as the native boy Jacob, who received assistance from Albany's magistrates, for which they were paid by the deacons of the Dutch Reformed Church in March 1701; see Venema, *Beverwijck*, 425n187.

143. The woman is not identified. Possibly, she is Waeleghlauwett's wife, three ac-

counts farther down this page. The same possibly applies to two additional cases, also farther down the same page.

144. This woman has been incorporated in TABLE 1 of the introduction, as of unknown origins.

145. Possibly, she is Waeleghlauwett's wife.

146. She is likely the same individual as listed on page [8], in September 1705, where her name is listed as Segh nae waes quae. This entry, dating from June or July of 1705, is the one occasion where Evert Wendell, while writing the woman's name, continues from page [18] onto page [19], in effect bridging the gap between two sections in the account book, that have different page numbers: page [17] has folio 9, page [18] has no number, and page [19] is marked as folio 1.

147. The *l*'s in this man's name make it unlikely that he was Mahican (BR). Other occurrences of this Schaghticoke sachem are in Dunn, *The Mohicans and Their Land*, 332–33; *DRCHNY*, 5: 228; and *AA*, 6: 257.

148. Despite extensive research, no identification of this individual has materialized. Researchers who have reconstructed much of the Schuylers' lineages reacted in the same vein (Peter and Florence Christoph, pers. comm., November 2003). The only reference to Cornelis/Cornelus Schuyler is in a family bible, where Abraham Schuyler (1663–1726) recorded his departure on December 16, 1709, for a journey to England "with Cornelus Schuyler," and his safe return on July 20, 1710. See Christoph, *Schuyler Genealogy*, 1: 30. It can not be excluded that Wendell incorrectly entered the name of another Schuyler, such as Cornelia (van Cortlandt) Schuyler, wife of Brant (1659–1752), fifth child of Philip Pieterse Schuyler.

149. Possibly, she is Waeleghlauwett's wife.

150. This older debt is not depicted within this account. The number of marks at the right indicates a total debt of ten skipple of corn.

151. The Catskill area, or the Indians residing there.

152. Nooses may possibly be the same woman as Onnosies, who sold land (with others) in Kinderhook in 1734; see Dunn, *The Mohicans and Their Land*, 324.

153. Relates to the next account.

154. This Korneles (Kornelis), Corneles (Cornelis), or Cees/Kees is most likely the prominent Mohawk Wolf clan sachem Tanigwaneg (fl. 1705–1744); see Sivertsen, *Turtles, Wolves, and Bears*, 90. He is also included in this account book as Tanawaneke, on page [109], in an account for his Mohawk wife, who remains unnamed (like his mother, here). The baptism records of Albany confirm this supposition: on April 25, 1709, Moses, son of two converted Indians, (Cornelis and Maria) was baptized. At that point, Cornelis's native name was registered as Thannawaneke, and that of his wife, Maria, as Karaghwine; see *Records of the Reformed Dutch Church of Albany*, 2: 54. Sivertsen lists his name as Thaneghwanege, and his wife's as Keragkwinon (but excludes the record of the baptism in appendix A, "Albany: Indian Baptisms and Marriages, 1689–1756"). Abraham Cuyler served as sponsor at the baptism, see the note on page [20]. Although there are a number of other Maria's in this account book, none seems to be the present Korneles's/T(h)anawaneke's wife. If this Korneles is indeed the later sachem of the Wolf clan, his mother (who is mentioned here) was Catrina, baptized with her son in Schenectady on October 5, 1700; see Sivertsen, *Turtles, Wolves, and Bears*, 90–91, 223. It seems unlikely that Cees *Dewelt* and Cees the savage, on pages [2] and [118], are the same individual as he appears in a predominantly Mahican context. That person has been counted as a Mahican, the present one as a Mohawk.

155. For another listing of Sander, see the account on page [75]; together they span the period between July 1701 and (probably) 1706. Although it is not certain that they all refer to the same individual, there are a number of appearances of this name in the primary sources. In September 1713 he was mentioned as living at Fort Hunter, and was

chosen to accompany Johannes Bleecker on a mission to Onondaga (with Tanigwanega, the present Tanawaneke/Cornelis). Fourteen months later, he was among those signing a deed for land west of the Mohawk River, to Margaret and Edward Collins; and in 1733 he was among a large group of Indian leaders signing a gift of land at the Mohawk Flats to the English Crown (again, together with a Cornelius). See *DRCHNY*, 5: 372; and Sivertsen, *Turtles, Wolves, and Bears*, 266. The baptism records of Albany and Schenectady also list a fair number of individuals with this name, but it is impossible to link the present individual to any of them without ambiguity.

156. The reference may be to page [45], a page *following* one that is labeled 23. However, the total debts appear to be different. It may be that the reference is to a folio 23, now missing from the account book.

157. "Kanossoodickhae in 'modern' Mohawk: kanonhsatekha' or 'burning house'" (GM). This individual appears frequently in the account book. For other cases, see pages [27], [45], [48], [49], [77], and [120]. Taken together, they span between the years 1697 and 1710. His wife was active on shared accounts, and that of her own. The entries on page [77] take up an entire page in the book, and they suggest that Canosedeckhaa died between January 1708 and February 1709. The activities of this Mohawk man were also reported by Armour although he mistranscribed the name as Canosedackhoe, which is not among the varieties of the name in the account book, *Merchants of Albany*, 67. Armour apparently overlooked this first account, as he stated that this Indian customer was active "from 1701 to 1710."

158. See note 156.

159. "Kaeijeenquereeko (in 'modern' Mohawk: kayenkwire'kowa, or 'Great Arrow') was a prominent name in Mohawk society. There were a number of chiefs of that name" (GM). This is possibly the same individual as Caienquierego, listed with other Mohawks on the roll call of Captain Abraham Schuyler's company of scouts in March of 1702/3. He had been in service since at least November 21, 1702. See Hastings, *Second Annual Report*, 477. This individual also appears elsewhere in the account book, see pages [25] and [43]. Taken together, the accounts span the years 1697 to 1706. All cases have slightly different spellings of the name: on page [25] he is listed as the brother of Aberham, or Cenderijockee.

160. Various members with the family name Lucassen (various spellings) appear in contemporary documents. Pearson does list a Claas Luykase Wyngaert (data, 1700–04), *First Settlers of Albany*, 8. He may have been a son of Luycas Wyngaert (various spellings), ibid., 155. There was also a Jan Luycassen Wijngaert, associated with the Schenectady area, who made his will in 1690; see Burke, *Mohawk Frontier*, 185n39, 199n4, 200. Claes Luijckesen is also mentioned on page [120], and he is listed on the last page of the account book, page [121]. An additional liaison between Evert and Claes Lucassen did exist, for Evert and his sister Hester were sponsors of Claas Lucasse Wyngaard at the baptism of their nephew Lucas (son of Johannes Lucasse Wyngaard and their older sister Susanna Wendell) on May 7, 1704. See *Records of the Reformed Dutch Church of Albany*, 2: 32.

161. Thehotsooen himself is not identified in the account book as an Oneida, although his wife is. This affiliation is suggested by Leder, where Tohotsjoge is listed as one of two Oneidas who came to inform Albany of the death of the Mohawk sachem onnagraooum in June 1707; see *LIR*, 201.

162. Although Wendell does not give sufficient information to make a positive identification of this individual, it is quite likely that the entry refers to Abraham Cuyler. There are two other cases in the accounts where Wendell indicates commercial contacts with Indian traders who had some connection to this Abraham. In July of the same year he registered an account with a Seneca man who "traded at Abberham Cuijler," see page [57]. And in September 1708 the mother of one of Wendell's Mohawk clients was

said to "stay at Aberham Cuijler's," see page [94]. Abraham Cuyler was godparent of the Indian boy Moses, son of Cornelis and Maria, baptized in 1709; see the note in the account of Cornelis, on page [19].

163. This predates any other account in the account book. It is used merely as a reference, possibly indicating that this Mohawk individual had been trading with the Wendells that year.

164. He may have been the same person as Kamichcareiade, who was mentioned by four Mohawks from Canada, who told the magistrates of Schenectady in September 1688 that this individual had informed them of the whereabouts of the governor of Canada; see *DRCHNY*, 3: 565.

165. Waenenpaeckes is among the Wendells' main Mahican customers. He and his wife appear frequently on these pages, with substantial accounts on pages [97], [99], [112], and [113]. Page [97] is folio 78 in this account. Together, the entries span between September 1705 and May 1718. His name appears in a variety of spellings, hers remains unknown. Following the shared account, here and on page [97], they both developed separate accounts with the Wendells, although the woman is also actively involved in her husband's account on page [99]. The account on page [97] is extraordinary, for one of the entries (dated ca. May 1709) contains a statement regarding her ownership of a "Negro boy," who she intends to sell. Despite the extensive nature of their interactions with the Wendells, no additional references to them have been located in other sources.

166. For Metewackam (also N(i)etewa(e/c)kam) see the note on page [8].

167. The status of the belt remains unclear.

168. Jonas Volkertse Douw (?–1736), son of the family's first settler, Captain Volkert Janse Douw (?–1683/4). Jonas's son Pieter is also listed in the account book, see page [120]. Pearson lists the year of his father's death as 1686, but this is clearly a mistake, because his widow (Doritee) asked to be administrator of Volkert's estate on January 8, 1683/4. See Van Laer, *CMARS*, 3: 412; and Pearson, *The First Settlers of Albany*, 43. Page [120] also mentions a Jan de Doo/Jan Doo (twice), probably Jan Andries Douw (see the note there).

169. In a deed dated May 1685, one of the Mohawk, "native proprietors" of land at Onisquetha, Onitsquathaa, or Onitquothaa, is listed as Tojonjow. See "Deed to 10,000 Acres," *DSSY*, 21–22: 13–14; and *ERA*, 2: 276–77. His wife does not reappear recognizably in the account book, but he is mentioned on page [62], where a Mohawk man, Thouwenjouw, escorts an unnamed Mohawk woman from Canada (with her son) to Wendell in 1705. This woman conveyed the greetings of "the priest" to Wendell. Previously, in 1700, David Schuyler reported in a letter to Governor Bellomont that while he was in Montreal, and made enquiries about the number of Indian inhabitants of Caughnawaga, one of his informants was "the son of Touyenijouw whose father [. . .] is one of our proselites." When Schuyler asked if the son would consider staying in New York, the young man answered that "he had a great inclination to be a Christian and that [was what] detained him in Canada," see *DRCHNY*, 4: 747.

170. A slightly aberrant way of referring to the name Rebecca. She reappears on pages [106], [107], and [118]; and if she is the same as Rapecke (which seems entirely plausible), she is also on page [34]. Including the latter entry, her activities span the period between 1697 and April 1724. Considering the number of times that the name was used to baptize American Indians in Albany and Schenectady, and the extensive period of time covered by the appearances in the account book, it is not certain that all accounts and appearances here refer to the same individual.

171. The sex glands of the beaver, used by Europeans in medicine and perfumes.

172. See also the note at the large account of Kahonck, on page [44].

173. Delivery on a singe day of such a quantity of goods suggests that this customer acted as a peddler (see TABLE 13).

174. The same identification of the woman, as the sister of Watcaro (various spellings), occurs on all her accounts on this page and on page [96]. The latter lists her own name as Catrin. Watcaro himself did not have an account with the Wendells, or it is no longer included in the account book.

175. See the note on page [21].

176. An interesting metaphor by Evert Wendell.

177. The same as Carhiaedsiecoo, he has additional accounts and appears otherwise on pages [67], [84], [90], and [110]. Together, these cover the period between 1697 and July 1710. In the last account, also latest in terms of the date (June–July 1710), Evert Wendell completely remitted this customer's debt. The entry on page [84] suggests he had some form of status in Mohawk/Canadian society, as a young Mohawk man from Canada was described as belonging to him. The reference and information contained in folio 62 (page [80]) in the line just above his name, clearly suggests that he lived in Canada. The entries on pages [90] and [110] corroborate this. No additional information on this individual has been located.

178. This is evidently his daughter's account. Also spelled Arijenhotens, the name of this Mohawk man appears in quite a number of accounts, covering the period from January 1701 to January 1707. He had a private account with the Wendells, a shared one with his wife, and his daughter and her husband shared an account. See page [50], listed as folio 16 just above this account, and pages [59], [76], and [120].

179. The first of three cases where the Wendells note such a denial on the part of a customer, or warn each other of that possibility. For an overview and brief discussion, see the introduction.

180. He reappears as Sohnerowane with another account of some volume on the next page, [24], see the note with additional information there. Together, these entries cover the period between (probably) 1697 and July 1703. He is also mentioned in the account of his brother Ogwasserooa on page [28], which covers the same period.

181. She remains unnamed here, and in another account of her husband. See page [24]. Together these accounts cover the period between (probably) 1697 and July 1703.

182. "Kanaetsakigto in 'modern' Mohawk: kana'tsakehte or 'she carries a kettle'" (GM).

183. This clearly identifies him as the Mohawk Sohnerowane, see page [24].

184. See notes for him on page [31], where he appears as Saequanekarij and most likely also as Saequarij. Page [31] is folio 13 in this account.

185. The appearance of Catrin on page [96], as the wife of "her last husband Saquanakaij," suggests she is the wife mentioned here, as on page [31]. For Catrin, see the note on page [96].

186. The origins of this part of the debt remain obscure, also when compared with the account on page [31], indicating that other transactions may have occurred that are not included in the account book.

187. Many occurrences of Roode (Rode, Rhode, etc.) are found in the primary and printed sources: as a Mohawk speaker (ca. 1687–1693), and a sachem in 1690. See in DRCHNY, 3: 483, 843; 4: 38; and DHNY, 2: 91. Johannes Wendell was sponsor at the baptism of Roode (June 23, 1695), when his age was listed as eighty years old. That individual was given the Dutch name Dirk. Sivertsen describes him as a Turtle clan sachem of the easternmost Mohawk village, Turtles, Wolves, and Bears, 20–21, 42, 210, 280n33. Several land dealings received his authorization, see the petition by Adam Vrooman stating that in 1685 Rode had "granted" two "flatts" to him along the Mohawk River; see AA, 2: 101. Roode was described as the "Chiefe Sachim of the Maquaes [Mohawks]" in June 1692, Public Record Office, Kew Gardens, CO 5/1082, p. 112 .

188. This appears to be the same individual as Sagnirroowanne on page [23]. "He signed a land deed to Evert and Harmanus Wendell and Abraham Cuyler on July 19, 1710. He signed with a wolf clan mark. See "New York council minutes," NYCM, ser.

A1894, 36: 10, f. 529" (GM). Sivertsen also lists the name as Sogharowane (but does not include him in the list of "Mohawk Signers of Deeds, 1700–1749," appendix F), *Turtles, Wolves, and Bears,* 73, 289n7. Evert Wendell, Ledger, 1711–1738, at the NYHS, records payments to Henderick, Esares and DeCaghnawadighko the Black [male] savage for that transaction with Schaghnerowane in January 1714. Snow lists a sachem of the Mohawk Wolf clan as Sharenhowaneh, *The Iroquois,* 63. Saghnirroowane is also mentioned on page [28], as the brother of Ogwasserooa. Possibly, he is the same as the Mohawk sachem Sidgsihowanne, who came to meet New York's new Governor John Nanfan in Albany on July 10, 1701; see *DRCHNY,* 4: 897.

189. She also appears in her husband's account on page [23].

190. The account book does not include a page with that number.

191. "Dekanijieendan may have been the Oneida speaker Doganitajendach(quo), who negotiated with the agent of Virginia in 1679" (GM). See *LIR,* 55, where October 31, 1679 is the listed date.

192. For this Mohawk individual, see the note on page [20].

193. A slight variation on Abraham, also commonly used to refer to European individuals. See, for instance, Abberham Cuyler, in this account book, on page [57]. Several natives appear with that name in the recorded "Indian baptisms" of the Dutch Reformed Churches in Albany and Schenectady. One of the earliest occurrences was in January 1699/1700, when Elizabeth Wendell (an aunt of Evert and Harmanus) sponsored the baptism of a native with the Christian name Abraam (whose parents were recorded as Jacob and Jacomyn), but none of the Indian names recorded at the time provide an indication that he, or any of the others, is the same as the present individual; see Sivertsen, *Turtles, Wolves, and Bears,* 81–82, 208–09, 211–12.

194. In the Mohawk's name, a *c* was inserted between the *o* and *k,* but has been removed.

195. In this instance, it is not entirely evident that Wendell was actually in Mohawk territory, also because this is the only time that such a trip is possibly recorded for 1706.

196. The item left with this client was the bag of gunpowder—not the peltry.

197. It is obvious that Wendell made an error in calculating the debt of Jassijdassijkoo. The debt developed in 1697, or from that year on, and did not amount to ten, but to twelve martens. The remaining balance in 1704 should have amounted to five martens, not three.

198. Although phonetically very similar to Dekarowade on page [50], the latter is clearly identified as a young Cayuga man, and Dekarowe as a Mohawk. Both descriptions are in the hand of Harmanus Wendell. For a remark by Gunther Michelson on the meaning of the name Dekarowade (or perhaps Dekarowe), see the note on page [50].

199. He also appears on page [37] to identify his wife. In combination with the occurrence here, they cover the period from 1697 to April 1698.

200. "Satsooriy (in 'modern' Mohawk: satshori) is not a name at all, but a remark. It means 'you slurp'" (GM). It renders the ascription of the debt more complicated: was Satsoorij an actual individual (misidentified by Wendell), or an alternate name for Swathoose's brother?

201. The word "martens" has been provided here, since the thirty-two vertical marks constitute the exact total debt of martens listed in this customer's account.

202. "Dekarijhondie in 'modern' Mohawk: tekarihontye' or 'the matter passes by.' He could well be the later Karighontie, alias Thom[as], a sachem of the Wolf clan in Canajoharie in 1734" (GM). Michelson refers to the Indorsed Land Papers; see "New York council minutes," NYCM, ser. A1894, 31: f. 87. On the next page, [28], he is guarantor for Sahorackwaghte, a young Mohawk. Together, the two occurrences cover the years 1697–1699. Dekarijhondie is possibly the same individual as tokaronde, listed with other

Mohawks on the roll call of Captain Abraham Schuyler's company of scouts in March of 1702/3. He had been in service since at least November 21, 1702. See Hastings, *Second Annual Report*, 477.

203. "Kakoensijwaecke in 'modern' Mohawk: kakonhsawakon or 'she holds up a face or mask'" (GM).

204. This indicates that Dekarijhondie was guarantor for Kakoensijwaecke, as he also did on at least one other occasion in the same year, see the following page, [28].

205. This comment was added later.

206. The entries here are part of the account of Caenoseedeckhae, whose activities fill the remainder of this page. The reference to folio 58 is either mistaken (as a substantial account does appear on the page directly across from folio 58, see page [77]), or that page is now missing from the account book.

207. Several accounts appear with the name Maria/Mary (various spellings), see pages [38] and [48].

208. See the note before the previous one.

209. This individual appears frequently in the account book: for other cases, see the note on page [19].

210. The total of 244 quarters is repeated on page [77], with a cross-reference to the present page. Both cases date from the same month and year. In converting the Indian's debt to quarters, the computation contains an element that is difficult to explain. Setting he value of martens in quarters at three quarters each, that brings the total here to $(3 \times 36 =)$ 108 quarters. Adding the quarters listed separately (sixteen), the total comes to 124 quarters. Dividing the remainder of the debt in quarters, $(244 - 124 =)$ 120, by the recorded number of ten beavers, results in a value of twelve quarters for each beaver. This is an extraordinary high rate—in this case, to the advantage of the Indian customer; if he were to deliver one beaver to Evert Wendell, a relatively high number of quarters would be deducted from his outstanding debt. The only other cases where the value of a beaver is listed in quarters states clearly that the rate was eight (sometimes six) quarters to the beaver; but in those cases it reflects the value of *actual money* that a Indian could take out for a debt of one beaver. The rate of eight quarters in money is listed twice in the last account on page [67], dated October 1708, and once on page [86], in an entry from October 1707. The only occurrence of a rate of six quarters in specie to the beaver is on page [69], the last account, dated September 1710. Yet, in 1699, eight quarters was also listed as the rate for one beaver, without the additional description that is was in money or specie, see page [39]. That Wendell allocated a favorable rate to this customer is confirmed by looking more closely at the value of martens in quarters. Throughout the accounts, a marten hide, when expressed in quarters, was consistently described as the equivalent of *two* quarters (sometimes with the addition that the quarters were taken out as money or in specie); this occurs at least seventeen times, in a period covering 1698–1714 (for examples, see the first account on page [4], the last account on page [16], again the last on page [46], and the first on page [76]). In the present computation, the only possible value for the customer's debt of martens is *three* quarters—in any other case, the totals simply do not add up.

211. This function of Caenoseedeckhae as an army scout in December 1705 or early 1706, is not corroborated by documentary evidence. On page [49] an entry occurs where Wendell traded with his wife, "when he went as a scout." That entry is undated, but appears to be from around January 1704. For a note on this individual, see page [19].

212. Here, Wendell wrote *Maqese,* instead of the normal renderings used in other places in the account book: *Maqaese, Maquase,* or *Maqaes.*

213. He appears with his own accounts on pages [23] and [24]. See especially the note on page [24]. His brother, Sagnirroowanne, was considerably more active, see the note on page [24] and the references there.

214. "Caeijhoekedee ('kentsyonkethe,' or 'Fish carrier') was and is a popular Cayuga name" (GM). Note that also his wife trades here, but not on her own account.

215. Another occurrence of either name has not been found on page [44], labeled folio 23, or elsewhere in the account book.

216. The item's value of three beavers indicates that this was not a piece of wampum (wampum tubes or pipes appear elsewhere in the accounts), but rather a (tobacco-)pipe. Note that a ceramic pipe would have had a considerably lower price than this amount.

217. The verb is quite difficult to decipher, my best reconstruction is provided here. The exact meaning also remains vague: the client had developed a debt of three beavers, and the result of the action was that his debt rose to four beavers. There is no indication that the account was ever settled.

218. The identity of this individual remains doubtful. He could be Johannes Barentse Bratt (?–1714), son of Barent Albertse Bratt, or possibly Johannes Janse Bratt (1684–?), although the latter's branch of the family lived outside the city of Albany itself. See Pearson, *The First Settlers of Albany*, 24.

219. The meaning of the closing remarks in the account remains unclear. In Dutch, it reads:

1705 den 18 Junij heeft hij mijn vooer gewesen dit
boven standen op Johannus bradt om daer
57 quarties voor desen booven standen schult

220. "Sahorackwaghte in 'modern' Mohawk: sahorahkwathe' is 'the bright sun'" (GM). For another account with this name, listed as Sahoorackwachte, see page [39]. There it is used to identify his mother, who developed a small account in the same year (1697).

221. For another account with this name, and a note, see the previous page, [27].

222. While there are several folios 19, see page [51]. The cross-reference there confirms the connection.

223. Like Arija and Arijawaasen, Wagrassero (various spellings) formed part of an intricate group of individuals who traded with the Wendells. Most of the members of the group were his direct relatives. They included his mother, his mother-in-law, his son Adam, and his wife's son (Daniel). Their accounts, activities, and debts accrued through the involvement of others (who fetched merchandise for them), are on pages [30], [32], [36], [51], [93], and [95]. Together, these fall in the exceptionally long period between 1697 and December 1721. He, and most of his relatives, also functioned as intermediaries by introducing other individuals to the Wendells. It is quite likely that he is the same as Wagrasshse who reported his findings after an intelligence mission to Montreal with Canawanegoe' (the report was made June 21, 1709); see *DRCHNY*, 5: 85. This is the only other reference to this individual that has been located.

224. Griet is identified (as Groet) on page [119] as Arija's wife. She frequently appears in the account book, see the note with Arije on page [30]. The only Griettie mentioned in the baptism records occurs at too late a date to be the same woman, as she had her son (an unnamed child by Adam) baptized in October 1724. See Feister, "Indian-Dutch Relations," 99; and Sivertsen, *Turtles, Wolves, and Bears*, appendix A, 216. The sponsors were Johannes and Anna (Kip) Wendell. But Grietie was often used as an abbreviated form of the female name Margarita/Margriet, of which there are considerably more occurrences in the baptism records.

225. She also appears on page [30], folio 12 in this account, again with an account of her own, covering 1697–1705.

226. "Kadareonichta in 'modern' Mohawk: ka'taronnihtha is 'she has a chimney made'" (GM). Comparison with another account in which she appears reveals a Seneca–Mohawk connection, see page [37].

227. Harmanus made a slip of the pen here, as he wrote *seewawant,* instead of *seewant.*

228. This word has no meaning, probably *dito* was intended.

229. For the accounts, activities, and debts of an intricate group around Wagrassero (various spellings), see the note on page [29].

230. Either 1703/4, or 1705/6 was intended.

231. The payment was not incorporated in the tally at the right side of the page.

232. "Arija (in 'modern' Mohawk: arya') means 'fish hook' in English. This was probably a pet name" (GM). Additional accounts of or connections to this Mohawk client are on pages [36], [41], [43], [46], [87], [106], and [107]. Page [46] is folio 15 in this account. Relatives of Arija (also Arije, Arya, Aria, Aerija, Areja) who maintained some form of commercial contacts with the Wendells, were his mother, wife, and son. Including these, the accounts cover the years 1697–1720. Arija and his direct relatives functioned in introducing a number of individuals, affiliated with them in various ways, to the Wendells. The entry on page [41], from 1704, indicates that he would have had a certain status in his community, and that this was recognized by the Wendells, as they describe another native customer as "living in the house of" Arija. He may well have been the father of Cornelius, later sachem of the Wolf clan, recorded in 1700 as Kornelus the son of Ari in the baptism records of Schenectady; see Sivertsen, *Turtles, Wolves, and Bears,* 90–91, 223. Also see the entry on page [106], for Cornelis's wife, described as Aria's son. Evidence exists of a Mohawk with the name Aria, or Arie, a noted war leader. On May 28, 1717, Alida Schuyler Livingston added to a letter from Livingston Manor that "Arie *de Wilt*" (Arie the savage) had just passed by with twelve or thirteen other American Indians, and that they carried three scalps and an Indian who they had captured in the Carolinas; see Livingston Family Papers, Correspondence of Alida Schuyler van Rensselaer Livingston, 1656–1720), GLC 03107. A delegation from Virginia, that was sent to Albany to discuss with Iroquois leaders a series of recent violent clashes, found in June of that year that "Aria, a Mohog that was Capt. of that company that was lately in Virginia" denied any hand in the raids in that colony; see *DRCHNY,* 5: 493. Other occurrences of the name are related to land deals between 1717 and 1733. See Sivertsen, *Turtles, Wolves, and Bears,* 79, and appendix F, 263; *AA,* 10: 53; and *DRCHNY,* 6: 16. It is by no means clear that all occurrences refer to the same individual as the one in this account book. He is certainly not the same as Arijawaasen or Arijenhotsen (both in various spellings) from this account book.

233. Folio 23 in the account book, on page [44], does not show a related account, but she is involved in transactions on page [43], a page that is labeled folio 22 (the second, consecutive page with that number).

234. Folio 23 in the account book, on page [44], does not show any related accounts.

235. "Sohoonachqae in 'modern' Mohawk: shonahkwa' is 'his spouse or marriage'" (GM). An additional account for this Mohawk and his wife is on page [85], where his name is listed as Johonnaghquaa. Page [85] is folio 66 in this account. Together, the accounts cover the period from 1698 to January 1709. The latter account contains strong evidence that this couple was involved in trade between Albany and Canada. His wife transported beaver to Wendell from Canada, and a Mohawk with connections to Canada (Sakadereuightha, see the note on page [66]) fetched merchandise for them.

236. For a discussion regarding this locality, see the note on page [4]. It is also mentioned on page [17].

237. See the notes for Catrin on page [24], listed as folio 6 just above this account, and page [96].

238. Sohoonachqae must have been intended.

239. "Saqaenakarie in 'modern' Mohawk: sakanakere' is 'there is plenty of it again'"

(GM). This is most likely the same individual as Saequarij, just above, and certainly the same as Saequanekarij, on page [24]. Together, the accounts cover the period from 1698 to September 1704.

240. Some illegible words.

241. He appears farther down the same page, and with another sizeable account on page [49]. Page [49] is folio 19, just above this entry and in the last line on this page. Together they span the period between 1697 and March 1703. His wife is active only on the first account on the present page.

242. Apparently, the five beavers were credited as three.

243. "Owanije (in 'modern' Mohawk: Awanie, Awanay) was mentioned as a Mohawk sachem in 1700 and 1702" (GM). See *DRCHNY*, 4: 728, 985. His connection to Wagrasseroo confirms his Mohawk ethnicity. There are no indications that his considerable debt was ever paid (apart from a small payment on a later debt, farther down the same account).

244. For the accounts, activities, and debts of an intricate group around Wagrassero (various spellings), see the note on page [29].

245. The total additional debt is entered in the column for beavers, although they should have been counted as martens.

246. This relatively small payment is not reflected in the tally of the account, as none of the vertical marks for the debt in martens is crossed out.

247. The one page labeled folio 23, page [44], does not show any related accounts.

248. The transaction of October 10, 1702, was entered at that point in time; the remainder of the account spans between the years 1697 and 1701.

249. Note that her husband, who she brought from Canada, traded on her account; see the last entries here.

250. "Kanadakonchoo in 'modern' Mohawk: kanatakonhon is 'in the middle of the village'" (GM). The name appears, but is crossed out, on page [35]. The same individual, listed as Cannadekonka, is clearly involved in an account on page [61]. Together, the accounts cover the period between 1697 and May 1709. His wife and daughter trade on the same account here, and on page [61]. Page [61] is folio 43 in this account.

251. The original reads a *mans lap*. For the term *lap*, see the glossary. In this instance, it possibly refers to a piece of cloth that Indian men used to cover their genitals.

252. "This was rather a place name near Crown Point on Lake Champlain," (GM) see Beauchamp, *Aboriginal Place Names of New York*, 73–74. This is certainly a possibility, but the account (and the extension of it farther down the page, involving Rotsie's daughter), shows there was also a (most likely female) Mohawk with that name who traded with the Wendells. "This could be either rotsiyo '*he* has good fish' or rotsi'io '*he* is weak'" (GM), emphasis added. A boy of twelve years old was baptized as Johannes in Albany (October 1700), when his native name was recorded as Rotsiho; see Siversten, *Turtles, Wolves, and Bears*, 53, 55, and appendix A, 212. It remains uncertain whether this client was a woman, see the following note.

253. "Dekaweeijeendigtachkoo in 'modern' Mohawk: tekaweyente'tahkon is 'the right side.' This is a female name" (GM).

254. The name originally ended with -quei, but was changed to -quee. Most likely, this is the same individual as mentioned on page [93], in an entry from 1709. There, his name is spelled Decaregjaghiaghquaa, but is mentioned only to identify his unnamed son.

255. If she is the same as Rabecken (which seems entirely plausible), she also appears on pages [21] (see the note there), [106], [107], and [118].

256. See the note with Roetsieijoo on the same page ([34]).

257. This could refer to Rotsie[ijoo], (above), her daughter, or both women. Since *sij* (modern Dutch: *zij*) can be singular and plural, this remains unclear, the more so because the verb is lacking.

258. See also the account of her mother, higher on the same page.

259. Crossed out here, he has an account (with active participation by his wife and daughter) on page [33] (see the note there), and page [61].

260. He also appears, with variations in his name, on pages [54] and [83]. These instances cover the period between 1697 and June 1707. His unnamed wife is active on this account, and the one on page [54]. Page [54] is folio 22 in this account. He may be the same as the Mohawk sachem Tananguriss who was present at an Indian conference in Albany, where the Mohawk, Oneida and Seneca nations reaffirmed the Covenant after French attacks in 1691; see *DRCHNY*, 3: 805.

261. This Mohawk man also appears with an account on page [43], where his wife is also active on that account. Together, the accounts cover the years 1697 to 1700.

262. For this Mohawk man and his relatives, see the note on page [30].

263. See the last account on page [29].

264. For the accounts, activities, and debts of an intricate group around Wagrassero (various spellings), see the note on page [29].

265. Areia's mother, a Mohawk, employed a Mahican woman to deliver the peltry.

266. "This could well have been the leading Cayuga sachem Tekahenyonk" (GM). See Fenton, "The Roll Call of the Iroquois Chiefs," 65. That would also support the reconstruction of the sentence, as the sachem would have been in a position to someone in his sphere of influence to bring him certain goods from a trusted source. On the other hand, this may be the individual mentioned as Thaeckenyackhaee on page [41] and, with slightly different names, in accounts on pages [44] and [75]. But in those cases, the environment in which the accounts are embedded suggests that individual was probably Mohawk; and no indication of Thaeckenyackhaee's position as a sachem can be found there.

267. All major individuals in, or related to, this account are Mohawk. It may be assumed that Wendell was in Mohawk country.

268. In the original, the last entry is written to the right of the other entries, between the tally for martens and the vertical mark for one *lap*. This was clearly done because of the lack of space in the account.

269. "I am not sure he was an Onondaga. Canadiorha was a traditional Mohawk name. For instance, there was a chief of that name in 1763" (GM). See Sullivan, *The Papers of Sir William Johnson*, 6: 50. Given the identification here in the account, his affiliation with the Onondaga has been maintained (also in TABLE 1 of the introduction).

270. This was Evert's older sister (1676–?), to whom other references are made on pages [101] (listed as folio 80 to the left of this account), and [119]—all cases relate to the same female Mohawk customer. See the remarks in the note on page [119]. For additional occurrences of the description "our savage," see the note with the first account on page [5].

271. This Mohawk man appears frequently in the accounts. Entries for him and his relatives can be found on pages [58], [60], [74], [86], [97], [115], [116], and [117]. He and his relatives (his wife, his wife's son, sister-in-law, and mother-in-law were actively involved in the trade) also functioned as intermediaries, introducing others (probably with some form of association to them) to the Wendells. Together, the accounts span the period between 1702 and February 1710. Despite the considerable activities of the group around this individual, no additional references to him or his relatives have been located in other sources.

272. No additional information has been entered.

273. This Mohawk man's name also appears on page [26] (see the note there).

274. The woman reappears, with an identification through both her sons, on page [55] listed as folio 38 in this account. Together the accounts span the period between 1704 and June 1710. Her son reappears as Nansendaghquee (one of two brothers, with alternate names added) on page [55], where he developed his own debt with the Wendells.

275. For another account with her name, as Kadareonichta, see page [29]. Combining this entry and the one on page [29], some interethnic connections appear. The son of this Seneca woman, Nansendaghqua, had a wife/companion whose mother was Mohawk.

276. Sara's account is crossed out here, but repeated in the following entries. There were numerous Indian women with this Christian name, who were baptized in Canada, Albany, or Schenectady. The information here is not sufficient to further identify her.

277. All numbers between brackets were blotted away.

278. "Aeshaerijkoo in 'modern' Mohawk: a'share'kowa is 'big knife.' This was also a common Mohawk name for a war chief" (GM). Note that he is clearly identified as a Seneca (also see the notes with the locality where the arrangement was made, and the sachem mentioned), an affiliation that has been maintained in TABLE 1 of the introduction. The Canadian client named Ashareiake on page [90] is apparently a different individual, since he was described as young more than ten years later. Also, Gunther Michelson identified that name as Onondaga.

279. "Oriewaes in 'modern' Mohawk: orihwase' is 'news.' This would hardly have been a name but rather a statement" (GM).

280. Wendell had a group of native customers whose place of residence is listed as Canosedaken. The other examples can be found on pages [57], [70], [104], and [105]; together they span the years 1705–1710. Without exception, the name appears in accounts with customers identified as Senecas. With regard to this locality, a situation similar to that of Caughnawaga existed. Documentary evidence shows the existence of at least two Iroquois villages with this name. One Canosedaken was situated in the homelands of the Senecas in Iroquoia, the other was described in September 1700 as being home of "the Indians about Mont Reall. . . . [in] the Castle called Canossodage"; see DRCHNY, 4: 799, 805. The Canadian village was also mentioned in 1695 and 1698, in both cases as "Canessedage, a fort where praying Indians of Canida live"; ibid., 120, 493. Gunther Michelson confirms the identification of one of the locations of this village: "This was originally an Onondaga mission at the Lake of the two Mountains near Montreal, Quebec. Later, Mohawk became the dominant language. It still exists today." See Beauchamp, *Aboriginal Place Names of New York*, 206. The village in Iroquoia is clearly identified in 1726. On September 13, New York Governor William Burnet announced to the sachems of the Six Nations that he would "send a proper person to stay among the Sinnekes this Winter," and two days later he appointed Evert Bancker "commissionary among the five [sic] nations," who was to "reside till April either at Canosedaqui or Onahe." See DRCHNY, 5: 797. The particular village Wendell referred to can only (most likely) be established by the instance here, and the one on page [57]. Since one of the witnesses to the agreement, Caienquaragtoo, can be identified as a Seneca sachem in Iroquoia (see note 282), Wendell most likely described that location. The Seneca Aennossockte is evidently the same individual as Josquassoo, which allows for a likely identification of the locality listed on page [57] as the Seneca village in Iroquoia.

281. The sentence ends abruptly.

282. This witness can be identified as the leading Seneca sachem Cagenquarichten (various spellings), also called Blawbeck or Blewbeck (fl. 1699–1726). For a detailed description of his diplomatic activities, where it is concluded that "by the 1720s [he] was regarded as a good friend of the English," see Halpenny, Hamelin, and Cook, *The Dictionary of Canadian Biography*, 2: 111–12. One of his appearances in Albany, as Wakajenquarachto, was in 1702. See DRCHNY, 4: 985–89. Gunther Michelson disagrees: "Kayen'kwarahton, 'disappearing smoke,' was a famous Seneca war chief during the American Revolution, not a sachem. However, this is also a traditional Mohawk name. For instance, John Smoke Johnson, the grandfather of the Mohawk poetess Pauline Johnson bore this name." See Fenton, "The Roll Call of the Iroquois Chiefs," 66–67; and Graymont, *The Iroquois in the American Revolution*, 123.

283. "Anonhso'kte' in 'modern' Mohawk is 'the end of the house' and was a traditional Mohawk name. During the American Revolution there was a war leader of that name, Isaac Anonhso'kte'" (GM). See Graymont, *The Iroquois in the American Revolution,* 254. Note that he is clearly described as a Seneca, an affiliation that has been maintained. For additional accounts that confirm his Seneca identity, see pages [41] (where he is listed as Tannassecha), [57], and especially [92]. On page [57], a Tennessocthaa is listed as residing at Canosedaken, in the context of this account book almost certainly the Seneca village in Iroquoia, not the mission settlement close to Montreal. In this account, his wife and mother are active; the one on page [57] shows him escorting a big customer. Together, the accounts cover the period from July 1699 to August 1710.

284. An additional account for this woman is found on page [56], where she is described as a "black savage," and her name is rendered Osheea. Her residence is further described there as Caenaederhaa. In all likelihood, the name refers to a Cayuga village. Together, the accounts cover the period between 1704 and 1708. In the present account, she introduced a woman to the Wendells. This is repeated on page [56].

285. He also appears on pages [54] (see the note there), [56], and [100].

286. Documentary references to a Mohawk political and military leader Jannetje/Jannetie (fl. 168?–1691) exist. On December 31, 1691, the New York Assembly was informed that the "Brothers Jannetie and Warigio" had been among those killed by Indian allies of the French, along with others of "the best Indians very well known to us"; see *DRCHNY,* 3: 817. In 1686 his native name was listed as Onnachragewaes; see *LIR,* 104. Considering the support he must have given to the interests of people in Albany, it is possible that his wife would be referred to in this fashion. Marij may be the same woman as Marijae (various spellings) on pages [27] and [48].

287. Her son developed a more substantial account in the same year, see page [28].

288. There are several references to this locality in the pages of this account book. In all but one of these cases, the Indian traders who resided in this village are identified unambiguously as Seneca women. The only exception to this pattern is found on page [58], where Wendell entered the account of Caienjawie, an Indian woman whose origins he does not state. The other references appear on pages [55], [83], and [104]. Together with the present instance, they cover the period from 1704 to 1710. Identification of this village, as a settlement of the Senecas in Iroquoia, is apparent also in the only contemporary reference to this locality in the primary sources. In June 1700 Johannes Groenendyk and Abraham Provoost reported to Robert Livingston that they had visited "the farthest castle of the Sinnekes called Sjaunt," where an English captive from Virginia, Charles Smith, had pleaded with them to effect his release; see *DRCHNY,* 4: 691.

289. The Dutch reads *houwen.* Considering the other occurrences of such descriptions with the verb *houden,* that have all been translated as "to stay [at]," this seems plausible here as well. *Houwen* would then be a corruption of *houden* (the substitution of a *d* with a *w* in verbs occurs quite often). But it can also mean "to cut" (tree branches, twigs, reed, etc.; or to plough land), a possibility that cannot be completely excluded.

290. This uncle Evert (1660–ca. June 1702) must be the brother of Hieronimus, father of Evert and Harmanus; see the introduction. His cousin Evert Wendell recorded several transactions with Indian clients who had some connection to his uncle when he was still alive (page [42]) and, after his death, with his aunt (this entry, plus those on pages [56] and [68]). The latter entries state that the respective accounts were with Indian clients who were in some fashion connected to the wife of Evert's uncle, Elizabeth Glen. See Talcott, *New York and New England Families,* 381. Evert Wendell also recorded transactions with references to an uncle Hans (or Johannes). He was probably either Johannes Sanderse Glen, or Johannes Teller. See the note on page [84].

291. "Kanasquiesackhe in 'modern' Mohawk: kanahskwisakhe,' or 'looking for a burden animal or a captive'" (GM). On pages [42], [47], and [48], the name is listed as Dekanasquijesackha, Dekanasquiesackha, Dekansqueisackha, and Dekansquesackha.

On pages [106] and [107] this Mohawk man's name is stated as Kanosquisackhe, Knos-quisackhe, and Cannasqusakje. Taken together, the accounts cover the period 1698–1726. The accounts of his wife are included in this. This unnamed woman appears with her own accounts on pages [48], [106], and [107], and they both trade on one on page [47]. His cousin (or nephew) trades, also on his own account, on page [47]. Yet, the second sequence of names may refer to a different individual: "Kanosquisaekhe in 'modern' Mohawk: kanonhsakwisakhe,' or 'going to look for a house'" (GM). As neither of the two possibilities can be excluded, he has been counted as a single Mohawk individual in TABLE 1 of the introduction, and his wife and cousin (or nephew) are counted as such. In 1717 a prominent individual among the Mohawks signed a deed for the Wolf clan, for land at Schoharie, as Canasquisacha. See Sivertsen, *Turtles, Wolves, and Bears*, 79, and appendix F.

292. Here, a note or number has been wiped out, and the same occurs in the next line.

293. It appears that this whole list of goods was delivered on credit on a single day. The delivery suggests that this customer acted as a peddler (see TABLE 13). He appears in the same fashion on pages [42] (twice), and [45].

294. "Kanaequathoo in 'modern' Mohawk: kanakhwahton or 'missing spouse'" (GM). He is likely the same individual as Canaquatho, a "Mohogg of the uppermost Castle," who reported to Albany in May 1695 that he had detected a "scheme among the Canadian Indians and the Governor of New France"; see *DRCHNY*, 4: 125. He could possibly be the same Mohawk who, with others, sold a parcel of land near Schenec-tady to Jan Hendricks van Baal in August 1672. The name appears as Canaghko in an eighteenth-century transcription of the document; see NYSL, SC 16676–30. He signed with a mark of the Turtle clan. In a printed version, without the marks, the name is Ca-nachko; see Leonard, "The La Grange Family," *DSSY*, 24: 7–33.

295. "Brant, or Brandt, was persuaded [in August 1700] by Henry [or Hendrick, or Hendrik] and other Protestant Mohawks not to go and live in Canada" (GM). See *DRCHNY*, 4: 731. Henry, one of the "Four Indian kings" is in an account on page [10], where his name is listed as Hendereck. If this Brant was indeed the prominent Mohawk sachem of the Bear clan, he would later also be one of the four Indian visitors of En-gland. He was baptized on December 20, 1694, when his age was listed as around twenty; and his Indian name was recorded as Thowariage (his later ceremonial name would be Saquainquaragton). His wife would have been Margaret/Margriet, Indian name Kviethentha; see Sivertsen, *Turtles, Wolves, and Bears*, 37, 284n2. But perhaps another Mohawk individual was listed here: on January 1, 1696, Tarogiagetho was baptized as Barent, which can easily be rendered as Brant; ibid., 210. All other appearances of Brant in the baptism records are too late in time to be applied to the present individual. He has been counted as a Mohawk individual in TABLE 1 of the introduction.

296. Here, Wendell wrote *Maqusse*, instead of the normal renderings used in other places in the account book to indicate Mohawk (e.g., *Maqaese, Maquase*, or *Maqaes*).

297. For this Mohawk man and his relatives, see the note on page [30].

298. See the note for Thackaeijack, on page [36]. He reappears on pages [44] and [75]. The latter page is folio 57 in this account. Together, these accounts span the period between October 1699 and October 1707.

299. The reference to folio 73 (see page [92]) shows that he is the same as the Seneca man Josquassoo or annosktoo. For a note on that individual, see page [38]. The listing here of Kawessat as a second name is puzzling; he probably also appears many years later on page [93], as Cawesaet, a "big Seneca."

300. He does not reappear elsewhere in the account book, but his brother-in-law and sister do.

301. It is not clear from this account book if this brother-in-law of dewannighrijeie

did indeed pay the remaining debt. He also appears (as DeCanjaeDeReghtToo) on page [66] with a substantial account, giving goods to the son of Sakadereiughthaa, a male (most likely) Mohawk trader with strong connections to Canada (see pages [67] and [85]). He also appears as dʼcanjadereghtoo on page [98] in an account of his wife (most likely, a sister of dewannighrijeie), where she is identified as a Cayuga. Together the accounts cover the period between October 1703 and November 1710. The relationship between Evert Wendell and this Indian trader continued for a considerable time. At the same time, Evert entered a note in English on the inside of the front cover of a Day Book, that on January 6, 1723/4, he had paid a large amount of goods "to Canjadereghto a Caghnawake [Caughnawaga] for that he surrendered a Negro boy which he had Taken in Vergenya [Virginia]." Evert's effort was later compensated by the commissioners for Indian affairs in Albany, who seem to have ordered the attempt to liberate the boy; see Evert Wendell, Day Book, 1717–1749, NYHS. The accounts in this manuscript suggest that at some time during these earlier exchanges, Canjadereghto was already living in Canada, or had connections there.

302. For a note on this individual, see page [39]. He also appears in the following account, and additional accounts of him and his relatives are on pages [47] (listed as folio 18 to the left of the next account), [48], [106], and [107].

303. Delivery on a singe day of such a quantity of goods suggests that this customer acted as a peddler. The instance has been incorporated as such in TABLE 13 of the introduction, and is the second occurrence on the same page.

304. He also appears in the account above.

305. It appears that Wendell did include the charges on the account, ignoring his remarks that this ought not to be done.

306. Although Wendell intended to charge twelve martens for the merchandise, he recorded a debt of thirteen martens.

307. The Dutch term *neef* does not differentiate between nephew and cousin.

308. At the time of this entry Evert Wendell, son of Evert Jansz. Wendell, an uncle of the writer was still alive—he died in June of 1702. For a reference to this individual, see the note on page [39]. His wife appears on pages [56] and [68].

309. It is quite complicated to attach a meaning to this interjection. It may be the name of the (likely Onondaga) individual from Kanende, whose account follows the entry. Alternatively, it could be the same individual as Adooho on pages [49] and [120], although that individual seems to be embedded in a Mohawk environment. An intriguing possibility is given by Gunther Michelson: "[This] does not appear to be a name. But there is a religious dance, the atonwa,ʼ which is a prominent feature at the Green Corn festival in August and the Midwinter festival in January. Could this be a reminder for Evert [Wendell] to attend this?"

310. This may simply be one of the various ways by which the Wendells referred to Canada. But it seems more plausible that Harmanus (the entry is in his hand) intended to describe the young Indian's residence in the Iroquois' homelands. About eight miles from the main Onondaga village, the Onondagas had a fishing station that also served as landing place; see Hodge, *Handbook of American Indians North of Mexico*, 1: 651. It was described, as such, in 1700, when its name was listed as Kaneende or Kanienda; see *DRCHNY*, 4: 649. Gunther Michelson submits a similar possible identification, also for the Onondaga area: "ka-ne-en'-da is given as 'port of Onondaga at Butternut Creek.'" See Beauchamp, *Aboriginal Place Names of New York*, 146. It seems likely that all references describe the same locality. The customer has been counted as Onondaga in TABLE 1 of the introduction.

311. He also appears on page [35] as Sasijijan (see the note there).

312. He also appears on pages [20] (see the note there), and [25]; the latter case only serves to identify his brother.

313. Evidently, a mistake by Harmanus (the account is in his handwriting). Con-

sidering the tally on the right, the arrangement must have been that if the customer did not return the bottle that contained the rum, he was to pay another marten.

314. Dekaniha reappears as Dekaenijhae on page [120], where part of this account is repeated; he is the same individual as Aedekanijhaa on pages [82] and [88], and Aedecanijhaa on page [72]. Together, the accounts span the period between 1699 and May 1708. He is likely the same as Dekanyhaha, a Mohawk who had just arrived in Albany from Canada and was questioned in July 1704; see Richter, *Ordeal of the Longhouse*, 218, 364n10.

315. As noted in the introduction, Evert's mother Ariaantje continued to trade with American Indians after the death of her husband. This entry, combined with those on pages [102] and [107], indicate that her involvement extended until at least 1709.

316. The only folio 16 in the account book, on page [34], does not show any related accounts.

317. Cresteia is mentioned only to identify his wife, an Oneida woman. The involvement of Areia's wife could signify that Cresteia was a Mohawk. He has been incorporated as of unknown origins in TABLE 1 of the introduction, where his wife has been included as an Oneida.

318. For this Mohawk man and his relatives, see the note on page [30].

319. "Kahonk, identical in 'modern' Mohawk, is 'wild goose'" (GM). Considering the period of time covered by this account and the one on page [21], it is likely that he is the same individual as Kahonckhae. Taken together, the accounts span the period between February 1697 and January 1708. The two accounts constituted a more than respectable amount of merchandise and debt, the greatest part of which was never redeemed.

320. This is the earliest occurrence of a name that reappears, with various spellings, on pages [41] (see the note there), and on [75]. On the occasion of this first delivery, Wendell noted the young Mohawk's alternate name, but did not repeat it elsewhere.

321. He and his wife reappear in the following account: the man as sochtaghcoo, and the woman remains unnamed.

322. This is evidently an additional account of thoghtachcoo and his wife, from the previous account. Together, the accounts cover the period between September 1700 and July 1704. The balance of the previous account had been paid.

323. "Dekannasoorae is not on my list of Mohawk personal names. But this is the name of an Onondaga orator and diplomat who lived for many years before and after the year 1700" (GM). This would be the Onondaga chief Decannesora/Teganissorens. For a good overview of his life, see *Dictionary of Canadian Biography*, 2: 619–23. Jennings, et al. contains a brief description of this individual, *The History and Culture of Iroquois Diplomacy*, 252. Richter notes that he was labeled both Oneida and Cayuga, and shows that he probably lived up to 1732, *Ordeal of the Longhouse*, 386n40.

324. Since it follows two consecutive pages that are numbered 22, and considering the appearance of an account referred to directly from page [61] as being on folio 23, the possibility must be considered that the second page 22 was misnumbered.

325. Page [61], listed as folio 43 in this account, contains an entry that lists the name "oghquesen or Canaghkwase," clearly for the same individual. Together, the accounts span the period between February 1701 and March 1719. "The first name, ohkwesen, means 'partridge' in 'modern' Mohawk. The second name means 'long barrel.' We may have here a recent name change or perhaps a mix-up of similar-sounding names. It is interesting to note that an individual by the name of 'Canaquese' was also known in 1654 and 1663 as 'Smiths Jan' or 'the Dutch Bastard'"(GM). See *DRCHNY*, 13: 264; and Grassmann, *The Mohawk Indians and their Valley*, 153–54. The *Dictionary of Canadian Biography* provides an overview of this individual's recorded activities (fl. 1650–1687), under 'Flemish Bastard' it states: "Indian name unknown," 1: 307–08. See Meuwese, "Flemish Bastard," 573. In a deed in May of 1685, one of the Mohawk native proprietors of land at Onisquetha, Onitsquathaa, or Onitquothaa, is listed as Ochquese; see "Deed to

10,000 Acres," *DSSY*, 21–22: 13–14; and *ERA*, 2: 276–77. For the same note, see Sivertsen, *Turtles, Wolves, and Bears*, 10, 275n21. In citing the pages where the name occurs in the Wendell account book, Sivertsen mistakenly states "44, 61," where she should give 45, 61. Sivertsen concludes that this Mohawk "became a communicant of the church in 1691 and died sometime before March, 1710"; ibid., 10. Yet, the account on page [61] for oghquesen or Canaghkwase has a last entry for March 9, 1719. And, as she herself reports, possibly the same individual (Canaghquase) signed a deed to Myndert Schuyler, and others, for lands at Schoharie in June 1717; ibid., appendix F, 263. The use, on that occasion, of the wolf in his mark possibly constitutes an expression of his clan affiliation.

326. As a security against the debt.

327. For this Mohawk man and his relatives, see the notes on pages [19] and [77]. Page [48] is listed as folio 19 in this account.

328. Delivery on a singe day of such a quantity of goods suggests that this customer acted as a peddler (see TABLE 13).

329. Neither she, nor her sister, reappear in the account book. Wendell's remark remains intriguing: did he not understand the woman's name, or was she unwilling to give it to him? Was she perhaps in a particular stage of her life, maybe as an adoptee, where she could not yet claim a personal name?

330. For this Mohawk man and his relatives, see the note on page [30].

331. As noted earlier, on page [30], the one folio 23 in the account book (on page [44]) does not show a related account, but she is involved in transactions on page [43], a page that is labeled folio 22, the second, consecutive page with that number.

332. In four cases, the Wendells described Indian customers as "black" (*swart*) or "blackish" (*swartigh, swartaghge*). For a listing and discussion, see the introduction.

333. The reference must be to Canoeawee.

334. For a note on this individual, see page [39]. He and his relatives also have accounts on pages [42], [48], [106], and [107].

335. See the preceding note, on page [47].

336. For this Mohawk man and his relatives, see the notes on pages [19] and [77]. Page [27] is listed as folio 9 in this account.

337. "Aennestoodde in 'modern' Mohawk: anenhstote' or 'standing corn'" (GM). Note that the woman is clearly described as Cayuga. The Mohawk affiliation of her husband has been maintained, also in TABLE 1 of the introduction.

338. A woman with the same or similar name appears on pages [27] and [38]. It is unlikely that they are the same individual: on page [27] a Marija is listed as the sister of Canosedeckhae (in December 1701), the present entry from 1700 lists Marijae as his wife.

339. A following, and closing, account for Arent can be found on page [85], listed as folio 66 in this account. There, he is described as staying at Canosedeckha, who is also mentioned here. Together, they span the period between December 1701 and September 1707. Two appearances of a (probably) Mohawk man (or possibly two men) named Arent are in the baptism records of Albany. Both took place in a period of time that allows for a possible identification: on September 10, 1699, an Arent served as sponsor at the baptism of Margriet, daughter of Asag and Maria; a few months later, on May 12, 1700, an Arent and his wife Agniet had their son baptized as Adam. All other occurrences of the name are too late to be connected to the accounts of the present individual; see Sivertsen, *Turtles, Wolves, and Bears*, 212.

340. Being a boy, it is very unlikely that this is the same Hendrick/Hendereck as listed on pages [10], [26], and [36].

341. As Watijandandieijoo, he has another account on page [32] (see the note there), listed as folio 14 in this account.

342. A folio 32 has not been located.

343. This section is in the right margin of the page.

344. For this Mohawk man and his relatives, see the notes on pages [19] and [77].

345. Adooho also appears on page [120] as Adohoo, where he is recorded as getting merchandise for Canoseedickhae's wife, probably in October of 1703. It is possible that he is also referred to on page [42] as A[d]owa, in 1700. But that entry seems to be connected to an Onondaga individual, while Adooho/Adohoo appears in a Mohawk context.

346. Also see the last note on page [27].

347. The sudden use of *New* Albany in 1701 cannot be explained. The only other occurrence appears on page [111], dated 1710.

348. "Dekarowade in 'modern' Mohawk: tekahronwate' or 'obstacle'" (GM). Note that he is clearly described here as Cayuga, an affiliation that has been maintained. Michelson's remark may possibly apply to Dekarowe, a Mohawk man, on page [26].

349. The name of this Mohawk man also appears on pages [23] (see the note there), [59], and [76]. An account predating this one, on page [120], identifies a daughter of his as Wierom Cast.

350. "CaghEnjockendase is probably Seneca" (GM). The reference to folio 18 reveals no relevant accounts of this individual on pages [36] or [47].

351. He does not reappear in the account book, but can be identified from other sources. In August 1703, the month before the present entry, Tarrigjories was one of two Mohawks who reported continuing French intrigues among the Senecas and Onondagas; see *LIR*, 190. This is almost certainly the same individual as Tarraghioris, chosen to join Johannes Bleecker on a mission to Onondaga in September 1713. The document places this individual at the second castle of the Mohawks, or Canajoharie; see *DRCHNY*, 5: 372. The year before, he was described as "Terachjoris, sachem of the upper Castle," Canajoharie, when he came to greet the new missionary William Andrews to Albany on November 15, 1712; see *DHNY*, 3: 901. In March 1711 Tarigjoris was one of the three Mohawks sent by the sachems to invite Hendrick Hansen from Albany to take command of the fort that was to be built there (Fort Hunter at Tiononderoge; the "lower castle"), and come to live with them; see *LIR*, 218. It is possible that he is the same as one of those to sign the 1717 deed for lands at Schoharie, where his name is listed as Targiors/Targions. Sivertsen states that his signature or mark possibly resembled a turtle, possibly indicating his clan affiliation, *Turtles, Wolves, and Bears*, 79, and appendix F, 267. Considering the time frame, it is less likely that he also signed a deed for lands at Canajoharie in May 1732. Also, the mark on that deed is listed as a bear; ibid., 121–12, 267.

352. As a security against the debt, although this seems unwarranted since the amount of goods taken on credit was small, and there are no indications that he developed other debts with the Wendells.

353. For the accounts, activities, and debts of an intricate group around Wagrassero (various spellings), see the note on page [29], listed as folio 11 in this account. Page [95] is listed as folio 76, to the left of this account.

354. Here, a sketch of a human head is inserted. It appears that Wendell initiated the sketch to document some physical characteristic of the Seneca boy, but for unknown reasons decided against it, or lacked time to finish. See PLATE XI.

355. There is no apparent connection between the computation here and the account for Soghsiecoowao, at the left side of it. His mother does not reappear recognizably in the account book.

356. Aedam reappears as Adam on page [63], with the same identification through his father. Together, the accounts span the period between January 1708 and September 1714. Several Indians appear as Adam in the recorded Indian baptisms of the Dutch Reformed Churches in Albany and Schenectady, but there is no indication that any of those is the same as the present individual. See also the note for his father, and the group around that individual, on page [29].

357. Clearly a different individual from Thrghijoores, a Mohawk on page [50]. The accounts partially cover the same time, but are unrelated.

358. The outlines of the person's head is sketchy, but it is evident that Wendell depicted an animal tattoo on the neck of the Seneca man. Its shape resembles other drawings of smaller fur bearing animals in the account book (fisher and otter), but it is not clear what animal was intended here. See PLATE X.

359. Other possible translations of the Dutch *bedarde* (modern equivalent: *bedaarde*) are "modest" and "tranquil."

360. The name may also end with -ko*g*e, the handwriting is not entirely clear. He also appears in the (earlier) account, below this one, as a boy. There, he settled the existing account, and in the present one took out credit for three martens again. The new debt appears to have been left unredeemed.

361. Gunther Michelson first stated: "Sattkattstoghka, as given on [72], in 'modern' Mohawk: satkatston or 'you make soup.' This is a misunderstanding or a joke." Note that he is clearly described as Oneida, an identification corroborated by the listing of Anit-soondi, an Oneida sachem, who visited Albany for a conference with Governor Bellomont, August 27–8, 1700; see *DRCHNY*, 4: 728. This is very similar to Aennetsoendeija, or anetsondeian on page [72], the other name of this individual. In a second personal communication, in December 2003, Gunther Michelson agrees with this identification. Taken together, the entries on pages [52] and [72] span between the years 1704 and 1707.

362. Wendell was uncertain here as to whether this is her name, or that of her father. The name does not reappear in the account book.

363. "Dekanesthejendaghqua in 'modern' Mohawk: tekananhstayentahkhwa' or 'what is used to put corn down'" (GM). Note that he is clearly described here as Seneca, an affiliation that has been maintained, also in TABLE 1 of the introduction. His wife is recorded here as trading on his account, like his brother and son. His second, new name for this individual lends further credence to his identification as a Seneca. The last part of that new name is extremely hard to decipher, but if the second suggested version is correct, it is quite similar to the name Owenano, recorded for a Seneca sachem in 1702 during an extended Indian conference in Albany that lasted between July 9 and August 19. The first transaction on this account coincides with this particular conference; see *DRCHNY*, 4: 985–89.

364. Following the reference in the manuscript, he reappears on page [55] as Oeka-dee, where he introduces the son of another Seneca man. Page [55] is listed as folio 38 in this account. Together, the occurrences cover the period between 1705 and September of 1708.

365. This drawing of a beaver is slightly different from others in the account book—the right half of body was left out.

366. The first letter of what, most likely, is a first name is unclear. It appears to be an *f*, but in Dutch this is not a given name. The most immediate possibility is Frans, but it is equally possible that Wendell meant an *h*. Hans might be a reference to a number of men whose first name was Johannes, because the diminutive Hans was (and is) often used as a nickname. This includes some relatives of the Wendells.

367. The same account appears with the same identification on page [64], listed as folio 46 to the left of this account. The one difference between the two accounts is that in the second one, the debt from the last entry is attributed to another woman, who she accompanied.

368. For this individual, see the account below and on page [64], listed as folio 46 to the left of the next account. Together, the accounts cover the period between September 1702 and August 1710. He attempted to take out credit for his wife's account, but see the passage about that on page [64].

369. Actually, three names are listed.

370. Of all three names, only Aeredonquas reappears: among other occurrences, he is Aeriedonquaes in the account of his sister, above. Also see the note there.

371. On page [64], he is described as usually living in Canada.

372. The debt of one beaver was incorporated into the tally, to the right, but it has been crossed out. Since the Seneca man did return, it seems reasonable to assume that he retained the gift.

373. He also appears on pages [35] (folio 17 in this account), and [84].

374. His brother does not reappear in the account book, but the Mohawk thotquerijese has two very substantial accounts on page [76]. His wife shared those, and received merchandise to sell for Wendell. An individual described as her son paid part of the debt. Together, the appearances cover the period between July 1703 and October 1710. It is possible that he is the same as one of those who signed the 1717 deed for lands at Schoharie, where his name is listed as Totquaorese/Totquanese/'Tot-quaiorese. Sivertsen states that his signature, or mark, was a turtle, probably indicating his clan affiliation, *Turtles, Wolves, and Bears*, 79, and appendix F, 267.

375. He also appears on pages [38], [56], and [100]. Taken together, the accounts cover the period 1704 to July 1710; the entry on page [100] is about his wife's son, Caghneghtjakoo, and dates from September 1709. Both Oskeea, a woman he is recorded as escorting to Wendell, on pages [38] and [56], and his wife's son Caghneghtjakoo, are listed as Seneca's living in Cayuga. For Oskeea this is the case on page [38], where she is further described as "black."

376. See page [100].

377. This word has become illegible; it may be assumed that it expressed a (kin?)relation of the unidentified individual to Catquerhoo.

378. The woman reappears with an identification through one of her sons on page [37], although the latter's name is listed in a different form, Nansendaghqua.

379. Quite clearly, the suggestion here is that the woman had two sons with very similar names: Sendaghqua and Nansendaghqua. For the latter, see slightly above; Nansendaghqua is mentioned on page [37], also to identify his mother. However, farther down the present account, two different names appear for her sons.

380. This woman has been incorporated into TABLE 1 of the introduction, as of unknown origins.

381. Evidently, the Wendells were somewhat confused about the exact identity of the two sons; it is even possible that the latter use of the term "other" refers to a second name for of one of the sons, not another son. Neither of these two names reappears in the account book.

382. She does not have another account in the account book. The present account reports, some lines below, that she had died by September 4, 1708.

383. The Wendells described as *groot* (big) a limited number of Indian clients. They are all Senecas, two men and two women: see pages [57], [83], and [93]. Although the most linear interpretation of the description would be to assume that Evert and Harmanus simply indicated the physical stature of the client, it is also conceivable that they intended to describe the relative status or prestige of the customer within his or her community. In 1709, however, when describing "the highest sachem of the Seneca country," Evert used "highest" (*opperste*) not a Dutch equivalent for "biggest"/"supreme," "grandest," or "greatest." See the note on page [98].

384. He is also mentioned in the account of his brother Dekanesthejendaghqua on page [53], as Okade.

385. It remains uncertain if she is the same as Sackhoowa, a few lines below.

386. For a discussion of this Seneca village, see the note on page [39].

387. The sentence ends here, and it is immediately followed by a new entry.

388. This young Onondaga man also appears on page [79], in an account that coin-

cides with the latter part of this account. Page [79] is listed as folio 61 in this account. On the same page, he is shown to escort at least two, possibly three, customers to Wendell.

389. This locality was most likely situated in Cayuga territory, since Wendell had stated in an account on page [38] that Oskeea was a "black" Seneca woman who lived in Cayuga. The man who escorted her to the Wendells is mentioned on page [100], where it is stated that his wife's son was also a Seneca living with the Cayugas. No additional information on this village has been located. It is unlikely that Wendell referred to the same location in an entry for 1707, on page [81], when he registered the account of a Seneca man who lived in Canadedaerkoo. The same applies to account from May 1707 on page [59], where a Seneca woman is documented as living in Canendedaerhaa. Also see the notes on pages [59] and [81].

390. He also appears on pages [38], [54] (see the note there), and [100].

391. This account is also on page [38] (see the note there).

392. Another account that includes this Mohawk's name is on page [59], where the name is listed as orghiaedecka. "Orghiaedecke in 'modern' Mohawk is aronhiatekha' or 'burning sky,' for many years a prominent Mohawk sachem's name. One Arughiadekka was an influential Canajoharie sachem in 1745" (GM). See Wallace, *Conrad Weiser*, 226. It is very plausible that a sachem, with that name, resided in Canada. In 1701, a New York colonial official reported that "one of our Indians called Orojadicka" had been living in Canada for two years; in April 1711 he accompanied a French delegation to Onondaga that was to propose that the Iroquois allow the French to build a fort on the northern shores of Lake Ontario. On that occasion, he was described as "Orighjadikha[,] Sachim of the Maquase [Mohawk] Canada Praying Indians," and the next month a delegation from Albany hurried to Onondaga to fence off this "design by Oriojadricko"; see *DRCHNY*, 4: 907; 5: 243, 246. If the account book documents trade with the same individual, it is instructive to note that both he and his white Seneca wife (see page [59]) continued to cultivate commercial connections with Albany in the same period.

393. The wife would be Elizabeth Glen. For further information on this uncle, see the note on page [39], above. His wife did indeed outlive her husband. She apparently continued to develop contacts with Indian clients, and another entry lists her on page [68].

394. See page [92].

395. See PLATE IX.

396. For a discussion of this individual, the same as the Seneca Aennossockte, see the note on page [38].

397. For a discussion of this Seneca village, see the note on page [38]. The name also appears on pages [70], [104], and [105].

398. Abraham Cuyler (?-1747) was the second child of Hendrick (1637-1691), the first settler of that family; see Pearson, *The First Settlers of Albany*, 36. Abraham served as commissioner for Indian affairs between 1728 and 1734, thus sharing the office with Evert Wendell for a number of years; see Howell and Munsell, *History of the County of Albany*, 42. Besides their combined presence at the meetings of the commissioners, and their possible practice of referring indigenous customers to each other, a number of additional connections can be established between Abraham Cuyler and Evert Wendell. Most significantly, he was among those who, together with Evert, were requested by the Oneida sachems to accompany them on a mission to Canada; see *CCM*, 231. One of Abraham's daughters, Catherina, was sponsor at the baptism of Harmanus, son of Evert Wendell and Engeltje Lansing on July 2, 1731. See Pearson, *The First Settlers of Albany*, 36; and *Records of the Reformed Dutch Church of Albany*, 3: 42. Finally, he served in the same capacity at the baptism of Moses, the son of two converted Indians (Cornelis and Maria) on April 25, 1709. Cornelis's Indian name was registered as Tannawaneke—most likely the same individual found in the accounts on page [19] as Korneles (Kornelis) and on page [109] as Tanawaneke, whose unnamed wife had an account with Evert in 1710.

Another contact with Wendell, recorded in the account book, can be found on page [94]. It is possible that Wendell also referred to Abraham on page [20], see remarks in note 162.

399. The Dutch term used, *groot* (big), can refer to either the man's physical stature or his relative standing within his native community. See page [55], and note 383.

400. Aennaedsoenes reappears once in this account book, on page [100] to identify his brother, Soeiae or Osseraecoe, in September of 709. A brother of Aennaedsoenes also appears in the present account, but the two occurrences do not necessarily mean they are the same individual. See the following note.

401. The word is very hard to decipher, it is either *aensoet* or *achsoet*. It is not possible to give a translation of *aensoet*. It may be an expression, describing an affectionate relationship between the Cayuga Aennaedsoenes and Radewackeree. One of the meanings of the verb *aanzoeten* is 'to influence someone/something in a lovely fashion.' On the other hand, it may simply be a way of referring to his brother, who is mentioned in the next line. A note card, dated January of 1966 by Brasser and Sturtevant on the sketches and text in the account (see the note below, and PLATE VIII), provides an intriguing possibility. While Brasser's direct transcription of the word is mistaken, in that he adds an *s* to the word, he reads the word as *achsoet* (I have not duplicated the added *s*) and suggests it could be linked to the Seneca word *ʔakso:t*, or "my grandmother"; see NAA, Photo Lot 81R.

402. Probably the same brother as the one referred to, two notes above this one: Soeiae or Osseraecoe.

403. They probably represent Aennaedsoenes and his brother, or (perhaps) his *aensoet/achsoet*. The pattern of the tattoos is quite similar, see PLATE VIII. It appears that both have a clan symbol on the side of their face in the shape of a bird. A note card by Sturtevant and Brasser, with a photograph of these sketches in the account book, describes them as "show[ing a] tattoo on left cheek, neck ornament [or tattoo], [and] hair ornament"; see NAA, Photo Lot 81R. The notes are dated January of 1966, and the transcription and translation contain a number of mistakes and omissions (the word *gemp* was not transcribed at all).

404. Joseph, of which this clearly seems to be a rendering, was among the names used when Indians were baptized in Albany and Schenectady. It is uncertain if he is the same person as the Mohawk sachem, Joseph or Tanograthask/Dehanochrakhas. An important Mohawk leader (fl. 1693–1702), he is documented as welcoming Governor John Nanfan to Albany on July 10, 1701, with Cornelis, Gideon, and Hendrick (the same sachems who were recorded as participating in a Council there from July 12–19); see *DRCHNY*, 4: 60, 364, 995, 897; *LIR*, 178; and *AA*, 4: 135.

405. Gideon, of whom this clearly seems to be a rendering, was among the names used when Indians were baptized in Albany and Schenectady. He does not reappear in this account book, but Wendell maintained connections to a Giedeion at a much later date: an account with the commissioners for Indian affairs, shows that Evert made a payment of rum to a native with this name (and to an Anthony) in September 1724; see Evert Wendell, Ledger, 1711–1738, NYHS, f. 112. It is uncertain if he is the same person as the Mohawk sachem Gideon, or Tonidoge, documented as welcoming Governor John Nanfan to Albany on July 10, 1701, with Cornelis, Joseph, and Hendrick; see the note with Jisep/Joseph, above. In November 1733 Gidion was among the Tiononderoge (the lower castle) sachems giving land around Fort Hunter to the English Crown; see *DRCHNY*, 6: 15–16.

406. For a discussion of this locality, see the note on page [39]. As indicated there, this is the only instance where Wendell refrained from providing a ethnic affiliation of a woman from this Seneca village.

407. "Sooquentssoowaa is Seneca" (GM).

408. This Mohawk man, described here as young in the earliest account with his

name, developed into a customer of some importance to the Wendells, and as an intermediary by fetching merchandise for other customers. His additional accounts are on pages [83] (listed as folio 65 in this account), and [111]; in the latter, he is referred to as Caheghtsiede. He collects goods for others on pages [60], [74], and [83]. His unnamed wife is active on his account on page [83], and her debt is summarized with his on page [111]. Together, the occurrences cover the period between 1705 and June 1710.

409. The account book does not contain a page with that number.

410. Entries for him and his relatives are listed in a note on page [36].

411. Intended to indicate that any transaction, after this point in the account, occurred after the customer had been given a bill stating his debt.

412. At first, looking at the computations in the last entries of this account, it seems that Caheghtsiedauw had a debt of forty-seven or forty-eight martens. In that case, one beaver weighing two pounds would equal three martens ($48/16 = 3$). But the total number of marks for martens comes to sixty-four (see the tally in the main part of the account). That brings the value of one beaver of that weight to four martens ($64/16 = 4$). This is corroborated by the next account of this individual, on folio 40 (page [83]). There, Evert states explicitly that the conversion rate was four martens for each beaver weighing two pounds.

413. The *r* in this individual's name makes it unlikely that he was Mahican (BR), although his father (the Greyhead or Wassewaencke/Wassewaecke), is listed as a Mahican in the "register."

414. "The name 'Taijenoekee' is similar to Indian names recorded for Hendrick, or Henry, the first Mohawk sachem with that name," (GM). At the time of his baptism, in July of 1690, his native name was recorded as Tejonihokarawe, and its meaning interpreted as "open the door"; see Sivertsen, *Turtles, Wolves, and Bears*, 24. In February 1755, Taijenoekee was listed as the alias of another Indian and then later as "Hendrick the Mohawk chief"; see *DRCHNY*, 7: 55.

415. If "brother" is taken to be that of a sibling, the *r* in this individual's name makes it unlikely that he was Mahican (BR). Aeshentheree's wife has a small account immediately following this.

416. Wendell ascribes an explicit ethnic affiliation to this Indian woman, ToeWist-Toewee, which gives plausibility to the supposition that Canendedaerhaa was a Seneca village. This is further corroborated: "ToeWistToewee is Seneca 'towistowi,' or 'sand-piper'" (GM). No additional information concerning a village with this name has been located. Hamell suggests the name could be Seneca for "snipe," predominantly associated with western Seneca communities, at least for the last half of the seventeenth-century (pers. comm., October 2004). The locality appears on page [81] as Canadedaerhoo, the place of residence of a Seneca man, in 1707.

417. The first of three cases where the Wendells query a customer about the extent of a debt, or urge each other to do so. For an overview and brief discussion, see the introduction.

418. The name of this Mohawk man appears on pages [23] (see the note there), [50], [76], and [120].

419. The only folio 16 in the account book, on page [34], contains no relevant accounts.

420. No additional transaction were recorded.

421. For another account with this individual's name, recorded as Orghjaedikhaa, see page [56] and the notes there.

422. It is not entirely clear what specific locality Evert Wendell (the entry is in his hand) intended to enter here. There are indications that the village was located in Canada. In that case, it may be a rather maimed version of Caughnawaga. Orghiaedecke, who escorted this particular Seneca trader to Wendell, can very likely be identified as a sachem of the Canadian Mohawks, see the note on page [56]. In addition, Oquenjonquas

himself escorted a French boy to Wendell, probably an American Indian as indicated by the entry immediately following Oquenjonquas's. Gunther Michelson submits another identification: "ca-wa-o-ge is given as 'Mohawk village east of 4th Mohawk castle.'" See Beauchamp, *Aboriginal Place Names of New York*, 122. The present entry does not preclude either identification.

423. He, and two others, who were explicitly described as French Indians on pages [65] and [107], and have been included, as such, in TABLE 1 of the introduction.

424. Entries for him and his relatives are listed in a note on page [36].

425. A page with that number is no longer part of the account book.

426. Additional accounts are on pages [58] (see the note there), [83], and [111]; another appearance is on page [74].

427. In 1634, a Dutch envoy who traveled among the Mohawks noticed the presence of dogs in a native village and seemed to indicate their inclusion in the beaver hunt. The editors of his journal, however, consider it unlikely that Indians would have used dogs in this specific fashion; see Gehring and Starna, *A Journey into Mohawk and Oneida Country*, 5–6, 35n43. Domesticated dogs were present in native villages in the Northeast. See Feest, "Virginia Algonquians," *HNAI*, 15: 258–59; Heidenreich, "Huron," *HNAI*, 382; and Russell, *Indian New England*, 56–57, 223n16. The first and last support the occurrence of dogs in hunting activities.

428. "Atsenhaa in 'modern' Mohawk: otsenha is '[man-made] fire'" (GM). An additional account for this Mohawk man is on page [96]. He and his wife are also mentioned on pages [76] and [83]. Together, these instances cover the years 1707–1710.

429. An account for the same individual, shared with his wife and daughter (like the one here), is on page [33] (see the note there); his name also appears, but is crossed out, on page [35].

430. An account of the same individual is on page [45] (see the note there).

431. The one folio 23 in the account book, on page [44], does not show a related account; a number of transactions of this individual appear on page [45], a page without a number. Note that the unnumbered page [45] immediately follows a page numbered [22].

432. Hester (1686–?), a younger sister of Evert and Harmanus, apparently kept a personal trade book of her dealings with American Indian customers; references to her book also appear on pages [87], [95], and [107], which covers the period 1714–1718. See Pearson, *First Settlers of Albany*, 158; and Talcott, *New England and New York Families*, 380, 389.

433. Danijel reappears as Daniell on page [107], listed as folio 87 in this account; the cross-references in the account, and the way he is identified, remove any doubt that it is the same individual. Both occurrences show considerable accounts, together they span the period between December 1705 and September 1714. The baptism records from Albany show two individuals who may be identical to the Danijel here. A Mohawk woman, Neeltie Kawachkerat (probably the wife of the Wolf clan sachem Ezras Kanneraghtahare), had her seven-year-old son baptized with that name on April 4, 1696. He may have died before 1720; a fifteen-year-old young man was baptized with the same name on February 7, 1692, his Indian name was recorded as Sognihoä. See Sivertsen, *Turtles, Wolves, and Bears*, 24, 38, 44, 208, 211.

434. This appears to mean: on the young man's account or bill, or that of his father.

435. The meaning of the last entry, clearly connected to the entry for June 23, 1708, remains unclear. Since Wendell did not enter a specific number of martens, the line may have served as a reminder of the debt from 1708. The transaction is restated on page [95], dated September 18, 1709. There, it is entered as Waghrosraa's debt: a shirt for a pistol.

436. "Ohonsaioenthaa in 'modern' Mohawk: ohonhsayontha' or 'she invites to her land'" (GM).

437. This annotation cannot be connected to any other account or transaction.

438. Her appearances here, on page [80], listed as folio 62 to the left of the next account, and on page [110], allow us to attempt a reconstruction of her complicated (and somewhat confusing) family situation. In the present account she is described as the wife of Tharencoo, her son being Warhosse Rode, but the name of the father of this boy is listed as SaadecaeeRehos; the account on page [80] is dated 1½ years later, but does not elucidate the situation since only the boy's name is restated. The cross-references between page [80] and the final account from 1710, on page [110], connects the name Carghiedsiecoo to her husband. He is documented elsewhere in the accounts as maintaining strong connections to Canada, see the note with Karighijaetsijkoo on page [23]. As the latter's occurrences cover the same period of time as those of the present Mohawk woman, it is possible that she found in him a new partner, or that he had acquired a new name. Also see the note with SaadecaeeRehos, three notes below.

439. For an extensive note on this Mohawk individual, see [21], the first account.

440. The boy's name is listed as WaerhoesRoodee in the next account. For another account with this name, recorded as Waerhosradee, see page [80].

441. "SaadecaeeRehos in 'modern' Mohawk: shatekenhrons or 'the one who despises it'" (GM). At a first glance, this name for the boy's father conflicts with the name listed just above: Tharencoo. But (on a speculative note) it could mean that when Wendell inquired about his father's name, Warhosse Rode/WaerhoesRoodee stated that his (Mohawk) father disapproved of him and his mother trading at Albany.

442. It appears that the boy put down the axe as a security against the debt, while his mother later redeemed it.

443. "Thehoghtaghqueesren in 'modern' Mohawk: tehotahkwishron or 'using his strength'" (GM).

444. In February of 168½ Jellis (1670–?) was apprenticed to Evert's father, Hieronymus. He was a son of the family's first settler, Jacobus Gerritse van Voorst. Pearson states that he moved to Schenectady around 1700, after his marriage to Elizabeth van Eps, *First Settlers of Schenectady*, 245. From this town, Indian traders were often transported to Albany with their packs of furs and peltry, an activity that was often the subject of regulation in Albany's ordinances.

445. The "old" woman has been incorporated into TABLE 1 of the introduction, as of unknown origins.

446. Conceivably, an account with a French *coureur de bois*. The presence of such transient traders from Canada, in the area between Albany and Montreal, had been reported since the times of New Netherland. From the 1670s, they came to Albany in increasing numbers. See Hinderaker, *Elusive Empires*, 34–36; and Trelease, *Indian Affairs*, 246–47, 250–51. For an evident case in Schenectady in the 1680s, see Burke, *Mohawk Frontier*, 121–22. A "Jan the Frenchman" also appears in the correspondence between Alida and Robert Livingston. In a letter dated March 20, 1698, Alida reports from Albany that "Jan the Frenchman" had given advice on what Robert was to exchange in Canada ("pipes and discs," most likely wampum), and that Jan would be allowed to "go with the Canadian prisoners"; see Livingston Family Papers, Correspondence of Alida Schuyler van Rensselaer Livingston, 1656–1720, GLC 03107. Another of her letters clearly implies that this Jan was sent with strouds to Canada, shortly thereafter, ibid., June 24, 1698. In the present account, Wendell refers to a previous entry, regarding merchandise already delivered on credit to the Frenchman, but this belongs to a part of the account book that is now missing.

447. A folio 31 is no longer part of the account book.

448. See the note on page [21].

449. Adam also appears (as Aedam) on page [51], with the same identification through his father (see the note there).

450. He does not appear to be identical to Caanonda, on page [84]; there, the name is either a reference to a locality, or the second name of a native customer from Canada

(with evident Mohawk connections). "Oendack in 'modern' Mohawk: ontak' or 'kettle'" (GM). Note that he is clearly identified as an Oneida, an affiliation that has been maintained.

451. He also appears on page [54], like his unnamed sister.

452. A remarkable communication. In many other cases, customers' wives were allowed to take out quite some credit with the Wendells. The reason for Evert to decide against it in this particular case remains obscure, but the entry is in his handwriting.

453. She also appears on page [54], like her brother Aeraedonquas/Aedonquas.

454. This woman has been incorporated into TABLE 1 of the introduction, as of unknown origins.

455. He and two others who were explicitly described as French Indians (on pages [59] and [107]) have been included, as such, in TABLE 1 of the introduction.

456. Sharing the account here, his wife reappears with her own on page [69], listed as folio 51 in this account; they are both mentioned in an additional account on page [86]. Together, the entries span the period between June 1706 and October 1710. Many elements in the accounts strongly suggest they lived in Canada, also see the note with Senjaad'riesen in this account.

457. In the same month, possibly on the same day, he is mentioned to identify a Mohawk from Canada as his son-in-law, see page [86]. That relative also occurs in the account of Oghsiknoendoo, who is described as Canadian. Another occurrence in the sources links Senjaad'riesen to Canada—and in a significant way—on July 9, 1702, as a "Canada Maquase [Mohawk] Sachem, Sinjaderise" was among those to greet newly arrived Governor Cornbury to Albany. He carried proposals for prolonged neutrality during Queen Anne's War, with the aim to continue trade; see *DRCHNY*, 4: 978–83. If this is the same individual, which seems very likely, the entries show that five years later he and his direct relatives were actively engaged in commerce between Albany and Canada. Both accounts in the book (dating from the same month) have a connection to Aequaenaghtaa/Aquanaghtaa and his wife, as Senjaad'riesen and his son-in-law (Soe-Haahies) fetched merchandise for them.

458. On eight occasions, the Wendells used the word *tonties* (also *tonies, toniets,* or *tonieties*) to describe a set of items sold on credit. Almost all occurrences are connected to the trade with Canada. In most cases, Indians bought the item in large quantities, varying between nineteen and seventy pieces. A strict translation of the Dutch word *tontie* is a "small keg or cask," see the glossary. The untranslated Dutch term is supplied on all occasions.

459. For an instructive note on this individual, see page [41]. He also appears on page [98].

460. "Sakadereiughta is definitely Mohawk, and identical with Sagoderiechta" (GM). The latter name is recorded in a deed of Mohawk lands near Schenectady to Jan Hendricks van Baal in July of 1672. There, he signed with the mark of the Beaver clan. For the eighteenth-century transcription, see NYSL, SC 16676–30. For a published version, without the marks, see Leonard, "The La Grange Family," *DSSY*, 24: 7–33. Sakadereiughta appears in the pages of this account book on pages [67] and [85]. Together, these accounts cover the period between June 1706 and August 1710. The account on page [67] shows him trading on the same day as DeCanjaeDeReghtToo/Dekanijadereeghkoe, principal trader on the present account, and recorded here as giving a shirt to Sakadereiughta's son. Two aspects link Sakadereiughta to Canada through DeCanjaeDeReghtToo/Dekanijadereeghkoe: the latter is identified on page [41] as a brother-in-law of a "boy staying in Canada" (October 1703), and on page [67] a Mohawk from Canada fetched goods for him (December 1708).

461. Delivery on a singe day of such a quantity of goods suggests that this customer acted as a peddler (see TABLE 13).

462. See PLATE VII.

463. See the notes on the same individual on page [66], he also appears on page [85]. He is one of only two customers whose account takes up an entire page in the book. The other case is that of Canosedeckha, on page [77].

464. Delivery on a singe day of such a quantity of goods suggests that this customer acted as a peddler (see TABLE 13). He reappears two times on this page in the same fashion.

465. Intended to indicate that this transaction occurred after the customer had been given a bill stating his debt.

466. Johannes Becker served as treasurer of the corporation of Albany in 1693, and (before that) as assessor and alderman. See *AA*, 2: 120, 126. According to Pearson, this Johannes is the oldest child of Jan Juriaense Becker, the first settler of this family. No dates for his birth or death are available. It is unlikely, but possible, that this entry refers to Johannes's son, also named Johannes, since he was baptized on August 4, 1691, and would have turned seventeen at the time of this entry; see Pearson, *First Settlers of Albany*, 16.

467. He also appears on pages [23] (see the note there), [84], [90], and [110].

468. The meaning of this passage remains obscure.

469. This is a mistake. The line should read: "and one pair of shoes."

470. He reappears on page [71] as Coenjaesquaa, where Wendell ascribes two, different affiliations to him. Page [71] is listed as folio 53 in this account. There, Wendell insists: "but he is a Seneca," adding "who always stays with me." He has been incorporated as a Seneca in TABLE 1 of the introduction.

471. Speakers of some Iroquoian languages referred to the Miami Indians as Twightwighs. For this synonym of the Miami's, residing during this time between the southern tip of Lake Michigan and the Ohio River, see *HNAI*, 15: 688.

472. Elizabeth Glen. Another reference to her is on page [56].

473. D'waddierhoe also appears on page [112], listed as folio 92 in this account, as Dewadierhoe. There, Wendell describes him as a debtor in 1710, and lists Thussighrondie (Detroit) as his place of residence. Together, the accounts document his modest, regular trading contacts with Evert Wendell in Albany in June 1706, 1708, and 1710.

474. The two bearskins reappear in his account on page [112].

475. From the setup of the page, it seems that he is the one escorting the young Ottawa man from the account above his, to Wendell.

476. See PLATE VI. A note card by Sturtevant and Brasser (with a photograph of this drawing in the account book) describes it as "show[ing a] tattoo (snake?) on left cheek, ear ornaments, choker(?) [or tattoo] on neck"; see NAA, Photo Lot 81R. The notes are on a card dated January 1966. Brasser states that the reference (of *ottewawesen*) could not apply to the Ontario Ottawa "used around Albany ca. 1706." Since Wendell applied the term *Tweghtteghen* just a few lines above this account (one also dated 1706), which is recognized as an Iroquoian identification of the Miami Indians, Ottawa seems correct.

477. It seems very unlikely that he is the same as the Mahican man magh-maghcees on page [16]; there is, for instance, no correlation between the two individuals' debts.

478. An example of the fluidity and state of flux of native identities and allegiances in this period of time. Given the statement of his residence, he has been incorporated as an Ottawa individual in TABLE 1 of the introduction. The last name listed here suggests that he may be the same individual as Nondaresochte, documented in roughly the same time frame, and with a distinct connection to Montreal. In a letter from that city dated April 2, 1714, Johannes Roseboom, Jr. informed Evert Wendell that he had passed the request to pay Nondaresochte on to Monsieur Cologne. No information about his origins is provided, the circumstances and the amount remain unspecified; see Roseboom, misc. papers, NYHS, April 2, 1714.

479. As a security against the debt.

480. For a note on this man and his wife, see page [65]. They also appear on page [86].

481. *Omlaag*, combined with the pronoun *van*, is used to describe a location (distinct from other usages that describe variations in height or elevation). Janny Venema, confirms the local, contemporary use in Albany of the term in that sense: from below, or south of the town (pers. comm., February 2004). Delivery on a singe day of such a quantity of goods suggests that this customer acted as a peddler (see TABLE 13). Apparently, he never paid his debt. A specific ethnic affiliation of Aekoetts (e.g., Catskill, Esopus, or other) cannot be determined, and, as such, he has been incorporated under the generic Mahican label in TABLE 1 of the introduction.

482. This clearly refers to Nicholas Bleecker, third child of Jan Jansen Bleecker (1641–1732), the first settler of that family. See Pearson, *The First Settlers of Albany*, 19; and Reynolds, *Hudson-Mohawk Genealogical and Family Memoirs*, 1: 128–29. Nicholas was deeply involved in the fur trade. In 1699, he was commissioner for Indian affairs, and in that capacity made a journey to Onondaga with Johannes Sanders Glen. The journal of that mission, made in March and April of that year, contains interesting information regarding diplomatic contacts with native leaders; see *DRCHNY*, 4: 558–60. In 1707, he was accused of having made an illegal agreement with Deputy Sheriff John Kilnie. Although the exact nature of the deal was never revealed, it is likely that Nicholas could count on some form of protection from the official if he was caught in the practice of illegal trading activities; see *AA*, 5: 168. The accusations did not end his official involvement in the management of relations with American Indians, for he was reappointed commissioner and served between 1728–38 and 1742–45. His term in this office thus partially overlapped with that of Evert Wendell; see Howell and Munsell, *History of the County of Albany*, 42. Like most commissioners, he also received at least one military commission, in his case as an ensign in Captain Johannes Roseboom's company in Albany. For the commission (listed under April 28, 1715), see *CCM*, 424. It is very likely that the Niecklas who housed the Oneida man Soghseerowanna in the same month as this particular entry, as reported by Wendell on page [72], is the same individual. He certainly is the same person as listed on the final page of the account book, page [121].

483. Other drawings are on pages [57] and [68]; sketches are on pages [1], [51], [52], and [104]. Though the drawing here is far less natural than the one on page [68], it contains considerably more detail and it is the only one in which tattoos on an individual's upper chest are explicitly included. See PLATE V. A note card by Sturtevant and Brasser with a photograph of this drawing describes it as "show[ing a] facial tattoo (2 diagonals and snake(?)), ear ornaments, neck ornament [or tattoo], perhaps knife-like tattoo (or paint) on chest"; see NAA, Photo Lot 81R. The notes are on a card dated January 1966. For a similarly adorned Iroquois individual presenting a miniature portrait of the Oneida Good Peter in the late eighteenth-century, see Fenton, "Northern Iroquoian Culture Patterns," *HNAI*, 15: 312. The Oneida man has a tattoo that resembles the one depicted here.

484. A fascinating description: while Wendell starts the account for a Cayuga (man), he then adds to this description that his background is Seneca, and that he always stays with Evert to trade. He was entered without such comments in an earlier account (in June 1706) as a Cayuga man, and with the name Nacoeghnajasquei, see page [68]. Both accounts are in Evert Wendell's hand. One of his brothers is described in this account as Cayuga, see Caunquienen.

485. This reference is either incorrect, or the page is now missing; the balance on his account in 1706 is zero, see page [68] which has page number 50, and the page numbered 23 (on page [44]) shows no related accounts.

486. Wendell uses a peculiar term here, *ouwenaghtenghen*. Literally, it can be translated as "oldish." There is no indication that it denotes anything other than the translation provided here.

487. This name is perhaps similar to the name Tawienneha, recorded for a Seneca sachem in 1702 during an extended Indian conference in Albany, which lasted between July 9 and August 19, *DRCHNY*, 4: 985–89. The name does not appear elsewhere in the account book.

488. "SoghseeRowanna in 'modern' Mohawk: shoserowane' or 'great winter/year'" (GM). Note that he is clearly described as Oneida, an affiliation that has been maintained.

489. Wendell does not indicate whether this is a Dutch name or nickname for this Oneida, but that possibility must be considered. In that case, it could refer to either his pigmentation that gave him the appearance of someone pertaining to the Hottentot in Africa (which, considering the cases of "black" and "blackish" Indians in the accounts, seems a possibility), or to the native's manner of speaking. Apparently, the Hottentot language sounds as a stammer to the unaccustomed ear. A final meaning of the nickname can be a rough, unpolished, uncivilized person. Yet, Hottentot was not an entirely unknown surname in the Dutch Republic. Gruys describes more than six thousand of such poems, and one edition celebrated the marriage of Jan Hottentot in Amsterdam on September 12, 1747, *Dutch Occasional Poetry*. One of the poems in the edition, printed for the occasion, was by his brother C. Hottentot; see Municipal Archives of Amsterdam, F Hot 1.

490. This most likely refers to Nicholas Bleecker, see the note on page [70].

491. For another account of the same individual, see page [52]. It contains the same combination of names for this client, spelled there as Satkatsteghcooe and Aennetsoendeija.

492. As a security against the debt.

493. He also appears on pages [43] (see the note there), [82] (listed as folio 64 in this account), [88], and [120].

494. Delivery on a singe day of such a quantity of goods suggests that this customer acted as a peddler (see TABLE 13).

495. Other accounts with this name, allowing for variations in spelling, appear on pages [74], [115], [116], and [117]. The last page is listed as folio 40 in this account. Together, they span the years between 1701 and 1707. His wife has her own account, on page [115]; his mother appears to trade on his account, on page [116]; a woman fetches merchandise for him, on page [115]; and his sister-in-law (his wife's younger sister) is given the responsibility for her deceased sister's debts, on pages [74] and [115]. Possibly, this is the same Mohawk individual as "Onighreende[,] one of the principal owners" of land deeded on May 1685. See "Deed to 10,000 Acres," *DSSY*, 21–22: 13–14; and *ERA*, 2: 276–77. It is almost certainly the same individual as Onogradicha, chosen to join Johannes Bleecker on a mission to Onondaga in September 1713. He refused, however, stating that he was too ill to participate (although the European correspondent reported: "But we could not see it"). That document places this individual at the second castle of the Mohawks, or Canajoharie; see *DRCHNY*, 5: 372.

496. For a brief discussion of this phenomenon, see the introduction. Throughout the text, similar statements about the Wendells and two Indian women can be found: see pages [5]–[7], [12], [36], and [105]–[106] (the occurrences on pages [5] and [36] have additional information in notes). This occurrence, and the one on page [94] about Johannes Lansing, are the only ones that do not relate to the Wendells. Stephanus Groesbeeck (?–bur. July 17, 1744) was a trader in Albany and last child of Nicholas Jacobse Groesbeeck (1624–?[will probated on January 3, 1706/7]), the first settler of the family; see Pearson, *The First Settlers of Albany*, 56. Stephanus was connected to Evert Wendell in a number of ways. They were both included in the request of the Oneidas for interpreters for their expedition against Canada in 1709; see the section titled "trading accounts" in the introduction. He functioned as commissioner for Indian affairs without interruption for more than fifteen years, from 1728 to 1744, and Evert shared the office

with him for a number of years; see Howell and Munsell, *History of the County of Albany*, 42. Stephanus was a godparent for Evert, son of Evert Wendell and Engeltje Lansing, baptized on January 13, 1722/3. On that occasion, Stephanus's wife Elisabeth also served as sponsor—a role she had already fulfilled at the baptism of Ephraim, another child of Evert and Engeltje; see *Records of the Reformed Dutch Church of Albany*, 2: 85, 98. This Elisabeth had married Stephanus in 1699 and was a sister of Evert Wendell's wife, Engeltje Lansing; see Pearson, *First Settlers of Albany*, 70.

497. Entries for him and his relatives are listed in a note on page [36]. Page [86] is listed as folio 67 in this account.

498. No account of this nature, referred to as being on a page across from this one, has been located; the page numbers do not show gaps around this page.

499. Additional accounts are on pages [58] (see the note there), [83], and [111]; another appearance is on page [60].

500. The sentence disappears into the bound sections of the page (final segment of the name added); Schenectady was intended.

501. Other accounts with this name appear on pages [73] (see the note there), [115], [116], and [117].

502. The exact construction of this transaction, and the relationships between the individuals, are elucidated by comparing the major account on page [115]. The present account lists the woman as purchasing a blanket on credit, at a very steep price. Apparently, she was expected to travel to Schenectady to pay corn for this blanket and (switching to page [115]) for another debt—that of her sister, Onoghradieha's wife, who had died in the meantime. The unnamed sister's account on page [115] covers May 1703 to June 1706. The entry here probably dates from July 1707. The woman's own account on page [115] is also substantial.

503. By the time of this entry the Mohawk village in Iroquoia had been abandoned. It must, therefore, refer to the village close to Montreal, meaning the old Onondaga man had traveled a considerable distance to Albany.

504. Suckcughoieghtie may have lived until at least May 1708, when (as the account states) his debt with Wendell was paid.

505. Annahriesaa, or TaenNaahariesie, also appears in accounts on pages [84] and [91], allowing for varying ways of spelling. Page [91] is listed as folio 72 in this account. Page [84] features both Annahriese and Annahariese as his new name, and Sacksareeij as his previous name. Taken together, they span the period between October 170(6?) and November 1710. He is identified as the younger Seneca brother of Decakedoorens, a Mohawk living in Canada, on page [84]. The account for Sajacaawecha, also on page [84], suggests he is their father. The Wendells also described the latter as a Mohawk living in Canada. The present account also lists Annahriesaa, or TaenNaahariesie, as living in Canada, but the one on page [91] states that he had returned to live in Seneca country in 1708. For Gunther Michelson's description of the *Mohawk* name Annahariesen, see the note on page [91]. This individual has been counted as a Seneca in TABLE 1 of the introduction.

506. The original number was six, and was changed to seven.

507. An American Indian, with the Christian name Sander, was among the sachems of the Mohawk village of Tiononderoge, where Fort Hunter later would be erected; see *DRCHNY*, 6: 15– 16. It is therefore highly unlikely that he would live in Canajoharie, which was farther upstream on the Mohawk River. Wendell may have intended to make mention of the residence of his mother. For Sander, see page [19], and the note there.

508. The Mohawk village Canajoharie. Situated along the Mohawk River, farther away from Albany than the first Mohawk castle at Tiononderoge (later Fort Hunter) it was commonly known as the second, or upper castle. The analogy between the descriptive name of upper castle and the Mohawk name Canajoharie can also be deduced from two other entries in the accounts: on page [101] Wendell describes the debts of "the

female savage who [stays] at our Susan[na]," adding that she lives in Canadeohare that, when rendered phonetically, closely resembles the name listed here; the same woman reappears towards the end of the book, on page [119], where her residence is listed as the "upper castle" (*bovenste kasteel*). In this particular case, it is impossible to determine whether the village was home to both Sander and his mother, or either of them alone, but see the remarks in the previous note.

509. The *r* in this individual's name makes it unlikely that he or she was Mahican (BR).

510. He certainly reappears on pages [41], referred to as folio 22 in the next line, and [44]; possibly on page [36] (see the note there).

511. A large number of American Indian women were baptized in Albany and Schenectady (and Canada), and received this Christian name.

512. See the note on page [54].

513. No related account has been located on page [48], [49], [51], or [52]; all are numbered 19.

514. Her debt for the stroud blanket was crossed out; she either returned it, or paid Wendell.

515. This stipulation is not repeated elsewhere.

516. Four martens, for each shirt, must have been intended.

517. The specific remark, that she could also return the merchandise, suggests that she may have attempted to resell the items elsewhere. Her debt was crossed out; she either returned the clothing, or paid Wendell.

518. Accounts for this Mohawk man are on pages [60] (see the note there), and [96]. He is also mentioned on page [83].

519. The remainder of this entry is empty; day or account was intended.

520. The name of this Mohawk man appears on pages [23] (see the note there), [50], [59], and [120].

521. "Thaijadoores in 'modern' Mohawk: thaya'torens or 'he splits the body open.' It is remarkable that a prisoner is given such a prominent name. *Vide* "Tachiadoris, the greatest of the Maquas Sachims. He died in 1691" (GM). See Richter, "Rediscovered Links in the Covenant Chain," 45–85; *DRCHNY*, 3: 783. This prisoner, now adoptee, could trade on his own account. There are no indications that he is the same individual as the Mohawk Tanijijooris on pages [35], [54], and [83], or Tijedores on page [79], most likely an Onondaga.

522. Possibly, a case of English influences on some expressions. The original reads: *alst hem lickt,* an unusual construction in Dutch.

523. Although Wendell seems to make an error in this subtotal (to his own disadvantage), he is consistent: the following two transactions add up to four additional martens, and the total tally does indeed state ten martens.

524. In most other cases, the statement *to sell* is followed by the remark *for my account.* That does not occur here.

525. For this Mohawk man and his relatives, see the notes on pages [19] and [77]. Page [27] is listed as folio 9 in this account. He is one, of only two customers, whose account takes up an entire page in the book. This page is shown in PLATE 11. The other case is that of Sakadereiughthaa on page [67].

526. Delivery on a singe day of such a quantity of goods suggests that this customer acted as a peddler (see TABLE 13). Canosedeckhaa is also documented (some lines above) as going to Canada for Wendell.

527. These two lines were added, vertically, in the lower right hand corner of the page.

528. An account from 1707, that contains his name spelled d'Cackkeedooren, appears on page [84]. It specifies his father's debt, and the one following it details his younger brother's account, whose name is listed as Sacksareeij or Annahriese. That brother is described as a Seneca living in Canada, but an entry on page [91] states that he had

returned to Seneca country in 1708. For an entry by Evert documenting Evert's mother as the recipient of beaver furs weighing 40 pounds from Dekakedooren in 1710, see Wendell, Ledger, 1711–38, NYHS. The account here has not been crossed out.

529. "Canaghquajeese in 'modern' Mohawk: kanahkwayesen or 'easy marriage'" (GM). Considering this identification, and as this is a new name in May 1707, it is highly unlikely that he is the same individual as Canaghquese (or Oghquese) on pages [41] and [61], and/or Cangquasen on page [86].

530. As indicated in note 12 of the introduction, this individual is most likely Evert's younger brother Johannes (1684–1743). For another entry in connection with Hans, see page [87]. It is possible that an additional entry on page [54] refers to the same brother. Evert may simply have made a writing error when he noted that the young Seneca man Caijassee, also known as Canissoe, in July 1702 was lodged at Hans,' when he wrote "at ans." Johannes Wendell, sometimes mentioned as "Johannes Hieronymi filius Wendell," served as constable for at least one term in Albany's first ward (from 1711–12). See Pearson, *First Settlers of Albany*, 158; Talcott, *New York and New England Families* (380, 389); and *AA*, 6: 266.

531. Delivery of such a quantity of goods on a singe day suggests that this customer acted as a peddler (see TABLE 13).

532. For another account in his name, see [56]. The accounts following this one show him escorting two, possibly three, Indian customers to Wendell.

533. The year has been derived from the next account.

534. This suggests that tijedores occupied a position of some prestige or authority. Judged by the affiliation of the individuals involved or named, also in the surrounding accounts, he may have been an Onondaga.

535. Presumably, the reference is to Oranij.

536. From the context (the date of the account, the nature of the previous accounts, and the role of Oranij there), it appears that this young Onondaga man was escorted by Oranij as well.

537. As a security against the debt.

538. See folio] 90, and page [110] (and the cross-reference there). That identifies the present account as Carghiedsiekoo's (various spellings).

539. For two other, earlier, accounts that include this name, see page [62]. There, it appears that he is indeed her son, and that she is listed there as a Mohawk from Canada.

540. "Brother Manes" is a reference to Harmanus Wendell, see the introduction. A considerable part of the early entries in this volume are in his hand. Other references to him are on pages [93] and [119].

541. Johanna is a typical Dutch name for women—hardly a father. It may simply be a mistake, and the word *of* should have been in written between father and Johanna.

542. A reference to Hieronymus Wendell. Since he had died in (or before) June 1697 this small remark represents a significant indication of the long periods of time that native customers were allowed to retain (part of) their debts with the Wendells. Or, stated from a different perspective, the extraordinary extent to which indigenous traders were able to negotiate their responsibilities as debtors. Even this Canadian Mohawk, who left a (relatively small) debt unredeemed for a decade, was not barred from further participation in commercial exchanges with members of the Wendell family. On the contrary, the notes here and on page [62] clearly indicate that his trade (and that of his relatives) was quite extensive.

543. Several Dutch, German, and Spanish coins were referred to as *doller*'s, or *daalder*'s. Its value in the account book excludes the possibility that it is the Dutch lion dollar, a silver coin bearing the figure of a lion, which was also current in New York in colonial times. Its nominal value in the Dutch Republic was between thirty and forty-two stivers (or between 1.50 and 2.10 Dutch guilders/florins)—far less than the

value of one beaver listed here. See Van Gelder, *De Nederlandse munten*, 284. The *Oxford English Dictionary* also gives the Spanish peso or "piece of eight" (consisting of eight *reales*) as a possible meaning; the peso was widely used in the North American colonies. Yet, its value also excludes that it was referred to here—in this case because the value was of multiple beavers, not just one. In three instances an account book of trade, with American Indians in or around Kingston, New York, between 1711 and 1729, recorded the *doller* as a form of payment by native clients. Only one of these transactions lists a direct value of the payment: an undated entry, from the period 1715–1719, shows a debit transaction of one *doller*, valued at twenty-two Dutch guilders; see Philip John Schuyler Papers, Account Book, 1711–1729, NYPL, reel 30.

544. Literally: "a beaver's side." This may possibly mean one half of a fur.

545. "SasseNowanense appears to be Mohawk, possibly Oneida" (GM).

546. This young Onondaga man's age seems to preclude a connection to the ceremonial name of an Onondaga sachem, Skanaawadi; see Snow, *The Iroquois*, 63.

547. The total debt consisted of two components: three beavers were for the purchase of merchandise on credit, and six beavers for which the Mohawk trader and Wendell had entered into a separate agreement. Possibly, the goods representing the six beavers were a consignment of items that the Indian client was to transport to the north or northwest, and resell there for his own (and Wendell's) account. If he were to return to Wendell with the latter's share of the proceeds (the six beaver pelts), TowaaHodieshenthoo's obligation would have been met. The account book contains no evidence that part of the debt was ever satisfied.

548. He also appears on pages [43] (see the note there), [72], [88], and [120]. Page [88] is listed as folio 69 in this account.

549. An individual with this name appears in documentary sources from Albany under various names: La Fleur or Lafleur, or with an alias, as in "Lafleur, alias Rene Poupar" and "Rineea Papar Lafleur." Sources indicate that between 1687 and 1692 he lived north of the city, close to the site of present-day Saratoga. See *AA*, 2: 95–97; "New York council minutes," NYCM, ser. A1894, 36: f. 6; and ibid., 38: f. 90. At times, his residence was recorded as "the Stille Water," a reference to a place north of Albany where the Hudson River widened to such an extent that the water appeared placid. The area was settled in the mid-eighteenth-century; see Horn, "Stillwater," 1483. By 1714, part of the city's lands north of the gates was described as "over against where La Fleur formerly lived"; see *AA*, 7: 15–16.

550. Additional accounts are on pages [58] (see the note there), and [111]; other appearances are on pages [60] and [74]. Page [58] is listed as folio 40 in this account, and page [111] as folio 91 (also see the cross-reference there).

551. He also appears on page [35] (see the note there), and [54].

552. Delivery on a singe day of such a quantity of goods suggests that this customer acted as a peddler (see TABLE 13). Caaheghtsiedawee is also documented (some lines down) as going to Canada for Wendell.

553. Accounts for this Mohawk man are on pages [60] (see the note there), and [96]. His wife is mentioned on page [76].

554. It is not clear what "others" refers to.

555. "Ohoonsiewaanens in 'modern' Mohawk: ohonhsowanen or 'great world'" (GM). Note that the woman is described as Onondaga. The *Dictionary of Canadian Biography* also describes Ohonsiowanne as an Onondaga sachem, claimed by the French as their "zealous partizan" (fl. 1699–1704), 2: 502. In fact, the present entry, stating the death of her husband, is for 1707. This Onondaga appears very frequently in documentary evidence. See, *DRCHNY*, 4: 491, 558, 564, 572, 998; ibid., 9: 708, 742–45; and *LIR*, 194, 198.

556. The Dutch term used, *groot* (big), can refer to either the woman's physical stature or her relative standing within her native community. See page [55], note 383.

557. This Mohawk man, living in Canada, had one son who was described as Mohawk (living in Canada, and among the Senecas, see page [78]), and another one listed as Seneca, see the account and notes below.

558. For an account of this individual, see page [78] and the note there.

559. For an account of this individual, see page [74] and the note there. He also appears on page [91]. His other name, Sacksareeij, does not reappear in the account book.

560. "Caanondaa could possibly be a Seneca place name. 'Modern' Seneca: kanonta'a or 'small town'" (GM). If this is a references to this place, it is the only instance it appears in the account book. If it is a person's name, as is suggested by the way Evert Wendell used it here, it is very unlikely that he is the same as the Oneida man Canaanda on page [64]. TiocaghneeRadeie has been incorporated as Canadian in TABLE 1 of this introduction. His obvious connections to Carghiaedsiecoo (or Karighijaetsijkoo on page [23], other occurrences on pages [67], [90], and [110]) confirm this individual's ties with Canada.

561. He also appears on pages [23] (see the note there), [67], [90], and [110]. The term Wendell used to describe the relationship between this Mohawk man and the "young Mohawk who lives Canada" is *belangt bij*. Not a Dutch expression, it appears to be an adapted form of the English "belongs to." The relation is not further described.

562. Evert used the description *oom*. In contemporary Dutch, this term did not refer strictly to uncles the genealogical sense, trusted business associates were also addressed in that fashion. By 1707 there were no Wendells with that given name. If Evert was referring to a family member, he would have been the husband of one of his aunts of the second generation of Wendells: possibly Johannes Sanderse Glen (second husband of Dieuwertje), or Johannes Teller (husband of Susanna). Both resided in Schenectady. Page [118] contains two additional instances where an uncle Hans is mentioned (one undated entry, and one from April 1698). Together with Harmanus Wendell, he purchased trading goods from Barboores and Abraham de Peyster.

563. Note that although the "young savage from Canada" *stays with* Noquaresen, he *belongs to* Carghiaedsiecoo. The latter had strong connections to Canada. The entry shows that the young Indian was in the company of a Canadian Mohawk escorter.

564. Arent also appears in an account on also [45], also with a connection to Canosedeckha(a).

565. See page [31]. This reference removes any doubt that the first customer here is the same as Sohoonachqae on page [31], although the name has a different first character on the two occasions.

566. See notes on the same individual on page [66].

567. He reappears two accounts below as Sohasie. While the specifics of the name are quite different, the occurrence in the account of Oghsiknoendoo coincides exactly with a specific day that he is recorded as trading with the Wendells (September 2, 1708).

568. Senjaad'riesen was mentioned on page [65] (see the note there).

569. For a note on this Mohawk man and his wife, both with strong connections to Canada, see page [65]. She also appears on page [69].

570. "This appears to contain the Mohawk root ahkwehsen in it, 'partidge'" (BR). Even with the addition of "the elder," it remains unclear if this may be the same individual as oghquese or Canaghquese (or Canaghkwase) on pages [45] and [61]. For a note on that individual, see page [45], where Gunther Michelson gives the same translation of this Mohawk name. The added "elder" suggests that there also was, or had been, a younger Canghcuasen. His wife has been incorporated into TABLE 1 of the introduction, as of unknown origins.

571. He also appears on page [88] as Oghseaknoendoo, where he introduces a young customer to the Wendells. Together, the accounts span the years 1707 and 1710.

572. See the note with SoeHaahies, two accounts above.

573. Entries for him and his relatives are listed in a note on page [36]. Page [74] is listed as folio 56 in this account.

574. A divergence seems to be present between the way the debt of hops is described here, a few lines farther down in the account, and the depicted total to the right. The account states 1 and 2 *notas* of hops, but the tally lists debts of 2 and 3 *notas*.

575. A folio 33 is no longer part of the account book.

576. For the likely identification of this Hans as a brother of Evert Wendell, see note 12 of the introduction. Another entry connected to a Hans can be found on page [78], and possibly an additional one on page [54].

577. For this Mohawk man and his relatives, see the note on page [30].

578. He also appears on pages [43] (see the note there), [72], [82], and [120].

579. "Dekaquarendightha is Mohawk" (GM). The connection to Oghseaknoendoo suggests he may have been living in Canada, but he has not been counted, as such, in TABLE 1 of the introduction.

580. "Oghseaknoendoo in 'modern' Mohawk: oskenonton or 'deer'" (GM). The other account in this book, on page [86], lists Oghsiknoendoo as a young Mohawk man from Canada.

581. "The carrying place" is also mentioned on page [93], in 1709. Traveling from Albany towards Montreal, one would have encoutered two of such places in the direction of Lake Champlain. A trip to the west would involve at least three such points; see *LIR*, 172–76; and Norton, *The Fur Trade in Colonial New York*, 13. It is not clear to which one Wendell refers to here, or in the case on page [93]. It is interesting that among the pieces of clothing Indian clients found worth acquiring, one also finds such personalized items as Evert Wendell's nightcap (the entry is in Evert's hand).

582. "Decannoessoekee in 'modern' Mohawk: tekanonhsoken or 'two houses adjoining'" (GM).

583. "Quanakaraghto in 'modern' Mohawk: kanakarahton is 'lost [walking] stick'" (GM).

584. "Ashareiake is 'cutting knife,' Onondaga" (GM). He is not the same as the Seneca man Aeshaerijkoo on page [38].

585. For additional occurrences of this type of description, see the introduction.

586. Carghiaedsiekoo appears regularly in the pages of the account book, see the note on page [23].

587. "D'caiendanharij or D'caiendanhawy is 'wood bringer,' Mohawk" (GM). D'caiendanharij is mentioned here only to help identify his mother, who remains without a name.

588. The account of a Seneca man on page [57] that lists the name Anadeias shows no connections to the present one.

589. "Annahariesen in 'modern' Mohawk: a'nenharishon or 'trembling vine'" (GM). Note that the individual is clearly described as a Seneca, an identification conclusively supported by accounts on pages [74] (see the note there), and [84]. He has been incorporated, as such, in TABLE 1 of the introduction.

590. Since the total debt in beavers amounts to twelve, fourteen have been entered in the tally, and three of these have been crossed out. It is possible that at least part of the crossed out debt derived from the gun that the customer borrowed and returned.

591. For a discussion on this individual, see the note on page [38]. For folio 39, see page [57].

592. It is likely that the raccoon is an expression of the value of items that the Seneca man borrowed.

593. This woman, who is also mentioned in the entries immediately above this one, has been incorporated into TABLE 1 of the introduction, as of unknown origins.

594. The Bleecker family (also spelled Bleeker/Blecker) was one of the most prominent families in Albany—also in relation to the fur trade. In this particular case, it is

impossible to determine what individual Wendell referred to. It could either be the first settler, Jan Jansen Bleecker, or any of his sons who had reached maturity by 1703 (e.g., Johannes, Rutger, Nicholas, or Hendrick). Wendell's entries provide clear evidence that he was connected commercially with both the elder Bleecker, see page [9] and the note there, and his son Niecklas/Nicholas, see pages [70] (and the note there), and [72].

595. Very likely, this man (probably Mohawk) is also mentioned on page [34], as karigijagrachquee, to identify his unnamed sister, who had developed a debt in 1697.

596. Harmanus Wendell.

597. "The carrying place" is also mentioned on page [88] in 1708 (see the note there).

598. No additional identification of this individual has been located. Considering his role in this transaction, however, one may speculate that he was an agent of the Wendells. His family name could be a normal surname, or an allusion to his capacities as a writer or record-keeper, which are some of the meanings of *schrijver*. He may have been a descendant from the tailor and innkeeper Jan Schrijver (note the difference from de Schriver), recorded in New Amsterdam during the 1650s and 1660s. See Fernow, and O'Callaghan, *The Records of New Amsterdam*, 1: 133; 5: 82.

599. For the accounts, activities, and debts of an intricate group around Wagrassero (various spellings), see the note on page [29].

600. The Dutch term used, *groot* (big), can refer to either the man's physical stature or his relative standing within his native community. See the note on page [55].

601. There is a strong resemblance here with Kawessat, one of the names of another Seneca man. See page [41], and the note there.

602. The Dutch reads *coort* (modern Dutch: *koord*), which can be cord, rope, or string. In any of these cases, the object's price is remarkably high.

603. This individual partially redeemed his debt by returning part of the merchandise. It seems unlikely that he is the same as the Canadian Mohawk man Waerhoesroodee (various spellings) on pages [62] and [80].

604. For a discussion of the contacts between this individual and Evert Wendell, see page [57] and the note there. It is possible that Evert also referred to Abraham on page [20].

605. References to Indians staying at, or trading with, individual traders occur with some frequency in the account book, but this statement is uncommon. For a brief discussion of this phenomenon, see the introduction. Throughout the text, similar statements about the Wendells and two native women can be found: see pages [5]–[7], [12], [36], and [105]–[106] (the occurrences on [5] and [36] have additional notes). This statement, and the one on page [73] about Stephanus Groesbeeck, are the only ones that do not relate to the Wendells. At the time Evert registered this account there were two traders in Albany named Johannes Lansing, and they were father and son. One of these Johannes Lansinghs is included in the list of names on page [121]. Johannes the elder (?–February 26, 1728/9) was the third child of the first settler of the family, Gerrit Lansing. He may have named the younger Johannes (September 4, 1687–1771?) after himself. See Pearson, *First Settlers of Albany*, 70; and Reynolds, *Hudson-Mohawk Genealogical and Family Memoirs*, 1: 72–74. Evert had strong connections to both men, since Johannes the elder was to be (about one month after this entry) his father-in-law when Evert married Engeltje (1690–1769). Johannes's son served as sponsor at the baptism of Ariaantje, Evert's third child, on May 19, 1717; see Pearson, *First Settlers of Albany*, 70; *Records of the Reformed Dutch Church of Albany*, 2: 77. The younger Johannes served as commissioner for Indian affairs between 1728 and 1746, occupying the office in years when Evert also served in that same capacity; see Howell and Munsell, *History of the County of Albany*, 42.

606. "Kaghtsweghtjoenie: kahswenhtyonni or 'belt of wampum.' If this individual lived long enough, he could have become the famous Onondaga chief of that name, a.k.a. 'Red Head,' who was mentioned, for instance, in 1752" (GM). See Sullivan, et al.,

The Papers of Sir William Johnson, 1: 365. Aslo note that a Seneca sachem with the name Kagswoughtioony was an active diplomat in the 1750s. He died before June 1756. See *DRCHNY*, 6: 966; 7: 133.

607. No account with that balance has been located on the only remaining folio 16, page [34].

608. For the accounts, activities, and debts of an intricate group around Wagrassero (various spellings), see the note on page [29]. Page [51] is listed as folio 19 in this account.

609. Delivery on a singe day of such a quantity of goods suggests that this customer acted as a peddler (see TABLE 13).

610. The same identification appears twice on page [22] (see the note there). The transfer of the debt to "the Indian corn book" is also entered there. A female customer with an (almost) identical name (Catrien) appears on page [107], but the entry is undated, and it is not clear that she is the same individual. The identification of the woman here as the wife of "her last husband Saquanakaij," helps us to place her also in this man's accounts, where his wife is active on their shared accounts, see pages [24] and [31]. It suggests Saquanakaij had died during the time between the latest of the other accounts, September 1704, and the present account in January 1709. Together, her appearances cover the period between 1698 and March 1710.

611. Another account for this Mohawk man is on page [60] (see the note there). He and his wife are also mentioned on pages [76] and [83].

612. He and his wife, who remains unnamed, also appear on pages [20] (see the note there), [99], [112], and [113]. Page [20] is listed as folio 2 in this account, and page [99] as folio 80.

613. The woman indicates that she has some form of proprietary rights over the "Negro" boy. That, and the fact that she intends to sell him, evidently suggests that the boy was her slave. This is a remarkable annotation by Wendell: as far as can be ascertained, it is the earliest documented case (May 1709) of an African who had been enslaved to an American Indian from the Northeast. In addition, it is noteworthy that a Mahican woman apparently claimed these rights over the boy. The racial description of the boy is explicit, but the remainder of the line in the Dutch text is confusing because of the use of the preposition *aen* (to): *Zij seght dat sij een negher jonghen heeft die aen vercoopen sall in Junij nastcomenden.* The sentence is unclear, possibly as a result of quick annotating on the part of Evert Wendell. In addition to what appears the most likely translation, two alternate constructions may be considered: *Zij seght dat sij een negher jonghen heeft die [sij g]aen vercoopen [sall removed] in Junij nastcomenden* (she says she has a Negro boy who they will sell this coming June), or *Zij seght dat sij een negher jonghen heeft die [sij] aen [mij] vercoopen sall in Junij nastcomenden* (she says she has a Negro boy who she will sell to me this coming June). The latter seems the more plausible alternative.

614. This debt is repeated on page [99], where it is redeemed. For a brief discussion on the appearances of hogs in this account book, see the note on page [2].

615. Entries for him and his relatives are listed in a note on page [36]. Page [86] is listed as folio 67 in this account.

616. This constitutes the only case in the document where a native individual is recorded explicitly as offering services (here, manual labor); possibly to gain access to commercial exchanges, earn some additional income, or to help pay off existing debts. There is no indication that she traded, or had otherwise developed a debt with the Wendells, before this account. Information connected to her son Eghnidaa, indicates that he was probably Mohawk. "Eghnidaa in 'modern' Mohawk: enhni'ta or 'moon'" (GM). Note that his mother is described as Cayuga, and that the following account shows her escorting another Cayuga woman to the Wendells. The woman and her son were possibly mentioned in a baptism record of one year earlier. On February 8, 1707/8, the Indian couple, Ary/Arien and Maria had their child Catharina baptized. On that

occasion, the son's Indian name was recorded as Egnidea/Egnietha, and Kajada for the mother. See Pearson, "Extracts From the Doop-Boek," 19: 70; and Sivertsen, *Turtles, Wolves, and Bears,* 214, 228. One of the sponsors at the baptism was Ezras, or Sonihomane/Sonihowane (the second variety of his name is listed in the baptism records of Albany). He may be the same individual who appears on these pages as Essaraes, in an undated entry on page [117].

617. Although the Cayuga woman remains without a name, d'canjadereghtoo appears on page [41] as Dekanijadereghkoe, the brother-in-law of Dewannighrijeie (see the note there). He also appears on page [66].

618. It appears, in making the tally to the right, Wendell overlooked the value of the cask of rum.

619. Most likely, they borrowed goods to the value of one raccoon.

620. This daughter of a Seneca sachem is listed with the balance of her account on page [114] (in August 1710), but with a substantially different name: Cahenquathaa. Page [114] is listed as folio 94.

621. Wendell's description is confirmed: "this is kanonkeridawih, a Seneca sachem" (GM). See Fenton, "Roll Call of the Iroquois Chiefs," 67. The name also appears on page [104] as Coghcaaradawen, and on page [114], as Caghqueriedawee. This account, likes the others, relates to the years 1709–1710. Several cases document a traditional name for the Seneca Doorkeeper who was sachem in the Seneca village that was farthest to the west. For identification of Kanonkeridawih as the Snipe clan Doorkeeper, see Hamell and Dean-John, "Ethnology, Archeology, History and 'Seneca Origins,'" 4.

622. On July 30, Albany's Common Council had issued an ordinance prohibiting the selling of "Liquor or anything Else" to Indians if it occurred on credit or against a pawn. Harmanus Wendell was one of the city's aldermen when the regulation was proclaimed; see *AA*, 5: 138.

623. The drawing of a bear covers the word, but "stockings" is almost certainly the word used.

624. Entries for Aijadatha (and his relatives) on page [47] seem unrelated to this one.

625. He and his wife, who remains unnamed, also appear on pages [20] (see the note there), [97], [112], and [113]. Page [97] is listed as folio 78 in this account, and page [113] as folio 93.

626. This is a cross-reference to page [97], where his name is listed as WaenEnpackes.

627. Wendell stated that 'Wannapackes's debt was 74 guilders, and half a guilder (ten stivers). The tally excludes the ten stivers.

628. This debt was also recorded on page [97]. See the note on page [2] for general remarks on hogs.

629. Jansen was, and still is, one of the most common surnames in the Dutch language. Yet, consultation of a wide array of published primary sources indicate that there was only one Jansen with this first name: Andries Janse Witbeck, oldest child of Jan Thomase (alias Van Witbeck), who had immigrated from Holstein, Germany. See Pearson, *First Settlers of Albany,* 153–54. In July 1684 Andries made a deposition in court where he stated his age as 30 years, which would place his birth in 1654; see Van Laer, *CMARS*, 3: 469. The island, mentioned in the next line, where Wannanpackes kept his pig may have been either Papscanee Island or Schodack Island, both in the Hudson south of Albany. The will of Andries Jansen's father recorded his residence as Paepsackane, and he had bought a part of Schodack Island from the Mahican owners with Volkert Janse Douw, who would later become Andries's father-in-law, in 1663. For the will, see Pearson and Van Laer, *ERA*, 3: 483–85. For the possession of Schodack Island, see Dunn, *The Mohicans and Their Land,* 286.

630. This debit transaction consisted of the payment of two pigs, valued at eighty guilders, minus Evert's payment of seven guilders from Wannapackes to Andries Jansen.

631. In the text, Wendell totals the debt at eighteen guilders, yet the tally to the right adds five stivers (one-quarter of a guilder) to this amount.

632. "Handbelt" is the direct translation of the Dutch *hant bant* (in modern Dutch *handband*), presumably referring to a type of wampum belt worn at the wrist, or close to the hand. Alternately, it could be a strung wampum belt about the size of one hand, a measure representing about four inches (see the note on page [4]).

633. This most likely describes the value of certain goods, rather than the purchase (on credit) of a raccoon pelt.

634. He also appears on pages [38], [54] (see the note there), and [56].

635. "Caghneghtjakoo in 'modern' Mohawk: kahnehtyakon or 'a cut-down pine'" (GM). Note that he is identified by Wendell as a Seneca (living in Cayuga), an affiliation that has been maintained in TABLE 1 of the introduction.

636. A brother, likely this same one, also appears in the account of Aennaedsoenes on page [57], in October 1707.

637. As a security against the debt.

638. For the identification of this Mohawk village, see the note on page [75].

639. For notes on Susanna and the Indian woman, see pages [36] and [119]. Page [36] is folio 18 in this account.

640. He also appears in the "register," and on pages [5], [7], [13], and [106]. See the note on page [5]. Page [7] is folio 5 in this account.

641. This Mahican man also appears on pages [8] (see the note there), and [16]. The latter is folio 8 in this account.

642. The written account puts the debt for the stockings at ten guilders, but the tally shows nine guilders and ten stivers (ten stivers represents half a guilder).

643. An unusual system to depict the debt is used here: the beaver is drawn, but money has been entered with a plus sign for ten guilders (folio 10), and a minus sign for half a guilder (ten stivers). Since the client paid forty-eight guilders, five plus signs are circled and two vertical marks have been added to account for the remainder of two guilders. A somewhat similar system can be found on page [112].

644. This Mohawk, living in Seneca country, traded on the same day as two Seneca women. See the following two accounts. Both women received goods to sell on Evert's behalf.

645. Presumably to record additional debts, Evert (these accounts are all in his hand) reserved space below the account, but it has not been used.

646. Originally, twelve was entered here, then changed to thirteen.

647. It seems unlikely that the transactions took place in this village. Presumably, it is a reference to the hometown of the customer. For this locality, clearly associated with the Senecas, see the note at [38].

648. The outlines only contain a depiction of this Seneca man's hairstyle and what appear to be some facial markings. See PLATE XIII. A note card by Sturtevant and Brasser, with a photograph of this sketch, describes it as "show[ing] ear ornaments, perhaps tattoo on right cheek," NAA, Photo Lot 81R. The notes are on a card dated January of 1966. Mistaken transcriptions on the card are: July, instead of *folij* (folio), and Canowaacightuca instead of Canowaacightuea.

649. This Seneca sachem also appears in accounts on pages [98] (see the note there), and [114].

650. Johannes Roseboom (?–Jan 24, 1744/5) was the first child of Hendrick Janse Roseboom, the first settler of his family. It is unlikely that this entry, or the one on page [119], refers to the Johannes of the third generation. This younger Johannes (son of second Johannes) was born in 1694, which makes him too young to be trading on his own account; see Pearson, *First Settlers of Albany,* 92–93. The Johannes who Evert referred to here, was a recognized merchant also active in the Indian trade. Roseboom and Evert Wendell were both among the select group of men who were requested by

the Oneida leaders to accompany them to Canada as interpreters in 1709; see *CCM*, 231. Also, Johannes served as commissioner for Indian affairs between 1728 and 1734, partially overlapping Evert's terms; see Howell and Munsell, *History of the County of Albany*, 42. The liaison was also cultivated on a more personal level, since Johannes was godfather of Evert and Engeltje's first child, Johannes; see *Records of the Reformed Dutch Church of Albany*, 2: 65.

651. The description of Osiestout/Sonieno/Sonienone as one who "stays with" him/her, suggests Waiesaa had a position of some status.

652. For a discussion of this Seneca village, see the note on page [39].

653. The preposition here could be: for, by, with, or to.

654. "Canossaase in 'modern' Mohawk: kanonhsase or 'new house'" (GM). Note that he is described by Wendell as a Seneca, an affiliation that has been maintained in TABLE 1 of the introduction.

655. Canaghcoonia may have been an Oneida war leader, later sachem. The Oneida captain Canniaghkennie was recorded returning from fighting in the south, against the Ondadeonwas, in September 1701; see *DRCHNY*, 4: 918. A captain of unidentified origins is listed as Canochquonnie, clearly expressing Anglophile tendencies in promising to apply his personal influence among the Praying Indians in Canada; see *LIR*, 166. By 1708, his tendencies were feared to be swaying: Wraxall mentions Canachquenjie, an Oneida chief sachem, "on who all the Castle depends," in May 1708, *An Abridgment of Indian Affairs*, 55. There he is described as "becoming under the influence of Jesuits." "Canaghcoonia in 'modern' Mohawk: kanahkonnya' or 'marriage concluded'" (GM). Note that the customer's identification as an Oneida has been maintained. It may be the ceremonial name for one of the Oneida sachems of the Wolf clan, Kanongweniyah; see Snow, *The Iroquois*, 63.

656. He also has an account on page [12], where his name is listed as Osaawaawans.

657. No page is missing, but page number eighty-five was skipped in the sequence.

658. He appears in the "register" on pages [2], [5] (see the note there), [7], [13], and [101]; his wife was described by the Wendells as "our female savage." Besides her own account here, she is active on a shared account on page [13].

659. The person described is the son of the sister of the Wendells' Indian woman, "our female savage." The mother is described as having had the son with "Jan the savage," most likely the same as Waskaemp on page [3].

660. It is not certain that he is the same individual as the one with the same name in the "register," and on page [3] (see the note there).

661. She reappears on pages [21] (see the note there), [107], and [118]; and if she is the same as Rapecke (which seems entirely plausible), she is also on page [34].

662. For a note on this individual, see page [39]. He also appears in the next account, and he and his relatives also have accounts on pages [42], [47], [48], and [107].

663. As it stands, the entry is illogical: it could be reconstructed as "Cornelis's wife Debit, he [Cornelis] is Aria's son." A Mohawk with the name Cornelius, later sachem of the Wolf clan, was described as the son of Arie in the baptism records of Schenectady; see Sivertsen, *Turtles, Wolves, and Bears*, 90–91, 223. He was baptized in October 1700, and died probably after 1744. While Sivertsen states that the present account book of the Wendells locates a Cornelius in 1720, the present entry is without a specific date and the name is spelled differently; ibid., 90, 292n23. For a differentiation between this Cornelis, and an individual with the name of Cees, see the notes on pages [2] and [19]. For Areia or Arija and his relatives, see the note on page [30].

664. Another account of this customer (identified in the same fashion) is on page [62] (see the note there). Page [62] is folio 44 in this account.

665. Although this description appears only once, it is an indication of the level of detail to which the Wendells were sometimes informed about the familial background of their customers. The stepfather was probably Waghrosraa, since he was still

actively trading long after Daniell was described as the son of Waghrosraas wife. See page [95].

666. Additional accounts of, or connections to, Areia or Arija are noted on page [30].

667. Evert's brother-in-law was the only child of Philip Schuyler, and grandson of Philip Pieterse Schuyler. Born in New York City on September 21, 1692, he later became surveyor. In 1714, he married Elsie (or Elsje) Wendell, Evert's younger sister. See Pearson, *First Settlers of Albany*, 98; and Talcott, *New York and New England Families*, 380, 389. Reynolds lists his date of birth as September 11, 1691, *Huson-Mohawk Genealogical and Family Memoirs*, 1: 33. Whether he lived in Schenectady at the time of his marriage is unclear, but he certainly was an inhabitant there in February 1723/4, when the authorities in Albany identified him as one of the Indian traders in Schenectady who were not to be given a license to continue their trade; see *AA*, 8: 293. This particular entry strongly suggests that, at the time of its recording, Nicolaes was already in Schenectady, and functioned in some fashion as conduit for trade between Mohawk clients and his mother-in-law Ariaantje. Legal complications did not stop Evert from cultivating relations with his brother-in-law: on September 25, 1726, Nicolaes was sponsor at the baptism of Evert's daughter Engeltje; see *Records of the Reformed Dutch Church of Albany*, 3:23.

668. For Ariaantje, Evert's mother, see the introduction and entries in the trade book on pages [43] and [102]. It is interesting to note that Ariaantje's commercial contacts with her female debtors, at least in this case, were conducted through both a European, and an American Indian intermediary. This particular Schuyler was her son-in-law, and Areja (or Arija) was one of the Wendells' most important commercial contacts among the Mohawks.

669. She, and two others who were explicitly described as French Indians, are on pages [59] and [95], and have been included, as such, in TABLE 1 of the introduction.

670. She reappears on pages [21] (see the note there), [106], and [118]; and if she is the same as Rapecke, which seems entirely plausible, also see page [34].

671. An Indian woman with an almost identical name (Catrin) appears on page [96], and through the identification of her husband, is also recognizable on pages [24] and [31], but it is not certain that she is the same individual.

672. For a note on this person, see page [39]. He and his relatives also have accounts on pages [42], [47], [48], and [106].

673. A significant, but very different connection, between Evert's mother (Ariaantje), and an Ezras and his wife Canastasi Koukoni/Koaroni (Neeltje(n) as a Christian name), can be established. In October 1711 Ariaantje became godparent of their daughter, who they christened Ariaantjen. An Esras, who was witness at a baptism in Schenectady, was probably the same individual as Sonyowaene, also the Bold (or Naughty) Boy, see page [118] (and the note there). There were various Mohawk sachems with the name Esras, or variations thereof. Sivertsen lists three in 1717, and two or three in 1733, *Turtles, Wolves, and Bears*, 79, 123–24. One of these probably received a payment in merchandise, from Evert Wendell in 1714, related to the transfer of land by another Mohawk in 1710. There the name is listed as "Esares *de wilt*" (Esares the savage). See the notes with Hendereck and Sohnerowane on pages [10] and [24].

674. Initially, page number eighty-nine was written here, it was later changed to (the current) eighty-eight.

675. "Atsakanhaa in 'modern' Mohawk: atshakanha' or 'Eastern Algonquian'" (GM). This suggests that the young man's father had been adopted into an Onondaga lineage. If so, it must have happened years before the present account; in reports of conferences in Albany with Governor Bellomont (August 1700), and Governor Cornbury (July–August 1702), an Onondaga sachem is listed as Otsagane and otsakana; see *DRCHNY*, 4: 728, 986, 989, 993.

676. This name is probably derived from the respect that many Indians in the area had held for Arent van Curler (1620–1666). He was assistant commissary, secretary, bookkeeper, magistrate, and *commies* (commercial agent of the proprietor) of Rensselaerwijck. For an overview of his life, see Jacobs, *New Netherland*, 396–97; and Van Laer, "Documents Relating to Arent van Curler's Death," *DSSY*, 3: 11–29. Following his death, Mohawk and other Iroquois orators often addressed New York's governors as "Corlaer." For an example from 1688, see *DRCHNY*, 3: 559. Besides Corlaer's wife, an additional account, in a different manuscript, documents exchanges with "Corlaer's sister"; see Wendell, "E. Wendell's French Savages B[ook]," NYSL. The account is appears to relate to the 1710s. That transaction leaves her indebted for four guilders, and (together with an existing debt) her total debts come to eleven guilders. The account is located on the inside of the item's back cover (all pages have been removed from in between the covers). As Wendell makes a reference here to both Corlaer's and his wife's debt in "the small book," he may have intended that manuscript.

677. "Tanawaneke in 'modern' Mohawk: thanawaneken or 'his two adjoining swamps'" (GM). This is almost certainly the Mohawk leader Cornelis, see the note on page [19]; it is possible that he reappears on page [106].

678. He also appears on pages [23] (see the note there), [67], [84], and [90]. The decision to remit his whole debt was recorded in Evert's hand. The cross-references here, and on pages [23] and [80], allows an acknowledgment of his presence on the account on the latter (folio 62 in this account).

679. This is the only instance in the account book where the Wendells drew beavers, and depicted numbers in the body of the animals. See PLATE IV.

680. This (most likely) describes the value of certain goods, rather than the purchase (on credit) of a beaver pelt.

681. For the only other occurrence of *New* Albany, in 1701, see page [50].

682. Additional accounts are on pages [58] (see the note there), and [83]. The latter is folio 65 in this account; other appearances are on pages [60] and [74].

683. An earlier account of this individual is on page [68] (see the note there).

684. Thussighrondie was one of the contemporary Indian names for the area around the French trading post in Detroit. Established in 1701, it attracted native traders and settlers from a wide variety of Indian nations. This Onondaga man appears to have been among them. See *LIR*, 196; and Richter, *Ordeal of the Longhouse*, 210–16, 223, 238. Detroit's strategic position initially posed a considerable threat to Albany's western Indian trade. By the summer of 1708, however, some of the Miami Indians from the area (or the actual settlement) visited Albany and held a council with Governor Cornbury. They explained that "Goods were actually very sparse" in Detroit; see *DRCHNY*, 5: 65.

685. At first, this appears to be a mistake since the total is only one bearskin. A comparison, with the account on page [68], shows that an older debt of bearskins had probably not been fully paid.

686. Noting that this individual had paid off his earlier debt (see page [68]), and the one developed here, the Wendells may have left this space available in anticipation of further commercial exchanges. Such expectations may have been fed (at least partially) by d'waddierhoo/Dewadierhoe's potential (certainly from the Wendells perspective) as an inter-Indian conduit for trade. If such an exchange ever developed it was recorded elsewhere, because he does not reappear in later accounts, and the remainder of this page remained unused.

687. Although Wendell states that *hoedsewerke* is the Dutch name of this native trader, it is not a recognizable given or family name. If one takes a large degree of liberty with it, the name might be tentatively interpreted as *hoedenwerker*, meaning hatworker. The active involvement of Dewadierhoe (or d'waddierhoe) may signify that *hoedsewerke* was connected to the Onondagas, with Detroit, or with both. *Hoedsewerke* has been incorporated in TABLE 1 of the introduction, as of unknown origins.

688. He, and his wife (who remains unnamed), appear regularly, see the note on page [20].

689. Again, an unusual method of visualizing the debt on the account (for a similar case, see page [102]). Each x represents ten guilders (11 x = f110, x = f10); each slash is one guilder (6 x = f6, / = f1). Rendered by the symbols, however, the total is not 126 guilders, but 116.

690. He and his wife (who remains unnamed) appear regularly in the account book, see the note on page [20]. Page [99] is folio 80 in this account.

691. See the note with the cross-reference to page [98].

692. For a note on this Seneca sachem, see page [98]. He also appears on page [104].

693. This is a cross-reference to page [98], but Wendell listed a very different name there for the sachem's daughter: Schadseeaaee. However, the balance of the account on page [98] is clearly transported here. Together, the accounts cover from August 1709 to August 1710.

694. Literal translation of *parck huijt*. The tally to the right lists *parckmentshuijt* (parchment skin). A main distinction was made in two types of (beaver) furs: freshly trapped, cleaned, and prepared furs were referred to as parchment beaver (French, *castor sec*), whereas hides that had been used and worn by Indian suppliers were known as coat beaver (French, *castor gras*). The latter were of considerably higher value. See Ray and Freeman, "'*Give Us Good Measure*,'" 19–20; and Carlos and Lewis, "Property Rights and Competition in the Depletion of the Beaver," 134, 144, 147n3.

695. It is plausible that the Wendells reserved space here for additional commercial exchanges with this daughter of the Seneca sachem, see [98]. If those ever materialized they were recorded elsewhere.

696. Other accounts with this name (with various spellings) appear on pages [73] (see the note there), [74], [116], and [117]. For the death of his wife, keeper of the present account, see page [74].

697. This promise by her sister (Aeijewases's wife) is also on page [74]. One of her own accounts immediately follows the one here, and another one is on page [116]. Other entries for aiewase/arijawasen, and his relatives are described in the note on page [36].

698. This is the child's fare for a wagon ride, most likely between Albany and Schenectady.

699. Entries for him and his relatives are described in the note on page [36].

700. The customer's sex has not been determined.

701. Probably intended to state that a payment was made to settle a debt with the value of one shirt.

702. The use of the names of her father and husband (to identify this woman) is repeated on page [118], where the whole account is restated. The man's name does not seem to reappear elsewhere, as Cenderijockee (the "savage name" of Aberham, on page [25]) is too different from this one; also, the latter's account seems unrelated to the one listed here, and on page [118].

703. Other accounts with this name appear below this one, on pages [73] (see the note there), [74], [115], and [117]. For a sketch depicting the situation with his wife's debt, see the note on page [74].

704. He reappears as Aequeras on the next page, [117], in an account (involving his wife and his mother) spanning the period between August 1703 and September 1704.

705. Entries for him and his relatives are listed in a note on page [36].

706. He is also mentioned on page [116] as going to Canada with Onogradieha in July 1703.

707. This entry is somewhat ambiguous, but seems to indicate that one of the Wendells purchased meat for this Indian customer.

708. A Mohawk woman, Rachel, sponsored the baptisms of Hendrick and Cornelius in Albany on October 5, 1700. Both have been identified as sons of Arie and Catrina; see

Sivertsen, *Turtles, Wolves, and Bears*, 90–91. Lacking additional information, this Rachel has been incorporated in TABLE 1 of the introduction, as of unknown origins.

709. Other accounts with this name appear on pages [73], [74], [115], and [116]. Page [73] is listed as folio 55 in this account.

710. The number has become illegible; the tally to the right lists two separate totals as one-quarter of debt.

711. An Uncle Hans is also mentioned slightly lower on the same page, and on page [84]. A note regarding the possible identity of this person accompanies the latter instance.

712. Barboores, the name of the merchant who sold the goods, may very well refer to Jean Barbary (also Barbarie). He is listed as a member of the council in New York, during 1709, as Mr. Barberie; he was present in a meeting with the Iroquois in September of 1722 where the building of military outposts on Iroquois lands was discussed. There, his name is recorded as John Barbary, Esqr.; see *LIR*, 202, 231. Matson describes John Barbarie as participating in the illegal, direct trade with Amsterdam in 1701, "The 'Hollander Interest,'" 255, 265n33. By 1713, he was among the major exporters in the city of New York; see ibid., *Merchants and Empire*, 222.

713. Shilling was probably intended.

714. Shilling was probably intended.

715. An additional account, farther down the present page, enables us to date this account as July 1704. For a delineation between this Mahican individual and the Mohawk Tanawaneke, see the notes on pages [2] and [19].

716. See notes 562 and 711.

717. The final part of the last name has disappeared into the binding of the account book, at the right side of the page, but the identification is evident. Abraham de Peyster did indeed have substantial business dealings with the Wendells, both in Albany and New York City. He is shown to have been in Albany as early as 1682, when he acted as a referee in (at least) two court cases; see *CMARS*, 3: 230, 245–47, 255, 259.

718. Shilling was probably intended.

719. "Sonyowane in 'modern' Mohawk: sho'nyowane' or 'his great palm/hand'" (GM). Given the nickname that follows in the account, "the bold [or naughty] boy," it is tempting to combine the inherent meaning of the two names, but that is a highly speculative. It seems entirely likely that this Sonyowaene is the same individual as Essaraes, see page [107]. Although there were a number of individuals who were baptized with that name (or variations thereof), the baptism records of Schenectady contain a likely identification: an American Indian is recorded as sponsor at a baptism with the name Ezras, his Indian name is recorded as Sonihowane, see the note on page [107]. This hypothesis is confirmed by Sivertsen, who adds much more information, since this Ezras was part of the Mohawk Turtle clan. See Sivertsen, *Turtles, Wolves, and Bears*, 26, 27, 225, 228. He may also have been the same individual as Sahonioneane, listed on the roll call of Abraham Schuyler's company of scouts on March 3, 1702/3; see Hastings, *Second Annual Report*, 477. He had been in service since, at least, November 21, 1702.

720. The Dutch reads *de Stouden Jongen*. *Jongen* is "boy," and the adjective (*stout*, in modern Dutch) can be used in both senses.

721. "Aederijhoores in 'modern' Mohawk: aterihorens or 'he splits the matter'" (GM).

722. The nickname or alias is written *Platfoet*. Its equivalent in modern Dutch would be *platvoet*.

723. The Dutch reads a *wije kam*, probably meaning that it had wide openings in between the combs teeth. Evert Wendell is documented as purchasing "combs for savages" from one of his relatives; see Evert Wendell, Day Book, 1717–1749, NYHS, f. 31. For a thorough, and richly illustrated, discussion of (re)uses of European combs among American Indians, see Baart, "Kammen / Combs," 175–88.

724. "Cees is the same as Korneles, Cornelis, Tanawaneke, Tanigwanega" (GM). As explained in a note on page [2], this appears to be a different Mahican individual.

725. This account is an exact copy of the one on page [116] (see the note there).

726. The upper, second, or farthest Mohawk castle was Canajoharie.

727. She reappears on pages [21] (see the note there), [106], and [107]; and if she is the same as Rapecke (which seems entirely plausible), also on page [34].

728. Left empty, probably "money of this province."

729. He is also mentioned by Evert on pages [80] and [93], in entries dating from 1703 and 1709.

730. The Dutch reads *het verste castel*, or "the farthest castle": a reference to the Mohawk village Canajoharie. It was located higher up the stream of the Mohawk River than Tiononderoge. For additional information on this locality, see the note on page [75].

731. See the entry and note on page [104].

732. The Dutch reads *het bovenste castel*, or "the upper castle": a reference to Canajoharie, the village of the Mohawk farthest removed from Albany.

733. The Indian woman is most likely the same individual as the one mentioned on page [101], where two identifying elements are repeated: her tendency to stay with Wendell's sister Susanna, and her residence in Canajoharie or the upper castle. On page [36], an entry can be found for a native woman who Evert describes as "our Susanna's female savage." The dates in that account fit perfectly between those here and on page [101], which allows for the assumption that the same individual is referred to there as well. Notice, however, the significant change in the descriptions. The possessive "our Susanna's female savage," on page [36], is chronologically located between the two other references which contain the more neutral statement that the Mohawk woman "stays at our Susanna's," here and on page [101].

734. This old woman has been incorporated into TABLE 1 of the introduction, as of unknown origins.

735. Johannes Van Allen, youngest son of Pieter Van Allen. He is probably the same as Jan van Allen on page [1] (see the note there). A Willem Van Hallen appears on on the final page of the account book, page [121].

736. This entry is undated, extremely unclear, and most likely overwritten with another sentence. This Evert Wendell Sr. could refer either to Evert Jansz. Wendell, or his son Evert who may have begun referring to himself as senior when the younger Evert (of this account book) began trading on his own account.

737. See the note on her, and her husband Johannes Vinhagel, on page [121].

738. For a brief discussion concerning this individual, see the note on page [20]. The same individual is also among those listed on the final page of the account book, see page [121].

739. The name of this Mohawk man appears on pages [23] (see the note there), [50], [59], and [76]. His daughter and her son shared a later account, covering 170(4?)–1706, see page [50].

740. For this Mohawk man and his relatives, see the notes on pages [19] and [77].

741. Adohoo is also listed on page [49], as Adooho. See the note there.

742. He also appears on pages [43] (see the note there), [72], [82], and [88].

743. This Johannes (1668–1747) was the youngest son of Philip Pieterse Schuyler. Johannes was a distinguished military leader, and Mayor of Albany from 1703 until 1706 (a function in which he is listed here). He also served as commissioner for Indian affairs, an office he occupied from 1710 to 1720, and again between 1732 and 1734. See Howell and Munsell, *History of the County of Albany*, 41–42; and Pearson, *First Settlers of Albany*, 98. His mayoral office helps to identify him here without further qualifications. This entry must therefore be dated between 1703 and 1706. Johannes married Elsie Staats Wendell (1650s?–1737) in April 1695, who was a widow from her marriage to Johannes Wendell,

the brother of Evert's and Harmanus's father. Evert was also connected to other members of the Schuyler lineages, see the notes on pages [18] and [107].

744. Perhaps "sheriff" was intended.

745. Perhaps, "Christian queen" was intended.

746. Although Harmanus clearly made the calculations in Dutch guilders, in the tally he used the symbol of the English pound.

747. The text reads *la*[*c*?]*en*, in which my insertion of a *c* or *k* serves to finalize the only likely reconstruction of the word.

748. For a remark on Jan de Doo, see note 752.

749. Johannes was a brother of Pieter Douw, mentioned on the same page. Both were sons of Jonas Volkertse Douw, see notes 168 and 752. There is no context, or further information which allows us to determine the nature of this entry. Johannes is also listed on page [1] as having brought a letter from an unidentified person to Wendell.

750. Pieter (also Petrus) Douw (1692–1775), son of Jonas Volckerts Douw; see Pearson, *First Settlers of Albany*, 43–44. See the note concerning his father, on page [20]. If this Pieter is the one described above, the (proposed) contract must be dated around 1710 at its earliest, when he would have been eighteen years old.

751. Possibly Jan Andries Douw, documented in Albany in 1678–1690, then moved to New York City; see Pearson, *First Settlers of Albany*, 43.

752. Apparently, this is a fragment of a draft of a sale contract for a lot and house in the city of Albany. No finalized version of it has been located, and it may never have been approved. Pieter Doo can be identified as Petrus Douw (1692–1775), son of Jonas Volkertse Douw, but the identity of Jan Douw is somewhat more obscure. He may have been the Jan Andriese Douw who was in Albany between 1678 and 1690, who afterwards moved to New York City and whose relationship to the other Douws remains unknown; see Pearson, *The First Settlers of Albany*, 43–44. The notes in the account book do not allow more precision.

753. Evert Wendell did indeed have a house on Joncker Street, so the contract may have affected him directly. This entry could therefore be the result of his attempt to quickly copy its contents.

754. Lacking any context (or date) it is difficult to attach any meaning to the name. It does not seem to reappear in the accounts. The individual has been incorporated in TABLE 1 of the introduction, as of unknown origins.

755. It may have been the result of one of Evert Wendell's many public functions in his governance of Albany, a conclusion supported by the inclusion of the constable in the list. It also may have been connected to a court case in which he practiced as a lawyer. Alternately, it could be a listing of a group of merchants from Albany, and its surroundings, organizing themselves in the face of a local or provincial dispute; or a (partial) listing of the Albany county militia, or a company thereof. The absence of any reference to military ranks argues against the latter possibility. The presence of individuals from outside the city excludes the possibility that it constitutes a listing of individuals from a particular city ward.

756. This is either Johannes, the elder (1668–1747), or Johannes, Jr. (1697–1741). But since the name of Jackop (or Jacobus) Schuyler is also included in this list, and considering that this Jacob died in 1707 (see the note there), and as the list can be dated between October 1704 and October 1705 (possibly up to that same month in 1706), it is very unlikely that Johannes Schuyler, Jr. is listed here. He would have been a mere seven to ten years old. See Pearson, *The First Settlers of Albany*, 97–98.

757. This individual is also mentioned on pages [20] (see the note there), and [120].

758. Since the list dates from 1704–05, and possibly 1706, this is either Melgert (ca. early 1670s–1720), son of Melgert Wynantse VanderPoel (1646?–1710), or Melgert senior himself. Around 1712, the younger Melgert moved to Kinderhook, southeast of Albany. See Reynolds, *Hudson-Mohawk Genealogical and Family Memoirs*, 1: 252–52.

759. He is also mentioned in an account on page [70], and most likely on page [72]. On page [70], he is identified as the third child of Jan Jansen Bleecker (1641–1732).

760. The list is in the Evert Wendell's handwriting.

761. While the text clearly reads Vinhagel, the name is most often written Vinhagen. This Johannes (1670s?–1750) is most likely the son of Jan Dirckse Vinhagen. Very little is known about Johannes. In March of 1706 he married Maria Van Tright (ca. early 1680s– after 1722), who is mentioned on page [120].

762. The only son of Jacob Tyssen Van Der Heyden, and Anna (Hals) Van Der Heyden. His father came to Beverwyck in 1654, having emigrated to New Amsterdam the previous year from Holland. Dirk was referred to as a tapper of Rensselaerwyck, also proprietor of land in Albany. Derck (or Dirk) married Rachel Jochemse Keteluyn on March 9, 1687, and he was buried on October 13, 1738. See Reynolds, *Hudson-Mohawk Genealogical and Family Memoirs*, 1: 97–98.

763. A Johannes Lansing also appears on page [94], see the note there for a description of the father and son with the same name.

764. Isaac, born on May 14, 1677, married Jannetje Beeckman on June 27, 1703; he died in January 1772. Son of Gerrit, who was a son of the founder of this lineage, Gerrit Frederickse Lansing. See Reynolds, *Hudson-Mohawk Genealogical and Family Memoirs*, 1: 72–74.

765. First son (?–1753) of Hendrick Coster; see Pearson, *First Settlers of Albany*, 35.

766. The appearance of Jackop, or Jacob(us), Davidse Schuyler in this list lends further plausibility to the conclusion in the note with Coenraet Ten Eyck (see note 782) regarding the time frame in which the list was created: between October 1704 and October 1705, possibly up to October 1706. This Jacob (born January 1675) died on March 22, 1707. He first married Cat(a)lyntje Wendell (daughter of Johannes of the second generation) in 1700, about whom very little is known, and then her cousin Susanna Wendell (daughter of the second-generation Evert Wendell, therefore a cousin of the author of the list) on June 3, 1704. See Pearson, *First Settlers of Albany*, 98; and Talcott, *New York and New England Families*, 378, 381.

767. This is probably the first child of Sybrant Van Schaick (1653–1685), the third child of the first settler of that name, Captain Goosen Gerritsen Van Schaick. Goosen was born in 1677, and was buried on May 29, 1725. See Pearson, *First Settlers of Albany*, 123; and Reynolds, *Hudson-Mohawk Genealogical and Family Memoirs*, 1: 71–72.

768. Willem Van Allen (1670s?–1753), son of Pieter Van Allen (?–1674), married Maria Van Petten in November 1695. See Pearson, *Early Settlers of Albany*, 112.

769. According to Pearson, Harmanus made his will in 1750 and it was probated in 1756, *First Settlers of Albany*, 94.

770. A son of Jochem Staats (the family name was often recorded as Staets), Pearson lists his year of birth as before 1685, *First Settlers of Albany*, 105. He wrote a will in January 1748. Barent was a freeholder in Rensselaerswijck. For the list of freeholders in Albany city and county in June 1720, see *DHNY*, 1: 241–46.

771. The combination of Anthony and Anthony, Jr. in the same list makes it likely that the individual listed here is the son of Anthony Van Schaick, Sr. (1655?–1737). Reynolds puts the year of his father's birth at around 1665, *Hudson-Mohawk Genealogical and Family Memoirs*, 1: 71–72. Another Anthony Van Schaick (1681–1756), in Albany at the same period of time, was a son of Sybrant (1653–1685) and Elizabeth (Van Der Poel) Van Schaick. He married Anna Catherine Ten Broeck on October 19, 1707, and she died in 1756; they had six children, ibid., 1: 71–72.

772. Anthony the elder (1655?–1737) was among the wealthiest Albany merchant-landowners. As stated earlier, Reynolds estimates his year of birth at around 1665.

773. The eldest son (ca. before 1691–?), and the heir of Tjerk Harmense Visscher (?–February 9, 1725). In 1716, Jacob was recorded as owning a lot in Albany; see Pearson, *First Settlers of Albany*, 144.

774. Hendrick Vrooman (1687–?), son of Adam (1649–1730), brother of Wouter. Married Geertruy (surname unknown), and then Maria, daughter of Barent Wemp. He was constable of Albany in 1705, although later he moved to Schenectady. Hendrick's grandfather, with the same first name, had been killed in the French and Indian raid on Schenectady on February 8, 1690; see Burke, *Mohawk Frontier*, 136. The only other Hendrick in the direct line, is the present Hendrick's son (from his second marriage) born in Schenectady on August 4, 1722. See Pearson, *Early Settlers of Schenectady*, 278. It is then likely he is the Hendrick Vrooman that was one of the five carpenters from Schenectady to sign an indenture with Governor Robert Hunter in 1711, agreeing to build a fortification among the Mohawks (later known as Fort Hunter). See *DRCHNY*, 5: 279–80. None of the other carpenters appears in this list, or elsewhere in this account book.

775. Information on this individual is sparse. He is probably the (first?) son of Pieter Quackenbos, brick maker, who in 1668 bought Adriaen Van Ilpendam's brickyard in Albany. See Pearson, *Early Settlers of Schenectady*, 146–47.

776. Wouter Vrooman (1680–1756), son of Adam (1649–1730), and bother of Hendrick. Married Marytje, daughter of Isaac Casparse Hallenbeck of Albany, on September 24, 1707. See Pearson, *Early Settlers of Schenectady*, 278. Wouter Vroman is listed as a freeholder in Schenectady in June 1720; see *DHNY*, 1: 241–46.

777. Likely, this Pieter (1690–1759) was a son of Frans Winne (ca. 1659?–before 1720), although Pieter would have been between fourteen and sixteen years old at the time this list was made; see Pearson, *First Settlers of Albany*, 152. A Peter Winne was listed as a freeholder in Schaghticoke in June 1720; see *DHNY*, 1: 241–46.

778. A reference to Johannes, a younger brother of Evert Wendell. Entries connected to a Hans and "brother Hans" can be found on pages [78], [87], and (possibly an additional one) [54].

779. This surname is often recorded as Ketelhuyn, Ketelhuyn, even Ketel or Kittle. Daniel was a son of Joachim/Jochem, who settled in Rensselaerwijck in or before 1649. Daniel married Debora, daughter of Cornelis Viele, on August 16, 1695. According to Pearson, he settled in Schaatkooke as early as 1708, *Early Settlers of Schenectady*, 99; Burke states that this was probably after 1709, *Mohawk Frontier*, 211–212n21. Daniell Ketlyne was listed as a freeholder in Schaghticoke in June 1720; see *DHNY*, 1: 241–46. Daniel and Harmanus Wendell were involved in some dealings concerning land in Schaghticoke. In 1713, Harmanus had acquired a lot and sold it to Ketelhuyn for eighty pounds, but on July 30, 1719, Ketelhuyn returned the property to Wendell, the price having dropped to sixty-five pounds; see *AA*, 7: 18, 8: 237.

780. Probably the oldest child of Jan Bronck, the latter a son of Pieter, and the first settler with that surname. Pieter, mentioned in Jan Bronck's will, may have been born sometime between 1683 and 1685. Pearson provides little information on a Pieter Bronck, although he indicates that Pieter resided in the Catskill-Coxsackie area, and married Anna (also Annetje) Bogardus on November 17 or December 2, 1705. See *First Settlers of Albany*, 27.

781. According to Pearson, this could be either Cornelis Gysbertse Van Den Bergh, of Rensselaerswijck, son of Gysbert Cornelise (this Cornelis made his will on March 3, 1714, proved July 6, 1717); or Cornelis Claase Van den Bergh of Westchester County (d. on February 14, 1738), son of Claes Cornelise. It is also possible that he was Cornelis Willemse (grandson of Gysbert Cornelise), born before 1685, who made his will on November 24, 1706, proved April 18, 1707. See Pearson, *First Settlers of Albany*, 118. One of the men with this name was listed as a freeholder at Half Moon (just north of Albany, across from the Mohawk River) in June of 1720; see *DHNY*, 1: 241–46.

782. Coenraedt Ten Eyck (1678–1753) was, among other occupations, primarily active as a silversmith in Albany. He manufactured various products that were used in commercial exchanges with the Indians; see Wilcoxen, "Indian Trade Silver On the New York Frontier," 1356–1361. The inclusion of his position as constable is instrumental in

establishing the date of the present listing. In October 1704 he was appointed assessor and constable of the first ward; a year later he was named high constable. This function (most likely) came to an end when he was elected assistant alderman for the first ward, in September 1706; see *AA*, 4: 195; 5: 126, 141. Consequently, it is likely that the list was drawn up between October 1704 and October 1706, and more likely between October 1704 and October 1705 (Stefan Bielinski, pers. comm., October 2004).

783. This could either be Robert Livingston (1654–1728), originator of one the most influential lineages in the New York province, or his nephew Robert Livingston, Jr. (1663–1725); see Pearson, *First Settlers of Albany*, 75.

References

MANUSCRIPTS

Beauchamp, William S. Papers on Iroquois Personal names (microfilm #643). American Philosophical Society.

Evert Wendell's license to practice law; from Lieutenant Governor Hunter, April 1717. Manuscripts and Special Collections. New York State Library.

Gratz Collection. Historical Society of Pennsylvania.

Indenture of land to the Dutch Church in Albany, conveyed to the deacons Jan Lansing and Evert Wendell, March 15, 1688/9. Manuscripts and Special Collections. New York State Library.

Indian Deed to Jan Hendricksen van Bael, July 18, 1672. Manuscripts and Special Collections. New York State Library.

Livingston. Family Papers. Gilder Lehrman Collection, The Gilder Lehrman Institute of American History. New-York Historical Society.

Livingston. Papers. Gilder Lehrman Collection, The Gilder Lehrman Institute of American History. New-York Historical Society.

Livingston, Robert. Papers. Gilder Lehrman Collection, The Gilder Lehrman Institute of American History. New-York Historical Society.

New Netherland Papers. Bontemantel Collection. Astor, Lenox and Tilden Foundations. New York Public Library

New York Council Minutes. New York Colonial Manuscripts. New York State Archives.

Notarial Archive, inv. no. 6108 (notary Pieter Schabaalje) Gemeentearchief, Municipal Archives, Amsterdam, Netherlands.

Petition to Governor of New York, April 29, 1726. Manuscripts and Special Collections. New York State Library.

Photo Lot 81R, Evert Wendell, Account book (extracts) with Sketches of American Indians, 1700–1709 (photocopies). Smithsonian Institution, National Anthropological Archives.

Resolutions and copies of other writings of the [Albany] Church Council, 1699–1734 (microfilm, AFM-331, reel 19). Manuscripts and Special Collections. New York State Library.

Roseboom. Papers. New-York Historical Society.

Staats. Family Papers, 1654–1910. Joachim Staats, Account Book, 1681–1711 [1720] (microfilm #3635). From the *New York State Library*, Albany, NY. *Manuscripts and Special Collections*, SC 15250. Gemeentearchief, Municipal Archives, Amsterdam, Netherlands.

Schuyler, Philip John. Papers. Astor, Lenox and Tilden Foundations. New York Public Library.

Stuyvesant-Rutherford. Papers. New-York Historical Society.

Van Nuys, William. Papers. New-York Historical Society.

Van Rensselaer, Kilaen. Papers. New-York Historical Society.

Wendell. Family Papers. Astor, Lenox and Tilden Foundations. New York Public Library.

Wendell, Ephraim. Correspondence. Manuscripts and Special Collections. New York State Library.

Wendell, Evert. Account Book, 1695–1726. New-York Historical Society.

Wendell, Evert. Account book, 1732–1746. New-York Historical Society.

Wendell, Evert. Day Book, 1711–1749. New-York Historical Society.

Wendell, Evert. Docket book, 1723–1740. New-York Historical Society.

Wendell, Evert. Ledger, 1708–1750. New-York Historical Society.

Wendell, Evert. Ledger, 1711–1738. New-York Historical Society.

Wendell, Evert. Ledger, 1717–1749. New-York Historical Society.

Wendell, Evert. Manuscripts and Special Collections. New York State Library.

Wendell. Family Papers, ca. 1620–1921. Houghton Library, Harvard University.

Wendell, Johnannes Harmanus. Manuscripts and Special Collections. New York State Library.

Wendell, Mr. and Mrs. Evert. Papers. New-York Historical Society.

Published Sources

Anon. "Albany in 1694." *Dutch Settlers Society of Albany Yearbook* 6 (1930–1931):9–12. Albany, NY: Dutch Settlers Society, 1927.

Anon. "Deed to 10,000 Acres [to] Teunis Slingerland from the Mohawk Indians." *Dutch Settlers Society of Albany Yearbook* 21–22 (1945–1947): 13–14. Albany, NY: Dutch Settlers Society, 1948.

Anon. *Nieuwe Ordonnantie ende Instructie voor de Ghezworene Wisselaers ende Collecteurs van alle ghebilloneerde soo Goude als Silvere Penningen.* Brussels: Eugenius Henricus Fricx. 1698.

Anon. *Records of the Reformed Dutch Church of Albany: Excerpted from the Year Books of the Holland Society of New York for 1904–1908, 1922–1926.* Baltimore, MD: Genealogical Publishing Co, 1978.

Armour, David A. *Merchants of Albany, New York: 1686–1760.* New York: Garland Publishing Co, 1986.

Axtell, James. *Beyond 1492: Encounters in Colonial North America.* New York: Oxford University Press, 1992.

Baart, Jan. "Kammen/Combs." In *"One Man's Trash is Another Man's Treasure": The Metamorphosis of the European Utensil in the New World,* edited by Alexandra Van Dongen, 175–188. Rotterdam, Netherlands: Museum Boymans-van Beuningen, 1995.

Bangs, Jeremy D. *Indian deeds: Land transactions in Plymouth Colony, 1620–1691.* Boston, MA: New England Historic Genealogical Society, 2002.

Beauchamp, William M. *Aboriginal Place Names of New York.* Albany, NY: New York State Education Department, 1907.

Bielinski, Stefan. "How a City Worked: Occupations in Colonial Albany." In *A Beautiful and Fruitful Place: Selected Rensselaerswijck Seminar Papers,* edited by Nancy Anne McClure Zeller, 119–136. Albany, NY: New Netherland Publishing, 1991.

———. "A Middling Sort: Artisans and Tradesmen in Colonial Albany." *New York History* 72 (1992):261–90.

———. "The New Netherland Dutch: Settling in and Spreading Out in Colonial Albany." In *The American Family: Historical Perspectives,* edited by Jean E. Hunter and Paul T. Mason, 1–15. Pittsburgh, PA: Duquesne University Press, 1991.

Bonvillain, Nancy. "Iroquoian Women." In *Occasional Publications in Northeastern Anthropology,* edited by Nancy Bonvillain, 47–58. *Studies on Iroquoian culture,* no. 6 Rindge, N.H.: Department of Anthropology, Franklin Pierce College, 1980.

Bragdon, Kathleen J. *The Columbia Guide to American Indians of the Northeast.* Vol. 2, *The Columbia Guides to American Indian History and Culture.* New York: Columbia University Press, 2001.

Brandão, José A. "The Covenant Chain." In *The Encyclopedia of New York State.* Edited by Peter Eisenstadt, 416. Syracuse, NY: Syracuse University Press, 2005.

Brandão, José A., and William A. Starna. "The Treaties of 1701: A Triumph of Iroquois Diplomacy." *Ethnohistory* 43 (1996):209–244.

Brasser, T. J. "Riding on the Frontier's Crest: Mahican Indian Culture and Cultural Change." Paper 13, Natural Museum of Man, Ethnology Division, Ottawa, Canada, 1974.

———. "Mahican." In *Northeast.* Edited by Bruce G. Trigger, 198–212. Vol. 15, *Handbook of North American Indians,* edited by William C. Sturtevant. Washington, DC: Smithsonian Institution, 1978.

Braund, Kathryn E. Holland. *Deerskins and Duffels: Creek Indian Trade with Anglo-Americans, 1685–1815.* Lincoln, NE: University of Nebraska Press, 1993.

Brock, Leslie V. *The Currency of the American Colonies, 1700–1764: A Study in Colonial Finance and Imperial Relations.* New York: Arno Press, 1975.

Burke, Thomas E. *Mohawk Frontier: The Dutch Community of Schenectady, New York, 1661–1710.* Ithaca, NY: Cornell University Press, 1991.

Carlos, Ann M., and Frank D. Lewis. "Property Rights and Competition in the Depletion of the Beaver: Native Americans and the Hudson's Bay Company, 1700–1763." In *The Other Side of the Frontier: Economic Explorations into Native American History,* edited by Linda Barrington, 131–149. Boulder, CO: Westview Press, 1999.

Carothers, Neil. *Fractional Money: A History of the Small Coins and Fractional Paper Currency of the United States.* New York: Wiley & Sons, 1930.

Christoph, Florence A., ed. *Schuyler Genealogy: A Compendium of Sources Pertaining to the Schuyler Families in America.* 2 vols. Albany, NY: Friends of Schuyler Mansion, 1987–1992.

Christoph, Peter R., ed. *The Leisler Papers, 1689–1691: Files of the Provincial Secretary of New York Relating to the Administration of Lieutenant-Governor Jacob Leisler.* Syracuse, NY: Syracuse University Press, 2002.

Christoph, Peter R., and Florence A. Christoph, eds. *Books of General Entries of the Colony of New York, 1674–1688. Orders, Warrants, Letters, Commissions, Passes and Licenses issued by Governors Sir Edmund Andros and Thomas Dongan, and Deputy Governor Anthony Brockholls.* Baltimore, MD: Genealogical Publishing Com, 1982.

Christoph, Peter R., and Florence A. Christoph, eds. Charles T. Gehring, trans. *The Andros Papers, 1679–1680. Files of the Provisional Secretary of New York During the Administration of Governor Sir Edmund Andros 1674–1680.* Syracuse, NY: Syracuse University Press, 1991.

Corwin, Edward T., ed. *Ecclesiastical Records of the State of New York.* 7 vols. Albany, NY: J. B. Lyon, 1901–1916.

Day, Gordon M. "Western Abenaki." In *Northeast,* edited by Bruce G. Trigger, 148–59. Vol. 15, *Handbook of North American Indians,* edited by William C. Sturtevant. Washington, DC: Smithsonian Institution, 1978.

———. *In Search of New England's Native Past: Selected Essays.* Edited by Michael K. Foster and William Cowan. Amherst, MA: University of Massachusetts Press, 1998.

Demos, John. *The Unredeemed Captive: A Family Story from Early America.* New York: Vintage Books, 1994.

Donck, Adriaan van der. *Beschryvinge van Nieuw-Nederlant.* Amsterdam, 1655.

Dunn, Shirley W. *The Mohican World, 1680–1750.* Fleischmanns, NY: Purple Mountain Press, 2000.

——. *The Mohicans and Their Land, 1609–1730.* Fleischmanns, NY: Purple Mountain Press, 1994.

Ezzo, David A. "Female Status and the Life Cycle: A Cross-Cultural Perspective from Native North America." In *Papers of the 23rd Algonquian Conference,* 137–144. Ottawa, Canada: Carlton University, 1992.

Feest, Christian F. "Virginia Algonquians." In *Northeast,* edited by Bruce G. Trigger, 253–70. Vol. 15, *Handbook of North American Indians,* edited by William C. Sturtevant. Washington, DC: Smithsonian Institution, 1978.

Feister, Lois M. "Indian-Dutch Relations in the Upper Hudson Valley: A Study of Baptism Records in the Dutch Reformed Church, Albany, New York." *Man in the Northeast* 24 (1982): 89–113.

Fenton, William N. "The Roll Call of the Iroquois Chiefs: A Study of a Mnemonic Cane from the Six Nations Reserve." Smithsonian miscellaneous collections, vol. 111, no. 15. Washington, DC: Smithsonian Institution, 1950.

——. "Northern Iroquoian Culture Patterns. In *Northeast,* edited by Bruce G. Trigger, 296–321. Vol. 15, *Handbook of North American Indians,* edited by William C. Sturtevant. Washington, DC: Smithsonian Institution, 1978.

Fenton, William N., and Elisabeth Tooker. "Mohawk." In *Northeast,* edited by Bruce G. Trigger, 466–80. Vol. 15, *Handbook of North American Indians,* edited by William C. Sturtevant. Washington, DC: Smithsonian Institution, 1978.

Fernow, B., comp. *Calendar of Council Minutes, 1668–1783. New York State Library Bulletin 58.* Harrison, NY: Harbor Hill Books, 1987. First Published in 1902.

Fernow, Berthold, ed. *The Records of New Amsterdam, 1653–1674.* Translated by Edmund B. O'Callaghan. 7 vols. New York: Knickerbocker Press, 1897.

Foley, Denis. "The Mohicans: Alcohol and the Fur Trade." In *The Continuance—An Algonquian Peoples Seminar, Selected Research Papers, Mohican Seminar 1,* edited by Shirley W. Dunn, 131–41. Vol. 501, *New York State Museum Bulletin.* Albany, NY: University of the State of New York, 2004.

Gallay, Alan. *The Indian Slave Trade: The Rise of the English Empire in the American South, 1670–1717.* New Haven, CT: Yale University Press, 2002.

Gehring, Charles T., trans. and ed. *Fort Orange Court Minutes, 1652–1660.* Vol. 16, *New Netherland Document Series,* pt. 2. Syracuse, NY: Syracuse University Press, 1990.

Gehring, Charles T., trans. and ed., and William A. Starna, ed. *A Journey into Mohawk and Oneida Country, 1634–1635: The Journal of Harmen Meyndertsz van den Bogaert.* Syracuse, NY: Syracuse University Press, 1988.

Goddard, Ives. "Dutch Loanwords in Delaware." In *A Delaware Indian Symposium,* edited by Herbert C. Kraft, 153–60. The Pennsylvania Historical and Museum Commission, Anthropological Series. Harrisburg, PA: Commonwealth of Pennsylvania, 1974.

Grassmann, Thomas. *The Mohawk Indians and Their Valley, Being a Chronological Documentary Record to the End of 1693.* Schenectady, NY: Eric Hugo Photography and Printing, 1969.

Graymont, Barbara. *The Iroquois in the American Revolution.* Syracuse. New York: Syracuse University Press, 1972.

Grumet, Robert S. "Sunksquaws, Shamans, and Tradeswomen: Middle Atlantic Coastal Algonkian Women During the 17th and 18th Centuries." In *Women and Colonization: Anthropological Perspectives,* edited by Mona Etienne and Eleanor Leacock, 43–62. New York: Praeger, 1980.

Gruys, J. A., ed., and A. Nieuweboer, comp. *Dutch Occasional Poetry of the 16th through 18th Centuries: A Catalogue.* CD-ROM. Leiden, Netherlands: IDC Publishers, 2000.

Halpenny, Francess G., Jean Hamelin, and Ramsay Cook, ed. *The Dictionary of*

Canadian Biography. 14 vols. Toronto, Canada: University of Toronto Press, 1966–1998.

Hamell, George R., and Hazel Dean-John. "Ethnology, Archeology, History and 'Seneca Origins.'" Paper presented at the 1987 Annual Conference on Iroquois research. Rensselaersville Institute, 1987.

Hannay, William Vanderpoel, comp. "Burial records: First Dutch Reformed Church Albany, N.Y., 1654–1862." *Dutch Settlers Society of Albany Yearbook* 8–9 (1932–1934):1–145.

Hart, William B. "Black 'Go-betweens' and the Mutability of 'Race'; Status, and Identity on New York's Pre-revolutionary Frontier." In *Contact Points: American frontiers from the Mohawk Valley to the Mississippi, 1750–1830,* edited by Andrew R. L. Cayton and Fredrika J. Teute, 88–113. Chapel Hill, NC: University of North Carolina Press, 1998.

Hastings, Hugh. *Second Annual Report of the State Historian.* New York: Wynkoop Hallenbeck Crawford, 1897.

Heidenreich, Conrad E. "Huron." In *Northeast,* edited by Bruce G. Trigger, 368–88. Vol. 15, *Handbook of North American Indians,* edited by William C. Sturtevant. Washington, DC: Smithsonian Institution, 1978.

Herndon, Ruth Wallis, and Ella Wilcox Sekatau. "Colonizing the Children: Indian Youngsters in Servitude in Early Rhode Island." In *Reinterpreting New England Indians and the Colonial Experience,* edited by Colin G. Calloway and Neal Salisbury, 137–73. Boston, MA: Colonial Society of Massachusetts, 2003.

Hinderaker, Eric. *Elusive Empires: Constructing Colonialism in the Ohio Valley, 1673–1800.* Cambridge, England: Cambridge University Press, 1997.

Hodge, Frederick Webb. *Handbook of Indians North of Mexico.* 2 vols. Washington, DC: Government Printing Office, 1907–10.

Hodges, Graham Russell, and Alan Edward Brown, ed. *"Pretends to Be Free": Runaway Slave Advertisements from Colonial and Revolutionary New York and New Jersey.* New York: Garland Publishing Co, 1994.

Hodges, Graham Russell. *Root and Branch: African Americans in New York and East Jersey, 1613–1863.* Chapel Hill, NC: University of North Carolina Press, 1999.

Horn, Field. "Saratoga County." In *The Encyclopedia of New York State,* edited by Peter Eisenstadt, 1354–57. Syracuse, NY: Syracuse University Press, 2005.

——. "Stillwater." In *The Encyclopedia of New York State,* edited by Peter Eisenstadt, 1483. Syracuse, NY: Syracuse University Press, 2005.

Howell, George R., and Joel Munsell. *History of the County of Albany, N.Y., from 1609 to 1886.* New York: W. W. Munsell & Co, 1886.

Hunter, William A. "History of the Ohio Valley." In *Northeast,* edited by Bruce G. Trigger, 588–93. Vol. 15, *Handbook of North American Indians,* edited by William C. Sturtevant. Washington, DC: Smithsonian Institution, 1978.

Jacobs, Jaap A. *New Netherland: A Dutch Colony in Seventeenth-century America.* Leiden, Netherlands: Brill Academic Publishers, 2005.

Jacobs, Jaap A., and Martha D. Shattuck. "Bevers voor drank, land voor wapens. Enkele aspecten van de Nederlands-Indiaanse handel in Nieuw-Nederland/Beavers for Drink, Land for Arms: Some Aspects of Dutch-Indian Trade in New Netherland." In *"One Man's Trash Is Another Man's Treasure": The Metamorphosis of the European Utensil in the New World,* edited by Alexandra van Dongen, 95–113. Rotterdam, Netherlands: Museum Boymans-van Beuningen, 1995.

Jennings, Francis. *The Ambiguous Iroquois Empire: The Covenant Chain of Indian Tribes with English Colonies, from its Beginnings to the Lancaster Treaty of 1744.* New York: Norton, 1984.

———. "Susquehannock." In *Northeast,* edited by Bruce G. Trigger, 362–67. Vol. 15 of
Handbook of North American Indians, edited by William C. Sturtevant. Washington, DC: Smithsonian Institution.

Jennings, Francis, William N. Fenton, Mary A. Druke, David R. Miller, eds. *The
History and Culture of Iroquois Diplomacy: An Interdisciplinary Guide to the Treaties of the Six Nations and their League.* Syracuse, NY: Syracuse University Press,
1985.

Kawashima, Yasuhide. "Indian Servitude in the Northeast." In *History of Indian-White
Relations,* edited by Wilcomb E. Washburn, 404–6. Vol. 4, *Handbook of North
American Indians,* edited by William C. Sturtevant. Washington, DC: Smithso-
nian Institution, 1988.

Kenney, Alicia P. "Dutch Patricians in Colonial Albany." *New York History* 49
(1968):249–283.

Landy, David. "Tuscarora Among the Iroquois." In *Northeast,* edited by Bruce G.
Trigger, 518–24. Vol. 15, *Handbook of North American Indians,* edited by
William C. Sturtevant. Washington, DC: Smithsonian Institution, 1978.

Lauber, Almon W. *Indian Slavery in Colonial Times Within the Present Limits of the
United States.* New York: Columbia University Press, 1913.

Leder, L. H. ed. *The Livingston Indian Records, 1666–1723.* Gettysburg, PA: Pennsylvania Historical Society, 1956.

Leonard, Vreeland Y. "The La Grange Family." *Dutch Settlers Society of Albany Yearbook* 24 (1948–1949):7–33.

Lunn, Jean. "The Illegal Fur Trade Out of New France, 1713–60." *Canadian Historical
Association Annual Report,* 1939: 61–76.

Mann, Barbara A. "Haudenosaunee (Iroquois) Economy." In *The Encyclopedia of
Native American Economic History,* edited by Bruce E. Johansen, 120–34. West-
port, CT: Greenwood Press, 1999.

Marshe, Witham. "Journal of the Treaty Held with the Six Nations by the Commissioners of Maryland and Other Provinces at Lancaster in Pennsylvania, June
1744." *Collections,* Ser. 1, vol. 8. Boston, MA: Massachusetts Historical Society,
1801.

Matson, Cathy D. "'Damned Scoundrels' and 'Libertisme of Trade': Freedom and
Regulation in Colonial New York's Fur and Grain Trades." *The William and Mary
Quarterly* Ser. 3, 51 (1994):389–418.

———. "The 'Hollander Interest' and Ideas about Free Trade in Colonial New York."
In *A Beautiful and Fruitful Place: Selected Rensselaerswijck Seminar Papers,*
edited by Nancy A. McClure Zeller, 251–68. Albany, NY: New Netherland Publishing, 1991.

———. *Merchants and Empire: Trading in Colonial New York.* Baltimore, MD: Johns
Hopkins Press, 1998.

McCusker, John J. *Money and Exchange in Europe and America, 1600–1775: A Handbook.* Chapel Hill, NC: University of North Carolina Press, 1978.

Megapolensis, Johannes. "Kort ontwerp van de Mahakuase Indianen in Nieuw-
Nederlandt, haer landt, statuere, dracht, manieren en magistraten, beschreven in
't jaer 1644." In J. Hartgers. *Beschryvinge van Virginia, Nieuw-Nederlandt, Nieuw
Engelandt en d'Eylanden Bermudes, Berbados en S. Christoffel,* 1–15. Amsterdam,
Netherlands: 1651.

Merritt, Jane T. *At the Crossroads: Indians and Empires on a Mid-Atlantic Frontier,
1700–1763.* Chapel Hill, NC: University of North Carolina Press, 2003.

Merwick, Donna. *Possessing Albany, 1630–1710. The Dutch and English Experience.*
Cambridge, England: Cambridge University Press, 1990.

Meuwese, Mark. "Flemish Bastard." *The Encyclopedia of New York State,* edited by
Peter Eisenstadt, 573. Syracuse, NY: Syracuse University Press, 2005.

Miller, John. *New York Considered and Improved.* Edited by Victor H. Paltsits. Cleveland, OH: Burrows Brothers, 1903.

Mossman, Philip L. *Money of the American Colonies and Confederation: A Numismatic, Economic and Historical Correlation.* New York: American Numismatic Society, 1993.

Munsell, J., ed. *Annals of Albany.* 10 vols. Albany, NY: J. Munsell, 1850–1959.

Narrett, David E. *Inheritance and Family Life in Colonial New York City.* Ithaca, NY: Cornell University Press, 1992.

Nash, Gary B. *The Urban Crucible: The Northern Seaports and the Origins of the American Revolution.* Abr. ed. Cambridge, MA: Harvard University Press, 1987.

Nettles, Curtis P. *The Money Supply of the American Colonies Before 1720.* Madison, WI: University of Wisconsin, 1934.

Norton, Thomas E. *The Fur Trade in Colonial New York, 1686–1776.* Madison, WI: University of Wisconsin Press, 1974.

O'Callaghan, Edmund B., comp. *Calendar of Historical Manuscripts in the Office of the Secretary of State, Albany, N.Y.* 2 vols. Repr. Ridgewood, NJ: Gregg Press, 1968. First published 1865.

———, comp. *Calendar of New York Colonial Manuscripts: Indorsed land Papers in the Office of the Secretary of State, 1643–1803.* Rev. ed. Harrison, NY: Harbor Hill Books, 1987. First published 1865 by Weed, Parsons and Co.

———, ed. *Documentary History of the State of New York.* 4 vols. Albany, NY: Weed, Parsons, and Co, 1849–1851.

O'Callaghan, E. B. and Berthold Fernow, eds. *Documents Relative to the Colonial History of the State of New York.* 15 vols. Albany, NY: Weed parsons, and Co, 1853–1887.

Parmenter, Jon W. "The Significance of the 'Illegal Fur Trade' to the Eighteenth-Century Iroquois." In *Aboriginal People and the Fur Trade: Proceedings of the 8th North American Fur Trade Conference,* edited by Louise Johnston, 40–47. Rooseveltown, NY: Akwesasne Notes Publishing, 2001.

Pearson, Jonathan. *Contributions for the Genealogies of the Descendants of the First Settlers of the Patent and City of Schenectady.* Repr. Baltimore, MD: Genealogical Publishing Co., 1976. First published 1873.

———. *The First Settlers of Albany County, N.Y., 1630–1800.* Repr. Baltimore, MD: Genealogical Publishing Co., 1976. First published 1872.

———. "Extracts From the *Doop-Boek,* or Baptismal Register of the Reformed Protestant Dutch Church of Schenectady, N.Y." *New England Historical and Biographical Register* 19 (1865):70–315.

Pearson, Jonathan and A. J. F. van Laer, trans. and ed. *Early Records of the City and County of Albany and Colony of Rensselaerswijck.* 4 vols. Vols. 2–4 revised by A. J. F. van Laer. Albany, NY: University of the State of New York, 1869–1919.

Pelletreau, William Smith, ed. *Abstract of Wills on File in the Surrogate's Office, City of New York, 1665–1800.* Vol. 25–41. New York: New-York Historical Society, 1893–1909.

Peña, Elizabeth Shapiro. *Wampum Production in New Netherland and Colonial New York: The Historical and Archaeological Context.* Diss., Boston University, 1990.

Pickering, Kathleen. "Articulation of the Lakota Mode of Production and the Euro-American Fur Trade." In *The Fur Tade Revisited: Selected Papers of the Sixth North American Fur Trade Conference. Mackinac Island, Michigan, 1991,* edited by Jennifer S. H. Brown, W. J. Eccles, and Donald P. Heldman, 57–69. East Lansing, MI: Michigan State University Press, 1994.

Ramsey, William L. "'Something Cloudy in Their Looks': The Origins of the Yamasee War Reconsidered." *Journal of American History* 91 (2003):44–75.

Ray, Arthur J., and Donald Freeman. *'Give us Good Measure': An Economic Analy-*

sis of Relations Between the Indians and the Hudson Bay Company Before 1763. Toronto, Canada: University of Toronto Press, 1978.

Reynolds, Cuyler. *Hudson-Mohawk Genealogical and Family Memoirs*. 4 vols. New York: Lewis Historical Publishing Co, 1911.

Richter, Daniel K. *The Ordeal of the Longhouse. The Peoples of the Iroquois League in the Era of European Colonization*. Chapel Hill, NC: University of North Carolina Press, 1992.

———. "Rediscovered Links in the Covenant Chain: Previously Unpublished Transcripts of New York Indian Treaty Minutes, 1677–1691." *Proceedings of the American Antiquarian Society* 92:45–85.

Richter, Daniel K., and James H. Merrell, ed. *Beyond the Covenant Chain: The Iroquois and Their Neighbors in Indian North America, 1600–1800*. Syracuse, NY: Syracuse University Press, 1987.

Russell, Howard S. *Indian New England Before the Mayflower*. Hanover, NH: University Press of New England, 1980.

Shattuck, Martha D. *A Civil Society: Court and Community in Beverwijck, New Netherland 1652–1664*. Diss., Boston University, 1993.

Sivertsen, Barbara J. *Turtles, Wolves, and Bears: A Mohawk Family History*. Bowie, MD: Heritage Books, 1996.

Snow, Dean R. "Eastern Abenaki." In *Northeast*, edited by Bruce G. Trigger, 137–47. Vol. 15, *Handbook of North American Indians*, edited by William C. Sturtevant. Washington, DC: Smithsonian Institution, 1978.

———. *The Iroquois. The Peoples of America*, edited by Alan Kolata and Dean R. Snow. Cambridge, MA: Blackwell Publishers, 1994.

———. "Mohawk Demography and the Effects of Exogenous Epidemics on American Indian Populations." *Journal of Anthropological Archaeology* 15 (1996):160–182.

———. *Mohawk Valley Archaeology: The Sites*. Matson Museum of Anthropology, Occasional Papers in Anthropology, vol. 23. University Park, PA: The Pennsylvania State University, 1995.

Starna, William A. "Assessing American Indian-Dutch Studies: Missed and Missing Opportunities." *New York History* 84 (2003):5–31.

Starna, William A., and José A. Brandão. "From the Mohawk-Mahican War to the Beaver Wars: Questioning the Pattern." *Ethnohistory* 51 (2004):725–750.

State of New York, the. *Colonial Laws of New York from the Year 1664 to the Revolution*. 5 vols. Albany, NY: J. B. Lyon, 1894–96.

Sullivan, Dennis. *The Punishment of Crime in Colonial New York: The Dutch Experience in Albany During the Seventeenth Century*. New York: Peter Lang, 1894–96.

Sullivan, James, Alexander C. Flick, Almon W. Lauber, Milton W. Hamilton, eds. *The Papers of Sir William Johnson*. 14 vols. Albany, NY: University of the State of New York, 1921–1965.

Talcott, Sebastian V. *Genealogical Notes of New York and New England families*. Albany, NY: Weeds, Parsons & Co, 1883.

Tooker, Elisabeth. "The League of the Iroquois: Its History, Politics, and Ritual." In *Northeast*, edited by Bruce G. Trigger, 418–41. Vol. 15, *Handbook of North American Indians*, edited by William C. Sturtevant. Washington, DC: Smithsonian Institution, 1978.

———. "Women in Iroquois Society." In *Extending the Rafters: Interdisciplinary Approaches to Iroquoian Studies*, edited by Michael K. Foster, Jack Campisi, and Marianne Mithun, 109–23. Albany, NY: State University of New York Press, 1984.

Trelease, Allen W. *Indian Affairs in Colonial New York: The Seventeenth Century*. Repr., with an Introduction by William A. Starna, Lincoln, NE: University of Nebraska Press, 1997. First published 1960.

Trigger, Bruce G. ed. *Northeast*. Vol. 15 of *Handbook of North American Indians*, edited by William C. Sturtevant. Washington, DC: Smithsonian Institution, 1978.

Van Dongen, Alexandra. *"One Man's Trash is Another Man's Treasure": The Metamorphosis of the European Utensil in the New World*. Rotterdam, Netherlands: Museum Boymans van Beuningen, 1995.

Van Gelder, H. Enno. *De Nederlandse Munten*. 8th ed. Utrecht, Netherlands: Het Spectrum, 2002.

Van Laer, A. J. F., trans. and ed. "Documents Relating to Arent van Curler's Death." *Dutch Settlers Society of Albany Yearbook* 3 (1927–1928):30–34.

——, trans. "Letters to Evert Jansen Wendel." *Dutch Settlers Society of Albany Yearbook* 4 (1928–1929):1–7.

——, trans. and ed. *Minutes of the Court of Albany, Rensselaerswijck and Schenectady 1668–1685*. 3 vols. Albany, NY: University of the State of New York, 1926–1932.

——, trans. and ed. *Minutes of the Court of Rensselaerswijck, 1648–1652*. Albany, NY: State University of New York, 1922.

——, trans. and ed. *Van Rensselaer Bowier Manuscripts, Being the Letters of Kiliaen van Rensselaer, 1630–1643, and Other Documents Relating to the Colony of Rensselaerswyck*. Albany, NY: University of the State of New York, 1908.

Van Laer, A. J. F., trans., Kenneth Scott and Kenn Stryker-Rodda, ed. *Council Minutes, 1638–1649, New York Historical Manuscripts, Dutch*. Vol. 4. Baltimore, MD: Genealogical Publishing, 1974.

Venema, Janny, trans. and ed. *Beverwijck: A Dutch Village on the American Frontier, 1652–1664*. Hilversum, Netherlands/Albany, NY: Uitgeverij Verloren/State of New York University Press, 2003.

——, trans. and ed. *Deacons' Accounts, 1652–1674: Dutch Reformed Church, Beverwijck/Albany, New York*. The Historical Series of the Reformed Church in America, 28. Rockport, ME: Picton Press, 1998.

——. *Kinderen van weelde en armoede: Armoede en liefdadigheid in Beverwijck/Albany*. Zeven Provinciën Reeks, 6. Hilversum, Netherlands: Uitgeverij Verloren, 1993.

Wallace, Paul. *Conrad Weiser: Friend of Colonist and Mohawk*. Philadelphia, PA: University of Pennsylvania Press, 1945.

Washburn, Wilcomb E., ed. *History of Indian-White Relations*. Vol. 4, *Handbook of North American Indians*, edited by William C. Sturtevant. Washington, DC: Smithsonian Institute, 1988.

White, Marian E. "Erie." In *Northeast*, edited by Bruce G. Trigger, 418–41. Vol. 15, *Handbook of North American Indians*, edited by William C. Sturtevant. Washington, DC: Smithsonian Institution, 1978.

White, Richard. *The Middle Ground: Indians, Empires, and Republics in the Great Lakes Region, 1650–1815*. Cambridge, England: Cambridge University Press, 1991.

——. *The Roots of Dependency: Subsistence, Environment, and Social Change Among the Choctaws, Pawnees, and Navajos*. Lincoln, NE: University of Nebraska Press, 1983.

Wilcoxen, Charlotte. "Indian trade silver on the New York frontier." *Magazine Antiques* 116 (December 1979):1356–61.

Wraxall, Peter. *An Abridgment of the Indian Affairs Contained in Four Folio Volumes, Transacted in the Colony of New York, 1678–1751*, edited by Charles H. McIlwain. Repr. New York: B. Blom, 1968. First published 1915.

Index

Note: Information presented in figures and tables is represented by *f* and *t*. Information in notes is indicated by n following the page number. The index provides no entries for the transcription.

A

Canghcuasen, 185

Canissoe (Seneca), 155

Canmincoodee (Onondaga), 158

Cannadekonka (Mohawk), 163. *See also* Kanadakonckoo

Cannasquaskje, 206

Canniaghkennie, 272n655

Canoeawee (Cayuga), 147

canoes. *See under* trade items disbursed

Canosedaken (Seneca village), 137, 158, 170, 202, 203, 244n280

Canosedeckhaa (Mohawk), 25, 30–31, 58*t*, 61*t*, 62*t*, 66*t*, 68*t*, 71*t*, 81n150, 148, 149, 150, 177, Plate 2. *See also* Kanossodickahe

Canosedeckhaa's wife / Canoseedickhae's wife (Mohawk), 33, 60*t*, 68*t*, 218

Canosedeckhae (Mohawk), 28

Canossaase, 203, 272n654

Canossora (Cayuga), 153

Canowaacightuea (Seneca), 202, Plate 13

Carghiaedsiecoo (Mohawk), 50*t*, 66*t*, 71*t*, 168, 184, 189, 237n177, Plate 4

Carghiedsiekooe, 208

Carrahoedee (Cayuga), 211

casks. *See under* trade items disbursed

Catquerhoo's wife's son, 156

Catrin (Mohawk), Watcaroos's sister, 33, 41, 48*t*, 52*t*, 64*t*, 68*t*, 121, 194, 206

Catskill Indians, 105, 227n63, 228n66
escorters, 50*t*
first transactions by, 46*t*
listed as Mahican, 12
as portion of total traders, 15*f*, 45*t*
sachem, 72*t*

Catskill River, 12

Cattelaemet, 108, 230n99

Cattenarockes, 51*t*, 175

Cattquierhoe (Cayuga), 48*t*, 138, 199

Caughnawaga, 13, 34, 61, 86n197, 89n229, 236n169, 244n280, 247n301, 255n432

Caunquienen (Cayuga), 171

Cawasthaa, 183

Caweke (Mohawk village?), 161, 255n422

Cawesaet (Seneca), 192

Cayuga
escorters, 48*t*–51*t*
first transactions by, 46*t*, 47*t*
guarantors, 52*t*–53*t*
Mohawk version of names, 13–14
percentage of traders, 45*t*
sachem, 72*t*
traders
children, 97
male, 97

as portion of total, 15*f*

women
account participation by, 48*t*
first transactions by, 47*t*

Cees (Mahican), 62*t*, 99–100, 111, 215, 216, 224n21, 224n23, 234n154, 277n724. *See also* Corneles; Korneles

Cees's wife (Mahican), 99, 111, 224n21

Ceghcaareedawee (Seneca), 42, 197. *See also* Caienkeriekoo; Kaeijeenquereeko

Ceghnae (Cayuga), 148

Ceijenquerij cooe, 143

Cendeijughquae's wife, 213, 216

Cenderijokee (Mohawk), 66*t*, 124. *See also* Aberham

Cettelum, Daniel, 221

Ceuwanwaas, 99, 111

Chaghnaawakee, 174. *See also* Caughnawaga

cider. *See under* trade items disbursed

city charter, trade items in, 22

Claes, Tryn, 79n93

clan relationships, documentation of, 40

Clasd, Joh, 219

client relations, Wendells' policies, 1–2, 5

clothing. *See under* trade items disbursed

cnoo, 94

Coenjaesquaa (Seneca), 171. *See also* Nacoeghnajasquei

Coetsiessee (Seneca), 50*t*, 171

Coghcaaradawen (Seneca), 42, 71*t*, 203, 270n621. *See also* Caghquerieda wee; Ceghcaareedawee

Collins, Edward, 235n155

Collins, Margaret, 235n155

Cologne, Monsieur, 76n43

colors, of textiles, 21, 80n101

Commissioners for Indian Affairs
commissioners, 229n80
Dutch dominance of, 8
Wendell family members as, 3, 4, 5, 229n80

Conowaroo (Seneca), 153, Plate 10

Coote, Richard (Lord Bellomont, Governor of New York), 33

copper wire. *See under* trade items disbursed

corn. *See also under* trade items disbursed
as debt, 48*t*
as payment, 48*t*
purchasing power of, 56*t*–57*t*

Cornbury, Governor, 229n81

Corneles / Cornelis, 224n21, 224n23. *See also* Cees; Korneles

Cornelis's wife, 205

Correlaer (Mahican), 207, 274n676

Coster, Anthony, 220

leeway, 31
Leeweeweet, Jan, 113
leniency, with debt, 66t–67t
Lievenston, Robert, 221
Limping Woman (Mohawk), 18, 52t, 58t
linguistics, 78n76
liquor. *See also under* trade items disbursed
    as popular trade item, 22
    values of, 56t–57t
Livingston, Robert, 245n288, 281n783
Livingston, Robert, Jr., 281n783
Loockermans, Govert, 75n22
looking glasses. *See under* trade items
    disbursed
"Lower castle" (Mohawk). *See* Tiononderoge
Luijckessen, Claes, 118, 220, 236n160
Luyckesen, Clas, 218

M

Mackanant / Mackenant (Mahican), 98, 103,
    226n43
Mackkockwassien (Ottawa), 64t, 169, Plate 6
Mackseckwant / Masequant (Mahican), 70t,
    226n43, 231n110
Maghack (Catskill), 72t, 99, 111, 227n63
Maghah / Magtsaput, 227n57
Maghcoes (Mahican), 34, 233n132
Maghmaghcees (Mahican), 70t, 114
Magtsaput. *See* Maghah / Magtsaput
Mahicans
    and Albany Indian residence restrictions, 8
    Algonquians as, 14–15
    corn as debit item for, 23
    debt of, 60t
    escorters, 48t–51t
    first transactions by, 46t, 47t
    land sales, 226n42
    language, 78n76
    miscategorization of, 12–13
    names, 78n76
    percentage of traders, 45t
    Schaghticoke residents noted as, 12
    traders, 98, 224n17
        female, 17, 99, 107, 224n22
        gender unknown, 5
        male, 76n43
        as portion of total, 15f
    unpaid accounts among, 25
    war with Mohawks, 7, 77n54
    Wendells' use of term, 224n17
    women
        account participation by, 48t
        first transactions by, 47t

Malkiet (Mahican / Ottawa?), 110, 229n79. *See
    also* Waelekeiet
Malsik, 98, 103, 224n17, 226n48, 226n49
Mamatmitt, 233n133
manuscript. *See also* account book(s)
    ascription of origins in, 13, 45t
    clan relation documentation in, 40
    completeness of, 9–10
    dates of transactions in, 1
    description of, 9–11
    entry authors, 10
    entry format, 10–11
    family relation documentation in, 40
    names in, 13–14
    organization, 11
    page numbers, 10, 92
    provenance, 2, 78n65
    scholarly value, 1
    significant aspects of, 11–43
    traders in, 12–16, 15f
    trading accounts in, 16–21
Maqseequant, 231n110. *See also* Masequant
Marij, Jannetije's wife, 138
Marija, Dekarijhondie's sister, 126
Marijae, 149
markings, in account book, Plate 1
markings, on persons, 38–39
Marrijae (wife of Canosdeckhaa), 33
marten. *See under* furs
Masequant (Mahican), 71t, 112. *See also*
    Maqseequant
MassenantSeet (Mahican), 206
matrilinearity, 41
mediators, 44
Metewackam, 119, 228n71
Metewacom / Etowaucum / Etow Oh Koam /
    Nicholas (Mahican), 228n71
Metstaeharae (Mohawk village), 98, 223n10
Miami Indians, 13, 34, 259n471
Minichque, 229n81
mink. *See under* furs
miscategorization, of Mahicans, 12–13
mixed ethnicities, 35–36
mobility, of Indians, 34–35
Mohawk
    corn as debit item for, 23
    escorters, 48t–51t
    first transactions by, 46t, 47t
    guarantors among, 27, 52t–53t
    land sales, 6, 77n52
    peddlers, 28, 61t
    percentage of traders, 45t
    sachem, 72t
    trade, 5

Mohawk (*continued*)
traders
female, 3, 17, 97
as frequent, 12
male, 1–2, 74n12
as portion of total, 15*f*
sex undetermined, 10
as travelers, 30
version of names, 13–14
villages, 223n10
war with Mahicans, 7, 77n54
Wendell family and, 5
women, first transactions by, 47*t*
Moll, Anties, 69*t*, 108, 230n90
money. *See also* trade items disbursed, quarters
bills issued by Wendells, 1
in trade, 32–33
use of, 1
Montgomerie, John (Governor), 6
month, transactions by, 20*f*
Montreal, 12, 19
moustaches, 38

N

Nacoeghnajasquei (Cayuga / Seneca?), 169.
See also Coenjaesquaa
Naeckaepen (Mahican), 98, 228n69
Naeckapen (Mahican), 106, 228n69
Naermoes, 227n63
Naernis (Mahican / Catskill?), 98, 105,
227n57
Naghnacamet (Mahican), 41, 110, 200
Naghnacamet's wife (Mahican), 204
Naghnaehamet (Mahican), 98, 226n45
Naghnaehamet's sister (Mahican), 98
Naghnaehamet's wife's son (Mahican), 66*t*, 98
Naghnaekmet (Mahican), 25, 48*t*, 103,
226n45
Naghnahamett (Mahican), 71*t*
Naghnakamet's sister (Mahican), 48*t*, 105,
227n59
Naghnekampemet, 68*t*, 104, 227n56
Naghnekampenit (Mahican), 98
names
linguistics and, 78n76
in manuscript, 13–14
new, 39, 154, 178, 184
nicknames, 39
practices, 39–40
Nannaelaemit, 49*t*, 53*t*, 58*t*, 66*t*, 99, 111, 114,
233n133
Nansendaghqua's mother (Seneca), 137, 156

Nansendaghquee, 243n274. *See also*
Sendaghqua
Narmoes, 227n57
NasaeDekee (Onondaga), 206
Naughty Boy, 39, 216. *See also* Sonyowaene
Neemamet's wife, 49*t*, 102
Nemamet's wife (Mahican), 98
Netewakam (Mahican), 98
new names, 39, 154, 178, 184
Nicholas. *See* Metewacom / Etowaucum /
Etow Oh Koam / Nicholas
nicknames, 39
Niecklas, 172
Nietewaekam, 14, 53*t*, 71*t*, 106, 228n71
N(i)etewa(e)kam, 228n71
Nietewakam (Mahican), 42, 58*t*, 106, 107
Nietewapewa (Mahican), 66*t*, 70*t*
Niettewapwaee, 58*t*, 62*t*, 68*t*, 106, 108, 228n66,
229n87, 230n89
Niettewapwaee's sister, 106
Nondaresochte, 76n43, 259n478
Nooseewalamit, 98, 108
Nooses, 116, 234n152
Noquaresen (Mohawk, from Canada?), 71*t*,
184, 266n563
Norton, Thomas E., 43
notas, 23, 95
numbering, of pages, 92
Nutkathaa (Mahican village?), 103, 226n46

O

Oekaedee's wife, 157
Oekedee, 53*t*
Oekedee's wife, 41
Oendack (Oneida), 165, 258n450
Oghquese / Oghquesen (Mohawk), 145, 163,
248n325. *See also* Canaghkwase
Oghseaknoendoo / Oghsiknoendo (Mohawk,
from Canada), 50*t*, 186, 188, 258n457,
267n580
Ogwasserooa (Mohawk), 127
Ohonsaioenthaa (Indian, Canadian), 164,
256n436
Ohonsenowae (Seneca), 154
Ohoonsiewaanens (Onondaga), 72*t*, 265n555
Ohoonsiewaanens's wife (Onondaga), 183
Oiaewaekos (Seneca?), 171
OkaajatHie (Indian, Canadian), 167
Okade (Seneca), 154
OndeRiesaghtoo (Mahican), 76n43
One-Eyed Savage, 114
Oneghriedhaa's sister in law (Mohawk), 18

Van Rensselaers, 226n42
Van Schaijek, Anthonij, 220, 279n767
Van Schaijek, Gosen, 220
Van Schaijek, Sybrant, 279n767
Van Slyck, Jacques Cornelissen, 75n24
Van Thrijght, Marija, 218
Van Voorst, Jacobus Gerritse, 257n444
Van Voorst, Jelles, 164
Verbrugge, Gilles, 75n22
Versteeg, Dingman, 10, 78n70
Vinhagel, Johannes, 220, 279n761
Visscher, Hester, 231n111
Visscher, Johannes, 227n63
Visscher, Tjerk Harmense, 279n773
Visser, Jackop, 221, 279n773
Visser, Johannes, 6
vlenningh, 95
voeteling, 95
vret. *See under* trade items disbursed
vret, 95
Vrooman, Hendrick, 280n774. *See also*
    Ffroman
Vrooman, Wouter, 280n776

W

Waeleghlauwett (Schaghticoke), 72*t*, 116,
    226n42. *See also* Waniglawett
Waeleghlauwett's wife (Schaghticoke),
    233n143
Waelekeiet (Mahican), 35, 107, 229n79,
    231n105. *See also* Malkiet
WaenEnpackes / WaenEnpaeckes (Mahican),
    23, 58*t*, 62*t*, 68*t*, 119, 195, 236n165. *See*
    also Wanapakes / Wannapackes
WaerhoesRoodee (Mohawk), 62*t*, 64*t*,
    164, 180. *See also* Warhoose Rode;
    Warhosse Rode
WaerhoesRoodee's father (Mohawk), 66*t*
WaerhoesRoodee's mother (Mohawk), 62*t*, 64*t*
Waghrosraa (Mohawk), 61*t*, 71*t*, 152, 163, 193,
    272n665
Waghrosraa's son (Mohawk), 165
Waghrosraa's wife's son (Mohawk), 136
Wagrassero (Mohawk), 25, 66*t*, 128, 132,
    240n223
Wagrassero's mother (Mohawk), 52*t*, 128
Wagrassero's wife's mother (Mohawk), 68*t*, 129
Waiesaa (Seneca?), 71*t*, 203
Walitgaes, 48*t*, 52*t*, 98, 103, 224n17, 226n48,
    226n49
Wallingas, 226n48
Wamosie (Mahican), 48*t*, 99, 111, 224n22

Wamosie's sister, 99
Wamossij (Mahican), 62*t*, 99, 111, 224n22
Wampanoags, 85n192
wampum
    as collateral, 97
    of Niettewapwae, 230n89
    owed or received, 100, 102
    traded, 106
    as unpopular trade item, 22
Wanapakes, 60*t*, 210. *See also* WaenEnpackes /
        WaenEnpaeckes; Wannanpackes
Wanapakes's wife, 60*t*
Wanckpaee (Mahican), 98, 224n17
Waniglawett (Schaghticoke), 226n42. *See also*
        Waeleghlauwett
Wannanpackes (Mahican), 5, 28, 36, 68*t*,
        198. *See also* WaenEnpackes /
        WaenEnpaeckes; Wanapakes
Wannanpackes's wife (Mahican), 210
Warhoose Rode (Mohawk), 51*t*, 257n441. *See*
        also WaerhoesRoodee
Warhosse Rode's mother, 164
wars
    King William's, 5, 12, 43
    Mohawk and Mahican, 7, 77n54
    Queen Anne's, 6, 7, 8, 12, 20, 20*f*, 43, 77n60
Waskaemp (Mahican), 41, 100, 225n29,
        225n30, 226n41
Wassewaencke. *See* Greyhead / Wassewaencke
Watcaro's sister (Mohawk), 33, 41, 48*t*, 52*t*, 64*t*,
        68*t*, 121, 194, 237n174, 269n610
Watijandandieijoo (Mohawk), 131, 149
Watjandondieijo, 60*t*, 132
Wemp, Barent, 280n774
Wendell, Abraham, 5–6, 75n37, 76n39
Wendell, Anna, 76n47
Wendell, Ariaantje Harmense Visscher, 3, 5,
        10, 73n6, 206, 248n315, 273n668
Wendell, Diver / Diewer, 75n33
Wendell, Elizabeth, 238n193
Wendell, Elsie, 74n12, 273n667
Wendell, Engeltje, 75n34
Wendell, Ephraim, 6, 227n63
Wendell, Evert, Jr., 2, 3, 4–5, 73n4
Wendell, Evert
    client relations, 1–2
    commercial activities, 4, 5–6, 75n36, 76n43
    family history, 2–3
    fur trade involvement, 1, 5–6, 9
    gifts from, 29, 64*t*–65*t*
    identification as author, 2, 3
    Indian affairs involvement, 5, 6, 77n52
    manuscript entries, 10–11

A Note
on the Author

K EES-JAN WATERMAN, M.A., studied Early Modern History at the University of Amsterdam, and American History at the Catholic University of America, Washington, D.C. He has published on trade between Europeans and Indians and on Dutch ethnicity in colonial New York. As an independent historian, he works in publishing and lives in Leiden, The Netherlands. He has provided English translations of seventeenth- and eighteenth-century Dutch documents to the Huguenot Historical Society, New Paltz, New York. He is now preparing for publication, together with J. Michael Smith, another significant (albeit smaller) account book of trade with American Indians in the area around Kingston, New York. Dating from the early eighteenth century, that manuscript is also compiled in Dutch.

www.ingramcontent.com/pod-product-compliance
Lightning Source LLC
Chambersburg PA
CBHW061754260326
41914CB00006B/1108